RIGHTS, REGULATION, AND THE TECHNOLOGICAL REVOLUTION

Rights, Regulation, and the Technological Revolution

ROGER BROWNSWORD

OXFORD
UNIVERSITY PRESS

This book has been printed digitally and produced in a standard specification in order to ensure its continuing availability

OXFORD
UNIVERSITY PRESS

Great Clarendon Street, Oxford OX2 6DP

Oxford University Press is a department of the University of Oxford.
It furthers the University's objective of excellence in research, scholarship,
and education by publishing worldwide in

Oxford New York

Auckland Cape Town Dar es Salaam Hong Kong Karachi
Kuala Lumpur Madrid Melbourne Mexico City Nairobi
New Delhi Shanghai Taipei Toronto

With offices in

Argentina Austria Brazil Chile Czech Republic France Greece
Guatemala Hungary Italy Japan South Korea Poland Portugal
Singapore Switzerland Thailand Turkey Ukraine Vietnam

Published in the United States
by Oxford University Press Inc., New York

Reprinted 2011

ISBN 978-0-19-927680-6

Acknowledgements

I am not sure how far back it would be necessary to go to locate the seeds of all the ideas that have grown into this book—certainly to the 1980s and probably even earlier. At all events, I formally started work on the book in the academic year 2003–2004 when I had the benefit of a Leverhulme Trust award. Without that award, it would have been much more difficult properly to get started and it is a pleasure to acknowledge the Trust's invaluable support.

When I say that I formally started work on the book in 2003–2004, I did not actually start writing it then. Rather, I started writing a number of papers that I intended to serve as building blocks for the book. Some of those papers, although not in the order in which they were written, are conspicuously present in the finished version. They are: (Chapter 1) 'Regulating Human Genetics: New Dilemmas for a New Millennium' (2004) 12 Medical Law Review 14–39, and 'Red Lights and Rogues: Regulating Human Genetics' in Han Somsen (ed) *The Regulatory Challenge of Biotechnology* (Cheltenham: Edward Elgar, 2007) 39–62; (Chapter 2), 'Bioethics Today, Bioethics Tomorrow: Stem Cell Research and the "Dignitarian Alliance"' (2003) 17 University of Notre Dame Journal of Law, Ethics and Public Policy 15–51, 'Three Bioethical Approaches: A Triangle to be Squared' (Tokyo, September 2004) (available at <http://www.ipgenethics.org/conference/transcript/session3.doc>), and 'Stem Cells and Cloning: Where the Regulatory Consensus Fails' (2005) 39 New England Law Review 535–71; (Chapter 3) 'Informed Consent: To Whom it May Concern' 15 Jahrbuch für Recht und Ethik (2007) 267–89; (Chapter 4) 'Cloning, Zoning, and the Harm Principle' in Sheila McLean (ed) *First Do No Harm* (Festschrift for Ken Mason) (Aldershot: Ashgate, 2006) 527–42, and 'Happy Families, Consenting Couples, and Children with Dignity: Sex Selection and Saviour Siblings' (2005) 17 Child and Family Law Quarterly 435–73; (Chapter 6) 'Ri-Connessione Interpretativa, Rivoluzione Riproduttiva, e Stato di Diritto' (Interpretive Re-connection, the Reproductive Revolution, and the Rule of Law) (2005) 10 *Ars Interpretandi* 141–75; (Chapter 8) 'Genetic Databases: One for All and All for One?' (2007) 18 King's Law Journal 247–73; (Chapter 9) 'Code, Control, and Choice: Why East is East and West is West' (2005) 25 Legal Studies 1–21; (Chapter 10) 'Neither East Nor West, Is Mid-West Best?' (2006) 3 *Script-ed* 3–21 (available at <http://www.law.ed.ac.uk/ahrb/script-ed/issue3-1.asp>); and, in Chapter 11, I return to where I started by revisiting 'What the World Needs Now: Techno-Regulation, Human Rights, and Human Dignity' in Roger Brownsword (ed) *Human Rights* (Oxford: Hart, 2004) 203–34.

During the last three years, I have taught an inter-collegiate London LLM module that has been very closely linked to the themes of the book. Each year, it has been my good fortune to teach a small group of students who have been energized by debates at the interface of regulation and technology. Each year, I have thought, 'I surely cannot be as lucky as I was last year in recruiting such a terrific group of students'; but my luck has continued. Without the patience and enthusiasm of these students, with their cosmopolitan backgrounds, the project would have been a lot less pleasurable and a whole lot more difficult. I am indebted to them.

I have lost track of the many helpful conversations and communications that I have had while I have been working on the book. However, some that particularly stick in my mind have been with Heidi Li Feldman, Jonathan Glover, Neil Gunningham, Richard Ireland, Graeme Laurie, Colin Scott, Elaine Snell, Han Somsen, Paul Street, Mark Taylor, and Karen Yeung. To these friends and colleagues, I extend my considerable thanks.

Last, but by no means least, it scarcely needs saying that I have benefited over the years from countless conversations and collaborations with my many-times co-author Deryck Beyleveld. In this book, there are strong echoes of our recent work on human dignity, consent, and precaution but there are also threads in the discussion that go right back to our first joint book, *Law as a Moral Judgment* (1986). In other words, although the library catalogue will show *Rights, Regulation and the Technological Revolution* as under my sole authorship, this is a book that belongs very firmly to a body of jurisprudence that was crafted during an extraordinary couple of decades that were the Sheffield years.

Contents

Table of Cases

AUSTRALIA

CANADA

EUROPEAN COURT OF HUMAN RIGHTS

EUROPEAN COURT OF JUSTICE

EUROPEAN PATENT OFFICE

FRANCE

UNITED KINGDOM

UNITED STATES OF AMERICA

WORLD TRADE ORGANIZATION

Table of Legislation

EUROPEAN COMMUNITIES LEGISLATION AND INSTRUMENTS

INTERNATIONAL LEGISLATION AND INSTRUMENTS

UNITED KINGDOM LEGISLATION AND REGULATIONS

UNITED STATES LEGISLATION

1

The Technologies of the 21st Century: Regulatory Challenge and Regulatory Opportunity

I Introduction

Speaking in the House of Lords in April 2006, Baroness Susan Greenfield remarked that 'the 21st century is offering society an unprecedented raft of challenges.'[1] The reason for this is that:

> [a]ll at once science is now delivering a diverse range of information technology, nanotechnology and biotechnology, with a speed and convergence that we could never have predicted even a decade ago.[2]

To this list of rapidly emerging technologies, Baroness Greenfield—indeed, of all people, the Baroness with her background in the neurosciences—might have added neurotechnology. The Baroness might also have said that, viewing this constellation of modern technologies from a regulatory perspective, we can detect not only a raft of challenges but also a range of opportunities. From such a perspective, the new technologies represent both regulatory targets as well as regulatory tools.

This book offers a commentary on the relationship between regulators and regulatees as the emerging technologies of our time achieve an ever greater penetration in our daily lives. For readers approaching this topic from a legal background, the commentary will confirm that these technologies are difficult regulatory targets—posing, in particular, problems relating to regulatory connection, regulatory effectiveness, regulatee compliance, and regulatory legitimacy. It will also suggest that, at the same time that regulators are struggling to articulate adequate frameworks to limit, license, and support these technologies, they will increasingly adopt a technological approach in order to complement and enhance, possibly even to replace, traditional legal strategies. Not surprisingly, one of the themes of this commentary is that, where regulators have difficulties

[1] Hansard, 20 April 2006, col 1219.
[2] ibid.

in controlling access to and use of modern technologies, these difficulties are, if anything, exacerbated where regulators themselves turn to the technology as a regulatory instrument.

In these introductory remarks, it is appropriate to say a few words about the three elements that give the book its title: that is, the sense of a 'technological revolution'; the idea of regulation (which will take us again to the contrast between technology as a regulatory target and as a regulatory tool); and the notion of rights (and, by implication, the threat to rights presented by the development of new technologies). It is also appropriate, in a book that is aimed primarily at a legal audience, to underscore the significance of the anticipated displacement (by technology) of traditional legal strategies for social control. Even if we are getting used to the idea that new technologies, particularly new information and communication technologies, have transformed the business of practical lawyering, even if we agree with Richard Susskind that 'we are on the brink of a shift in [the] legal paradigm, a revolution in law',[3] the revolution that I am contemplating goes well beyond this comfort zone. To put the point rather dramatically, we can say that if the Rule of Law is to be displaced by the Rule of Technology, this might or might not prove a more effective regulatory strategy but it certainly represents a radically different approach, not just within the law, but in the whole basis of social channelling and ordering.

II A Technological Revolution?

According to the President's Council on Bioethics:[4]

> [w]e have entered upon a golden age for biology, medicine, and biotechnology. With the completion of (the DNA sequencing phase of) the Human Genome Project and the emergence of stem cell research, we can look forward to major insights into human development, normal and abnormal, as well as novel and more precisely selected treatments for human disease. Advances in neuroscience hold out the promise of powerful new understandings of mental processes and behavior, as well as remedies for devastating mental illnesses. Ingenious nanotechnological devices, implantable into the human body and brain, raise hopes for overcoming blindness and deafness, and, more generally, of enhancing native human capacities of awareness and action.... In myriad ways, the discoveries of biologists and the inventions of biotechnologists are steadily increasing our power ever more precisely to intervene into the workings of our bodies and minds and to alter them by rational design.[5]

When we add developments in information and communication technology into this mix, we might think that this golden age is also an age of

[3] Richard Susskind *The Future of Law* (Oxford: Oxford University Press, 1996) at 41.
[4] President's Council on Bioethics *Beyond Therapy* (New York: Dana Press, 2003).
[5] ibid 5–6.

revolutionary proportions. Pierre Baldi[6]—one who takes such a view—contends that:

> We are witnessing a revolution brought about by scientific and technological advances, one in which change occurs at an accelerated pace. By 1945 we had the ability to destroy life on a large scale. By 2045, only a hundred years later, we ought to be able to create life from scratch, both in real space and in cyberspace.[7]

At this point, Baldi pauses to ask: 'why call it a revolution, and why is there acceleration?'[8] To which question(s), he offers four responses.

First, although there was a great deal of progress in the basic sciences before 1950, it is only since then that there has been an acceleration in the biological and computer sciences, 'these [being] the sciences that study what we are made of and how we can somehow replicate ourselves'.[9]

Secondly, 'we are in the process of passing some key thresholds, such as sequencing the human genome and developing computers with brainlike processing speeds'.[10]

Thirdly, although the taxonomy of human biology is complex, 'it has an inherent, discrete, and finite nature at the molecular level';[11] we have the computing power to handle the relevant classifications; so that our understanding of the structure and function of the human genome will be realized and will lead on to 'the more challenging problem of understanding all protein networks and metabolic pathways'.[12] With such knowledge and understanding, medicine becomes a science.

Finally, Baldi cites the development of the internet, a move that 'is greatly accelerating the pace and volume of information propagation'.[13]

What these interacting developments in information technology and biotechnology signify, claims Baldi, is:

> [t]he end of our evolutionary odyssey. As in a simulation of artificial life played in the material world, natural evolution has been building increasingly sophisticated information-processing systems up to the current threshold, where the most complex systems are getting ready to take on a life of their own. All the things that have been created and molded by evolution stand a chance of being seriously challenged.[14]

What should we make of this? Do the changes that we are witnessing truly constitute a technological revolution?

For two reasons, any claim that a technological revolution is taking place is problematic. First, there is the question of how we conceive of a 'revolution'. Would we agree, for example, with the proposition that the '[d]igitization of information may truly be called revolutionary, as it led to a momentous change in the

[6] Pierre Baldi *The Shattered Self* (Cambridge, Mass: MIT Press, 2002).
[7] ibid 163. [8] ibid. [9] ibid. [10] ibid.
[11] ibid. [12] ibid. [13] ibid. [14] ibid.

production, storage and dissemination of content'?[15] Or would we share the view, apparently held by many Americans, that nanotechnology is on the way to becoming the next industrial revolution?[16] Just how momentous does a particular development need to be before it qualifies as 'revolutionary'? And, does it need to be (at least, prospectively) a beneficial development—that is to say, are revolutions necessarily progressive?[17] Secondly, in which sector of science and society is it claimed that the technology is revolutionary? Is this a claim about the nature of the underlying science, or about the penetration and impact of the technology, or about the way we relate to it, and so on?

Taking up the first of these difficulties, a standard conception of a 'revolution' will emphasize both the speed of change and the radical nature of that change. Baldi, as we have seen, plays on both the acceleration of technological development as well as the creative powers that the new technologies promise to vest in humans. Whether or not we characterize such changes as 'revolutionary' will hinge on both how demanding a conception of a 'revolution' we employ—if Copernicus, Newton, and Darwin set the standard, we will be lucky to see a single revolution in our lifetime, let alone a sequence of revolutionary changes—and how we read the changes relative to that conception.

Even if we operate with a shared conception of a revolution, we might be looking for the technological revolution in different places. For example, one person might deny that the development of the internet amounts to a technological revolution because there was no great leap forward in the underlying science; it was simply a matter of connecting up technologies that were already available. However, against this, another person might claim that the internet is a prime example of a technological revolution because its impact on social life has been both speedy and transformative—indeed, the internet is a prime example of what some commentators would term a 'disruptive' technology, that is, a technology the introduction of which replaces an incumbent technology as well as impacting on social practices that are proximate to the technology.[18] Similarly, whereas one

[15] Rik Lambers 'Code and Speech. Speech Control through Network Architecture' in Egbert Dommering and Lodewijk Asscher (eds) *Coding Regulation* (The Hague: TCM Asser Press, 2006) 91, at 104.

[16] Compare Ronald Sandler and WD Kay 'The National Nanotechnology Initiative and the Social Good' (2006) 34 Journal of Law, Medicine and Ethics 675; and the French National Consultative Ethics Committee for Health and Life Sciences, Opinion No 96 ('Ethical Issues Raised by Nanosciences, Nanotechnologies and Health', 2007) p 6 (where it is suggested that the nano revolution is of a technological rather than an, as yet, scientific nature).

[17] Compare (on the notion of a 'rebound revolution') Geoffrey Hunt 'Nanotechnoscience and Complex Systems: The Case for Nanology' in Geoffrey Hunt and Michael Mehta (eds) *Nanotechnology: Risk, Ethics and Law* (London: Earthscan, 2006) 43.

[18] See Mathias Klang *Disruptive Technology* (Göteborg: Göteborg University, 2006). Thus, at p 8:

> Printing presses replaced the scriptoria and also changed the role of the scribe. Railways replaced canals and also changed the way in which social organization around the canals functioned. Railroads did not only make an impact on the barge pilot but also on the bargeman, lock keeper, canal owners, canal-side innkeepers, barge builders, waterway engineers and the horse trade

person might claim that the science underpinning human genetics and genomics is truly revolutionary, another might deny that there has been a revolution because, thus far, the penetration of the science into routine social life has been modest. There is also the possibility that the development of the new technologies might be seen as culturally revolutionary. According to Margaret Somerville,[19] for instance:

> [A]t present, in secular societies we are in search of a new story. Some of the factors that have caused the collapse of our old story result from the extraordinary advances in science and technology, whether information technology, the neurosciences, nanotechnology, artificial intelligence or molecular biology and genetics. The possibilities these advances open up are mind-altering, society-altering and world-altering and, depending on how we use them, could radically alter our human nature or even annihilate us. We have become very sensitive to the threats that these new technologies present to our physical existence and our planet. Our contemporary search for ethics shows, I believe, that we are becoming much more sensitive than we have been to their threats to our human spirit—the deeply intuitive sense of relatedness or connectedness to all life, especially other people, to the world, the universe and the cosmos in which we live; the intangible, invisible, immeasurable reality that we need to find meaning in life and make life worth living. In short, the human spirit is the metaphysical reality (that which is beyond the physical) that we need to fully live fully human lives.[20]

Putting this observation another way, Somerville suggests that the 'widespread search for ethics can be seen as an early 21st century revolution in conscience and consciousness'.[21] Clearly, it matters whether we are looking for a revolution in science or in commerce, culture, or conscience.

In the light of these remarks, it will be appreciated that there is no simple answer to the question of whether a technological revolution was underway as we crossed into the new millennium. Claims that announce revolutionary change

(most barges were horse drawn). This process is not only one of historical interest. Examples of disruptive technologies are all around us. It is, in fact, a continual process. Digital cameras are replacing photographic film, flash drives replace floppy disks, DVD players replace VHS players. Each change brings social and economic effects to a larger or smaller degree. This disruption brings with it new possibilities of communication and control as well as disruption. (References omitted)

See, too, Manuel Castells *The Internet Galaxy* (Oxford: Oxford University Press, 2001); Egbert Dommering 'Regulating Technology: Code is not Law' in Egbert Dommering and Lodewijk Asscher (eds) *Coding Regulation* (The Hague: TCM Asser Press, 2006) 1; and, for a helpful distinction between 'low end' and 'high end' disruptive technologies, see Robert Best and George Khushf, 'The Social Conditions for Nanomedicine: Disruption, Systems, and Lock-In' (2006) 34 Journal of Law, Medicine and Ethics 733.

[19] Margaret A Somerville, 'Searching for Ethics in a Secular Society' in UNESCO *Ethics of Science and Technology: Explorations of the Frontiers of Science and Ethics* (Paris, 2006) 17.

[20] ibid 18.

[21] ibid 17.

certainly need to be treated with caution.[22] As Adam Burgess, writing about the 'mobile (ie cell phone) revolution' puts it:[23]

> Beyond levels of usage, the impact on social consciousness and everyday life of different technological innovations is... impossible to measure. How are we to compare the impact of the introduction of electricity with the impact of the Internet, or the telegraph with the cellular phone? What can be suggested is that the particular claims for a contemporary communications 'revolution' are difficult to sustain.[24]

Having said that, no one surely would deny that the changes that we now see as a raft of technologies become mutually enabling and interactive are significant both for their technological innovation and for their social and cultural impact. Indeed, one of the themes of this book is that the development of these technologies is highly significant for the future of law and the way that we regulate social life. If regulation by legal prescription, by rules issued by legislative assemblies and courts, gives way to regulation by technological design-in or design-out, it matters little whether we agree that this amounts to a technological revolution—for the displacement of law by technology is a sea change however we view it.

III Regulation

The relationship between law and regulation is unclear. Is law to be understood as a broader enterprise than regulation, or is it narrower? In the regulatory literature, it is generally accepted that regulation signifies something like:

> [t]he sustained and focused attempt to alter the behaviour of others according to standards or goals with the intention of producing a broadly identified outcome or outcomes, which may involve mechanisms of standard-setting, information-gathering and behaviour-modification.[25]

If regulation is primarily about channelling behaviour, then legislation is certainly a species of regulation. However, to the extent that regulators rely on instruments and strategies other than legislation in their sustained and focused attempts to

[22] Compare Monroe E Price 'The Newness of New Technology' (2001) 22 Cardozo Law Review 1885. Similarly, Nikolas Rose in *The Politics of Life Itself* (Princeton NJ: Princeton University Press, 2007) declares himself to be 'wary of epochal claims' (at 7); nevertheless, he recognizes that the changes taking place in biological, medical, and social thought (around the ideas of molecularization, optimization, and subjectification) coupled with the rise of somatic experts (such as bioethicists, genetic counsellors, and the like) and the development of a bioeconomy are reshaping our lives such that 'things will not be quite the same again' (at 5). For more on the distinction between innovation and penetration, as well as the persistence of the old alongside the new, see David Edgerton *The Shock of the Old: Technology and Global History Since 1900* (London: Profile Books, 2006).

[23] Adam Burgess *Cellular Phones, Public Fears, and a Culture of Precaution* (Cambridge: Cambridge University Press, 2004).

[24] ibid 59.

[25] Julia Black 'What is Regulatory Innovation?' in Julia Black, Martin Lodge, and Mark Thatcher (eds) *Regulatory Innovation* (Cheltenham: Edward Elgar, 2005) 1, at 11.

alter the behaviour of others, regulation is broader than law. On the other hand, to the extent that regulation does not encompass such tasks as constitution-making and dispute-resolution, then law is broader than regulation.[26] We might infer, therefore, that while law and regulation intersect with one another, they are not co-extensive.

While these preliminary remarks about the relationship between law and regulation make a start in clarifying the nature of regulation, there is a good deal more work to be done. In particular, I need to declare my working concept of regulation and my understanding of how we call regulators to account before introducing the ideas of regulatory style, regulatory mode, regulatory pitch, regulatory phasing, and regulatory range.

(i) The core concept

Regulation, as I have implied, has become an unwieldy concept.[27] It is unclear who counts as a regulator and what counts as regulation. However, let me cut through this by declaring that, for the purposes of this book, we should understand the concept of a regulator narrowly (as an agent or agency of government authorized to control and channel conduct in a specified field)[28] and the concept of regulation broadly (as encompassing whatever measures regulators take to control and channel conduct in the desired way). It follows from these stipulations that the regulatory complex that is the reference point for the questions addressed in this book is constituted by whatever controlling or channelling strategies government (and its agents) employ.

As I have said, while the stipulated concept of a regulator is narrow, the stipulated concept of regulation is relatively broad. With regard to the former, by limiting regulators to agents or agencies of *government*, the controlling and channelling strategies of non-governmental agents or agencies are not to be treated (for present purposes) as the actions of regulators. This is significant because some of the most innovative controlling and channelling strategies have been developed and employed by just such non-governmental parties.[29] This is particularly so with product design. Of course, all products have their limits and compatibilities. However, where products are designed for obsolescence or one-off use (such as

[26] Here, I am drawing on the standard functional analysis of 'law-jobs' theory: see Karl N Llewellyn 'The Normative, the Legal, and the Law-Jobs: The Problem of Juristic Method' (1940) 49 Yale Law Journal 1355.

[27] See, eg, Julia Black 'De-centring Regulation: Understanding the Role of Regulation and Self-Regulation in a "Post-Regulatory" World' (2001) 54 Current Legal Problems 103.

[28] This stipulation is not so narrow as to exclude regional and supranational *governmental* bodies or agents. However, it does exclude, at all levels, local, regional, and international, the channelling strategies of non-governmental organizations, corporations, trade associations, consumer groups, the professions, netizens, and the (non-governmental) rest.

[29] See, eg, Colin Scott 'Regulatory Innovation and the Online Consumer' (2004) 26 Law and Policy 453.

crops carrying the terminator gene), or where they have designed-in compatibility (such as herbicide-resistant crops that function only with a particular herbicide or DVDs that will play on a limited number of DVD players) and the like, the producer is seeking to control and channel the purchaser's use of the product. The function is regulative; but, given my stipulations, the producer is simply not a regulator.

If government, wanting to control or channel a certain kind of behaviour, determines that the desired conduct is best achieved by product design, then producers might be co-opted into government's regulatory scheme and, to this limited extent, producers (qua agents of government) become regulators (surrogate regulators, as some might put it).[30] For example, if government wants motorists to wear seat belts, and if it thinks that product design is the best regulatory approach, then it might make available funds to automobile manufacturers whose cars are then designed in such a way that they are immobilized until the seat belts are engaged. Where government initiates such a product design change, the sense in which manufacturers act as government agents is straightforward. However, if the change is initiated by safety-conscious automobile manufacturers and then this move is, so to speak, 'adopted' by government the agency relationship is less clear-cut. Such nice questions, however, need not detain us.[31]

By stipulating that regulation covers any form of controlling or channelling strategy, a relatively broad notion of regulation is in play. Governments, to be sure, perform many functions, some of which would not fall within this conception of regulation. However, wherever government seeks to steer the conduct of a group in a particular direction, we can treat its efforts as regulation. To return to the example of seat belts, it follows that government regulates where it enacts a criminal law requiring motorists to wear their seat belts; but, equally so, government regulates if it runs a public education campaign alerting motorists to the risks of not wearing a seat belt or building up pressure to wear seat belts, or charging motorists for their medical expenses where they have been injured in a road traffic accident while not wearing their seat belts, or adopting a product-design solution. No matter which strategy, or combination of strategies, government selects, its objective is to control and channel the conduct of motorists in relation

[30] Compare Rik Lambers 'Code and Speech. Speech Control through Network Architecture' in Egbert Dommering and Lodewijk Asscher (eds) *Coding Regulation* (The Hague: TCM Asser Press, 2006) 91 (the state using ISPs and private nodes as surrogate regulators of internet content).

[31] I am mindful that my narrow conception of a regulator will be seen as unhelpful for some theoretical purposes—in particular, by those who seek to map the post-regulatory state. There is also the view that, if we are 'to secure a better understanding of core state governance functions and the relationship between them and other ordering processes', then we must 'have better tools to understand the pervasiveness of non-state law and non-hierarchical control processes' (see Colin Scott 'Regulation in the Age of Governance: The Rise of the Post-Regulatory State' in J Jordana and D Levi Faur (eds) *The Politics of Regulation* (Cheltenham: Edward Elgar, 2004) 145, at 167 et seq). In a sense, it is precisely such an understanding that I am after; but, in order to see the wood, I am eliminating some of the trees.

to the wearing of seat belts; (in my stipulated terms) these are the activities of a regulator and its channelling measures are regulation.

(ii) Assessing regulatory positions and practices

Broadly speaking, regulators are liable to be called to account in two fundamental ways. First, the question might be whether the objective or purpose associated with a particular regulatory intervention is appropriate or justifiable—that is to say, the question is whether regulators are trying to do the right kind of thing. Secondly, even if it is conceded that regulators are trying to do the right kind of thing, we might question whether they are setting about securing their regulatory objectives in the right kind of way. When we ask whether regulators are proceeding in 'the right kind of way', our question might be whether the intervention is likely to achieve its regulatory purposes—our question, in other words, is whether this particular intervention will work, whether it will be effective. Alternatively, our question might be more concerned with the legitimacy of the means adopted by the regulators: here, we do not doubt that the regulatory intervention will work, but we remain to be persuaded that it passes moral muster.[32] It follows that, if regulators are to have a complete answer to their critics, they must show that their regulatory interventions are backed by legitimate regulatory purposes, that the regulatory means employed are legitimate, and that the interventions are actually effective.

In order to fine-tune the question of whether regulators are trying to do the right thing, let me distinguish between the 'legitimation' of regulatory purposes and practices and the 'legitimacy' of such purposes and practices.

Where regulators seek to 'legitimate' their objectives, they might appeal to a broad range of public interest or national interest purposes (economic, medical, educational, security, and so on) which they claim merit respect on the part of their regulatees. For example, it might be claimed by regulators that a bespoke regulatory framework for online contracting needs to be put in place in order to extend consumer choice and to open up new market opportunities for small businesses, or that a population-wide national DNA database needs to be established in order to detect criminals and to improve the level of public security. It should not be assumed, however, that the same legitimating reason must be presented to each segment of regulatees. Indeed, where there is a plurality of constituencies, a regulatory position might be legitimated in more than one way. Thus, as Ian Ayres and John Braithwaite rightly observe:

> When the state acts as an umpire between interest groups under a liberal-pluralist model, it is hard put to find a general justification that appeals to the plurality of interests, and it generally fails to do so. When the rules are indexical, everyone hates the umpire. Tripartism can solve this problem by differentiating legitimation. In the classic case of the

[32] See, in particular, Karen Yeung *Securing Compliance* (Oxford: Hart, 2004).

industrial agreement, the trade union uses one set of arguments to explain to the workers why they should stick with the deal; the industry association uses a radically different set of arguments and appeals to different values to secure the consent of its members. When agreements are differentially legitimated in this way, the players are more likely to make the agreement work than when the state is stuck with finding a legitimating message that is generalizable.[33]

Having said this, a differentiating legitimation strategy is likely to come apart if the various reasons offered are contradictory rather than complementary.

While legitimation envisages a broad set of potentially justifying reasons for regulatory action, we engage a much narrower class of justifying reasons if we question the 'legitimacy' of regulatory purposes and practices. Here, the question is whether an adequate moral or ethical justification is available. So, for example, it might not be enough for regulators to present an intervention as one that promises to assist medical research (and, in due course, to deliver therapies for major human diseases); if the research in question is judged to violate moral or ethical standards—for example, by violating human rights or compromising human dignity—regulatees will seek to engage regulators as to the (moral or ethical) legitimacy of their actions. To put this another way, whereas regulators might purport to 'legitimate' their actions by appealing to a wide range of public interest reasons, they must appeal specifically to moral or ethical reason if they are to defend the 'legitimacy' of their actions.[34]

It should be said that the fact that claims to legitimacy operate within a restricted band of justifying reasons does not altogether preclude the possibility of a differentiating *legitimacy* strategy (paralleling the differentiating *legitimation* strategy to which Ayres and Braithwaite draw attention). For example, there might be situations in which regulators can answer utilitarians with consequential welfare-maximizing reasons and, at the same time, respond to rights theorists with deontological autonomy-respecting reasons. However, one of the main claims in this book is that the ethical plurality is so deeply contested and conflictual (especially in relation to modern biotechnology) that regulators (whether they rely on an undifferentiated generalizable standard or a differentiating approach) will struggle to persuade all regulatees as to the legitimacy of their position and practices.

In a later chapter,[35] I will suggest that we should treat regulatory effectiveness as a question of degree. If we think about the matter in such terms, rather than asking whether a particular intervention is effective or ineffective, we will ask how

[33] Ian Ayres and John Braithwaite *Responsive Regulation* (Oxford: Oxford University Press, 1992) 87.

[34] Given this distinction between legitimating reasons and legitimacy reasons, it follows that the 'regulatory pitch' associated with the former might tap into any dimension of practical reason (other than threats); but, where the regulatory pitch is moral, the question of regulatory legitimacy is engaged. See further below at 16–18.

[35] Chapter 5.

well it is working in holding a regulatory line or moving things towards the regulatory objective. I will also explain how regulatory effectiveness, so understood, relates to regulatory economy and regulatory efficiency. However, at this introductory stage, it suffices to think about effectiveness simply in terms of whether, and how well, a regulatory intervention is serving its intended purpose.

Once we distinguish between, on the one hand, the legitimation (and legitimacy) of regulatory purposes and, on the other, how effectively the particular regulatory intervention is serving its intended purpose, it is clear that we can (and should) evaluate the position at more than one point of the regulatory cycle. In general, we can think of the cycle in terms of direction, detection, and correction;[36] that is, the cycle starts with regulators setting the standard (giving regulatees direction), then monitoring the impact of their intervention (particularly detecting cases of non-compliance), and then correcting for both individual deviation or some more systemic design failure.

When we assess the *legitimacy* of a particular regulatory intervention, our first thought is likely to concern the legitimacy of the particular regulatory position—in other words, to consider whether regulators are doing the right thing in giving a negative steer (to deter, discourage, and disincentivize the targeted behaviour), or a positive steer (to promote, encourage, and incentivize the targeted behaviour), or simply to take a neutral permissive line. However, we should not stop here. We should also ask whether the allied practice, relating to the monitoring or enforcement of the standard, is legitimate.[37]

When instead, we assess the *effectiveness* of a particular regulatory intervention—at any rate, when we assess the position a posteriori—the question is whether the intervention (which is already underway, the standard already having been set) is working as intended.[38] Hence, when we assess the effectiveness of a regulatory intervention, we will tend to focus on matters of compliance and resistance, of correction and revision.

Having distinguished between judgments of legitimacy and judgments of effectiveness, it is important nevertheless to remember that we are assessing two potentially related aspects of just the one regulatory intervention. Accordingly, we should not be altogether surprised if our inquiries into the effectiveness of regulation sometimes lead us straight back to questions of legitimacy; for one source of regulatee resistance is precisely that the standard set is not regarded as legitimate.

[36] Roughly speaking, this is in line with the thinking of the so-called 'cybernetic' model of regulation: see, eg, Christopher Hood *Regulation Inside Government* (Oxford: Oxford University Press, 1999) 45–6. Compare, too, Andrew Murray and Colin Scott 'Controlling the New Media: Hybrid Responses to New Forms of Power' (2002) 65 Modern Law Review 491, which is discussed below at 14–15.

[37] Again, see Karen Yeung, n 32 above.

[38] In principle, of course, we might also assess a regulatory intervention a priori, making an effectiveness judgment in relation to a particular standard adopted by the regulators but not yet tested in practice.

(iii) Regulatory styles: smart and stupid

Regulators are sometimes confronted by a moral panic—for example, a panic about dangerous dogs,[39] dangerous weapons, dangerous drugs, or dangerous people (whether paedophiles or maverick cloners), or the like—coupled with the demand that a criminal law prohibition should be immediately put in place. When public concern articulates itself in this brute form, clamouring for the enactment of a law against the perceived danger, the realpolitik might make it difficult to resist. Nevertheless, to submit to such pressure, to react in a knee-jerking way, is the mark of a low-intelligence regulatory response.[40] Against such a style, intelligent regulators understand that this is no way to operate; they are aware that such a response might be counter-productive; and they know that if we legislate in haste, we might well repent at our leisure.[41]

If the regulatory style is to be 'smart' and 'responsive', it is essential that regulators become more imaginative, breaking the deadlock between those who advocate more regulation and those who advocate less, abandoning any idea that 'one regulatory size fits all', developing a sensitivity to the differing motivations and attitudes of regulatees, and recognizing the limits of single instrument approaches.[42] Thus, it needs to be appreciated that traditional command and control interventions—whether or not in the face of a moral panic—are not always an effective form of response. Having taken this first step towards an intelligent approach, the next step is for regulators to be aware of the range of regulatory instruments and the importance of putting in place an optimal mix. Hence, writing in relation to environmental protection, Neil Gunningham and Peter Grabosky argue that single instrument 'approaches are misguided, because all instruments have strengths and weaknesses; and because none are sufficiently flexible and resilient to be able to successfully address all... problems in all contexts'.[43] Instead, Gunningham and Grabosky maintain that 'a better strategy will seek to harness the strengths of individual mechanisms while compensating for their weaknesses by the use of additional and complementary instruments. That is,... that in the large majority of circumstances (though certainly not all), a mix of instruments is required, tailored to specific policy goals'.[44] Of course, regulatory style is not enough; unless there is also regulatory substance, regulation is unlikely to be adequate to its task.

[39] See, eg, Christopher Hood and Martin Lodge 'Pavlovian Innovation, Pet Solutions and Economizing on Rationality? Politicians and Dangerous Dogs' in Julia Black, Martin Lodge, and Mark Thatcher (eds) *Regulatory Innovation* (Cheltenham: Edward Elgar, 2005) 138.

[40] Although as Hood and Lodge (n 39 above) argue, such a response might not be entirely stupid; ironically, it might 'reflect a rational strategy to economize on rationality' (ibid 154).

[41] A caution famously stated in Patrick Devlin *The Enforcement of Morals* (Oxford: Oxford University Press, 1965).

[42] Generally, see Neil Gunningham and Peter Grabosky *Smart Regulation* (Oxford: Clarendon Press, 1998); and Ian Ayres and John Braithwaite *Responsive Regulation* (Oxford: Oxford University Press, 1992).

[43] Gunningham and Grabosky (n 42 above) at 14.

[44] ibid 14–15.

Nevertheless, other things being equal, smart regulators are likely to outperform stupid regulators.

If intelligent regulators are to choose wisely from their repertoire, if they are to select the smartest option, they need to be aware of the principal regulatory *modes (or modalities)*, the different regulatory *pitches* that are available, the options that they have for the *phasing* of regulatory interventions, and the variables within the regulatory *range*. In what follows, I will speak briefly of these matters of mode, pitch, phasing, and range.

(iv) Regulatory modes

In the Orwellian dystopia, Oceania, 'actions are not regulated by law or by any clearly formulated code of behaviour. In Oceania, there is no law'.[45] If law is not the regulatory mode, then how are the citizens of Oceania regulated? As is well known, the answer is that Oceania is a certain kind of surveillance society:

> A Party member lives from birth to death under the eye of the Thought Police. Even when he is alone he can never be sure that he is alone. Wherever he may be, asleep or awake, working or resting, in his bath or in bed, he can be inspected without warning and without knowing that he is being inspected. Nothing that he does is indifferent. His friendships, his relaxations, his behaviour towards his wife and children, the expression of his face when he is alone, the words he mutters in sleep, even the characteristic movements of his body, are all jealously scrutinised. Not only any actual misdemeanour, but any eccentricity, however small, any change of habits, any nervous mannerism that could possibly be the symptom of an inner struggle, is certain to be detected. He has no freedom of choice in any direction whatever.[46]

In part, the pressure for conformity comes from fellow members. As Julia, Winston Smith's soulmate confesses, she knows that the Two Minutes Hate, the denials and contradictions of Newspeak, and all the rest of the repressive apparatus is a lot of nonsense; but she also knows 'when to cheer and when to boo'.[47] However, it is the intrusive presence of the telescreens that ensures round-the-clock monitoring; and, although Oceania is depicted as a society that has gone backwards rather than forwards technologically speaking, it is this aspect of its regulatory approach that has given it such a bad name.

Seminally, Lawrence Lessig has identified four regulatory modalities (or modes of regulation), that characterize the activities of regulators back in the real world. These four modalities are: the law, social norms, the market, and architecture

[45] George Orwell *Nineteen Eighty-Four* (London: Penguin Books, 1989) 219–20. For a modern version of the surveillance society, see Kirstie Ball, David Lyon, David Murakami Wood, Clive Norris, and Charles Raab *A Report on the Surveillance Society* (September 2006), and see ch 8 below.

[46] Orwell (n 45 above) at 219.

[47] ibid 163.

(or, code).[48] The wearing of seat belts is one of Lessig's illustrative examples. He states:

The government may want citizens to wear seatbelts more often. It could pass a law to require the wearing of seatbelts (law regulating behavior directly). Or it could fund public education campaigns to create a stigma against those who do not wear seatbelts (law regulating social norms as a means to regulating behavior). Or it could subsidize insurance companies to offer reduced rates to seatbelt wearers (law regulating the market as a way of regulating behavior). Finally, the law could mandate automatic seatbelts, or ignition-locking systems (changing the code of the automobile as a means of regulating belting behavior). Each action might be said to have some effect on seatbelt use; each has some cost. The question for the government is how to get the most seatbelt use for the least cost.[49]

When a smart regulatory style is adopted, then regulators will consider direct and indirect strategies, choosing and combining strategies in whichever way promises the optimal ratio of regulatory input to desired regulatory output.

In a helpful paper that extends and elaborates on Lessig's four regulatory modes, Andrew Murray and Colin Scott consider the best terms in which to identify the four modalities. They discuss how the modalities might be combined and, most importantly for present purposes, they highlight three dimensions that are fundamental to whatever strategy is adopted.[50]

On the first point, Murray and Scott reclassify the modality of law as one of 'hierarchy', that of social norms as one of 'community', that of markets as one of 'competition', and that of architecture as one of 'design'. There is more at stake here than terminological nicety, particularly where theorists are seeking out a classificatory scheme that will cover the maximum range of regulatory instruments or strategies. However, a map of this kind is not the object of the present exercise. For the purposes of the commentary in this book, what matters is a distinction between two ideal-typical regulatory regimes. One ideal-typical regime, the 'East Coast' model as I will refer to it, operates very much like a traditional Rule of Law regime by engaging (more or less successfully) with the practical reason of regulatees. The other ideal-typical regime, the 'West Coast' model as I will refer to it, secures a regulated pattern of behaviour without any such engagement with the practical reason of regulatees. In these terms, the first three of Lessig's modalities, whether classified in Lessig's own terms or in accordance with Murray and Scott's reclassification, are variations on the East Coast ideal-type; and the fourth

[48] Lawrence Lessig *Code and Other Laws of Cyberspace* (New York: Basic Books, 1999) ch 7; and Lessig 'The Law of the Horse: What Cyberlaw Might Teach' (1999) 113 Harvard Law Review 501, 507–14.

[49] *Code* (n 48) 93–4.

[50] Andrew Murray and Colin Scott 'Controlling the New Media: Hybrid Responses to New Forms of Power' (2002) 65 Modern Law Review 491. See, also, Andrew Murray *The Regulation of Cyberspace* (Abingdon: Routledge-Cavendish, 2007).

of Lessig's modalities, again whether classified in Lessig's own terms or in accordance with Murray and Scott's reclassification, is that of the West Coast.[51]

With regard to the second point, it is undoubtedly correct to think of smart regulation, just as Neil Gunningham and Peter Grabosky propose,[52] in terms of tailored responses using the optimal mix of regulatory modalities. It is not just in relation to the environment that such regulatory conjunctions have been advocated and developed. For example, David Garland describes a number of new crime prevention strategies in very similar terms:

> The key phrases of the new strategy are terms such as 'partnership', 'public/private alliance', 'inter-agency co-operation', 'the multi-agency approach', 'activating communities', creating 'active citizens', 'help for self-help', and the 'co-production of security'. The primary objective is to spread responsibility for crime control onto agencies, organizations and individuals that operate outside the criminal justice state and to persuade them to act appropriately.[53]

However, recognizing that smart regulation invites working towards the optimal mix of regulatory approaches does not have real bite until we take on board the third point made by Murray and Scott.

Following a cybernetic model, Murray and Scott present each regulatory modality as having three components (or dimensions), namely: some goal, standard, rule, or norm to which the system refers; some mechanism for monitoring or feeding back information about performance; and some mechanism for realigning the system when its operation deviates from its intended goal. The importance of this third point is that it enables us to see precisely where and how a particular ingredient in the regulatory mix is intended to contribute to the total regulatory impact. For example, it is not just that regulators might employ the traditional legal mode in conjunction with, say, social pressure; rather, the strategy might be to use the traditional legal mode to set the standard but then leave it to social pressure (the community) to monitor compliance (performance) and possibly even to respond to non-compliance (deviation).

For those who are used to thinking in traditional regulatory terms, it is easy enough to relate to the three dimensions identified by Murray and Scott, but the habits of a lifetime in the law offer some resistance to adopting their cybernetic language. Far from being unhelpful, this tension paves the way for a necessary sharpening up of the contrast between the East Coast ideal-type and that of the West Coast. If we are operating with the West Coast ideal-type, we will think purely in terms of a designed environment (and/or controlled regulatees) with a required

[51] Compare Andrew Murray *The Regulation of Cyberspace* (Abingdon: Routledge-Cavendish, 2007) at 37, where he divides the modalities of regulation into two families, one socially-mediated, the other environmental. While, within the former family, we have law, markets, and norms, within the latter family, we have architecture. In my view, however, the essential nature of the family resemblance is not drawn out until we understand the significance of the regulatory pitch: see below at 16–18.

[52] Gunningham and Grabosky; (n 42).

[53] David Garland *The Culture of Control* (Oxford: Oxford University Press, 2001) 124–5.

pattern of behaviour. In one dimension, regulators identify the required pattern (this is what they want their regulatory targets to do or not to do); in a second dimension, they monitor whether the control system is producing the required pattern; and, in a third dimension, they respond (by fixing the problem) where the system needs to be adjusted. To state these three dimensions in the language of the East Coast ideal-type is not simply to use a more familiar language (at any rate, to lawyers), it is to revert to a fundamentally different paradigm. Stated in such East Coast terms, the first dimension is to adopt and declare a regulatory position; the second is to monitor responses to that position and to exert pressure for compliance; and the third is to take enforcement steps against regulatees who do not comply.

Before proceeding, it is as well to underline the importance of the first dimension for the East Coast ideal-type. Quite simply, the rule or standard that represents the regulatory position is promulgated. If we take a Fullerian view, we are already a long way towards acting in accordance with the Rule of Law.[54] On the East Coast, legalism at least lets regulatees know where they stand.[55] By contrast, on the West Coast, those who are controlled stand only where their regulated environment allows them.

(v) Regulatory pitch

If, following Lessig, we think of regulation as having four possible modalities each of which, following Murray and Scott, has three functional dimensions, then our thinking about the regulatory complex is already pretty sophisticated. However, this analysis does not yet make explicit the significance of what I will term the 'regulatory pitch'.[56]

The idea of 'regulatory pitch' refers to the way in which regulators seek to engage with their targets. Essentially, three pitches are available, namely: moral, practical, and behavioural.[57]

Where the pitch is moral, regulators seek to engage with the targets' moral reason. Here, regulators seek not merely to 'legitimate' their general purposes but to assert the 'legitimacy' of the particular standards set.[58] The moral pitch might appeal to the *authority* of the regulator (the authoritative pitch), the *substance* of the regulation (the substantive pitch), or the *procedures* that led to the adoption of the particular regulation (the procedural pitch). Where the authoritative pitch is made, regulators claim either that they have some special moral insight (so that

[54] Lon L Fuller *The Morality of Law* (New Haven: Yale University Press, 1969).

[55] Compare Judith N Shklar *Legalism* (Cambridge, Mass: Harvard University Press, 1964).

[56] For broader comments about regulatory pitch in relation to the nature of regulation, see Roger Brownsword 'Red Lights and Rogues: Regulating Human Genetics' in Han Somsen (ed) *Regulating Biotechnology* (Cheltenham: Edward Elgar, 2007) 39, 42–3.

[57] Unless regulators are wholly misguided in their approach, this suggests that the 'rules of engagement' will pan out in a broadly similar way when viewed from the perspective of regulatees.

[58] For the distinction between 'legitimation' and 'legitimacy', see above at 9–10.

their regulatory pronouncements are necessarily morally underwritten) or that they are properly charged with regulatory responsibilities and merit respect for that reason. Where the pitch is substantive, the paradigmatic claim is that the particular regulatory position adopted is legitimate, as being in line with some given moral principle. However, it might also be argued that, even if the particular regulatory position is controversial, it merits respect because it belongs to a body of regulation that, generally speaking, is in line with some given moral principle. Or, again, it might be argued that, whatever the moral credentials of the regulation, particular or general, there is good reason to respect it because the negative consequences of challenging the regulatory order are more serious from a moral point of view. Where the moral pitch is procedural, the paradigmatic claim is that, even if the particular regulatory position is controversial, it merits respect because it is the outcome of a process that is fair. And, in the face of intense scepticism about either appeals to moral authority or to substantive moral legitimacy, a procedural turn is invited.[59]

Where the moral pitch, in whichever articulation, successfully engages regulatees, it is accepted either that the regulatory position is morally legitimate, or that it merits respect, or that compliance (where channelling takes this form) is morally obligatory.

Where the pitch is practical, regulators seek to engage with the targets' practical reason (but not specifically the moral aspect of practical reason). What regulators rely on is the more diffuse claim that there is 'good reason' for compliance; and channelling will have the desired effect where targets share the sense of good reason (even if there is no one reason that targets uniformly recognize as good).[60] Accordingly, no particular reason within practical reason is privileged although, in practice, the practical pitch will often appeal to the self-interest, especially the economic interests, of targets.[61]

Where the pitch is behavioural, no attempt is made to engage with either moral reason in particular or practical reason in general. All that matters is that the channelling device employed engages with the targets in such a way as to achieve

[59] See ch 4 below; and Deryck Beyleveld and Roger Brownsword *Consent in the Law* (Oxford: Hart, 2007) ch 10.

[60] Compare Jürgen Habermas 'Introduction' (1999) 12 Ratio Juris 329 at 330:

> [T]hough modern law requires from its addressees nothing more than norm-conformative behavior, it must nevertheless meet the expectation of legitimacy [*sic*], so that it is at least open to people to follow norms, if they like, out of respect for the law.

[61] It is important to appreciate that the question of choice is pervasive in the traditional legal form of regulation. Background rules set the standard and present the choice; but the way in which (smart) enforcement agencies/agents respond to their regulatees might often depend upon whether they (regulatees) are perceived to be 'compliers' by disposition or 'evaders'. In relation to compliers, enforcers might adopt a more flexible, cooperative, and light touch approach; but, in relation to evaders, an altogether stricter approach might be adopted. In other words, regulatees not only have a choice with regard to the background question of compliance but also as to the kind of enforcement (and inspection) regime that they invite. For extended discussion of the dynamics of such enforcement relationships, set in the context of game theory, see John T Scholz 'Cooperation, Deterrence, and the Ecology of Regulatory Enforcement' (1984) 18 Law and Society Review 179.

the desired pattern of behaviour. Hence, if the desired outcome is that x is done, the doing of x is all that matters. Those who do x need have no reasons for doing x; and regulators who employ a behavioural pitch need give no reasons. From this perspective, there is no difference between a robot doing x and a human doing x (albeit for no reason); in each case, the channelling strategy works; the desired pattern is achieved.

(vi) Regulatory phasing

Regulation might be 'first phase', 'second phase', or even 'third phase', and so on, in the following sense. Where regulation is first phase, its purpose is to control, confine, and channel ex ante the particular aspect of practice that is its target. Where such first phase regulation is successful, practice operates (by and large) in accordance with the rules (let us assume a rule-based approach) laid down by the regulatory order. For example, regulators who are concerned about the potential use of psychoactive drugs for cognition or performance enhancement might put in place a set of first phase prohibitions that seek to nip any such drug use in the bud. Where, by contrast, regulation is second phase, no attempt (or, at any rate, no successful attempt) is made to control, confine, or channel some given aspect of practice; regulators have abandoned such ex ante first phase intervention. Instead, second phase regulation operates ex post, endeavouring to compensate for, or adjust in response to, the consequences of a practice that cannot be controlled by first phase regulation.[62] So, for example, if first phase regulation fails to prevent the use of drugs as cognition or performance enhancers, a second phase regulatory strategy might try to lay down the parameters for acceptable use (implying that some use will remain prohibited). If second phase regulation is not feasible, regulators might even delay intervention until a third phase, seeking to channel conduct in a context where the (third phase) consequences of the (second phase) consequences (themselves being the consequences of first phase deregulation) invite a regulatory response.[63]

In this light, the well-known disagreement between Francis Fukuyama (who is ostensibly pro-regulation in relation to biotechnology) and Gregory Stock (who is anti-regulation) can be read as concerning the futility (or not) of first phase

[62] A clear example of this is the shift in emphasis from controlling crime to dealing, instead, with the effects or consequences of crime (for example, by regulating in relation to the fear of crime). See David Garland *The Culture of Control* (Oxford: Oxford University Press, 2001) 109 and 121 et seq. Indeed, as Garland goes on to argue, much of the new criminology can be understood as an adaptive response to the fact that crime is something we must live with. Within this adaptive response, we have the seeds of the techno-regulatory approach that I discuss in pt II of the book.

[63] This is not quite the same as the idea of regulatory 'sequencing'. Whereas sequencing is about a progressively tougher regulatory intervention, phasing is more concerned with when the decisive intervention is made.

interventions and the necessity to grapple with second phase consequences.[64] For Fukuyama, it is not too late to attempt first phase regulation; for Stock, the writing is on the wall and we would do better to address the implications of the (inevitable) biotechnological revolution. So, for example, if technology for the genetic enhancement of our offspring were to be developed to the point where it was safe and reliable, but prohibitively expensive for most parents, whereas Fukuyama might favour first phase gatekeeper regulation designed to control access to the technology, Stock's advice might be to apply our regulatory resources to second phase correction of those adverse social effects that seem likely to flow from technology being available only to a privileged elite.

In what follows, it is probably simpler to assume that we are dealing with first phase regulation (although the analysis is equally applicable to second or third phase regulation).

(vii) Regulatory range

In principle, whichever regulatory mode (or modes) are deployed, the desired channelling might be negative, neutral, or positive. Regulators might wish to channel conduct so that x is not done (negative channelling), or so that x is done (positive channelling), or so that agents have a choice between doing x or not doing x as they prefer (neutral channelling). Where traditional law-like regulation is employed, in its crudest form negative channelling presupposes a legislated rule that prohibits x; positive channelling a rule that requires x; and neutral channelling a rule that permits x. For example, in relation to the regulation of human genetics, legislation might prohibit reproductive cloning, permit therapeutic cloning, and require all citizens to contribute samples for a national genetic data base. Regulators, thus, may show human geneticists a red light or a green light, but the complexity of the intermediate positions is not captured by an amber light—at any rate, if it is captured, it is only in the general sense of cautioning that there is a lot more to the regulatory range than simple red light prohibitions and green light permissions.[65]

There is a great deal to be said about the regulatory range (even when we are thinking only about traditional law-like modes of regulation). However, using human genetics as the target practice, it will suffice for present purposes to identify four variables within the range.

First, where regulation prohibits some genetic practice, it might sanction non-compliance in more than one way. Prohibition might signify the creation of a criminal offence with penal sanctions—as with the statutory prohibition on

[64] Francis Fukuyama *Our Posthuman Future* (London: Profile Books, 2002); Gregory Stock *Redesigning Humans* (London: Profile Books, 2002).

[65] Compare Gary E Marchant and Douglas J Sylvester 'Transnational Models for Regulation of Nanotechnology' (2006) 34 Journal of Law, Medicine and Ethics 714, at 715–16 (for the distinction between permissive and prophylactic regulation).

human reproductive cloning in the UK—but this is not necessarily the case. For example, if legislation is introduced to regulate genetic discrimination, and if the model of existing anti-discrimination schemes is copied, then the prohibition will be in the form of a statutory tort. This will mean that the principal sanction for non-compliance will be a private law claim for redress, possibly with some pressure for conformity applied by regulators having supervisory responsibilities. Or, again, where prohibitions form part of a licensing scheme such as that centred on the Human Fertilisation and Embryology Authority (HFEA), the sanctions for non-compliance may be internal to that licensing scheme (for example, the revocation of a licence).

Secondly, where the regulatory position permits some genetic practice, this might be accompanied by various reservations and qualifications (permission with negative reservation) or by various measures aimed at encouragement and incentivization (permission plus facilitation).[66] When the HFEA is mandated to license research on human embryos if, and only if, such research is judged to be necessary, this signals that the permission is subject to negative reservation. However, negative reservation might also be manifested one step removed from the public law permission in private law. For instance, by refusing to treat 'designer baby' agreements as legally enforceable contracts or by rendering the tort regime more claimant-friendly in response to pharmacogenomic products, the background permission would be hedged with negative reservation. Importantly, however, the regulators might give the permission some encouragement by taking steps to facilitate the practice in question. Away from genetics, this regulatory approach has been very much in evidence in the steps taken to clear the way for the development of e-commerce.[67] In relation to genetics, the patent system is one of the keys to facilitation. For, whatever the ultimate *raison d'être* of patents, the working assumption is that the prospect of patent protection for inventive work encourages investment in research and development in genetics.[68] In this light, the debate about the patentability of inventive work around the human genome is not about prohibition versus permission but about permission subject to negative reservation versus permission plus facilitation. To the extent that the outcome is in favour of patentability, we have permission plus facilitation; to the extent that it is against patentability, we have permission subject to negative reservation.[69]

[66] Compare Andrew Murray *The Regulation of Cyberspace* (Abingdon: Routledge-Cavendish, 2007) 40–1 (dealing with the extent to which a permissive regulatory position opens itself to third-party challenge).

[67] cf Roger Brownsword and Geraint Howells 'When Surfers Start to Shop: Internet Commerce and Contract Law' (1999) 19 Legal Studies 287.

[68] See Amanda Warren-Jones 'Patenting DNA: A Lot of Controversy Over a Little Intangibility' (2004) 12 Medical Law Review 97.

[69] Compare the Nuffield Council on Bioethics *The Ethics of Patenting DNA* (London, July 2002).

Thirdly, to understand the character of the regulatory position, we need to attend to the regulatory *mix*. In the absence of a blanket prohibition under the criminal law or an unvarnished permission, the regulatory position is liable to mix elements of public and private law. To say that, in the UK, embryonic stem cell research is permitted is to say something rather significant—because, in many European countries, we have zones of regulated prohibition rather than regulated permission.[70] Nevertheless, so far as the UK is concerned, there is a good deal more to know: we need to know on what terms such research is permitted, whether the products of the research (for example, techniques that are developed for deriving and purifying embryonic stem cells) are patentable,[71] what sanctions apply if the informed consent of embryo donors is not obtained, whether the donors have any redress if the research is commercialized in a way that they did not expect, what the arrangements are for depositing and accessing stem cell lines at the national stem-cell bank,[72] and so on. In other words, the full *mix* of regulation needs to be kept in mind.

Fourthly, and finally, we also need to attend to the regulatory *tilt*, that is to say, we need to take into account the default position set by regulators. If the default position is set for prohibition, then the tilt is against permission. Conversely, if the default position is set for permission, then the tilt is against prohibition. Where the regulatory tilt is of the former kind, then ambiguities will be resolved in favour of prohibition and, similarly, where regulation is silent on a point, the presumption is that silence indicates prohibition. As in the standard caricature of German legal culture, the assumption is that in the absence of explicit permission, the activity is deemed to be prohibited. On the other hand, where the regulatory tilt is the other way, ambiguities will be resolved in favour of permission and silence will be read as indicating permission. Here, it is the caricature of English legal culture that applies, the assumption being that, in the absence of explicit prohibition, the activity is deemed to be permitted. As we will see, in due course, where the technology has moved on ahead of the express terms of the regulatory framework, the way in which judges read the tilt is highly material to their interpretation of the law.[73]

[70] See the review in Samantha Halliday 'A Comparative Approach to the Regulation of Embryonic Stem Cell Research' (2004) 12 Medical Law Review 40.

[71] For a critical view of the jurisprudence now emerging from the European Patent Office, see Graeme Laurie 'Patenting Stem Cells of Human Origin' (2004) European Intellectual Property Review 59.

[72] See 'Code of Practice for the Use of Human Stem Cell Lines' (version 3, August 2006). This code of practice, which is drawn up by a steering committee the membership of which reflects a range of disciplines and expertise, is presented as 'an evolving interim document' (ibid p 2). And, for an important analysis of a possible weakness at the interface between the Human Fertilisation and Embryology Authority and the UK stem cell bank, see Ryan Morgan 'A Lack of Foresight? Jurisdictional Uncertainties in the Regulatory Interface between the HFEA, the UK Stem Cell Bank and Beyond' (2007) 27 Legal Studies 511.

[73] See ch 6.

IV Rights

Participating some years ago at a symposium on the patenting of genetically engineered products—which was one of the first places in which modern genetics impacted on the law[74]—Baroness Mary Warnock spoke on the question of how ethicists might view modern technological developments.[75] She said:

> Technology has made all kinds of things possible that were impossible, or unimaginable in an earlier age. Ought all these things to be carried into practice? This is the most general ethical question to be asked about genetic engineering, whether of plants, animals or humans. The question may itself take two forms: in the first place, we may ask whether the benefits promised by the practice are outweighed by its possible harms. This is an ethical question posed in strictly utilitarian form.... It entails looking into the future, calculating probabilities, and of course evaluating outcomes. 'Benefits' and 'harm' are not self-evidently identifiable values. Secondly, we may ask whether, even if the benefits of the practice seem to outweigh the dangers, it nevertheless so outrages our sense of justice or of rights or of human decency that it should be prohibited whatever the advantages.[76]

It is implicit in these helpful remarks that, if we were dyed in the wool utilitarians, we would simply calculate the benefits and harms, acting on the option that promised to maximize the balance of benefit over harm. If we reasoned in this way, we would not take into consideration issues of justice or human decency; and nor would we take into account any question of rights—or at any rate, we would not take into account claimed violations of rights unless such claims were underwritten by utilitarian calculation. Thus, if we approached the technological revolution in this exclusively utilitarian spirit, while we would recognize the importance of setting a utility-maximizing regulatory environment, we would regard concerns about rights as largely irrelevant. Why, then, should we move beyond utilitarian reasoning, in the way that Warnock invites, to take on board considerations pertaining, in particular, to individual right?

There are at least three reasons for rejecting utilitarianism as the sovereign ethic to govern our deliberations about the legitimacy of developments in technology as well as the way that we regulate such matters. And, concomitantly, there are matching reasons for believing that individual rights should be taken seriously.

First, utilitarians have no deep defence of their axioms. To be sure, it is plausible to suppose that it is right to try to avoid causing pain or distress to ourselves and to others; and, other things being equal, it is plausible, too, to see the promotion of pleasure and happiness as a worthy objective. However, if we question why we

[74] See Roger Brownsword, WR Cornish, and Margaret Llewelyn (eds) *Law and Human Genetics: Regulating a Revolution* (Oxford: Hart Publishing, 1998).

[75] See Baroness Mary Warnock 'Philosophy and Ethics' in C Cookson, G Nowak, and D Thierbach (eds) *Genetic Engineering—The New Challenge* (Munich: European Patent Office, 1993) 67.

[76] ibid 67.

should accept these intuitively attractive guiding principles, utilitarians can give us no reason. In short, if we are not attracted by these principles, there seems to be no reasoned argument for being a utilitarian. Against utilitarianism, proponents of rights-based ethics believe that their views are not only intuitively more attractive (see the second point below) but, in some cases, susceptible of a deeper defence. Without doubt, any attempt to develop a deep defence of first ethical principles, whether utilitarian or rights-based, will be hugely controversial; but, insofar as a plausible reasoned defence (against all-comers, moralists, and amoralists) has been offered, it is in support of an ethic of individual rights.[77]

Secondly, although the starting points for utilitarian reasoning have a degree of plausibility, they soon lead to counter-intuitive results as the maximization of utility overrides the distribution of utility and the interests of individuals are sacrificed for the sake of the greater good. To some extent, the worst excesses of case-by-case act utilitarian reasoning can be tempered by taking a rule utilitarian approach. However, the adoption of a rule utilitarian approach sets up a tension within utilitarian thinking and, more importantly, it can never be as direct as a rights-based approach in ruling out the counter-intuitive overriding of individual interests. By contrast, a rights-based approach has an appeal against utilitarianism because those applications of utilitarianism that notoriously outrage our sense of justice and decency do so precisely because we are intuitively committed to an ethic that evinces respect for individual rights.

Thirdly, if the credentials of utilitarianism hinge on acceptance, then it must share the stage with rights-based reasoning. For, whether we test the ethical temperature locally, regionally, or internationally, the prevailing view is that, while it makes good (utilitarian) sense to support the research, development, and application of technologies that have a beneficial effect, such initiatives must always be compatible with respect for human rights and human dignity. As the Director General of UNESCO, Koïchiro Matsuura, put it when opening an international Round Table of Ministers of Science in October 2001, there is (within the group) a:

> [f]irm commitment to international solidarity in scientific progress, and to safeguarding human rights and human dignity from the misuse of science and technology, particularly in the life sciences.[78]

This has now been said and repeated so many times that I take it as axiomatic that the regulation of the technological revolution should ensure that the rights of individuals are fully respected.

[77] See the agency-based will-theory of rights seminally argued for in Alan Gewirth *Reason and Morality* (Chicago: University of Chicago Press, 1978) and elaborated in *Community of Rights* (Chicago: University of Chicago Press, 1996). We might contrast this with RM Hare *Moral Thinking* (Oxford: The Clarendon Press, 1981), in which a reasoned defence of utilitarianism is offered but only from an initial acceptance of moral reason.

[78] *Bioethics: International Implications* (Paris: UNESCO, 2003) p 2.

V A Community of Rights

If we accept that the development and application of modern technologies should be compatible with respect for individual rights, this gives us a particular critical vantage point. Even so, it is still a fairly broad vantage point, for there are many ethics that might claim to be rights-based; there are many ethics that might claim that they advocate taking the interests of individuals seriously.[79] Accordingly, where my commentary requires a more precise specification of the rights-based critical vantage point, I will refer to an ideal-type that I will term 'a community of rights'. As we proceed, I will have occasion to be more expansive about the nature of such a community. However, for the purpose of these introductory remarks, a thumbnail sketch will suffice.

First, because the community of rights is a particular kind of *moral* community, it must systematically embed a *moral* standpoint (in the formal sense). No doubt, there could be considerable debate about the precise specification of the generic characteristics of the formally-speaking 'moral', whether it is a moral standpoint or a moral community. However, I take it that a community of rights, as a moral community, must hold its commitments sincerely and in good faith, that it must treat its standards as categorically binding and universalizable, and that there must be an integrity and coherence about its commitments as a whole.

Secondly, because the community is a community of *rights*, the substantive moral approach embedded is rights-led, being committed to the protection and promotion of individual rights. In this respect, the community distinguishes itself from two other rival instantiations of moral community, these being utilitarian and duty-driven communities.[80]

Thirdly, a community of rights, so specified, might take quite a wide range of forms. Let me also stipulate, then, that in a community of rights, a will (or choice) theory of rights, rather than an interest theory of rights, is adopted.[81]

[79] For a particularly succinct version of the liberal version of such a rights-based community, see Justine Burley 'An Abstract Approach to the Regulation of Human Genetics: Law, Morality and Social Policy' in Han Somsen (ed) *The Regulatory Challenge of Biotechnology* (Cheltenham: Edward Elgar, 2007) 63, 66–8.

[80] For the most part, positions argued for in bioethical debates reflect one of three principal approaches, namely: utility-maximizing, rights-led, and duty-led. See, eg, Roger Brownsword 'Three Bioethical Approaches: A Triangle to be Squared', paper presented at international conference on the patentability of biotechnology organized by the Sasakawa Peace Foundation, Tokyo, September 2004 (available at <http://www.ipgenethics.org/conference/transcript/session3.doc>); 'Making People Better and Making Better People: Bioethics and the Regulation of Stem Cell Research' (2005) 1 Journal of Academic Legal Studies 3; and 'Cloning, Zoning and the Harm Principle' in Sheila AM McLean (ed) *First Do No Harm* (Aldershot: Ashgate, 2006) 527.

[81] On will and interest theories of rights, see HLA Hart 'Bentham on Legal Rights', in AWB Simpson (ed) *Oxford Essays in Jurisprudence* (Second Series) (Oxford: Clarendon Press, 1973) 171; and DN MacCormick 'Rights in Legislation' in PMS Hacker and J Raz (eds) *Law, Morality, and Society* (Oxford: Clarendon Press, 1977) 189.

Fourthly, it is a corollary of the third point that, in a community of rights, the paradigmatic bearer of rights is one who has the developed capacity for exercising whatever rights are held, including making choices about whether to give or to refuse consent in relation to the rights that are held.

Fifthly, a community of rights is to be understood as a reflective and interpretive society, not so much a finished product as an ongoing process. By this, I mean that it is a community that constantly keeps under review the question of whether the current interpretation of its commitments is the best interpretation. So, for example, the fact that a particular community of rights reviews technological developments by reference to its commitment to, inter alia, a right to individual freedom and well-being as well as a right to privacy, does not preclude it also reviewing its understanding of the scope and application of these rights.

Even with these specific features, the general concept of a community of rights might be articulated in a variety of particular conceptions (including, it should be said, a human rights conception). Accordingly, we might find conceptions of such a community with various epistemological bases (some more foundationalist than others), with different views about the status of non-paradigmatic rights-holders, with different arrays of recognized rights, with different approaches to conflicting and competing rights, and with different views about precaution, and so on.[82]

VI The Plan of the Book

It is trite to observe that modern technologies represent both a challenge and an opportunity—indeed, as Nick Bostrom has remarked, this is now a feature of the Western mainstream consensus.[83] Nevertheless, from a regulatory perspective, this truism points to two critical lines of inquiry. If the line of inquiry indicated by the idea of a regulatory challenge is to identify the problems of legitimacy and effectiveness presented by modern technologies, the line of inquiry prompted by the idea of regulatory opportunity is to consider the implications of modern technologies being taken up as regulatory tools. Broadly speaking, in the first part of the book, I focus on four types of regulatory challenge (concerning legitimacy, effectiveness, connection, and what I call cosmopolitanism); and, in the second part, I turn things round to focus on the question of regulatory opportunity.

In some respects, the regulatory challenges presented by new technologies are no different to the challenges faced by regulators whenever a particular activity is controversial or whenever compliance cannot be taken for granted. In the former

[82] Compare Deryck Beyleveld and Roger Brownsword 'Principle, Proceduralism and Precaution in a Community of Rights' (2006) 19 Ratio Juris 141.

[83] Nick Bostrom 'Technological Revolutions: Ethics and Policy in the Dark' in Nigel M de S Cameron and M Ellen Mitchell (eds) *Nanoscale* (Hoboken, NJ: Wiley, 2007) 129 at 131.

case, regulators will grapple with questions of legitimacy, and in the latter they will seek out strategies that are effective in limiting deviance. Whilst, in the case of some modern technologies, one senses that legitimacy is the hot spot—biotechnology is the obvious example—with others the hot spot seems to be effectiveness—the regulation of cyberspace might fit this description. However, all technologies have it in common that they advance at a pace that the law finds difficulty in matching. As John Braithwaite has remarked:

> The problem with [laws] is that they... have to be constantly updated to keep pace with scientific advances. Science always changes faster than any form of law because, by design, law aims for stability whereas science aims at growth and transformation by revolutionary paradigm shifts.[84]

In addition to questions of legitimacy and effectiveness, therefore, we need to consider the particular challenge of connection or regulatory sustainability.

The principal purpose of Chapters 2, 3, and 4 is to map the arguments that bear on the legitimacy of regulatory interventions. In Chapter 2, I identify three principal ethical forms (goal-orientated, rights-based, and duty-based) that support judgments of legitimacy. Often, debates about the legitimacy of regulatory responses to modern technologies are spearheaded by utilitarian (goal-orientated) and human rights (rights-based) standards. However, where such debates relate to biotechnology, and particularly where they relate to the regulation of human genetics, we find a three-way ethical opposition with each of the principal forms in play. Distinctively, in such contexts, we have seen the articulation of a dignitarian duty-based ethic that advocates caution, constraint, and conservativism in the face of the new technologies. Moreover, because this is an ethic that is agitated whenever particular technologies impact dramatically on our understanding of our essential humanity, we will find this three-cornered debate replicated in relation to the regulation of, say, neurotechnology and nanomedicine.

In Chapters 3 and 4, I deal with three key ethical concepts—namely, 'consent', 'harm,' and 'precaution'—that are regularly deployed in making assessments of the legitimacy of regulatory positions. My point is that these are not neutral concepts. To the contrary, what we make of consent, harm, or precaution, and the like, hinges on which of the three leading ethics we are presupposing.

In Chapter 5, I turn from the question of regulatory legitimacy to that of regulatory effectiveness. My intention here is to build on the general literature of regulation which gives us some insights into smarter and more effective ways of achieving our particular regulatory objectives. However, if we are to speak more specifically to the effective regulation of modern technologies, we need to concretize our regulatory intelligence in two stages. First, we need to understand the generic challenges that stand in the way of the regulability of modern technologies—the

[84] John Braithwaite *Corporate Crime in the Pharmaceutical Industry* (London: Routledge and Kegan Paul, 1984) 311.

outstanding difficulty being the pace of technological change, and concomitantly the challenge of regulatory connection, this important issue being reserved for discussion in Chapter 6. Secondly, we need to understand whether particular technologies present their own distinctive problems, much of this part of the discussion focusing on the regulation of information technology.

In the final chapter of the first part of the book, Chapter 7, I endeavour to put the questions of regulatory legitimacy and effectiveness in a larger regulatory context by setting national regulatory initiatives alongside regional and global regulatory regimes. Identifying the challenge here as one of regulatory cosmopolitanism, I consider two kinds of puzzle. One is how, as a matter of principle, we can regulate for universal values while also making exceptions for legitimate local difference; and the other is how national regulators can enforce their local standards in the face of regulatory tourism, international regulatory arbitrage, and the rapid growth of online provision that recognizes no national boundaries.

Having considered the challenges confronting regulators, in the second part of the book, I turn to the increasing adoption of modern technologies as regulatory tools. The opportunity presented by such technologies is obvious. For instance, in *R v Chief Constable of South Yorkshire Police, ex parte LS and Marper* (2004),[85] Lord Steyn endorsed the turn to technology in the following way:

> It is of paramount importance that law enforcement agencies should take full advantage of the available techniques of modern technology and forensic science. Such real evidence has the inestimable value of cogency and objectivity... It enables the guilty to be detected and the innocent to be rapidly eliminated from enquiries. Thus in the 1990s closed circuit television [was] extensively adopted in British cities and towns. The images recorded facilitate the detection of crime and prosecution of offenders.... The benefits to the criminal justice system [of DNA profiling] are enormous. For example, recent... statistics show that while the annual detection rate of domestic burglary is only 14%, when DNA is successfully recovered from a crime scene this rises to 48%.... [A]s a matter of policy it is a high priority that police forces should expand the use of such evidence where possible and practicable.[86]

With some 4 million profiles now held on the National DNA Database[87]—it was about 3 million when I first drafted this chapter—and with the average person being caught 300 times a day on CCTV,[88] we might see the United Kingdom as a pilot for technology-assisted criminal justice. But is this a regulatory opportunity that should be taken?

In Chapter 8, I draw together the development of the National DNA Database with that of the UK Biobank. The former database is for forensic purposes, the latter is for public health research purposes. The one is designed to assist in the

[85] [2002] EWCA Civ 1275, [2004] UKHL 39.

[86] [2004] UKHL 39, at paras 1–2.

[87] See Nuffield Council on Bioethics *The Forensic Use of Bioinformation: Ethical Issues* (London, 2007).

[88] See, eg, John Gibb *Who's Watching You?* (London: Collins and Brown, 2005).

investigation and elimination of crime, the other in the investigation and understanding of the genesis of major diseases. But, in both cases, we are relying on genetics to tighten our control. In the one case, we hope to channel citizens away from criminal behaviour and, in the other, we hope to channel citizens towards healthier forms of behaviour. It might seem innocuous. However, these are pointers to a regulatory approach that becomes more reliant on new technologies.

In Chapter 9, I draw a contrast between two ideal-typical forms of regulation, the East Coast and the West Coast, a contrast that I have mentioned earlier in this introductory chapter. The East Coast model, much like existing regulatory regimes relies mainly on law, social pressure, market signals, and the like. Technology is in the regulatory mix, but not in a systematic way. By contrast, the West Coast model relies exclusively on a technological fix. On the West Coast, the regulatory environment is technologically controlled such that the required pattern of behaviour is designed-in (or prohibited behaviour is designed-out). Assuming that the West Coast is a model of regulatory effectiveness, and assuming that the regulated pattern of behaviour meets whatever standard of legitimacy we want to specify, I consider the price that we pay for total control.

One of the objections to the West Coast is that regulatees have no choice but to act in accordance with the pattern that the technology dictates. In Chapter 10, I consider how, and why, the availability of choice matters for an aspirant moral community. In this light, we are left to wonder whether, where we substitute the Rule of Technology for the Rule of Law, we sign a death warrant not only for law but also for moral community.

Finally, in Chapter 11, I place the discussion (and narrative) in this book in the context of, so to speak, an underlying agenda that addresses issues of regulation and technology in a context of global governance. Although in this final chapter I pick up some of the underlying questions for further consideration, it is clear that there is a great deal more work to be done; regulation and technology is an open agenda that invites ongoing reflection. Having reached the last page of the book, readers will sense that there is much unfinished business. However, if we enter into the spirit of debate in a community of rights, this is as it should be.

Nevertheless, the book does offer a view. Stated shortly, that view is that the technologies of the 21st century, while presenting considerable challenges to regulators, also offer themselves as an opportunity for regulatory innovation. The fundamental mission that lies ahead for regulators is to respond to both the challenges and the opportunities in such a way that increments in regulatory effectiveness are not achieved at the cost of a diminution in legitimacy—or, even worse, at the cost of weakening the conditions that are essential for any aspirant moral community to have a meaningful purpose.

I

REGULATORY CHALLENGE

2

The Challenge of Regulatory Legitimacy I

I Introduction

Henk ten Have has rightly remarked that the 'current revolution in science and technology has led to the concern that unbridled scientific progress is not always ethically acceptable'.[1] Responding to this concern, the International Bioethics Committee (IBC) of UNESCO has been in the vanguard of attempts to forge a worldwide bioethical consensus, publishing three major instruments, namely: the Universal Declaration on the Human Genome and Human Rights in 1997, the International Declaration on Human Genetic Data in 2003, and most significantly—or, at any rate, certainly most ambitiously—the Universal Declaration on Bioethics and Human Rights in 2005.[2] Although the latest of these declarations is addressed specifically to 'ethical issues related to medicine, life sciences and associated technologies,'[3] it presents us with a starting point for thinking about the legitimacy not only of regulation directed at biotechnology but also of the regulation of neurotechnology and nanotechnology (at any rate, in its biomedical applications). Moreover, even if information technology does not seem like quite such an obvious candidate for a bespoke declaration on 'cyberethics',[4] there are clearly ethical concerns relating to IT (especially, human rights concerns),[5] and, as technologies converge and combine, the declaration might offer a useful reference point for debating newly arising ethical concerns.

[1] Henk ten Have 'UNESCO and Ethics of Science and Technology' in UNESCO *Ethics of Science and Technology: Explorations of the Frontiers of Science and Ethics* (Paris, 2006) 5–16, at 6.

[2] See Abdulqawi A Yusuf 'UNESCO Standard-Setting Activities on Bioethics: Speak Softly and Carry a Big Stick' in Francesco Francioni (ed) *Biotechnologies and International Human Rights* (Oxford: Hart, 2007) 85.

[3] UNESCO *Universal Declaration on Bioethics and Human Rights* (adopted by acclamation on 19 October 2005 by the 33rd session of the General Conference) Article 1.

[4] Compare Richard A Spinello *Cyberethics: Morality and Law in Cyberspace* (3rd edn, Sudbury, MA: Jones and Bartlett, 2006). Spinello employs three ethical approaches (utilitarian, contractarian rights-based, and Kantian duty-based), in conjunction with a post-Lessig range of regulatory options, to review four key issues: namely, freedom of online expression, intellectual property in cyberspace, internet privacy, and security.

[5] See Mathias Klang and Andrew Murray (eds) *Human Rights in the Digital Age* (London: Cavendish Glasshouse, 2005).

This chapter is in five sections. First, I sketch the general features of the declaration. Secondly, I identify and map three leading bioethical positions, each of which is compressed within the declaration. These positions, represented as the 'bioethical triangle',[6] generate a background ethical plurality that sets the scene for regulators. Thirdly, I comment on the increasingly important idea of human dignity, an idea which features strongly at two points of the bioethical triangle. In the fourth and fifth sections of the chapter, I offer two illustrative applications of the bioethical triangle: the first concerns the regulation of (human embryonic) stem cell research and therapeutic cloning and the second the recognition of proprietary entitlements in relation to human tissue and (detached) body parts.

To avoid any misunderstanding about the nature of the bioethical triangle, it is important to be clear about its relationship with what I see as the basic matrix that sets the form, rather than the substance, of ethical reasoning. I take it that the basic matrix—the matrix that sets the mould for ethical debates—involves three essential *forms*: namely, goal-orientated (consequentialism), rights-based, and duty-based forms. Each of these forms is open to a variety of *substantive* articulations, with various goals, various rights, and various duties being advocated. The bioethical triangle fully expresses the *form* of the matrix because it is constituted by a particular goal-orientated ethic, a particular rights-based ethic, and a particular duty-based ethic. However, the particular *substantive* articulations that are represented in the bioethical triangle are by no means exhaustive of all substantive ethical possibilities. In other words, the bioethical triangle should be viewed as a particular conjunction of ethical form and substance that reflects the way in which certain positions have come to dominate modern bioethical discourse and debate.

While the basic matrix always sets the formal pattern for debates about the legitimacy of regulatory positions and practices (that is, irrespective of the subject matter of the regulation), it is the bioethical triangle that sets the pattern for a great deal of substantive disagreement about the regulation of modern technologies (especially biotechnologies). However, the detail needs to be filled in; and, in Chapters 3 and 4, I will triangulate the pervasive (ethical and regulatory) principles of doing no harm to others, obtaining informed consent, and taking a precautionary approach to risk.

II The Universal Declaration on Bioethics and Human Rights

The Universal Declaration on Bioethics and Human Rights is in five principal parts. The first part, setting out the general provisions, speaks to the scope and the aims of the declaration. As we have said, the scope of the declaration is limited

[6] See Roger Brownsword 'Three Bioethical Approaches: A Triangle to be Squared', paper presented at international conference on the patentability of biotechnology organised by the Sasakawa Peace Foundation, Tokyo, September 2004 (available at <http://:www.ipgenethics.org/conference/transcript/session3.doc>) and 'Stem Cells and Cloning: Where the Regulatory Consensus Fails' (2005) 39 New England Law Review 535.

to medicine and the life sciences; and, in this sphere, it was already clear in the preliminary drafts that UNESCO would continue to press for recognition of:

> [t]he great benefit derived from scientific and technological developments, whilst ensuring that such development occurs within the framework of ethical principles that respect human dignity and protect human rights and fundamental freedoms, and... prevent practices contrary to human dignity.[7]

So, for example, in Article 2(d) of the final version of the declaration, one of the aims is said to be 'to recognize the importance of freedom of scientific research and the benefits derived from scientific and technological developments, while stressing the need for such research and development to occur within the framework of ethical principles set out in this Declaration and to respect human dignity, human rights and fundamental freedoms'.[8]

It is in the second, and longest, part of the declaration that we find the aforesaid ethical principles. Starting in Article 3(1) with the principle that '[h]uman dignity, human rights and fundamental freedoms are to be fully respected', and finishing in Article 17 with a principle of protection of the environment, the biosphere and biodiversity, this part of the declaration articulates familiar principles relating to the maximization of benefit and the minimization of harm (Article 4), the importance of individual autonomy (Article 5), and consent (Article 6), and requiring respect for privacy and confidentiality (Article 9). However, not all persons are robust individualists able to look after their own interests, and the declaration emphasizes the importance of respecting human vulnerability and integrity (Article 8), as well as setting out principles of equality (Article 10), and non-discrimination or stigmatization (qua 'violation of human dignity, human rights and fundamental freedoms') (Article 11). The declaration also conveys the sense of our essential connectedness (and, concomitantly, our mutual responsibilities) in a series of Articles that relate to solidarity and cooperation (Article 13), social responsibility and health (Article 14), benefit sharing (Article 15), and the protection of future generations (Article 16) and the environment (Article 17) (the latter of which has already

[7] See Article 2 of *Elaboration of the Declaration on Universal Norms on Bioethics: Third Outline of a Text* (Paris: 27 August 2004). Compare the preamble to the Universal Declaration on the Human Genome and Human Rights according to which, while 'research on the human genome and the resulting applications open up vast prospects for progress in improving the health of individuals and of humankind as a whole... [it is imperative]... that such research should fully respect human dignity, freedom and human rights'.

[8] Compare National Bioethics Advisory Commission *Ethical and Policy Issues in Research Involving Human Participants* (Bethesda, MD: August 2001) at i:

> Clearly, scientific investigation has extended and enhanced the quality of life and increased our understanding of ourselves, our relationships with others, and the natural world. It is one of the foundations of our society's material, intellectual, and social progress. For many citizens, scientific discoveries have alleviated the suffering caused by disease or disability. Nonetheless, the prospect of gaining such valuable scientific knowledge need not and *should not be pursued at the expense of human rights or human dignity.* (Emphasis added)

been mentioned). Last but not least, hidden away in the middle of this list, we find Article 12, according to which:

> The importance of cultural diversity and pluralism should be given due regard. However, such considerations are not to be invoked to infringe upon human dignity, human rights and fundamental freedoms, nor upon the principles set out in this Declaration, nor to limit their scope.

Arguably, this is one of the key principles of the declaration, seeking to lay down the ground rules for the relationship between cosmopolitan bioethical principles and local cultural identity. Or, to put this another way, Article 12, by striving to draw the line between non-negotiable global regulatory standards and negotiable local standards, foreshadows the challenge of regulatory cosmopolitanism that I deal with in Chapter 7.

In its third part, the declaration deals with the application of the principles. While Article 18 lays out the virtues of professionalism, honesty, integrity, and transparency in decision-making, coupled with consultation and participation, Article 19 sets out the need for ethics committees, and Article 21 speaks of the responsibilities of those engaged in transnational research activities, and the like. By contrast, Article 20 provides somewhat sparingly that 'appropriate assessment and adequate management of risk related to medicine, life sciences and associated technologies should be promoted'. One assumes that, if the precautionary principle as a general principle of application is implicated in the declaration, then this is where it is anchored.[9]

Broadly speaking, the fourth part of the declaration deals with the responsibilities of states (Articles 22 and 23) and UNESCO itself (Article 25) for the promotion, effectuation, and dissemination of the principles; and Article 24 provides, inter alia, for the responsibilities of states in connection with the spreading and sharing of scientific and technical knowledge.

Finally, in the fifth part of the declaration, we find a couple of Articles (Articles 26 and 28) that deal with matters of interpretation together with Article 27 which specifies the following terms on which the application of the principles may be legitimately limited:

> If the application of the principles of this Declaration is to be limited, it should be by law, including laws in the interests of public safety, for the investigation, detection and prosecution of criminal offences, for the protection of public health or for the protection of the rights and freedoms of others. Any such law needs to be consistent with international human rights law.

Hence, if regulators wish to derogate from the ethical principles set out in the second part of the declaration, they need special reasons—indeed, the double emphasis in Article 27 on countervailing rights and overarching international

[9] Arguably, Article 17 already implicates the precautionary principle in relation to the specific matters of environmental protection and sustainability.

human rights suggests that the special reasons would need to be of a kind that would be recognized in what I am calling a community of rights.[10]

Without doubt, the completion of the declaration is a significant milestone. Nevertheless, the drafting, which necessarily is at a high level of abstraction, glosses over two major difficulties. First, the line and the relationship between the cosmopolitan and the local is unclear (although, to some degree, these are problems that can be managed by adopting flexible notions such as 'the margin of appreciation', or the like). Secondly, a conflictual ethical pluralism is already written into the UNESCO cosmopolitan principles. Crucially, respect for human dignity not only sets limits on pushing ahead with the science, it is also open to an interpretation that puts it in tension with respect for human rights.

III The Nature of the Ethical Plurality and the Bioethical Triangle

If we were to try to tease out from the UNESCO Declaration the nature of the cosmopolitan commitments, we would find three competing ethics—the three ethical views that make up the bioethical triangle. These are: the utilitarian view, advocating the pursuit of human welfare (human health, wealth, and happiness); the human rights view; and the view of a constituency that we can term 'the dignitarian alliance'.[11] Each of these constituencies is rooted in a distinctive ethical type (respectively teleological or goal-orientated, rights-driven, and duty-driven), which articulates in its own way. Each constituency demands that regulators do the right thing; but each has its own gold standard for doing the right thing.

Occasionally, these three perspectives converge to invite regulators to act on a consensus. At present, this is the case with human reproductive cloning where there are overwhelming concerns about safety and risk. So, for example, Alan Colman, who was Research Director of PPL Therapeutics Ltd at the time of the successful and dramatic cloning of Dolly, has suggested that, if human reproductive cloning were to be attempted, it 'would quite likely join thalidomide in the teratogenic hall of infamy'.[12] Safety aside, there are also many other concerns—for example, concerns about subverting the cloned child's 'sense of an independent self';[13]

[10] See ch 1.

[11] See Roger Brownsword 'Bioethics Today, Bioethics Tomorrow: Stem Cell Research and the "Dignitarian Alliance"' (2003) 17 Notre Dame Journal of Law, Ethics and Public Policy 15.

[12] Alan Colman 'Why Human Cloning Should not be Attempted' in Justine Burley (ed) *The Genetic Revolution and Human Rights* (Oxford: Oxford University Press, 1999) 14, at 16.

[13] Lori B Andrews 'Is There a Right to Clone? Constitutional Challenges to Bans on Human Cloning' (1998) 11 Harvard Journal of Law and Technology 643, 655. See, also, on the widespread concern for the replicant's 'individuality', Ruth Deech 'Cloning and Public Policy' in Justine Burley (ed) *The Genetic Revolution and Human Rights* (Oxford: Oxford University Press, 1999) 95, 98; and (for a sceptical assessment) Dan W Brock 'Cloning Human Beings: An Assessment of the Ethical Issues Pro and Con' in Martha C Nussbaum and Cass R Sunstein (eds) *Clones and Clones: Facts and*

about the creation of confusion and ambiguity in familial relationships;[14] about the possibly disreputable purposes of cloners; about unnatural intervention in the human reproductive process; and, particularly so in Europe, about the dignity of human life and, concomitantly, the importance of ensuring that human dignity is not compromised.[15] In the event, as John Kunich has remarked, we find a 'degree of unanimity in opposition to cloning [that is] astounding, often uniting liberal and conservative, pro-life and pro-choice, and secular and religious people of various persuasions'.[16] Such three-way convergence is truly exceptional; more commonly, we find a two-way synthesis between utilitarian and human rights thinking.[17] However, too often for regulatory comfort, these perspectives generate competing and conflicting views (as is the case, for instance, with therapeutic cloning and human embryonic stem cell research which we discuss later in the chapter).[18]

1. *The Utilitarian Perspective*

Utilitarians count utility (encompassing individual pleasure and preference satisfaction, and the like, together with convenience and economy), the sum of utilities

Fantasies About Human Cloning (New York and London: WW Norton & Company, 1998) 141, 152–5.

[14] This consideration was highlighted by the House of Lords Select Committee in its report on *Stem Cell Research* (London: HMSO, 2002) HL Paper 83(i) (Report), Appendix 6 (Reproductive Cloning) para 6. Lawrence Wu 'Family Planning Through Human Cloning: Is There a Fundamental Right?' (1998) 98 Columbia Law Review 1461, 1496–1500 and 1509–10 argues that such fears are speculative and largely unfounded. However, his confidence in the individuation of the cloned child is aided by assumptions concerning a loving context, the child being informed as to its cloned status at the right time, and the fact that the child is cloned not being widely known.

[15] As the preamble to the Additional Protocol (dated 12 January 1998 at Paris) to the Convention on Human Rights and Biomedicine puts it, 'the instrumentalisation of human beings through the deliberate creation of genetically identical human beings is contrary to human dignity and thus constitutes a misuse of biology and medicine'. Similarly, see eg Rick Santorum 'The New Culture of Life: Promoting Responsible and Appropriate Medical Research' (2003) 17 Notre Dame Journal of Law, Ethics and Public Policy 151, 154–5 ('America has never been a nation of strict utilitarianism…And it is critical that we seek a responsible policy framework that will protect and enhance human dignity').

[16] John Charles Kunich 'The Naked Clone' (2002–2003) 91 Kentucky Law Journal 1, 3.

[17] See Roger Brownsword 'Regulating Human Genetics: New Dilemmas for a New Millennium' (2004) 12 Medical Law Review 14.

[18] All 191 members of the United Nations support a prohibition on human reproductive cloning. However, after four years of deliberation, during which time efforts were made to achieve a consensus covering the regulation of all uses of cloning technology (reproductive and therapeutic) in humans, the nations remained divided. On 18 February 2005, the Legal Committee voted 71 in favour, 35 against, with 43 abstentions, to recommend to the General Assembly that members should be called on 'to prohibit all forms of human cloning inasmuch as they are incompatible with human dignity and the protection of human life' (UN press release GA/L/3271: <http://www.un.org/News/Press/docs/2005/gal3271.doc.htm>). On 8 March 2005, the General Assembly accepted this recommendation, 84 members voting in favour of the (non-binding) UN Declaration on Human Cloning, with 34 against and 37 abstentions (UN press release GA/10333: <http://www.un.org/News/Press/docs/2005/ga10333.doc.htm>).

being aggregated in the credit column; and they count disutility (encompassing individual pain, suffering, and distress, and the frustration of preferences and the like, together with cost, inconvenience, and the general expenditure of resources), such disutilities being totalled in the debit column. For utilitarians, the maximization of utility and the minimization of disutility is all that counts; to do the right thing is to identify and adopt whichever option seems most likely to maximize utility or minimize disutility. Broadly speaking, Article 4 of the UNESCO Declaration—providing that '[i]n applying and advancing scientific knowledge, medical practice and associated technologies, direct and indirect benefits to patients, research participants and other affected individuals should be maximized and any possible harm to such individuals should be minimized'—speaks this kind of language.

Although utilitarians count the benefits/harms in relation to all those who are affected by an action, they restrict the calculation to those who are judged capable of experiencing pain or pleasure, having preferences and so on. Insofar as a human embryo is a pre-sentient life form, utilitarianism is not directly engaged—pre-sentient life fails to show interests in the relevant sense; and the logic of utilitarian thinking is that the same applies to post-sentient humans—as Lord Mustill famously remarked in the *Bland* case,[19] to talk about the 'best interests' of a human who is in a persistent or permanent vegetative state is to ignore the 'distressing truth' that he or she no longer has any interests in a material sense.[20] On the other hand, utilitarianism is directly engaged by sentient non-human life. Accordingly, in the *Harvard Onco-Mouse* case,[21] the utilitarian-minded examiners thought it perfectly sensible to weigh in the moral balance (that they took to be required by Article 53(a) of the European Patent Convention) the distress occasioned to a genetically engineered mouse.[22]

2. *The Human Rights Perspective*

For human rights theorists, the key is not positive or negative consequences so much as respect for individual human rights. Much of the history of bioethics hinges on ethical opposition to the idea that the interests of individuals may be legitimately sacrificed for the greater good. While Article 3(2) of the UNESCO Declaration emphatically confirms this opposition, insisting that '[t]he interests and welfare of the individual should have priority over the sole interest of science or society', which is to say that humans have rights and that they must be taken seriously, it remains moot who precisely qualifies for such protection. Like the utilitarians, human rights theorists do not usually recognize pre-sentient life

[19] *Airedale NHS Trust v Bland* [1993] 1 All ER 821.
[20] ibid 894.
[21] OJ EPO 10/1992, 590.
[22] See, further, ch 7 below.

as a bearer of rights.[23] Indeed, in the human rights tradition, an even more restrictive view is taken—even sentience does not suffice. Thus, in two recent decisions at Strasbourg, the European Court of Human Rights has declined to affirm that either a human embryo or a six month fetus is protected by the convention right to life.[24] If the embryo has no *direct* protective entitlement, the only caveats that will be imposed by this ethical approach relate to the need for free and informed consent by relevant rights-holders, such as women who donate eggs or couples who donate embryos, or they reflect any *indirect* or precautionary considerations.

It should be said, of course, that the caveats relating to free and informed consent are by no means trivial, unproblematic, or easily satisfied. Indeed, under pressure from proponents of human rights, these requirements have tended to become ever more demanding (particularly so in relation to the information to be supplied). For example, in Canada, there has been a lively debate concerning the adequacy of consent protocols where fresh embryos are sourced for stem cell research from IVF programmes. At issue is the question of whether we can be satisfied that the donor's consent is adequate when there is inevitably an element of situational and relational pressure in play and when a donor might not fully comprehend the sacrifice being made in giving up an embryo that might be utilized for her own reproductive purposes.[25] Depending upon the stringency of our conception of free and informed consent, we will be more or less readily satisfied as to such matters. In principle, however, human rights theorists are willing to be satisfied that all is well, that the consent clearance is adequate, and that embryonic stem cell research is ethically clean.

By now, we are well-versed in the tension between utilitarian promotion of the general good (where little or no attention is paid to the *distribution* of utility or disutility) and the constraints imposed if individual rights are to be respected.[26] Where human rights has made its mark, it is axiomatic, as we have just said, that best practice demands careful attention to free and informed consent, that the capacity for autonomous decision-making should be respected, that privacy and confidentiality should be protected, and so on. However, if bioethics was

[23] Compare the position presupposed by Carl Cohen in Carl Cohen and Tom Regan *The Animal Rights Debate* (Lanham: Rowman and Littlefield, 2001) at 35:

> To be a moral agent is to be able to grasp the generality of moral restrictions on our will. Humans understand that some acts may be in our interest and yet must not be willed because they are simply wrong. This capacity for moral judgment does not arise in the animal world; rats can neither exercise nor respond to moral claims.

[24] *Vo v France* (2005) 40 EHRR 12 (a 6 month fetus); *Evans v UK* [2006] ECHR 200 (7 March, 2006) (a human embryo).

[25] For critical assessment, see Jeffrey Nisker and Angela White 'The CMA Code of Ethics and the Donation of Fresh Embryos for Stem Cell Research' (2005) 173(6) CMAJ 621–2.

[26] For some vivid examples of researchers putting their projects before their research participants, see Aurora Plomer *The Law and Ethics of Medical Research – International Bioethics and Human Rights* (London: Cavendish, 2005) ch 2 (US human radiation experiments), ch 3 (UK Porton Down experiments), and ch 6 (research trials in developing countries).

once a two-way contest between utilitarians and human rights theorists, this is no longer the case.

3. The Dignitarian Perspective

Where a technology impacts on the human body, as is particularly the case with the human genetics applications of biotechnology, this is widely seen as raising concerns about human dignity. Even in the case of information and communication technology which, issues of (internet) content regulation apart, largely raises questions within and between utilitarian and human rights thinking, we find concerns about human dignity being expressed once a bio-application is proposed—witness, for example, the discussion by the European Group on Ethics in Science and New Technologies with regard to ICT implants in the human body.[27] At all events, what we now have is a third ethical constituency, an alliance of dignitarian views, making up the plurality.[28]

The dignitarian perspective condemns any practice, process or product—human reproductive cloning, therapeutic cloning, and stem cell research using human embryos being prime examples[29]—which it judges to compromise human dignity. Such condemnation (by reference to human dignity) operates as a 'conversation stopper';[30] but the dignitarians are not troubled—to say that something violates human dignity is the ultimate condemnation. The emergence of the new dignitarian view creates a genuinely triangular contest, the dignitarians disagreeing as much with the utilitarians as they do with the human rights constituency—with the former because they do not think that consequences, even entirely 'beneficial' consequences (that is, 'beneficial' relative to a utilitarian standard), are determinative; and with the latter because they do not think that informed consent cures the compromising of human dignity.

[27] Opinion No 20 of the European Group on Ethics in Science and New Technologies to the European Commission *Ethical Aspects of ICT Implants in the Human Body* (adopted 16 March 2005).

[28] Compare Roger Brownsword 'Biotechnology and Rights: Where are We Coming from and Where are We Going?' in Mathias Klang and Andrew Murray (eds) *Human Rights in the Digital Age* (London: Cavendish Glasshouse, 2005) 219; and Susan Millns 'Consolidating Bio-rights in Europe' in Francesco Francioni (ed) *Biotechnologies and International Human Rights* (Oxford: Hart, 2007) 71.

[29] See, eg, June Mary Zekan Makdisi 'The Slide from Human Embryonic Stem Cell Research to Reproductive Cloning: Ethical Decision-Making and the Ban on Federal Funding' (2003) 34 Rutgers Law Journal 463.

[30] See Dieter Birnbacher 'Do Modern Reproductive Technologies Violate Human Dignity?' in Elisabeth Hildt and Dietmar Mieth (eds) *In Vitro Fertilisation in the 1990s* (Aldershot: Ashgate, 1998) 325. Compare Nuffield Council on Bioethics *Genetically Modified Crops: the Ethical and Social Issues* (London, 1999) at 96 (those who contend that genetic modification is intrinsically wrong or unnatural present views that 'have something of an "unarguable" quality, inasmuch as no amount of information, explanation or rationalisation would move a person with such views from their position').

Insofar as the dignitarian view expresses a religious or a Kantian approach, the duty to respect human dignity (or not to compromise human dignity) will be treated as cosmopolitan; and, because the sharp end of dignitarian ethics is to identify which practices should be prohibited, it invites being regarded as imperialistic.[31] Insofar as it is communitarian, the dignitarian view might be of more limited range—for example, insisting on embryo protection at home but without arguing that all nations should do the same thing. Amongst its arguable cosmopolitan principles, dignitarianism decrees that human life should be protected and respected (from the point of conception onwards), that life should be recognized as having no price (hence, it should not be commercialized) and that life should not be instrumentalized (hence, it should not be commodified).[32]

While the third point of the bioethical triangle brings together a range of duty-driven approaches, each taking it as axiomatic that human dignity must not be compromised, the dignitarian alliance does not have a monopoly on the idea that human dignity should be respected. For human rights thinking also subscribes (albeit in a rights-led way) to the fundamental importance of human dignity. It is, thus, to the elusive concept of human dignity that we must shortly turn.

Before we do so, however, let me enter four short, but important, caveats about the bioethical triangle. First, let me repeat my introductory warning that the bioethical triangle is a particular substantive articulation of the underlying formal ethical matrix. So, while the dignitarian alliance is a particular articulation of a duty-driven ethics, it does not follow that all duty-driven ethics have dignitarian characteristics—in the next chapter, for example, we will note that, whereas the dignitarian view is generally dismissive of the significance of consent, this is by no means so with all duty-driven bioethics. Secondly, on closer inspection, we might well find that each of the three principal constituencies in the bioethical triangle can be broken down into sub-constituencies and, indeed, it might be argued (particularly in relation to the dignitiarian alliance) that some of these sub-constituencies have much less in common than the triangular representation implies. Thirdly, some ethical positions might reflect more than one point of the triangle. For example, the approach advocated by Mary Warnock, that we quoted in the previous chapter, operates with a utilitarian default position but then sets some limits to straight utilitarian calculation by reference to concerns about human rights and human decency. Whether or not such a synthesis is rationally defensible, there is no doubt that this is actually the working ethic that is adopted by many British policy makers. Fourthly, even allowing for sub-constituencies and for syntheses, there might be some ethics that are simply off this particular substantive map. One might wonder, for example, whether a feminist ethic is on

[31] Compare Roger Brownsword 'Cloning, Zoning, and the Harm Principle' in Sheila McLean (ed) *First Do No Harm* (Festschrift for Ken Mason) (Aldershot, Ashgate, 2006) 525.

[32] Compare Tim Caulfield and Roger Brownsword 'Human Dignity: A Guide to Policy Making in the Biotechnology Era' (2006) 7 Nature Reviews Genetics 72.

the map and, if so, where it is located. In her recent book, *Property in the Body*,[33] the feminist bioethicist Donna Dickenson argues for a sophisticated Lockean version of property rights in relation to various body parts and samples. Although this thesis involves the 'novel position ... that the most legitimate property in the body is that which women possess in their extracted reproductive tissue',[34] this reads very much like an ethic of rights. However, so long as there are traces of background limiting feminist convictions,[35] it makes no sense to try to shoehorn these views into a particular ethical constituency. Hence, if we were to try to go both broader and deeper, our map of bioethical debates might become significantly more complex. As ever, there is a trade-off: for present purposes, we can stick with relative simplicity, because this is what we need if we are to get our bearings in relation to the landmarks of the UNESCO Declaration.

IV Human Dignity

In debates concerning the ethics and regulation of biotechnology, human dignity is an idea that appears in two very different roles, in the one case acting in support of individual autonomy (human dignity as empowerment) and, in the other case, acting as a constraint on autonomy (human dignity as constraint).[36]

We can try to disentangle and clarify these two approaches to human dignity by taking one step at a time. First, we can identify the salient features of human dignity as empowerment; secondly, we can do the same with human dignity as constraint; thirdly, we can point to the contrast between human dignity, on the one hand, as a distinctive characteristic of individual persons that speaks to their moral entitlement and obligation and, on the other hand, as a collective good to be respected by a community; fourthly, we can anticipate where practical tensions are likely to arise between these approaches; and, finally, we can consider the possible extension of these rival conceptions of human dignity to matters of the environment.

1. Human Dignity as Empowerment

The conception of human dignity as empowerment is very closely linked with modern human rights thinking. In particular, human dignity is explicitly declared to be one of the foundational ideas in the Universal Declaration of Human Rights 1948,

33 Donna Dickenson *Property in the Body* (Cambridge: Cambridge University Press, 2007).
34 ibid 67.
35 For example, ibid 86, we read that 'both cord blood and the stem cell technologies share an *inherently anti-feminist view* [my emphasis] of organisms as "sets of replaceable parts"'.
36 The terminology here comes from Deryck Beyleveld and Roger Brownsword *Human Dignity in Bioethics and Biolaw* (Oxford: Oxford University Press, 2001). Compare Ronald Dworkin *Life's Dominion* (London, Harper Collins, 1993) especially at 233–7.

and its partner Covenants on Economic, Social and Cultural Rights 1966, and on Civil and Political Rights 1966. Thus, the preamble to each of these instruments provides that 'recognition of the inherent dignity and of the equal and inalienable rights of all members of the human family is the foundation of freedom, justice and peace in the world'; and Article 1 of the Universal Declaration famously proclaims that 'All human beings are born free and equal in dignity and rights'. That is to say, each and every human being has inherent dignity; it is this *inherent* dignity that grounds (or accounts for) the possession of *inalienable* human rights; and, because all humans have dignity, they hold rights equally. So understood, the injunction to respect human dignity is much more than a demand that we commonly make in contexts where we detect demeaning or degrading treatment, or where we are trying to give weight to an interest in privacy, it is perceived to be the infrastructure on which the entire superstructure of human rights is constructed.

If the inherent dignity of humans is the justifying reason for the possession of human rights, what is it precisely that dignity connotes? To say that humans have dignity, meaning that humans have a value, simply by virtue of being members of the human species will not convince even fellow humans. For any attempt to privilege the members of a particular species, including the members of the human species, merely by virtue of their species-membership will attract the charge of 'speciesism' —such a response is arbitrary and it plainly will not do. If humans have a value, it must be for a better reason than this.

Humans, let us concede, are different from rocks and stones; humans have the capacity to value their existence; they have preferences; and they have the capacity to make free and informed choices—or, at any rate, such is the phenomenology of human experience. When we are throwing pebbles on a beach, we need not worry whether we are acting against their preferences or interfering with their purposes, because quite simply they have none. Similarly, although computers are getting ever smarter, I do not yet pause to think that I might be acting unfairly by using my laptop more than my desktop computer. When, however, we discriminate between humans or throw them around, it is a very different matter. So, dignity, in the sense of the capacity to make one's own choices, or to value one's own preferences, and so on, distinguishes humans from inanimate objects and, quite probably, from most other non-human living things. However, we are still some way short of seeing how human dignity justifies human rights in anything more than a limited way.

From the mere fact that humans have the capacity to make choices or to value their preferences, it takes a leap to maintain that humans have a right to make choices and to act on them. Nevertheless, if we accept that human dignity (qua the capacity to make choices) is worthy of respect, then the following triple demand is invited: that one's capacity for making one's own choices should be recognized; that, other things being equal, the choices one freely makes should be respected; and that the need for a supportive context for autonomous decision-making should be appreciated and acted upon. Such demands may then be expressed as entitlements that are due to each human as of right.

2. *Human Dignity as Constraint*

Philippe Séguin, President of the National Assembly of the French Republic, remarked in the mid-1990s that the trend towards the enactment of bioethics laws (such as the three French Acts on bioethics of July 1994):

illustrates a growing awareness around the world that legislators must, despite the difficulties, act to ensure that *science develops with respect for human dignity and fundamental human rights*, and in line with national democratic traditions.[37]

This trend is further illustrated in many different instruments. From the Council of Europe's Convention on Human Rights and Biomedicine[38] through to the EC Directive on the Legal Protection of Biotechnological Inventions[39] we find ringing declarations in favour of human dignity; and, as we have said, respect for human dignity is treated as axiomatic in the three UNESCO Declarations. Insofar as these provisions simply reinforce the demand that human rights should be respected, they say little that is new. However, it is in these most recent appeals to human dignity that we find the new turn in the rhetoric of bioethics, specifically by reliance on human dignity as constraint.

In modern European bioethics, human dignity is articulated in a way that appeals to a coalition of Kantians, Catholics, and communitarians.[40] In fact, both interpretations—human dignity as empowerment and human dignity as constraint—can claim to be rooted in the seminal writing of Immanuel Kant, For, in Kant's work, we find not only the idea that humans have intrinsic dignity (which suggests a conception of human dignity as empowerment, albeit duty-driven rather than rights-driven)[41] but also that human dignity has no price and that humans owe themselves a duty of self-esteem (which might suggest a conception of human dignity as constraint). In *The Metaphysics of Morals*, Kant collects together the strands of his thinking as follows:

Every human being has a legitimate claim to respect from his fellow human beings and is *in turn* bound to respect every other. Humanity itself is a dignity; for a human being

[37] Philippe Séguin 'Speech by Mr. Philippe Séguin' in *Proceedings of the Third Session of the International Bioethics Committee of UNESCO, September 1995*, vol i (Paris: International Bioethics Committee of UNESCO, 1995) 119, 120 (emphasis added).

[38] This convention is sometimes referred to as 'the Bioethics Convention'. Its full title is Convention for the Protection of Human Rights and Dignity of the Human Being with Regard to the Application of Biology and Medicine: Convention on Human Rights and Biomedicine 1996. For analysis, see Susan Millns (n 28 above).

[39] Directive 98/44/EC; [1998] OJ L 213.

[40] Generally, see Jacob Rendtorff and Peter Kemp *Basic Ethical Principles in European Bioethics and Biolaw (vol I: Autonomy, Dignity, Integrity and Vulnerability)* (Copenhagen: Centre for Ethics and Law, 1999).

[41] For the significance of this distinction, see Deryck Beyleveld and Roger Brownsword 'Human Dignity, Human Rights, and Human Genetics' in Roger Brownsword, WR Cornish, and Margaret Llewelyn (eds) *Human Genetics and the Law: Regulating a Revolution* (Oxford: Hart, 1998) 69; and Deryck Beyleveld and Roger Brownsword (n 36 above).

cannot be used merely as a means by any human being... but must always be used at the same time as an end. It is just in this that his dignity (personality) consists, by which he raises himself above all other beings in the world that are not human beings and yet can be used, and so over all *things*. But just as he cannot give himself away for any price (this would conflict with his duty of self-esteem), so neither can he act contrary to the equally necessary self-esteem of others, as human beings, that is, he is under obligation to acknowledge, in a practical way, the dignity of humanity in every other human being. Hence there rests on him a duty regarding the respect that must be shown to every other human being.[42]

In these much-quoted remarks, modern writers can (and do purport to) find support for a variety of supposed applications of Kantian morality, not just in practical matters generally but specifically within the fields of bio-science and bio-commerce.[43] For, Kant's remarks, if taken literally, are an open invitation to claim that commercialization of the human body is an affront to dignity (by putting a price on something that is beyond price).

Thus, commodification and commercialization of the human body—whether in the form of trade in human organs or tissue, prostitution, surrogacy for profit, or patenting human genes—is just one of a number of practices that are regularly cited as instances of human dignity being compromised. Typically, human dignity as constraint also condemns sex selection and positive (eugenic) gene selection, germ-line gene therapy, embryo research and abortion, euthanasia and assisted suicide, genetic discrimination, and (perhaps top of its current list) human reproductive cloning. The list, however, is hardly closed; and there surely will be additions as technology opens up new bio-options and opportunities—for example, there are already indications that dignitarians are troubled by the idea of nanotechnologies being applied (in biomedical settings) for purposes that involve commodification of the body[44] and, similarly, of neurotechnologies being applied (most immediately in the form of smart drugs) to enhance cognition or to improve our mood.[45]

3. *Two Reference Points for Human Dignity*

When we order our thinking about human dignity, we can fix on two different reference points. One reference point is the idea that human dignity speaks to what is special or specific about humans, that is to say, what is intrinsically

[42] I Kant *The Metaphysics of Morals* (translated and edited by Mary Gregor) (Cambridge: Cambridge University Press, 1996) (first published 1797) 209.

[43] See, eg, W Wolbert 'The Kantian Formula of Human Dignity and its Implications for Bioethics' (1998) 4 Hum. Reproduction & Genetic Ethics 18.

[44] See, eg, Bert Gordijn 'Converging NBIC Technologies for Improving Human Performance: A Critical Assessment of the Novelty and Prospects of the Project' (2006) 34 Journal of Law, Medicine and Ethics 726, and 'Ethical Issues in Nanomedicine' in Henk ten Have (ed) *Nanotechnologies, Ethics and Politics* (Paris: UNESCO, 2007) 99.

[45] President's Council on Bioethics *Beyond Therapy* (New York: Dana Press, 2003).

and universally distinctive about humans. As Francis Fukuyama has put it, the demand made in the name of human dignity is one for equal recognition which implies 'that when we strip all of a person's contingent and accidental characteristics away, there remains some essential human quality underneath that is worthy of a certain minimum level of respect…'[46] This reference point is to be contrasted with the idea that human dignity speaks less to what is special about humans qua humans and more to what is special about a particular community's idea of civilized life and the concomitant commitments of its members. Here, appeals to human dignity draw on what is distinctively valued concerning human social existence in a particular community—indeed, on the values and vision that distinguish the community as the particular community that it is and relative to which the community's members take their collective and individual identity. In principle, each starting point has the scope to support human dignity as empowerment as much as human dignity as constraint. In practice, however, whereas the former tends to be closely associated with human rights movements aimed at giving individuals the opportunity to flourish as self-determining authors of their own destinies, the latter (as expressed by the dignitarian alliance) combines a (Kantian) view of what is distinctive about humans (their dignity) with views about what defines life as civilized (and, thus, respectful of human dignity) in a particular community.

4. *Practical Tension Between the Rival Approaches*

Once put into practical application, there are two particular hot-spots where we can anticipate a tension between human dignity as empowerment and human dignity as constraint.

First, because human dignity as constraint takes a more inclusive protective approach than human dignity as empowerment, there are likely to be tensions in relation to human life that lies beyond the direct protection of the latter. For example, in the cases already mentioned at the European Court of Human Rights,[47] it was human dignity as constraint that offered the more direct protective shield. Similarly, we will see (in pt V of this chapter) that, wherever the question of using human embryos for research comes up, it is the dignitarians (relying on human dignity as constraint) who argue against permissive regulation. And, again, if it is proposed to extend reproductive choice by appealing to human dignity as empowerment, it is human dignity as constraint that responds in defence of embryos that are subjected to screening procedures (for positive or negative selection).

[46] Francis Fukuyama *Our Posthuman Future* (London: Profile Books, 2002) 149. According to Fukuyama, although 'many would list human reason and human moral choice as the most important unique human characteristics that give our species dignity, I would argue that possession of the full human emotional gamut is at least as important, if not more so' (p 169).

[47] Above n 24.

Secondly, whereas human dignity as empowerment pushes for the extension of individual autonomy, human dignity as constraint takes a more limited view.[48] Whilst the former is protective of choices that are made on a free and informed basis, the latter limits autonomy to those choices that do not compromise human dignity. This kind of tension is perfectly illustrated by the famous French dwarf-throwing ('lancer de nain') case,[49] where the Conseil d'Etat, upholding the restrictions on dwarf-throwing in clubs, presupposed human dignity as constraint in insisting that the dwarves compromised their own dignity. Similarly, on at least one reading of the more recent *Omega* case,[50] the Bonn authorities closed the shooting arcade for reasons reflecting a conception of human dignity as constraint. In both cases, the argument in support of the autonomy of the dwarfs and games-players presupposed human dignity as empowerment.

5. *Human Dignity and the Environment*

In his book, *Crimes Against Nature*,[51] Robert Kennedy Jr launches a blistering attack on the Bush administration's reversal of established environmental protection policy—the principle that the polluter pays has, it seems, been turned on its head; the Environmental Protection Agency, Kennedy claims, has become more like a country club for America's polluters than a regulatory agency, and so on. At one point, Kennedy despairs of the weak enforcement against the meat barons:

> In violating our federal antipollution laws like the Clean Air and Clean Water Acts, the meat barons are stealing something that belongs to the American public—the purity of our land and waterways, healthy air, abundant fisheries. They have lulled people into accepting unhealthy, unsavoury meat and have gained a stranglehold on US commodity production that poses a genuine threat to our food independence and national security.

[48] Compare David Feldman 'Human Dignity as a Legal Value: Part I' *Pub. L.* (1999) 682, at 685, where it is rightly observed that human dignity can cut both ways:

> [W]e must not assume that the idea of dignity is inextricably linked to a liberal-individualist view of human beings as people whose life-choices deserve respect. If the state takes a particular view on what is required for people to live dignified lives, it may introduce regulations to restrict the freedom which people have to make choices which, in the state's view, interfere with the dignity of the individual, a social group or the human race as a whole. ... The quest for human dignity may subvert rather than enhance choice. ... Once it becomes a tool in the hands of lawmakers and judges, the concept of human dignity is a two-edged sword.

[49] Conseil d'Etat (27 October 1995) req nos 136–727 (Commune de Morsang-sur-Orge) and 143–578 (Ville d'Aix-en-Provence). See MC Roualt's note on the two decisions *Les Petites Affiches* (24 January 1996, No 11) 30, at 32. And, for reflections on the case, with dignity being interpreted as the essence of humanity, see B Edelman 'La Dignité de la Personne Humaine, un Concept Nouveau' Recueil Dalloz 1997, 23e Cahier, Chronique, 185, 187–8.

[50] *Omega Spielhallen- und Automatenaufstellungs- GmbH v Oberbürgermeisterin der Bundesstadt Bonn* (Case C-36/02) [2004] OJ C300/3. For comment, see Thomas Ackermann (2005) 42 CMLR 1107.

[51] Robert F Kennedy Jr *Crimes Against Nature* (London: Penguin Books, 2005).

But our battle is more than a fight to save American farming and fishing communities. It is a fight to preserve human dignity.[52]

Even though the gist of the critique is for restraint, Kennedy's rhetoric might be taken as an expression of the empowerment conception of human dignity. For so long as the sustainability of the environment is connected to the sustainability of autonomous human life, then the empowerment conception will argue for restraint. Hence, if agricultural biotechnology might have indirect negative effects from a human rights perspective, then at the very least it needs to be monitored.[53]

Having said that, we also hear in this rhetoric something akin to the voice of human dignity as constraint, possibly captured by a larger ethic of veneration.[54] And, this is by no means an isolated instance—witness, for example, the doubts about GM crops as they have been expressed in some European countries (for example, in Switzerland and Austria). In other words, rhetoric of this kind might well signal that a community defines itself by taking a protective attitude to non-human life and the natural environment—and, possibly, by placing certain technologies categorically off limits,[55] if not for the sake of human dignity as such, then in order to defend its particular view of civilized life.[56]

V Human Embryonic Stem Cell Research and Therapeutic Cloning

The ethics, and legitimacy, of so-called 'therapeutic cloning', or allied procedures involving the isolation and manipulation of human embryonic stem cells, are deeply controversial. Nations that are united in condemning human reproductive cloning and supporting its worldwide prohibition become divided when it is

[52] ibid 75.

[53] Compare the powerful presentation of this line of thinking in Laura Westra 'Environmental Rights and Human Rights: The Final Enclosure Movement' in Roger Brownsword (ed) *Human Rights* (Oxford: Hart, 2004) 107.

[54] Jean-Christophe Galloux, Arne Thing Mortensen, Suzanne de Cheveigné, Agnes Allansdottir, Aigli Chatjouli, and George Sakellaris 'The Institutions of Bioethics' in Martin W Bauer and George Gaskell (eds) *Biotechnology – The Making of a Global Controversy* (Cambridge: Cambridge University Press, 2002), where three ethical frames are identified—one organized around the principle of utility, a second around the principle of democracy, and a third around the principle of veneration.

[55] Compare Nuffield Council on Bioethics *Genetically Modified Crops: The Ethical and Social Issues* (London, May 1999) paras 1.32–1.50 (discussing the natural/unnatural boundary, taboos, and moral conservatism).

[56] Compare, eg, the *LICRA v Yahoo! Inc* case where an auction site hosted in the USA (although set up on a server in Europe) by Yahoo! offended local values in France by offering Nazi memorabilia for sale. See Douglas W Vick 'Regulating Hatred' in Mathias Klang and Andrew Murray (eds) *Human Rights in the Digital Age* (London: Cavendish, GlassHouse Press, 2005) 41; and Jack Goldsmith and Tim Wu *Who Controls the Internet?* (Oxford: OUP, 2006) ch 1.

proposed that therapeutic cloning, too, should be covered by the prohibition;[57] and, around the world, within nation states, a patchwork of regulatory provisions is to be found. In some jurisdictions, there are outright prohibitions; in others, the position is permissive but heavily qualified (for example, restricting researchers to the use of supernumerary human embryos); in others, the regulation is relatively liberal (notably that in the United Kingdom);[58] and, in yet others, we find a form of regulatory schizophrenia with prohibition coexisting with permission.[59]

In an attempt to map the various ethical positions and their regulatory articulations, we can start by sketching the perceived promise of human embryonic stem cell research. If this line of research promises significant therapeutic benefits, then we need to locate the dignitarian reasons for opposing it. This leads to a consideration of the coherence of the limits imposed by essentially permissive regimes on the creation and use of human embryos for research as well as the vexed debate about the moral status of the human embryo. Finally, we can review the positions taken up by the House of Lords Select Committee on Stem Cell Research[60] (in which it was accepted that strictly regulated use of human embryos for research is compatible with the principle of respect for the embryo) and, more recently, by the House of Commons Science and Technology Select Committee in its report on the use of human-animal cytoplasmic hybrid embryos for stem cell research.[61]

1. *The Promise of Human Embryonic Stem Cell Research*

For some years, so-called adult stem cells have been in clinical application in the form of bone marrow transplantations. Some researchers believe that adult

[57] All 191 members of the UN agree in principle that there should be a declaration banning human reproductive cloning. However, only a minority agrees that the ban should extend to all uses of cloning technology in humans. See n 18 above.

[58] eg in 2004 the regulatory authority (the HFEA) approved an application from Professor Ian Wilmut (who led the team that cloned Dolly the sheep) to undertake therapeutic cloning of human embryos with a view to understanding more about the early development of motor neurone disease: see Nuffield Council on Bioethics *Bioethics News* (Issue 43, 8 October 2004) (on file with author).

[59] Such 'schizophrenia' might be reflected in funding restrictions that do not map on to the legislative scheme of permission and prohibition; or in prohibition subject to quite unprincipled permissive exemption. For a helpful review of the regulatory scene in Europe, see Samantha Halliday 'A Comparative Approach to the Regulation of Human Embryonic Stem Cell Research in Europe' (2004) 12 Medical Law Review 40; and, more recently, the European Group on Ethics in Science and New Technologies, *Recommendations on the Ethical Review of hESC FP7 Research Projects* Opinion No 22 (20 June 2007) 29–31 and Table 1 at 32. For the US, see Shawn E Peterson 'A Comprehensive National Policy to Stop Human Cloning: An Analysis of the Human Cloning Prohibition Act of 2001 with Recommendations for Federal and State Legislatures' (2003) 17 Notre Dame Journal of Law, Ethics and Public Policy 217.

[60] See House of Lords Select Committee on Stem Cell Research *Stem Cell Research* (London: HMSO, February 2002) HL Paper 83(i) (Report) and 83(ii) (Evidence).

[61] House of Commons Science and Technology Select Committee *Government Proposals for the Regulation of Hybrid and Chimera Embryos* (Fifth Report of Session 2006–07) (HC 272–I, 5 April 2007).

stem cells have much greater plasticity than has hitherto been assumed and that it would be sensible (and less ethically problematic) to dedicate more research resource towards exploring such potential. However, the prevailing view is that embryonic stem cells hold the key to a therapeutic revolution and that, in consequence, this is where research energies should be focused.

To understand the excitement associated with stem cell research, we need to appreciate the special character of such cells. Briefly, stem cells are special because they are a potential source of new cells—for example, blood stem cells will replenish blood cells, neural stem cells will replenish brain cells, skin stem cells will replace skin, and so on. Human embryonic stem cells (hES cells), however, are special because they are still in a so-called pluripotent state. As pluripotent stem cells, hES cells have the potential to develop into any one of the 200 or so human cell types and, in natural development, they will duly specialize in this way. By contrast, even if adult stem cells (ie stem cells that have already developed to perform one or more specialized functions) have a degree of flexibility, the orthodox view is that their function in the human body is relatively stable. In other words, whilst say (adult) blood stem cells might be able to regenerate blood cells, they are not thought to have the capacity to regenerate brain cells; and, similarly, neural stem cells are not thought to have the capacity to regenerate blood cells.

If researchers were able to isolate, purify and culture hES cells, and if they were able to simulate the mechanisms by which such cells differentiate to become specialized adult stem cells, what benefits might this bring? The importance of such an advance in our knowledge is explained by James Thomson, the pioneering hES cell researcher, in the following way:

> As developmental biologists become more accomplished at directing hES cells to specific cell types, the differentiated derivatives of the cells should have an important role in developing new therapies. Large, purified populations of hES cell-derived cells, such as heart muscle cells or neurons, could be used to screen for new drugs. Purified, normal human cells would allow accurate screening of candidate drugs, greatly reduce the need for animal testing during the early screening process, and accelerate drug discovery. Differentiated derivatives of hES cells also could be used to test for possible toxic side effects of drugs identified by other methods, and hES cells would be particularly useful for identifying compounds that interfere with normal development.
>
> Finally, differentiated derivatives of hES cells could be applied to transplantation therapies for treatment of a range of human diseases.... Numerous diseases might be treated by this approach, including heart disease, juvenile-onset diabetes, Parkinson's disease, and leukemia.[62]

Interestingly, in contrast with the stem cell debate in the United Kingdom, Thomson identifies the drug development implications first, before going on

[62] James A Thomson 'Human Embryonic Stem Cells' in Suzanne Holland, Karen Lebacqz, and Laurie Zoloth (eds) *The Human Embryonic Stem Cell Debate* (Cambridge, Mass: MIT Press, 2001) 15, 21–2.

to highlight the possibility of cell-based transplantation therapies for serious diseases.[63] Nevertheless, there is an unmistakable promise of stem cell-based therapies for a very wide range of human diseases and disorders. Moreover, if the human embryos from which the stem cells were isolated were generated by a process of cell nuclear replacement (CNR) that used the patient's own tissue, this should dramatically reduce the risk that the cells developed for transplantation might be rejected. In idealised accounts, therefore, the promise is of a bespoke treatment regime—for example, a patient suffering from Alzheimer's disease supplies some tissue, say, skin cells; they are reprogrammed using CNR; embryonic stem cells are derived from the CNR-embryo and cultured to differentiate into millions of brain cells which are then transplanted into the patient.

Not surprisingly, then, where a positive view is taken, the general perception is that therapeutic cloning and stem cell research represent a field of very considerable medical significance.[64] Whether we are thinking about bespoke stem cells and their derivatives for transplantation or generic lines or collections for therapy as well as for drug-testing, it is conceivable that there could be major benefits resulting from this kind of research. This creates a pressure on regulators to pave the way for such research initiatives. But, are there any ethical counter-arguments and how might a permissive regulatory approach play relative to the bioethical triangle?

2. *Why Not Take a Permissive Approach?*

For both utilitarians and human rights theorists, the promised benefits of human embryonic stem cell research are positive considerations. On the negative side, there seem to be no real counter-weights: we assume that terminated embryos do not suffer and nor do they have rights; and, provided that those who donate eggs or embryos do so on the basis of free and informed consent, all is well.

Yet, are we looking hard enough for the negatives? First, are we being sufficiently careful to check for indirect damage to rights-holders? Maybe human embryos do not have rights; and, in this respect, they are comparable to other life-forms that do not have rights. However, one concern about the mistreatment of such life-forms is that it sets a bad example that leads, *indirectly*, to a weakening of respect for rights-holders. Granted, there is no straight-line connection. Notoriously, Hitler was a dog lover; and it might be that a person who is cruel to cats behaves perfectly properly when dealing with rights-holders. We really do not know. Secondly, there is the even less straightforward risk of the context

[63] We might also note the reluctance in Warnock (n 73 below) to make human embryos available for routine testing of drugs (in para 12.5).

[64] See Roger Brownsword 'Stem Cells, Superman, and the Report of the Select Committee' (2002) 65 Modern Law Review 568; and, even after many twists and turns, not to mention South Korean scandals, the optimism persists, see eg Ian Sample 'How Stem Cells Can Turn Back the Biological Clock' *The Guardian*, 15 June 2006, 15.

that sustains a community of rights being compromised. Just as individual acts of pollution cumulatively corrode the physical environment, might it be that resort to therapeutic cloning cumulatively changes the social environment in a way that undermines the conditions for a flourishing community of rights? Some commentators believe that genetic engineering poses an insidious risk of this kind. However, although therapeutic cloning might involve some genetic manipulation, it is not carried through into social relations in the way that would occur in reproductive contexts. If there is a risk here it is that people perhaps live longer or that, thanks to stem cell treatments for Parkinson's and Alzheimer's diseases, the quality of life for large classes of elderly people is considerably improved. These developments might have important economic consequences as well as consequences for the allocation of public health care resources; however, if there is some deeper threat to a rights-respecting community, it is unclear what it is. Accordingly, if the onus is on those who assert such indirect negatives, then the burden of proof is liable to be heavy (at any rate, for the time being). We might conclude, therefore, that therapeutic cloning seems to be ethically clean—unless, of course, one is a dignitarian.

Taking a dignitarian view (guided by a conception of human dignity as constraint), the ethical imperative is to avoid compromising human dignity; and the application is perfectly clear—the human embryo is to be directly respected. It matters not that the human embryo cannot experience distress or make its own choices. It is *not* like a rock or a stone. It is a living thing and a member of the human species. As such, it is protected by the overarching value of respect for human dignity. It has moral status and to treat it like a rock or a stone is to compromise human dignity. Once we have considered the details of a permissive regulatory approach, we can return to the dignitarian objection.

3. The Devil is in the Detail (of Permissive Regulatory Positions)

It is often said that human dignity is too vague an idea to be fit for regulatory purposes. In one sense, this is undoubtedly correct: any regulatory instrument that purports to restrain conduct where it would be 'contrary to human dignity' simply invites too many competing interpretations. In another sense, however, nothing could be more straightforward: for, if we adopt a dignitarian view, it is perfectly clear where the regulatory lines should be drawn—and, in particular, it is perfectly clear that regulators should prohibit the use of human embryos as research tools. Ironically, it is the translation of the utilitarian and human rights ethics into preferred regulatory positions that is more complex.

If we assume that therapeutic cloning and human embryonic stem cell research is to be permitted, regulators might hedge their permission in various ways—for example, by permitting only supernumerary embryos that would be destroyed anyway to be made available for research. Even in the United Kingdom, where the regulatory framework allows for the use of supernumerary embryos as well as embryos donated for research ab initio, and (in defiance of Article 18(2) of the Convention on Human Rights and Biomedicine) allows for the use of embryos specially created for research, there are restrictions. In particular, research is only to be licensed where the regulatory authority judges that it is necessary[65] (in the sense of it not being possible to do the research in any other way) as well as being necessary or desirable in relation to one of the approved statutory purposes.[66] Yet, why impose such restrictions? Would they (or more extensive restrictions) make sense from the perspective of utility or human rights?

Consider the logic of utilitarianism. Generally speaking, from a utilitarian perspective, the local context and culture will influence the particular contours of even a permissive regulatory regime. It follows that utilitarians might advocate some particular regulatory restrictions in some places at some times, but not in other places or in any place at other times. Nevertheless, how would we expect utilitarians to respond to the kind of restrictions mentioned?

First, utilitarians would surely accept efficiency arguments in favour of prioritizing the use of embryos that are surplus to requirement in IVF programmes and that will have to be destroyed anyway. Not only would it seem wasteful not to use such supernumerary embryos before turning to other sources, it might also chime in with public preference and sentiment. Against such utilities, there might be deficits if the embryos that are available to be sourced from IVF programmes are lower grade and not optimal for stem cell research. However, if the regulatory position merely prioritizes the use of supernumerary embryos provided that they are suitable for research, this does not hinder research and there is no real difficulty.

Secondly, if the regulatory position prohibits the creation of embryos specifically for research, this might prove a serious obstacle to stem cell research which relies on specially designed embryos as its research tools. To be sure, stem cell research would not grind to a standstill: therapies might be developed using adult stem cells (or even fetal stem cells); stem cell lines might be imported; and there would still be supernumerary embryos available for research. Nevertheless, if the prohibition seriously interferes with research, utilitarians would need some convincing that it makes sense. In this light, utilitarians would want to take a hard look at Article 18(2) of the Convention on Human Rights and Biomedicine (as, indeed, they would want some convincing that research should be confined to adult stem cells).

[65] Human Fertilisation and Embryology Act 1990, sch 2, para 3(6).

[66] Originally, there were five such purposes: see ibid sch 2, para 3(2). To clear the way for human embryonic stem cell research and therapeutic cloning, three further purposes were added by the Human Fertilisation and Embryology (Research Purposes) Regulations: SI 2001/188. Doubts having been expressed about whether the additional purposes cover basic stem cell research, the government declared its intention to legislate on this matter for the avoidance of doubt: see Department of Health *Review of the Human Fertilisation and Embryology Act* (Cm 6989, December 2006) 2.74; and appropriate provision is duly made in sch 2 of the draft Human Tissue and Embryos Bill 2007.

Thirdly, what would utilitarians make of the twin constraints of *necessity* (meaning that the research cannot be carried out without using human embryos—in particular, that it cannot be conducted using non-human animals) and *proportionality* (meaning that human embryos should not be used for 'trivial' research purposes, such as, to take the standard example, research into baldness)? On the face of it, neither restriction would make immediate sense. If research on human embryos causes no distress, while research on animals causes distress, Peter Singer and other like-minded utilitarians surely would be quick to point out that the argument of necessity cuts in the wrong direction.[67] They would also resist the intuition that so-called 'trivial' research purposes should be excluded. If undertaking such research generates more utility than not doing so, the argument of proportionality tries to rewrite the basic arithmetic of utilitarian calculation.[68] Having said this, where local conditions reveal strong support for constraints of this kind (irrational though they might seem to be to any straight-thinking utilitarian), the disutility of opposing these preferences would need to be taken into account.

Turning to human rights theorists, first, there is no particular rights-related reason to prioritize the use of supernumerary embryos. To be sure, the persons for whom such embryos are now surplus to reproductive requirement should not be precluded from donating their embryos; but this is not an argument for their prioritization.

Secondly, to prohibit the *donation* of embryos specifically for research impinges on the autonomy of the donors; and to prohibit the *creation* of embryos specifically for research impinges on the freedom of researchers. Why should such persons not be permitted to make a useful contribution to medical research? Indeed, if prospective beneficiaries of the research have a right that the state at the very least does not impede medical research unless there is a clear violation of right, patients' rights are infringed by such limitations.

What, then, of necessity or proportionality, or similar restrictions that are designed to reduce the use of human embryos or make them research tools of last resort? How do such constraints evince respect for rights? Under a standard articulation of human rights thinking, neither human embryos nor non-human animals have rights;[69] and, thus, there is no direct rights argument to favour one class of research resource over another. If there is some indirect argument here to support the necessity restriction, it needs to be teased out. As for the constraint

[67] See Peter Singer *Rethinking Life and Death* (Oxford: Oxford University Press, 1995) for Singer's thinking on the significance of sentience (sentient life to be valued more highly than non-sentient life) and purposive agency (purposive sentient life to be valued more highly than non-purposive sentient life).

[68] NB the argument of proportionality applied to research on animals is in line with utilitarian thinking: researchers should not subject animals to great distress unless such disutility is offset by the utility produced for the human beneficiaries of the research. Compare the reasoning of the examiners at the European Patent Office in the Harvard Onco-mouse application, OJ EPO 10/1992, 590.

[69] But note the precautionary argument to be considered in ch 4.

imposed by proportionality, human rights theorists certainly hold that more pressing rights should take priority over less pressing rights—which perhaps has some purchase on the priorities that should direct the efforts of the research community. However, this is quite different from holding that non-rights-bearing embryos should be used for research only where pressing human rights are at stake. Once again, unless an argument concerning the indirect impact on rights is to be teased out, proportionality makes no more sense as a restriction than necessity. Surprisingly, then, the logic of robust human rights thinking might be to take up an even more permissive regulatory position than that indicated by utilitarianism.

4. *The Moral Status of the Human Embryo*

Against a permissive regulatory approach, dignitarians stand on the protected moral status of the human embryo. On this question, dignitarians brook no argument; it is strictly non-negotiable; and there is little to be said other than that one accepts this view or starts somewhere else (as is the case with the utilitarian and human rights views). However, those who do start elsewhere often make a concession to the dignitarian position by recognizing the embryo as having a special status (albeit not a status that precludes embryo research). Yet, so long as we are eschewing the *direct* protection of dignitarianism, how can we render such a version of respect plausible? What kind of *indirect* or contingent considerations might be drawn into the utilitarian and human rights perspectives?[70]

First, as indicated already, negative utilitarians seek to minimize the sum total of distress. Whether the source of my distress is what I regard as inappropriate action in relation to myself, or in relation to others, it matters not. Nor does it matter that the 'others' in relation to whom I am experiencing distress would not themselves figure directly in a utilitarian calculation. The crucial fact is that I do count; I am distressed; and this must be weighed. What this amounts to, therefore, is that utilitarians must respect the attitudes of its membership insofar as they hold negative views about embryo research. However, if we have no qualms about embryo research, and if there are no other negative utilities to be detected, we would have no problem with proceeding.

Secondly, in some contexts, the consequences of treating a human embryo as if it were no more than a rock or a stone might be damaging to the way in which we respond to the claims made by those who do have moral status. In other words, utilitarians might be concerned that lack of respect for human embryos tends towards lack of respect for those who are sentient; and rights theorists might

[70] For a brave attempt to translate respect for human embryos into a reluctance to treat embryos as mere research objects coupled with a recognition that this is a potential person, see Karen Lebacqz 'On the Elusive Nature of Respect' in Suzanne Holland, Karen Lebacqz, and Laurie Zoloth (eds) *The Human Embryonic Stem Cell Debate* (Cambridge, Mass: MIT Press, 2001) 149.

worry that lack of respect for human embryos tends towards a weakening of respect for the entitlements of rights-holders. The fact that, in both utilitarian and human rights theories, there is a clear distinction between those, such as the human embryo, who do not have moral status and those who do is neither here nor there. If there is a reasonable belief that lack of concern for the one might lead to lack of respect for the other, there is a reason for acting with restraint in relation to human embryos.

Thirdly, there is the potentiality of the human embryo. On the one side, it is argued that potentiality is not actuality, that acorns are not yet oaks any more than students are already graduates or embryos already fetuses let alone born humans. From this it follows that whatever respect or recognition attaches to actual or achieved status cannot be read across to those still in the category of potentiality; and, thus, there is no reason why potential humans, merely by virtue of their potentiality, should be treated as though they are already actual humans. To this, the standard riposte is that we are dealing here, not with potentiality at large, but specifically with potential human life—and, this we are led to believe, is a special case. Clearly, this exchange is stuck in the mire. On the one side (the latter side as presented above), the potential for human life, the 'radical' potential, is seen as giving the embryo moral status.[71] It is not a matter of treating the embryo 'as if' it had moral status; quite simply, it already has what it takes to be accorded moral status in its own right. Such is the dignitarian position. On the other side, a more restrictive view of moral status is taken. The embryo does not qualify and the question is why potential qualification should be treated as sufficient. From utilitarian and human rights perspectives, therefore, potentiality is a poor argument for moral status (which, itself, does not hinge on the potential for human life). Nevertheless, from such perspectives, is there anything more that can be said about potentiality as a contingent consideration?

The potentiality of the human embryo might figure as a factor in indirectly protective arguments of the kind already sketched. Over and above such considerations, the potentiality of the embryo might be linked into a precautionary approach that results in a degree of protection. In the case of utilitarianism, the relevant threshold is sentience. Quite where this threshold lies is moot. However, if there is any risk of inadvertently crossing the line, the utilitarian may think it right to err on the side of caution. By drawing the line on embryo research at 14 days, the utilitarian might judge that English law takes an excessively cautious approach. Nevertheless, the fact that the embryo (all being well) is on the way to becoming a being with moral status must generate some caution unless we are entirely confident about the point at which that status is achieved. The human rights standard for moral status, however, is so far beyond the level of development achieved by the embryo that potentiality coupled with precaution

[71] See eg, John Keown 'Restoring Moral and Intellectual Shape to the Law after *Bland*' (1997) 113 Law Quarterly Review 481.

seemingly adds little to the argument for protection. Indeed, the logic of this approach suggests that it is not until we are dealing with children that we approach the threshold for moral status.[72]

5. *The Select Committee's Response to the Ethical Objection*

Where a permissive regulatory regime is proposed, dignitarians might express their opposition in two ways. First, in its stronger form, the objection is that the use of human embryos for research is unjustifiable and should be prohibited. On this view, human embryonic stem (hES) cell research, whatever its supposed benefits, is categorically wrong. In its weaker form, the objection is that supporters of embryo research cannot have it both ways; that is to say, they cannot claim that they respect the embryo (or recognize its special status) and, at the same time, claim that the creation or use of human embryos for research is justifiable—in other words, the weaker objection challenges the coherence of a position such as that taken by the Warnock Committee (whose recommendations ushered in the Human Fertilisation and Embryology Act 1990).[73] What did the House of Lords Select Committee on Stem Cell Research[74] have to say on these matters?

Although Article 18 of the Convention on Human Rights and Biomedicine which, inter alia, categorically prohibits the *creation* of human embryos for research, supports the objection in its stronger form, the United Kingdom has not yet committed itself to the Convention.[75] As for arguments based explicitly on respect for human dignity, although the Select Committee notes that appeals to this idea increasingly feature in international frameworks designed to set ethical limits for science and medicine, the committee effectively rejects it as an elusive notion which falls short of offering practical guidance when the aim of the exercise is to set limits to permissible research on human embryos.[76] As I have pointed out already, however, this particular piece of conventional wisdom is not entirely convincing: the dignitarians offer perfectly clear and precise practical guidance as to the limits of permissible research on human embryos—quite simply, no such research is permissible.

[72] For an argument that combines proportion with a more systematic form of precaution, see Deryck Beyleveld and Roger Brownsword *Consent in the Law* (Oxford: Hart, 2007) ch 4; and see further ch 4.

[73] *Report of the Committee of Inquiry into Human Fertilisation and Embryology* (the Warnock Committee Report) (London: HMSO, Cm 9314, 1984).

[74] See House of Lords Select Committee on Stem Cell Research *Stem Cell Research* (London: HMSO, February 2002) HL Paper 83(i) (Report) and 83(ii) (Evidence).

[75] But cf the approach of the Human Genetics Commission, urging the government to sign and ratify the Convention: see *Inside Information* (London: Human Genetics Commission, May 2002).

[76] Report, n 74 above, paras 7.3–7.7. Interestingly, whilst the committee fully supports the ban on reproductive human cloning in the Human Reproductive Cloning Act 2001, it does not rest on human dignity—rather it is the risk of physical abnormality coupled with the ambiguity of a cloned child's relationship with its parents that troubles the committee: Report, para 5.21 and app 6.

Clearly, the committee is starting at another point of the bioethical triangle, essentially accepting the broadly utilitarian position struck by Warnock and enshrined in the 1990 legislation. This not only serves to shut out human dignity as constraint, it excludes any serious engagement with the ethical objection in its stronger form and leads fairly rapidly to the committee's central conclusion, namely that 'the Committee is not persuaded, especially in the context of current law and social attitudes, that all research on human embryos should be prohibited'.[77] However, to the extent that the committee avoids engaging with the stronger ethical objection by rehearsing the position attacked by the weaker objection, what sense does it give to its commitment to respect the special status of the human embryo?

As a measure of its respect for the human embryo, the committee endorses the current 14 day limit for embryo research.[78] It underlines the sensitivity that is required where human tissue is handled,[79] and it argues that embryos, whether standard or CNR,[80] 'should not be created specifically for research purposes unless there is a demonstrable and exceptional need which cannot be met by the use of surplus embryos'.[81] The report also makes a pair of mutually reinforcing recommendations the aim of which is to minimize the use of embryos in research, namely: (i) that, where the Human Fertilisation and Embryology Authority (HFEA) grants licences for hES cell research, it should impose a condition requiring that any ES cell line generated in the course of the research should be deposited in a national cell bank; coupled with (ii) that, before granting any new licence for hES cell line research, the HFEA should be satisfied that no suitable cell lines are already available in the cell bank.[82] What are we to make of these concessions to the embryo?

From a utilitarian perspective, the 14 day limit, as we have remarked, might seem a touch over-cautious—the embryo surely is still some way from being sentient. Nevertheless, if such a restriction serves to maintain public confidence in the integrity of embryo research and its regulation, this may well be a measure worth taking. From a rights perspective, the attachment to a 14 day limit has no clear rationale. Even on a precautionary approach, the possibility that the embryo is already an agent does not markedly alter at this stage of what we understand to be its developmental path.

Why should the committee emphasize the need for human tissue to be handled sensitively? At least three considerations spring to mind. First, the insensitive handling of such material can cause offence—one only has to recall the notorious

[77] Report, para 4.21.

[78] Report, para 4.22.

[79] Report, para 4.25.

[80] That is, an embryo produced by the process of cell-nuclear replacement and stimulation of the engineered egg.

[81] Report, paras 4.28 (standard embryos) and 5.14 (CNR embryos).

[82] Report, para 8.29.

Kelly case[83] where removed body parts were incorporated in so-called works of art. From a utilitarian standpoint, there is good reason to avoid occasioning such gratuitous distress. Secondly, if the way in which the tissue is handled deviates from the expectations of the donors, this will be a matter that concerns both rights theorists (who will detect departures from the terms of the consent given)[84] and utilitarians (who will fear that bad publicity might interfere with the donation of embryos needed for utility-yielding research). Thirdly, insofar as the tissue contains information about the genetic make-up of any individuals who do have moral status, then both utilitarians and rights theorists will be concerned, the former about the consequential disutility and the latter about breaches of privacy and confidentiality.

The committee also insists that embryos should not be specifically created for research if surplus embryos are available and fit for the purpose; and it endorses the necessity principle written into the 1990 legislative framework. This amounts to the following two principles: (1) surplus human embryos are not to be used for research unless it is necessary (unless, in effect, the research cannot be carried out using animals); and (2) human embryos are not to be specifically created and used for research unless the research cannot be carried out using surplus embryos. But, why worry most about the creation of human embryos, then about the use of surplus human embryos, and least of all about non-human animals? As we have seen already, this order of protective priorities does not self-evidently cohere with either a rights perspective or a utilitarian approach.

Finally, it is worth observing that, although the committee is strongly opposed to those who are sources of human embryos treating their embryos as commodities to be sold, it does not relate its view on this matter to the question of respect for the human embryo.[85] Yet, it would have been perfectly plausible to have identified a stand against commodification or commercialization as one aspect of the respect due to human embryos.[86] Or, at any rate, this would have been a natural move to be made by a committee guided by the dignitarian perspective. That the committee was not so guided is overwhelmingly clear. Indeed, as we have said, its remarks on respect for human embryos fit best with a utilitarian bioethics shaped by a political sense of how far and how fast the public seems to be prepared to go with the latest technology.

[83] *R v Kelly* [1998] 3 All ER 741.

[84] cf Loane Skene 'Proprietary Rights in Human Bodies, Body Parts and Tissue: Regulatory Contexts and Proposals for New Laws' (2002) 22 Legal Studies 102, at 117–18, for the proposal that there should be a personal, but not a proprietary, right to permit our bodies, body parts, and tissue to be used for inter alia medical or scientific research. Consent for such use may be subject to express or implied conditions. Where conditions of this kind are flouted by researchers (or other recipients), it is suggested that, in principle, damages should be available (at 123). See, further, section VI below.

[85] Report, para 8.32.

[86] See, further, the analysis in section VI below.

6. *Another Select Committee, Another Question: Hybrids and Chimeras*

Although the regulatory environment in the United Kingdom was modified in 2001 to facilitate local human embryonic stem cell research,[87] work has been hampered by the difficulties of sourcing sufficient human eggs. However, if non-human animal eggs (such as eggs from cows or rabbits) might serve as second-best hosts for cell nuclear replacement and therapeutic cloning, and even if this is something of a long-shot, then why not permit the regulators to license stem cell research that utilizes such eggs?[88] Given that the regulatory position already permits the creation and use for research of embryos generated from enucleated human eggs with replacement human cellular content, is there any reason why it should not also permit the creation and use for research of embryos generated from enucleated non-human animal eggs with replacement human cellular content? Is the fact that the engineered egg involves a degree of animal-human mixing—that the intention is to generate a so-called human-animal cytoplasmic hybrid embryo—any reason for restricting the research?

Even though researchers sometimes bring together human and animal cellular features in their research models,[89] such hybrid and chimera models being both lawful and relatively common practice in the UK, the prospect of creating human-animal cytoplasmic hybrid embryos prompted debate on a spectrum of chimeras and hybrids. Taking the lead, the House of Commons Science and Technology Select Committee rightly identified the three points of the bioethical triangle as the key ethical constituencies.[90]

The utilitarian case for proceeding with the research is self-evident. As we have said, human embryonic stem cell research promises a major breakthrough in the manner and effectiveness of treating some of the most serious human diseases and disorders. Such research is held up by the shortage of human eggs. If eggs sourced from animals will serve instead, and if this will maintain the momentum of the research, the utility is obvious. Granted:

> [s]ome may argue that whilst they accept the creation of human-animal chimera or hybrid embryos for their immediate purpose (to produce embryonic stem cell lines), there are concerns at what may follow: perhaps in this case, that allowing scientists to create

[87] Human Fertilisation and Embryology (Research Purposes) Regulations 2001, SI 2001/188.

[88] Research undertaken by Professor Hui Z Sheng's team in China encourages the belief that this strategy might work: see 'Chinese Fusion Method Promises Fresh Route to Human Stem Cells' *Nature* 424, 711 (14 August 2003).

[89] See House of Commons Science and Technology Select Committee *Government Proposals for the Regulation of Hybrid and Chimera Embryos* (Fifth Report of Session 2006–07) (HC 272–I, 5 April 2007) paras 27–30.

[90] Report, n 89 above, paras 34–7. Compare the Academy of Medical Sciences *Inter-Species Embryos* (London, July 2007) at 28–30 (especially, para. 8.3.1, for consideration of the objection that 'the creation of human embryos containing animal material is unacceptable because it subverts the animal-human species distinction and undermines human dignity and human rights').

human-animal chimera or hybrid embryos may eventually result in the birth of such creations.[91]

Of course, if there was a possibility of such new life forms being born, or if such creations actually were born, the positive and negative impact of their possible or actual birth would need to be factored into the overall utilitarian calculation.

From a human rights perspective, too, there is a strong imperative to permit such research; indeed, it is eminently arguable that 'since such research promotes human rights through the development of treatments and thus enhances human capability', it should be 'actively encouraged'.[92] Reassuringly, since a human-animal cytoplasmic hybrid embryo, even if essentially human, is not yet a bearer of rights, then so long as there is no intention to take such embryos beyond 14 days' development (or, crucially, no intention to try to take such embryos to a live birth) there is no rights-based objection.[93]

Predictably, just as with embryo research itself, it is the dignitarian view that presents the most resolute ethical opposition to this new line of stem cell research. As the committee summarized the matter:

There is also an argument that research of this nature compromises *human dignity*, and it is this argument which has formed much of the opposition evidence we have received in this inquiry. For example, we heard from the Scottish Council on Human Bioethics (SCHB) that 'the creation of certain kinds of human-nonhuman embryonic combinations could seriously undermine the whole concept of human dignity'[Ev 57]. However, what is meant by the phrase human 'dignity' is vague. Professor Raanon Gillon told us that 'the concept of human dignity is a very complex one and people have different accounts of what they mean by it'[Q 211]. The SCHB told us that 'in this regard, it should be remembered that the concept of human dignity is not a scientific one. No individual will ever be able to prove whether or not a person possesses human dignity'[Ev 58]. Human Genetics Alert (HGA) is also against the creation of human-animal chimera or hybrid embryos because they feel that 'the strong public concern about the unnaturalness of creating human/animal hybrids is valid and must not be ignored'[Ev 132], an argument which generally fits into the dignitarian approach.[94]

It is not entirely clear how to interpret the dignitarian objection.[95] Given that dignitarianism categorically rejects the creation and use of human embryos for research, the characterization of a human-animal cytoplasmic hybrid embryo as

[91] Para 36.

[92] Para 35.

[93] Para 35. If animal-human chimeras, with essentially human capacities, were bred and born, they would need to be shown equal concern and respect alongside all other rights bearers. If the likelihood was that such life forms would be systematically discriminated against, then arguably such chimeras should not be developed at all; see Robert Streiffer 'At the Edge of Humanity: Human Stem Cells, Chimeras, and Moral Status' (2005) 15 Kennedy Institute of Ethics Journal 347.

[94] Report, n 89 above, para 37.

[95] For a helpful dissection of the dignitarian arguments, see Françoise Baylis and Andrew Fenton 'Chimera Research and Stem Cell Therapies for Human Neurodegenerative Disorders' (2007) 16 Cambridge Quarterly of Healthcare Ethics 195.

essentially human (whether because of the preponderance of its human cellular content or because of its possible viability for implantation and human live birth) entails that the use of such embryos compromises human dignity. If the embryo were not characterized as essentially human, as might be the case with a chimera (some of whose cells were human, some of whose cells were animal), this would call for the articulation of a fresh dignitarian principle—one that opposes the mixing of human cells with animal cells. But, as we have remarked already, the catalogue of dignitarian objection is not closed.

Faced with these rival ethical arguments, the committee did not underrate the depth of concern about, on the one side, delaying the research and, on the other, allowing it to proceed. However, rather like the House of Lords committee six years earlier, this Commons committee defaulted to a utilitarian approach in favour of research facilitation coupled with a recognition of the importance of both effectively engaging with the public and maintaining its confidence.[96]

VI Property in Human Tissue

Once upon a time, the question of whether regulators should recognize that people can have proprietary rights in relation to their own bodies, or in relation to parts of their bodies that have been removed, would have seemed wholly academic and of no practical importance. However, after the famous John Moore case,[97] it is clear that the question is far from academic; removed body parts might prove to be a resource of some considerable commercial value. And, in some future world, regulators might need to settle the position in relation to personalized body parts that have not yet been fitted. Yet, the fundamental question of property in one's own body parts is hotly contested. It is not so much that ethicists take one view and lawyers another, it is that ethicists dispute the question with fellow ethicists and lawyers with fellow lawyers.[98]

To be sure, some argumentation is wide of any possible mark. For example, it is clearly a non-sequitur to hold that, because A has a claim-right to his bodily integrity, it follows that A has a *property* right in relation to his removed

[96] One indication of the public view (broadly speaking, in favour of the creation and use of hybrid embryos as research tools) has been given by the public consultation carried out by the Human Fertilisation and Embryology Authority in summer 2007. See Ian Sample 'Human-Animal Embryo Study Wins Approval' *The Guardian* 4 September 2007, p 1. In the light of this outcome, the regulatory authority has announced that there is no fundamental reason barring the licensing of research that makes use of cytoplasmic hybrid embryos: see Mark Henderson 'Human-Cow Hybrid Research is Approved' *The Times* 6 September 2007, p 30.

[97] *Moore v Regents of the University of California* (1988) 249 Cal Rptr 494; (1990) 271 Cal Rptr 146, (1990) 793 P2d 479; cert denied (1991) 111 SCt 1388.

[98] For a careful examination of the issues, see, Stephen R Munzer *A Theory of Property* (Cambridge: Cambridge University Press, 1990) especially at 37–58 and Rohan Hardcastle *Law and the Human Body* (Oxford: Hart, 2007).

body parts.[99] Even if B does wrong by lopping off A's arm (against A's will), it does not follow that A has *proprietary* rights over the removed arm. Equally, it is a poor argument (against property) to hold that, where A donates body parts to B, donation entails that A has no property rights. Clearly, in a case of donation, A has no property rights ex post (otherwise this would not be a case of donation); but this says nothing about whether A has property rights in removed body parts *prior* to donation.[100] Indeed, one might wonder whether it is possible to 'donate' x without having ex ante property rights in relation to x. Again, it will not do to argue (against property) that, if we cannot have property in our own full bodies (because there is then no distance between me and my property), we cannot have property in our removed body parts; and nor will it do to argue that, if we have no right to commercialize our body parts (which some advocates of property rights might concede), we can have no kind of property entitlements whatsoever (that is, claiming implicitly that property is an all-or-nothing matter).

Yet, if we eliminate the spurious and the specious arguments, why should this still be such a contested question? After all, when the question is modified to become whether a person can have proprietary rights over human tissue taken from another person, there is much less disagreement; apparently, it is widely accepted that such a person can have proprietary rights. Yet, if someone other than me can have proprietary rights over tissue of which I am the source—I am tempted to say, 'over tissue that is *mine*'—then is it not exceedingly odd that I cannot have proprietary rights over that tissue—again, I am tempted to say, 'over *my own* tissue'? How can it be rational for regulators to permit me to have property rights over your tissue and for you to have property rights over my tissue while not recognizing either of us as proprietors of our own tissue?

In this part of the chapter, I will suggest that our responses to the property question[101] are driven by the particular ethical position that we take up in the bioethical triangle. After sketching how each of the principal ethical constituencies arrives at very different views about the property question, I consider what each of the three ethical constituencies might say about proprietary rights over spare body parts. One thing that they surely cannot say is that the disconnected body parts have been 'abandoned' (thereby surrendering whatever proprietary claims might otherwise have been made); for these are body parts that are waiting to be connected.

The ambitions of this section are modest. My point is that, once we understand how the debate about property and bodies is triangulated, we can get fairly

[99] As pointed out in JW Harris 'Who Owns My Body?' (1996) 16 Oxford Journal of Legal Studies 55.

[100] Compare the (unpersuasive) reasoning in *Greenberg v Miami Children's Hospital Research Institute, Inc* 2002 WL 1483266 (ND Ill); 264 F Supp 2nd 1064 (SD Fla 2003) (02-22244-CIV-MORENO (Miami)).

[101] It should be emphasized that this question is not whether the institution of private property can be justified but whether, assuming such an institution, its rules should recognize that people can have proprietary rights in relation to their own bodies, or their removed body parts.

quickly to the crux of the protagonists' differences; but, alas, this is not to say that we can get so quickly to an incontrovertible answer to the question itself.[102]

1. *Property Entitlements and Bodies*

What do each of the three ethical constituencies hold in relation to the question of property entitlements over our own bodies or our removed body parts? It is worth emphasizing that we are assuming that no one is arguing against the very idea of private property. The idea that an individual may hold property rights over, say, his house or clothes, is not at issue. The only issue is whether such property entitlements apply, too, to bodies and body parts. If we also make the standard assumption that the generic property right comprises a bundle of entitlements then, for present purposes, the two critical claims concern: (i) the right to control access to and use of a particular body or body part; and (ii) the right to exploit commercially a particular body or body part.[103] Finally, to get the matter into focus, the burning question is whether an individual should have property claims of this kind in relation to that individual's own body or removed body parts. What, then, does each of the ethical constituencies hold about this question?

First, for the utilitarian, there is no reason a priori to rule in or to rule out such property entitlements. If property rights are to be recognized, it will only be because, in the particular context, this makes good utilitarian sense. Generally, utilitarians will want to avoid two kinds of tragedy. One is the tragedy of the commons, where private property rights are insufficiently recognized as a result of which a particular resource is over-exploited and damaged. The other is the tragedy of the anti-commons, where too many private property rights are recognized as a result of which a particular resource is under-exploited, or where so-called 'patent thickets' obstruct the research and development of new technologies,[104] again with a loss to the community. Hence, for utilitarians the property puzzle is largely a matter of instating the profile of entitlements that promises to maximize the benefit obtained from the resource. In short, a (private) property-free zone

[102] Compare Deryck Beyleveld and Roger Brownsword 'My Body, My Body Parts, My Property?' (2000) 8 Health Care Analysis 87.

[103] Compare Donna Dickenson *Property in the Body* (Cambridge: Cambridge University Press, 2007) who, relying on the bundle of rights analysis of property, argues, at 12, that it is 'of enormous importance... that we think long and hard about which rights we want to protect. [This is because] proponents of commodification [here meaning commercialization], such as some researchers, universities and biotechnology companies, are prone to assume that once they acquire proprietary rights, those rights are complete and undifferentiated'.

[104] See, eg, Nuffield Council on Bioethics *The Ethics of Patenting DNA* (London, July 2002) (especially with regard to over-broad patents); and, for patent thickets now creating problems for nanotechnology, see Siva Vaidhyanathan 'Nanotechnologies and the Law of Patents: A Collision Course' in Geoffrey Hunt and Michael Mehta (eds) *Nanotechnology: Risk, Ethics and Law* (London: Earthscan, 2006) 225.

will rarely be right, but neither will a zone that is dense with (private) property entitlements.

Characteristically, utilitarians will have no objection to individuals exploiting the commercial value that they have in their bodies. Utilitarians will not resolutely oppose prostitution or the sex trade; and, provided that there could be adequate assurances about safety and provenance, a market in human organs might be defensible according to utilitarian criteria. However, where it is proposed that the individual sources of human tissue for research should have proprietary rights over their removed body parts, that is another matter. What utilitarians tend to sense here is a tragedy of the anti-commons as too many proprietary stakeholders interfere with the progression of the research and delay the delivery of its benefits. On the other hand, of course, if prospective participants are reluctant to step forward to donate their body parts for research, then this might occasion a rethink; in some contexts, utilitarians might be persuaded that the recognition of property entitlements is the price that must be paid to procure cooperation.

In the light of these remarks, it will be apparent that utilitarians do not have a simple red light or green light approach to property—any particular property proposal will need to be audited for its projected utility and disutility. It also follows that, where the projections are unclear, there might even be disagreement within the utilitarian ranks (depending upon which projections are thought to be most reliable).

For both rights theorists and dignitarians alike, the consequentialist approach of the utilitarians is to be rejected. Property in our own bodies and body parts is either a matter of entitlement or not and, whatever the position, it is categorically so. For the dignitarians, the position is pretty straightforward—or, at any rate, it is pretty straightforward in relation to any claimed right to exploit the commercial value of our bodies or body parts: quite simply, to recognize such a right would be to compromise our dignity as humans. In line with this view, Article 21 of the Convention on Human Rights and Biomedicine provides that: 'The human body and its parts shall not, as such, give rise to financial gain'. The partner claim, to have control over our own bodies and body parts, is less clear-cut. However, dignitarians will tend to see this kind of claim as involving the commodification of the human body and, for this reason, they will condemn it again as compromising human dignity.[105]

Although commercialization and commodification are closely related to one another, they should not be treated as identical; and the difference between the two concepts bears a brief word of explanation.[106] Where an object or resource is

[105] Compare Deryck Beyleveld and Roger Brownsword 'Articles 21 and 22 of the Convention on Human Rights and Biomedicine: Property and Consent, Commerce and Dignity' in Peter Kemp (ed) *Research Projects on Basic Ethical Principles in Bioethics and Biolaw* (papers from the Utrecht meeting, November 1997) (Copenhagen: Centre for Ethics and Law, 1998) 33.

[106] Contrast Donna Dickenson (n 103 above) ch 2, for a distinction between 'commodification' and 'objectification'. Broadly speaking, Dickenson uses 'commodification' in the way that I use

exploited for its commercial value, it is necessarily commodified; it is treated as a mere thing. Hence, commercialization presupposes commodification. However, this does not hold in reverse; for we might commodify a resource without commercializing it. For example, if we have a market for the sale of human babies, babies are both commercialized and commodified. But, if we permit social sex selection of babies, it is arguable that babies are commodified (treated as mere products, like consumables coming off a production line) but they are not yet commercialized.[107] In the same way, dignitarians might object that, even if human body parts are not commercialized, to recognize the individual's right to control access to such parts qua research resource involves an element of commodification and, hence, such property rights should be rejected.

This leaves the human rights constituency, the constituency from which there is most pressure for recognition of individual property rights in human bodies and body parts. Why should rights theorists so contend?

In relation to the commercialization of the human body or body parts, rights theorists see this as a matter of personal choice and life-style. Some rights theorists might put certain choices off limits (possibly selling oneself into slavery) but this goes against the grain of respect for individual autonomy. What rights theorists are most concerned about is that individuals who make risky choices should do so on the basis of a free and fully informed consent. If the consent is not in place or if we cannot confidently monitor the adequacy of consent, rights theorists might retreat to a more precautionary position—we see this move being made all the time, for example, in response to proposals put forward in test cases for the relaxation of prohibitions on physician assisted suicide.[108]

The case of a market for human organs is an interesting one.[109] In principle, a rights theorist will argue for an individual's freedom to sell, say, a kidney or a cornea. However, where sellers typically come from economically disadvantaged circumstances and buyers come from economically advantaged circumstances, there are concerns about background duress and foreground inducement.[110] If the baseline for fair dealing is given by a standard of global equity, it is quite likely that such transactions will fail to pass muster—the sellers might be under no

'commercialization'. However, our stipulative definitional differences are unimportant. We agree that, once the right of commercial exploitation is taken out of the property bundle, the argument that we should recognize property in bodies and body parts looks much less open to objection.

[107] Compare Roger Brownsword 'Happy Families, Consenting Couples, and Children with Dignity: Sex Selection and Saviour Siblings' (2005) 17 Child and Family Law Quarterly 435.

[108] In Europe, see *R(on the Application of Mrs Dianne Pretty) v DPP and Secretary of State for the Home Department* [2001] UKHL 61; *Case of Pretty v The United Kingdom* (2002) ECHR 2346/02, 29 April [2002] 35 Eur HR Rep 1. In North America, see *Washington v Glucksberg* 117 SCt 2258 (1997) 138 L Ed 2d 772 and *Re Rodriguez and Attorney-General of British Columbia* (1993) 107 DLR 4th 342.

[109] Compare Stephen Wilkinson *Bodies For Sale: Ethics and Exploitation in the Human Body Trade* (London: Routledge, 2003).

[110] See, further, Deryck Beyleveld and Roger Brownsword *Consent in the Law* (Oxford: Hart, 2007) ch 5.

foreground pressure, but their indigent circumstances involve a violation of basic rights standards and create an unacceptable situational pressure. It is less clear that inducements invalidate consent; even so, if the purchaser tempts the seller with an offer of big money, it is possible that the buyer's intention is to divert the seller from addressing the risks.[111]

As for property in removed body parts, rights theorists will think that sources are being exploited where researchers and others acquire property rights over the tissue downstream. Why should the sources, why should the many John Moores, not also share in the bounty? If the response takes a utilitarian shape, rights theorists will know that some irregularity is afoot.

It is clear, however, that for many rights-minded agents, the issue is not about sharing in commercial exploitation of the resource but about controlling its use. We see this very clearly in the *Greenberg* case[112] and it is fundamental, too, to the more recent *Catalona* case,[113] where the sources wanted the tissue to stay with a particular researcher rather than with the institution at which the researcher was originally employed.

Quite how rights theorists might vindicate property rights for tissue sources is a moot point. If rights theorists major on the right to control, then one argument relies on the immanent logic of the secondary purpose provisions in Article 22 of the Convention on Human Rights and Biomedicine. According to Article 22:

> When in the course of an intervention any part of a human body is removed, it may be stored and used for a purpose other than that for which it was removed, only if this is done in conformity with appropriate information and consent procedures.

The obvious question is why the donor's consent is needed in such circumstances. And the obvious answer is that the donor retains a proprietary right to control the use of the tissue.

Another argument is that the essential feature of a property right is 'preclusionary'. What this picks up on is the idea that a property entitlement operates in a preclusionary way (in the sense of a right to control access to or use of some resource simply by asserting one's proprietorial stake and without further reason). If this is so, then the application of property rights to agents' body parts seems eminently appropriate.[114] We need not push this matter any further. My purpose is not to rehearse arguments in support of the rights view so much as to indicate where it fits in the triangulation of property claims.

[111] For further discussion of this issue, see ch 3.

[112] Note 100 above. Similarly, see the case of PXE International, which was founded by Patrick and Sharon Terry after their children were diagnosed with PXE—recounted in Nikolas Rose *The Politics of Life Itself* (Princeton NJ: Princeton University Press, 2007) 151–3.

[113] *Washington University v Catalona* 437 F Supp 2d 985 (USDC Ed Mo 2006); WL 1758268 (20 June 2007) (8th Cir); for discussion, see Hardcastle (n 98 above) at 73–78.

[114] See Deryck Beyleveld and Roger Brownsword *Human Dignity in Bioethics and Biolaw* (Oxford: Oxford University Press, 2001) ch 8.

2. *Property and Spare Body Parts*

Imagine a future world in which each person's cord blood is stored at birth and then, using stem cell technology, a set of spare personalized body parts is cultivated and stored for each person. Assuming that cord blood is susceptible to a property regime, there might be some disagreement as to whether the mother or her child is the more eligible initial proprietor.[115] Arguably, too, persons at the facility where these spare body parts are cultivated and stored will have proprietary rights over them. However, the essence of the arrangement is that these are body parts for a particular person; and it is surely plausible to view such dedicated body parts as the property of that person. For that person already seems to be in a position to complain if the body parts are allocated to some other person without the intended recipient's consent. But what would each of our three ethical constituencies say about this idea?

Utilitarians, as always, would want to weigh the options. First, of course, utilitarians would want to be satisfied that the consequences of holding spare parts are conducive to the welfare of the majority. That utilitarians would be so satisfied is not a foregone conclusion. As Leon Kass (who has dignitarian reasons for rejecting such an option) has remarked:

> Even the most cursory examination of these matters suggests that the cumulative results of aggregated decisions for longer and more vigorous life could be highly disruptive and undesirable, even to the point that many individuals would be *worse off* through most of their lives, and enough to offset the benefits of better health afforded them near the end of life. Indeed, several people have predicted that retardation of aging will present a classic instance of the 'Tragedy of the Commons', in which genuine and sought-for gains to individuals are nullified, or worse, by the social consequences of granting them to everyone.[116]

If, however, utilitarians read the runes in a more positive way, then it becomes a matter of whether the appropriate covering framework is one in which individuals have proprietary rights over their own spare parts. On the face of it, this seems like a serious candidate; and, even if, in some contexts, it is not judged to be the optimal arrangement, utilitarians will certainly have it on their short-list.

For dignitarians, the very idea of a spare parts bank is almost certainly unacceptable. Once we hold spare body parts, it sounds as though we are commodifying humans; it sounds as though there is little difference between the way that we view our own bodies and body parts and the way that we view, say, our motor cars and car parts. Essentially, in both cases, when the parts wear out, whether it is a human heart or a car battery, they need to be replaced. Accordingly,

[115] See Dickenson (n 103 above) ch 4 (for the view that, contrary to the conventional wisdom, it is the mother who has the stronger claim).

[116] Leon R Kass *Life, Liberty and the Defense of Dignity* (San Francisco: Encounter Books, 2002) 261.

if we have a dignitarian concern to hang on to what is distinctively 'human' in our social and moral lives, we must resist any such banking proposal.

What about rights theorists? In this scenario, it is the right to control that seems to be fundamental. What the rights theorists will contend is that, applying preclusionary thinking, this is precisely the kind of case where the rights-holder asserts pre-emption over the body part by simply asserting that 'It is mine'. Moreover, two arguments that might trouble the rights theorists in other contexts do not apply here. One is the argument that the right to personal (bodily) integrity does not equate to a proprietary right, and the other is the argument about abandonment. With regard to the former argument, where body parts are embedded within the person, the physical integrity right can be presented as doing the protective work. Where this is the case, no one can take possession of, say, my heart or my kidney without violating my physical rights. However, where the body parts are detached from the body, they might be taken without any violation of a person's physical integrity. Hence, the right to physical integrity cannot do the protective work and we need a *proprietary* right for that purpose. As for the latter argument, concerning abandonment, that becomes an issue only where the body part has been discarded. However, as mentioned already, such an objection does not hold where the body part is destined for connection—in such a case, the body parts are spare (but committed to my future needs) rather than surplus to my future requirements. All in all, even though the spare body parts scenario is futuristic, it looks like an attractive context for the rights theorists to push their claims.

VII Conclusion

The matrix that sets the pattern for all ethical debates involves three basic *forms*: namely, goal-orientated, rights-based, and duty-based forms. Each form is a mould or a shell, open to substantive articulation in many different ways: different goals, different rights, and different duties may be specified. Nevertheless, in principle, the basic pattern of ethical debate, whatever the particular technological focus—whether it be biotechnology (and bioethics), ICT (and cyberethics), nanotechnology (and nanoethics), or neurotechnology (and neuroethics)—is governed by this matrix.[117]

Although, in principle, the matrix sets the pattern, in practice, it does not follow that the matrix is always fully expressed in debates about the ethics of new technologies. Often, we find only a two-sided debate with utilitarian cost/benefit calculations being set against human rights considerations. In general, unless there are major safety concerns, while utilitarians will assert the 'green light'

[117] Compare, eg, Fritz Allhoff and Patrick Lin 'What's So Specific about Nanotechnology and Nanoethics?' (2006) 20 International Journal of Applied Philosophy 179.

ethics of proceeding, a case of promotion (of the technology) modulated by a degree of precaution,[118] human rights theorists will take an 'amber light' approach insisting that the technological traffic pauses (to ensure rights clearance) before proceeding.

By contrast, in the present chapter, I have highlighted the way in which we have a three-cornered articulation of the matrix in relation to debates concerning the ethics of modern biotechnology. Here, in the shape of the bioethical triangle, we find the dignitarian alliance taking issue with both utilitarians and human rights advocates. While the latter can sometimes find a common position, it is much more difficult to reach an accommodation with the dignitarians. For, according to the dignitarian ethic, some technological applications are, quite simply, categorically and non-negotiably unacceptable. In this sense, of the three ethical perspectives, it is only the dignitarian view that is genuinely 'red light'.

Somewhat confusingly, the idea of human dignity underlies both the human rights and the dignitarian view. However, once this double-take is identified, it is easier to see which version of human dignity is being contended for or presupposed. Moreover, with the bioethical triangle as our reference map, we can track and locate the positions taken on particular issues such as the use of human embryos as research tools or the recognition of proprietary rights over removed body parts and tissues. But, of course, none of this makes it any the easier for regulators who are trying, against the backcloth of this contested plurality, to strike regulatory positions that meet the demands of all three constituencies. Nor, it seems, do regulators always find it easy to articulate the details of regulatory positions in a way that is entirely consistent with those sections of the plurality that they are privileging.[119]

[118] Compare Department of Biotechnology, Ministry of Science and Technology, Government of India *National Biotechnology Development Strategy* (2006) at 23: 'A precautionary, yet promotional approach should be adopted in employing transgenic R & D activities based on technological feasibility, socio-economic considerations and promotion of trade'.

[119] See, further, Roger Brownsword 'Ethical Pluralism and the Regulation of Modern Biotechnology, in Francesco Francioni (ed) *The Impact of Biotechnologies on Human Rights* (Oxford: Hart, 2007) 45.

3

The Challenge of Regulatory Legitimacy II

I Introduction

We saw in the previous chapter that the legitimacy of regulatory positions may be challenged from three critical ethical perspectives (captured by the bioethical triangle). By way of illustration, we considered how each perspective views a permissive regulatory approach to human embryonic stem cell research and a regulatory denial of property rights over our own bodies and body parts. The fact that each ethical perspective articulates its own line as to the legitimacy or not of particular regulatory positions on particular matters concerning the use of technology is precisely what one would expect. However, this does not exhaust the significance of either the bioethical triangle or the underlying formal matrix. For alongside the concepts of utility, human rights, and human dignity, we find a further set of key concepts—in particular, 'consent', 'harm', and 'precaution'—that are regularly deployed in making assessments of the legitimacy of regulatory positions. These are not neutral concepts. To the contrary, what we make of consent, harm, or precaution, just like who we count as a relevant 'other', hinges on which point of the bioethical triangle we are presupposing. In other words, the significance of taking, say, a utilitarian view is not simply that we judge the legitimacy of particular regulatory positions by reference to utilitarian standards, we also read the concepts of consent, harm, and precaution, and the like, through a utilitarian lens. We will deal with harm and precaution in the next chapter; but, in the present chapter, our focus is on consent.

Wherever we turn, we find consent being treated as of fundamental importance. For example, consent figures in the core ethical principles to which the Human Genetics Commission is committed;[1] consent is regarded as the fundamental principle that underlies the Human Tissue Act 2004; there is judicial support for the view that consent is one of the key principles underlying the Human Fertilisation and Embryology Act 1990;[2] and of course it is axiomatic that, wherever possible, dealings between medical professionals and patients or research

[1] See Human Genetics Commission *Inside Information* (London, May 2002) especially at 35–40.

[2] *Evans v Amicus Healthcare Ltd* [2003] EWHC 2161 (Fam) at para 37, Wall J.

participants should be strictly on the basis of informed consent.[3] In a culture that has shaken off paternalistic and status-based thinking, it should come as no surprise that autonomous individuals expect to be given the opportunity to consent or to refuse; those who perceive themselves to be stakeholders or interested parties are outraged when actions are taken without consultation and without their consent; and concerns about the legitimacy of proposed actions are assuaged by the assurance that nothing will be done without the prior consent of the parties affected. Consent is rightly watermarked into the justificatory currency of such a community.[4]

In this chapter, we start (in Part II) by sketching how consent is viewed from, respectively, a utilitarian, a human rights, and a dignitarian ethical perspective. Not surprisingly, each of these perspectives has a rather different take on consent and, unless we appreciate that consent is contested in this fundamental way, we are likely to be confused about such matters as its justificatory force and the conditions for its adequacy. Thereafter, we will place consent squarely within the rights perspective and consider some of its more problematic aspects as they would be debated within a community of rights. In Part III, we review the justificatory force of consent; in Part IV, the matter of third-party authorization; in Part V, the relationship between inducements and consent; and, in Part VI, the vexed question of ensuring that consent is properly *informed*.[5]

II Consent and the Bioethical Triangle

It is axiomatic in bioethics that those who are subjects of medical treatment or research should participate on the basis of free and informed consent. Thus, Article 6.1 of the UNESCO Universal Declaration on Bioethics and Human Rights provides that 'Any preventive, diagnostic and therapeutic medical intervention is only to be carried out with the prior, free and informed consent of the person concerned, based on adequate information'; and, in parallel language, Article 6.2 provides that 'Scientific research should be carried out only with the prior, free, express and informed consent of the person concerned'. This, however, is very much a version of consent that is driven by the human rights perspective. If,

[3] See, eg, Article 5 of the Convention on Human Rights and Biomedicine which states as a general rule that 'An intervention in the health field may only be carried out after the person concerned has given free and informed consent to it', the information in question relating to 'the purpose and nature of the intervention as well as [to] its consequences and risks'.

[4] Compare Roger Brownsword 'The Cult of Consent: Fixation and Fallacy' (2004) 15 KCLJ 223; and Deryck Beyleveld and Roger Brownsword *Consent in the Law* (Oxford: Hart, 2007).

[5] Compare John Harris 'Mark Anthony or Macbeth: Some Problems Concerning the Dead and the Incompetent when it Comes to Consent' in Sheila AM McLean (ed) *First Do No Harm* (Aldershot: Ashgate, 2006) 287. Harris remarks that there is 'the most staggering complacency about the assured role that consent in general and fully informed consent in particular plays in many contexts' (ibid).

by contrast, we take a utilitarian or a dignitarian view, we might think that consent is much less important. Accordingly, our first step towards clarifying consent is to review its significance from each of the three points of the bioethical triangle.

Utilitarians count utility and disutility; and, for utilitarians, utility and disutility is all that counts. As such, there is nothing special about consent or the lack of it. In general, it is easy to see the negatives in relation to consent collection. Obtaining consent might not always be practicable; where it is, it nevertheless incurs transaction costs; and, on some occasions, it might be downright distressful. Waiting for consents to be cleared might involve opportunity costs. Moreover, policies might be frustrated if, instead of saying 'yes', those who are asked to consent say 'no'. On the other hand, dealing on the basis of consent might ease matters ex ante, it might allay concern and weaken opposition, and it might be a convenient justificatory response ex post. Thus, for utilitarians, there is no golden rule requiring that the consent of those upon whom an action or decision impacts should be obtained. For example, requiring researchers or doctors to deal on an informed consent basis with research participants or others is not necessarily an improvement on compulsion, ignorance, or paternalism. The calculation always depends on context, convenience, contingency, and circumstance. Having said this, in a culture where preferences strongly favour the currency of consent, even if there is no golden rule requiring consent, utilitarians might well accept the sense of a general rule to this effect.[6]

Against the utilitarians, human rights theorists hold that what counts is respect for individual autonomy, entailing recognition of the right of individuals to make their own choices, to exercise control over their own person, property, and privacy, and to say 'yes' or to say 'no'. Taking individuals seriously, taking rights seriously, means taking consents and refusals seriously.

Viewed from a human rights perspective, consent by A might signal either a change of position or the creation of a new relationship. There is a tendency to focus more on the former than the latter, that is, on consent signalling A's willingness to modify his or her position in relation to the particular background scheme of rights and duties, permissions and immunities, and the like, that regulates his or her relationship with B (the recipient of the consent). As George Fletcher puts it:

> When individuals consent to undergo medical operations, to engage in sexual intercourse, to open their homes to police searches, or to testify against themselves in court, they

[6] Although consent has been proclaimed as the cornerstone principle of the UK human tissue legislation, the underlying rationale is essentially utilitarian. Thus, according to a House of Commons Research Paper (No 04/04 on the Human Tissue Bill), the government believes that the effect of the consent provisions will be to 'prevent a recurrence of the distress caused by retention of tissue and organs without proper consent', to 'help improve public confidence so that people will be more willing to agree to valuable uses of tissue and organs' (such as for research and transplantation purposes), and to 'improve professional confidence so that properly authorised supplies of tissue for research, education and transplantation can be maintained and improved' (p 4).

convert what otherwise would be an invasion of their person or their rights into a harmless or justified activity.[7]

The latter function (the creation of a new relationship), however, should not be ignored. Where A signals consent to the creation of a new relationship with B, this might be by virtue of some simple dynamic (such as the giving of a promise or agreement to an exchange of goods) or it might be by virtue of some more complex institutional set (as is the case, for example, if A invokes the law of contract or the law of marriage) or regulated scheme (such as one licensing assisted conception or physician assisted suicide). Where A thus signals consent, then other things being equal A is precluded from asserting that B may not justifiably rely on, or hold A to, the agreed change of position or the terms of the new relationship. Whether A signals a change of position or agreement to the creation of a new relationship, consent functions as a *procedural* justification (for the benefit of the recipient, B) rather than as a full *substantive* justification of the kind that would be appropriate if one were arguing for a particular human right itself.[8]

At the third point of the bioethical triangle, we have the duty-driven perspective of the dignitarians. For the dignitarians, it is human dignity, not consent, that fundamentally matters; and it is the interests of all members of the community that count, not merely those of the consenting community. The fact that all parties consent to participation in dwarf-throwing, or to playful killing at the Laserdrome, is irrelevant insofar as these activities compromise human dignity—as, indeed, it is irrelevant that all adult stakeholders consent to cooperating with, or carrying out, research that uses human embryos. The duty to respect human dignity is not switched off by the consent of others any more than it is switched on again by a withdrawal or a refusal of consent. Consent, for the dignitarian, is largely a sideshow.[9]

The general irrelevance to dignitarians of both 'benefit' and consent is nicely illustrated by the opposition of the indigenous Tongan people to the agreement made between Autogen, an Australian firm, and the Tongan Ministry of Health for the collection of tissue samples with a view to researching the causes of diabetes.[10] Given the high incidence of diabetes in Tonga, there was some prospective health benefit for the local community. However, there were difficulties in modifying the Western model of individual consent so that it accommodated local custom and practice. Before it was clear whether these consent difficulties could be surmounted, Autogen decided against proceeding with the project. However,

[7] George P Fletcher *Basic Concepts of Legal Thought* (Oxford: Oxford University Press, 1996) 109.

[8] See, further, Roger Brownsword 'The Cult of Consent: Fixation and Fallacy' (2004) 15 KCLJ 223.

[9] Compare Shayana Kadidal 'Obscenity in the Age of Mechanical Reproduction' (1996) 44 American Journal of Comparative Law 353.

[10] Here, I am drawing on Donna Dickenson *Property in the Body* (Cambridge: Cambridge University Press, 2007) ch 8.

the key point is that, even if the consent issues could have been resolved, indigenous Tongans have a sense of human dignity that militates against any actions that compromise the sanctity of the person, their life force, and their genetic legacy.[11] In other words, even if all the other objections were surmounted, the Tongans might still have judged it unethical to give up tissue samples.

Having said this, it should not be thought that all duty-driven perspectives regard consent as unimportant—we should recall that the dignitarianism of the bioethical triangle is simply a particular substantive articulation of the duty-based form that is available within the basic ethical matrix. Indeed, in their important (obligation-driven) analysis of informed consent, Neil Manson and Onora O'Neill take consent just as seriously as rights-led thinkers.[12] Moreover, at least two of the key themes in Manson and O'Neill's account correspond with the view that would be taken from a rights perspective. First, getting information across from agent, A, to another agent, B, is not just like copying data across from one disk to another (and, to this extent, the metaphors of 'conduits' and 'containers' for the transmission of information are unhelpful). When A informs B, this is a communicative transaction in the context of agency. It involves a degree of inter-subjective understanding, and a successful transaction presupposes respect for 'a wide range of epistemic and ethical norms, including norms of accuracy and honesty'.[13] Secondly, consent is to be understood as a waiver relative to a backcloth of rights, obligations and expectations—'[t]hese obligations and expectations [being] *presupposed* by informed consent practices'.[14] Hence:

In consenting, we *waive* certain requirements on others not to treat us in certain ways (sometimes this will include waiving rights), or we *set aside* certain expectations, or *license* action that would *otherwise* be ethically or legally unacceptable.... Where an act would *otherwise* wrong an individual or disrupt their legitimate expectations, that individual's consent can waive their right, or modify their expectations in particular cases, and so justify an act that would *otherwise* be unacceptable.[15]

So, we should not make the mistake of thinking that a duty-driven ethic in itself entails that consent is downgraded. However, as Manson and O'Neill recognize, where autonomy-limiting dignitarianism is in play, actions that are judged to degrade others will be treated as unacceptable, the consent of those degraded others notwithstanding.[16]

In the light of this short analysis, we can see that it is the human rights constituency that is most strongly committed to the significance of consent. Even here, it would be a mistake to say that consent is to be treated as a fundamental value

[11] Dickenson (n 10 above) especially at 167–8.

[12] Neil C Manson and Onora O'Neill *Rethinking Informed Consent in Bioethics* (Cambridge: Cambridge University Press, 2007).

[13] ibid 185.

[14] ibid 187.

[15] ibid 72–3.

[16] ibid especially at 20–1.

because consent is always parasitic upon rights.[17] Nevertheless, it is the human rights constituency that is consistently concerned that consent should be taken seriously. By contrast, the dignitarians, as we have just said, do not attach significance to consent (at any rate, not where human dignity is compromised); and, as ever, the utilitarians modulate their view as context and contingency require.

III First-Party Consent as a Justification

In clinical and research settings, the bioethical consensus is that there should be no intervention unless the person directly concerned has consented. So stated, first-party consent represents a necessary, if not a sufficient, condition; and, even if further conditions for legitimate intervention are set (as they tend to be, especially in the case of research participation) it is tempting to treat consent as the paramount condition for a legitimate intervention. Nevertheless, the question bears asking: in what sense does first-party consent justify action? More particularly, in a community of rights, what is the scope and strength of a consent-based justification?

Broadly speaking, in a community of rights, the function of consent is twofold. In one kind of case, the consenting agent, A, is precluded from raising a complaint about the conduct of the recipient agent B (B's 'wrongdoing' as it otherwise would be)—for example, this is the position in the standard case in which A consents to some surgical procedure to be carried out by B. In the other kind of case, A is precluded from denying that he or she is bound by the rules or terms (the rights and obligations) to which he or she has consented—as might be the case, for example, where A consents to donate some of her eggs for research in return for a reduction in the cost of her IVF treatment.[18] In the former case, A's consent functions to release B from some part of his or her usual obligations to A; in the latter case, A's consent functions to increase A's own obligations to B. In the former case, the recipient agent, B, appeals to A's consent by way of a defence; in the latter case, B appeals to A's consent in order to advance claims. In one case, consent functions as a shield, in the other as a sword. However, if the consent is not authentic, if it is not freely and adequately informed, it will serve no justificatory purpose of any description.

Consent, thus, functions as a justifying reason. However, precisely because B relies on A's authorization for the doing of x rather than on the rightness of the doing of x itself, it becomes clear that consent operates as a distinctive form of justification. In particular, we can isolate three distinguishing features of

[17] See Deryck Beyleveld and Roger Brownsword *Consent in the Law* (Oxford: Hart, 2007); and Roger Brownsword (n 4 above).

[18] For comment, see Mark Henderson 'Cheaper IVF for Women who Give Eggs to Research' *The Times* 28 July 2006, pp 1–2.

'consent as a justification'. First, consent functions as a 'procedural' rather than as a 'substantive' (or 'on the merits') form of justification. Secondly, as a procedural justification, consent amounts to a limited 'in personam' (or 'agent relative') response. Consent does not comprehensively justify the action as such; rather, the consenting agent is precluded from asserting that he or she has been wronged (or that he or she is not bound by the agreed rule-set, or the like). Thirdly, where consent is relied on as a shield, it justifies by way of negating a wrong rather than by way of overriding a right. Each of these features merits a word or two of explanation.

First, whereas a substantive (or 'on the merits') form of justification refers to some set of background standards characterizing (in the justificatory argument) particular acts as permitted (including required), a procedural justification refers to an authorizing act or decision. For example, if agent B contends that he is entitled to carry out human embryonic stem cell research because background standards (relating to the freedom of researchers and the status of human embryos) provide for the permissibility of these actions, he relies on a substantive justification. Such a contention might be contested—even in a community of rights, the scope of a right to research freedom might be contested and, likewise, there might be different views about the status of a human embryo.[19] By contrast, if agent B claims to be so entitled by reference to the consent of his employer, or his research sponsor, then the justification does not rest on background standards, contested or otherwise; rather, the claimed justification is procedural in the sense that B relies on some authorizing act or decision, not background standards, to assert the permissibility of the particular actions in question.

Secondly, where consent is relied on, it justifies 'in personam' (that is, only in an 'agent-relative' way). The consenting agent, but only the consenting agent, is precluded from asserting that he or she has been wronged. In other words, although agent A, who has consented to the doing of x by agent B, is precluded from asserting that the doing of x violates A's rights, this does not make the doing of x right *tout court* (ie right as against all comers). So, if the complaint about B's stem cell research activities comes from B's employer or his research funders (who have consented to B's activities), then B may respond that such complaints by such parties are precluded by their consent. However, none of this justifies the carrying out of the research as such. Other agents might have grounds for complaint to which it is no answer for B to rely on A's consent. In other words, even if A's consent gives B a complete answer to A, it might give B no answer at all to C.[20]

[19] Compare, eg, Barbara Billingsley and Timothy Caulfield 'The Regulation of Science and the Charter of Rights: Would a Ban on Non-Reproductive Human Cloning Unjustifiably Violate Freedom of Expression?' (2004) 29 Queen's LJ 647.

[20] For a rather different example of the justificatory limits of consent relative to a third-party complaint, see Nikolas Rose *The Politics of Life Itself* (Princeton NJ: Princeton University Press, 2007) 179: 'It is not clear that... identity damage [to a group or a family] can be countered by the usual ethical means of individual informed consent, for evidence from DNA taken from one or two willing individuals can be used to make [unwelcome] claims about groups'.

Thirdly, where B relies on A's consent as a justification, B relies on A's consent to negate what would otherwise be a wrong in relation to A. To put this another way, given that A's consent *authorizes* the action in question, it must follow that B, by doing the authorized act x, does no wrong to A. A's consent to B doing x entails that, as between A and B, the doing of x by B is permissible. This is to be distinguished from treating the doing of x by B as justified by reference to overriding rights, or all things considered as the lesser of two wrongs. In such a case, where A has not consented to the doing of x by B, and where the doing of x violates A's rights, then the doing of x, even if justified all things considered, involves a wrong to A.[21] For instance, if B has promised his wife, A, that he will do the weekly supermarket shopping on a particular Saturday and A has not consented to B not doing so, B may justify breaking his promise to A if he abandons his shopping in order to respond to an emergency, such as driving a pregnant (and about-to-give-birth) supermarket shopper C to the local maternity unit.

Putting these three distinguishing features together we have the following. In a community of rights, consent functions as a procedural justification, giving the recipient of the consent (B) a complete answer to the consenting agent (A); no wrong is done to the consenting (authorizing) agent (A) by the recipient agent (B); but it does not follow that the recipient agent (B) does no wrong to third-party agents (such as C). In the absence of consent, a wrong will be done to agents whose rights are violated even if, all things considered, the wrongdoing can be substantively justified as the lesser of two evils.

The attraction of consent as a justifying reason is not hard to understand. Quite simply, not only does consent provide the recipient, B, with a complete answer to the consenting agent, A, but it does so without the former having to engage contestable substantive justifications—or, at any rate, such 'on the merits' justifications do not have to be offered to the consenting party (even if such substantive justifications cannot be altogether avoided in relation to third parties).

Nevertheless, the life-line offered by consent as a justification should not be abused. If we are to take consent seriously, at a practical level, we must guard against the 'routinization' of consent; it will not do simply to direct a would-be consenting agent to 'sign here and here' or to 'just tick the box'. Steps should be taken to ensure that the standards governing the adequacy of consent are fully articulated and stringently applied. The collection of consent, however commonplace, should not be approached in a mechanical or a perfunctory manner. Equally, we must discourage lazy or casual appeals to consent. Where substantive justification is called for, we should settle for nothing less; in particular, we should not be satisfied with artificial procedural justifications that are tendered in their place.[22] Conversely, where substantive arguments are called for to support

[21] Mutatis mutandis, these comments apply to the case in which B relies on A's consent in order to hold A to the rules of the agreed set.

[22] For example, see the *Strunk* case discussed below.

condemnation of a particular act or practice, they should not be suppressed in favour of a more convenient procedural objection to the effect that no adequate covering consents are in place. In every way, procedural justification should respect the ideals of transparency.

In sum, we begin to understand the place of consent within a community of rights once we appreciate that it has an important role to play in justificatory arguments; and we refine that understanding once we distinguish between appeals to procedural and substantive considerations. However, we should not make the mistake of thinking that, even in a community of rights, consent as a procedural justification is the whole justificatory story.

IV Third-Party Consent as a Justification

In the paradigmatic first-party case, consent functions as a procedural justification, giving the recipient of the consent (B) a complete answer to the consenting agent (A); no wrong is done to the consenting (authorizing) agent (A) by the recipient agent (B); but it does not follow that the recipient agent (B) does no wrong to third-party agents (such as C). For instance, if B proposed a xenotransplantation to A, who consented to the procedure, A would have no complaint against B if the procedure exposed A to risks of which he was aware. If, however, the procedure exposed third-party agents (such as C) to risks of infection, and the like, the fact that A has consented gives B no answer to C. B will only have a consent-based justification relative to C, if C has also consented to the risk.

In the present section, the issue is not that of third-party harm but, rather, third-party consent on behalf of a first-party. Suppose that if, instead of A giving consent, it is third-party Z who purports to consent on behalf of first-party A: is it still the case that the recipient of the consent (B) has a complete answer to A?

In a straightforward case of express agency or proxy (where A expressly authorizes Z to act as A's agent), the consent given by third-party Z will be equivalent to that given by A; it will be no better than A's consent but neither will it be any worse; the justificatory effect of Z's third-party consent (for A) will be precisely the same as if A had given first-party consent. Of course, this assumes that Z operates within the terms of the authority given by A; if Z exceeds the terms of his authority, we have a more difficult case to resolve. However, this is not a path that we need to go down on this occasion.

Rather, the focal question here is what we make of the kind of case where Z purports to consent for A, but where A lacks the capacity to give a first-party consent. Where this is the case, A is not able to consent directly to the action that Z purports to authorise, but *neither is A able to consent to the authorization of Z.* Hence, if Z is acting without A's authorization, it is unclear why Z's consent, qua consent, should have any justificatory effect in relation to A—or, at any rate, it will be unclear in a community of rights (even if a utilitarian might see no particular difficulty).[23]

Both the Convention on Human Rights and Biomedicine and the UNESCO Universal Declaration on Bioethics and Human Rights make extensive provision for cases of this kind (whether the reason for the lack of capacity is minority or adult disease or disorder, or the like). In the former, Article 6 essentially sets two necessary and sufficient conditions for an intervention against a person who does not have the capacity to consent: the first is that the intervention must be for the direct benefit of that person; and the second is that the intervention must be authorized by the consent of an appropriate third party. In the latter, Article 7 is drafted in a slightly different way but it, too, envisages that the intervention will need third-party authorization with a view to promoting the best interests of the person concerned. And, in both cases, insofar as there is any possibility of involving the first party in the authorizing process, this should be encouraged.

What we see in these guidelines is a set of second-best options. If the person concerned has moments of lucidity or periodic capacity to consent, then the preferred approach is to obtain first-party consent (even if the first person's capacity is not rock solid). In the absence of first-party consent, the approach switches to making a judgment as to the best interests of the person concerned. In PVS cases, such as that of Tony Bland,[24] an approach that appeals to best interests is notoriously problematic;[25] but the problem is a more general one. A best interests justification is 'on the merits' and it is contestable at two levels, both as to its adoption as the guiding standard and as to the way that the idea of best interests is interpreted and applied in a particular case. It follows that, for even the most conscientious and conscionable decision-makers, the best interests standard presents difficulties in its interpretation and application.[26]

Even though the addition of third-party consent adds nothing where the first party lacks the capacity to consent, there is a temptation to appeal to third-party authorization in an attempt to improve the justificatory script. The well-known Strunk case[27] is such an example. There, the Kentucky Court of Appeal upheld a lower court ruling authorizing the removal of a kidney from Jerry Strunk to be transplanted to his brother Tommy. Jerry was 27 years old but, with an IQ of 35, he was mentally incompetent and not able to give a first-party consent; Tommy

[23] The justificatory power of third-party 'consent' will also seem problematic from certain kinds of duty-driven perspectives: compare Manson and O'Neill (n 12 above) especially at 192–4.

[24] *Airedale NHS Trust v Bland* [1993] 1 All ER 821.

[25] As Lord Mustill bluntly put it in the *Bland* case, it is not clear what it means to ask whether the withdrawal of support would be in the young man's best interests because the 'distressing truth which must not be shirked is that... [Bland] has no best interests of any kind' (at 894).

[26] Compare Robert H Mnookin 'Child-Custody Adjudication: Judicial Functions in the Face of Indeterminacy' (1975) 39 Law and Contemporary Problems 226. In the context, not of child custody, but of medical treatment and research, see PD Skegg 'Consent to Medical Procedures on Minors' (1973) 36 Modern Law Review 370.

[27] *Strunk v Strunk* 445 SW 2d 145 (Ky 1969).

was 28 years old but dying with kidney disease. On the face of it, Jerry had little to gain from undergoing surgery for the removal of a perfectly healthy kidney; but, by portraying the relationship between Jerry and Tommy in a certain way, the lower court was able to hold that the procedure was actually in Jerry's best interests. Whilst we might jib at this on the facts and hesitate to embrace the utilitarian justification that we sense to be lurking in the background, at least the lower court's reliance on Jerry's best interests makes no pretence that Jerry consented. The appeal court, however, sought to improve the justification by introducing the idea of a 'substituted judgment'—that is, the idea that a court could justify the medical procedure by reference to the authorizing judgment that Jerry would have made had he been mentally competent.

In a brilliant critique, Louise Harmon[28] has pointed out that, when a court makes a substituted judgment in relation to one Jerry Strunk, there is no 'Jerry Strunk as an actual competent agent' to which the judgment can be anchored. It simply cannot be done; and, to speak as though the substituted judgment tracks the preferences of a competent agent is highly misleading. By contrast, when a court makes a substituted judgment in relation to one who once was an ostensible agent[29]—to a Karen Quinlan,[30] a Nancy Cruzan,[31] or a Tony Bland[32]—it can seek to reconstruct the particular agent's profile and anchor its judgment in what seem to have been that agent's characteristic preferences. It *can* do this; but it does not follow that, the court's rhetoric notwithstanding, this is what it actually does. A court's exercise in substituted judgment might pay lip-service to the preferences of the party who once was an ostensible agent, while doing exactly what the court did in a case such as that of Jerry Strunk (in which there was not even the possibility of reconstructing the preferences of a party who once was an ostensible agent). In these cases, there is a distance between the flesh and blood person for whom the substituted judgment purports to speak and the generically 'reasonable' reference point for which the judgment actually speaks. Hence, as Harmon pointedly observes, in *Strunk*, the court makes its substituted judgment on behalf of a 'generic, reasonable idiot prone to give his organs away'.[33]

To put this more explicitly in the language of consent, where the court's substituted judgment speaks for a generic 'reasonable' agent, it fictionalizes consent. If Jerry Strunk consented to the removal of his kidney for the benefit of his brother, then no wrong was done to Jerry by the removal of the organ. However, to rest the justification on the ground that (incompetent) Jerry would have consented to the

[28] Louise Harmon 'Falling off the Vine: Legal Fictions and the Doctrine of Substituted Judgment' (1990) 100 Yale Law Journal 1.

[29] For this terminology and a taxonomy of agency, see Deryck Beyleveld and Roger Brownsword *Consent in the Law* (Oxford: Hart, 2007), especially ch 4.

[30] *Re Quinlan* 70 NJ 10, 355 A 2d 647 (1976).

[31] *Nancy Beth Cruzan v Director, Missouri Department of Health* 497 US 261, 110 S Ct 2841 (1990); 111 L Ed 2d 224.

[32] *Airedale NHS Trust v Bland* [1993] 1 All ER 821.

[33] Harmon (n 28 above) at 35.

procedure had he been a subject of consent who was minded to assist his dying brother is worse than a fiction, it is almost a fraud. If the procedure is to be justified by reference to Jerry's consent, it cannot get to first base unless Jerry either is a subject of consent who purports to consent or, although he is not now a subject of consent, he either once was so or is intermittently so, and his biography gives us a basis for treating him as consenting. If such a justification is not available, we need a substantive justification—for example, along the lines that Tommy has a positive right that Jerry should come to his rescue in the emergency. If there is a good substantive justification, then we should not rely on a bad procedural justification; and, if neither justification will fly, then we should not allow our sympathy for Tommy to distort our justificatory thinking.

Turning to a more recent case, the Clinical Trials Directive[34] recognizes the vulnerability of both children and adults who are unable to give first-party consent.[35] Article 4 sets out a protective regime for clinical trials on minors and Article 5 sets out a similar regime for adults who are not able to give consent. In the case of children, we read that the informed consent of the parents or legal representative must have been obtained and that such 'consent must represent the minor's presumed will';[36] in the case of adults who are incapable of consenting the informed consent of the legal representative 'must represent the subject's presumed will'.[37] In the United Kingdom's implementing regulations,[38] we read that:

> Informed consent given by a person with parental responsibility or a legal representative to a minor taking part in a clinical trial shall represent the minor's presumed will.[39]

Similarly, in relation to an adult:

> Informed consent given by a legal representative to an incapacitated adult in a clinical trial shall represent that adult's presumed will.[40]

What are we to make of such provisions? Quite rightly, one kind of concern is that the third party will fail to discharge his responsibilities to the first party—indeed, that in some cases, insofar as the first party has any kind of will it is precisely that the particular third party should *not* be entrusted to act as its representative.[41] Or, again, as Shaun Pattinson has observed, we might be concerned that, where

[34] Directive 2001/20/EC.

[35] The directive flags up these special cases at some length in recitals 3 and 4.

[36] Article 4(a).

[37] Article 5(a).

[38] The Medicines for Human Use (Clinical Trials) Regulations 2004, SI 2004/1031.

[39] Schedule 1, pt 4, para 13.

[40] Schedule 1, pt 5, para 12.

[41] Compare Jean McHale 'Law Reform, Clinical Research and Adults without Mental Capacity—Much Needed Clarification or a Recipe for Future Uncertainty?' in Sheila AM McLean (ed) *First Do No Harm* (Aldershot: Ashgate, 2006) 215 at 223: 'Whilst some individuals would be perfectly happy for their spouse or daughter to give consent on their behalf should they suffer from a degenerative mental disorder others might take a very different view...'.

there is a choice of legal representatives, researchers will head for the third party who looks most likely to consent.[42] However, my concern is with the temptation to elide presumed will with actual will and, concomitantly, with the question of whether the consent of the third party is thought to be doing any justificatory work qua consent.

In the light of the foregoing analysis, there are only two ways that we may legitimately interpret the role of the third party's authorization. On one view, the third party is making a best guess as to the will of the first party had the first party been able to consent. The justification is not that the first party has consented but that the third party speculatively asserts that the first party would have consented. This purports to be some kind of procedural justification. If the third party acts in good faith, and if there is some biographical evidence of the first party's will to support the assessment, it might even be a passable justification; but, even in the best kind of case, it is some way from the first-party paradigm. Alternatively, the third party is making a judgment about the welfare of the first party. Notwithstanding the rhetoric of consent, this is really a substantive justification within the paternalistic family.[43] What the third party is authorizing is an action that it judges the first party would have consented to if the first party had been seeking reasonably and rationally to protect and promote its own welfare interests.

Provided that we keep the analysis in mind, we should not be misled. We should be able to differentiate between a substantive justification in which a third party purports to speak for the welfare of the first party and a procedural justification in which a third party purports to construct a consent for the first party regardless of whether this seems to serve the welfare of the first party. Equally, we should appreciate that there is a wide gulf between respecting the autonomy of the first party by acting on actual first-party consent and acting on a speculative third-party statement that claims to represent or reflect the first party's will.

V Consent and Inducement

The relationship between consent and threat has been extensively debated; but the relationship between consent and inducement is much less well theorized.[44] Yet, particularly in relation to research projects, there is a distinct nervousness about offering financial inducements in order to procure the consent of prospective

[42] Shaun D Pattinson *Medical Law and Ethics* (London: Sweet and Maxwell, 2006) 374.

[43] Compare John Harris (n 5 above) at 297: 'The suggestion that it might be wrong to do something to or for children because they are not in a position to consent is simply absurd'. And, ibid at 301: 'Why then so many people have thought the concept of consent, or the extensive literature of informed consent, can in any way illuminate the problem of what to do, for or about [the incompetent] is, and remains, a mystery'.

[44] However, see the excellent discussion in Pattinson, (n 42 above) at 347–9.

participants.[45] For example, point 7 of the CIOMS guidelines (2002) provides that:

Payments should not be so large... or the medical services so extensive as to induce prospective subjects to consent to participate in the research against their better judgment ('undue inducement').

Apparently, the concern that consent might be tainted by inducements is not so great as to proscribe any kind of inducement. However, there is a worry that inducements might reach a level where they distort a person's judgment and, at that point, undermine the justification given by consent.[46] In a community of rights, would such concern be viewed as coherent?

In such a community, as we have seen, consent is understood as an authorization given by a rights-holder, licensing an act which otherwise would be a violation of right. Where a rights-holder consents to some right-protected activity, there is a risk to which the rights-holder is not otherwise exposed. This is not to say that rights-holders are never at risk of right violations unless they consent; alas, far from it. Rather, the point is that rights-holders who consent are exposed to the risk of actions about which they will have no legitimate cause for complaint (because they have authorized such acts). In a community of rights, it is imperative that rights-holders should not be treated as exposing themselves to such a risk unless their consent is free and informed.

Notoriously, the preconditions of free and informed consent are difficult to formulate.[47] To a considerable extent, the difficulties arise from the unstated background influence of rival utilitarian and rights-driven views, and we seem to be driven to a compromise position that requires the consent to be 'substantially' free and informed.[48] Plainly, however, this is not at all satisfactory. If we eliminate all background influences other than that of rights theory, it is easier to specify the conditions; but, even then, there is a tension between protecting the interests of the agent who appears to consent and the interests of the agent who in good faith relies on the consent.[49]

[45] A concern highlighted by the adverse events associated with the Phase One trial of TeGenero's TGN1412 monoclonal antibody drug at Northwick Park Hospital in March 2006. See Expert Scientific Group on Phase One Clinical Trials *Final Report: 20th November 2006* (London: Stationery Office, 2006).

[46] Compare Nuffield Council on Bioethics *The Ethics of Research Related to Healthcare in Developing Countries* (London, 2002) paras 6.25–6.32 for current thinking concerning the distinction between acceptable and unacceptable inducements.

[47] In a rather different context, compare the seminal account in Duncan Kennedy 'Distributive and Paternalist Motives in Contract and Tort Law, with Special Reference to Compulsory Terms and Unequal Bargaining Power' (1982) 41 Maryland Law Review 563.

[48] Seminally, see Ruth Faden and Tom Beauchamp *A History and Theory of Informed Consent* (New York: Oxford University Press, 1986).

[49] This is a recurrent theme in Deryck Beyleveld and Roger Brownsword *Consent in the Law* (Oxford: Hart, 2007).

But what of inducement? What would a community of rights make of this? Clearly, in a community of rights, there will be objections to the bribery and corruption of regulators, and the like. Public officers should not be offered inducements to turn a blind eye or allocate resources in a certain way. However, such objections are wholly unrelated to the adequacy of the consent given by the agent who is so induced. What we have to focus on is a situation in which the only objection is that the consent apparently given is defective and that the reason why it is invalid is because it was improperly induced. In such a situation, what would a community of rights make of transparent market-rate payments, not dressed up as 'expenses' or coyly offered as 'nominal'? Let me suggest that, in such a community, the following two points would be agreed.

First, provided that the recipient agent B is not already in breach of the consenting agent, A's, rights, then no matter how great the inducement offered by B to A, this does not militate against treating A's consent as free. What does militate against free consent is, paradigmatically, a threat to the consenting agent's generic interests in physical and psychological well-being.

Secondly, unless the effect of the inducement is to deflect A's attention away from the risks involved in giving consent, the mere fact that there is an inducement does not militate against treating A's consent as informed.

It follows that, in a community of rights, it would not be a cause for concern that the inducement brings about a change of mind on A's part, that A now agrees to participate when, without the inducement, A would not so agree. However, if the effect of the inducement is to cause A to give an ill-considered consent, this invites further inquiry. Certainly, if B offers the inducement with a view to rushing A into an ill-considered consent, the community of rights will want to protect A. However, if B acts in good faith and it is entirely A's fault that the risks and benefits are not properly considered, it is much less clear that A should be protected. A might come to regret having consented but it is not part of the culture of a community of rights to prevent agents making poor choices. Rather, the culture is to respect the autonomy of agents by creating a regulatory environment in which they are left to make their own free and informed choices.

Nevertheless, does this analysis take due account of the fact that participation in research is likely to expose the participant to a necessarily uncertain range of risks and that the participant is so exposed without any offsetting therapeutic benefit? Clearly, the nature of the risks, the element of uncertainty, and so on needs to be covered by the information supplied to participants and participants should not sign up on a false prospectus.[50] However, provided that the risks are clearly set out and participants are advised that they will derive no clinical

[50] See, further, 97–8 below for discussion of consent in the context of highly uncertain nanomedical applications.

benefit personally, the choice will be as informed as it can be and the fact that an inducement is offered simply constitutes an entry in the benefit side of what is otherwise a one-sided negative calculation.

If it takes inducements, whether financial or in kind, before agents will participate in research trials, it might be objected that only those who are most needy are likely to sign up; and that this highlights the way in which inducements exploit the more vulnerable members of the community. Where a community of rights is properly instantiated, we can assume that there will be no background injustice and that this kind of objection will not stick. However, this is a bit too convenient. If there is an element of background injustice, and if the pattern of recruitment clearly shows that the inducements are exploitative, then the community might take a less sanguine view of inducements. However, its reservations would not be that participants give flawed consents so much as that participants are unfairly exploited. There is also an important puzzle about the use of inducements in research trials that are carried out beyond the boundaries of a community of rights. For example, if it were known that participants in a research trial in Africa would receive ancillary care (for example, medication for AIDS), and if such care had been specified as a matter of research ethics governance, then it would be ironic if we questioned the validity of the consents given by participants.[51]

There is a good deal more thinking that needs to be done about this.[52] However, in general, it seems to me that, in a community of rights, the fact that researchers in good faith hold out inducements to prospective participants would not be seen as problematic; and the conventional wisdom that inducements should not be excessive or undue would be seen as a rather awkward way of expressing a concern, not that consent should be free, but that consent should be given only on a properly informed basis.

What, then, about the offering of inducements to patients in treatment contexts? Presumably, the fact that there has been less discussion about the use of inducements in such contexts is because, in most cases, the perceived personal

[51] For a general review of the responsibilities of researchers conducting their trials in developing countries, see Nuffield Council on Bioethics *The Ethics of Research Related to Healthcare in Developing Countries* (London, 2002). The council contends that the duty to alleviate suffering naturally extends to providing positive benefits (see para 7.13), from which it infers that, in some cases, ancillary care might be required (see paras 7.34–7.35). However, the emphasis here, as in the council's discussion of the difficult question of the sustainability of treatment after the completion of the research (see ch 9), is on the importance of the researchers addressing such questions before the research begins and then making their intentions clear to prospective participants. The council returned to these issues in *The Ethics of Research Related to Healthcare in Developing Countries: A Follow-Up Discussion* (London, 2005). On the particular question of ancillary-care responsibilities for conditions that are not directly related to the researchers' study, once again positive obligations are asserted albeit to be specified on a case-by-case basis (see paras 3.25–3.26).

[52] On the ancillary care issue, see Roger Brownsword 'The Ancillary-Care Responsibilities of Researchers: Reasonable but not Great Expectations' (2007) 35 JLME.

therapeutic benefit of the treatment is inducement enough. However, there are cases where inducements for maintaining the treatment have been proposed (for example, where a particular drug regime needs to be strictly observed over a period of time). And, where such inducements are proposed, I take it that the principal objection is that society should not be taxed to cover the additional costs of this kind of treatment. In other words, the principal issue here is not about the consent of the parties who are induced to take the treatment but about the equity of charging this back to the community.

Let us suppose, however, that a community of rights addressed the question of inducement and consent in the context of *treatment*. Would it stick to the two guiding principles that I have suggested it would adopt for *research* contexts? The short answer is that I believe it would.

The first principle holds that inducements (not being negative threats) do not militate against consent being freely given. The fact that the inducement acts to procure consent to a risky activity does not signal that a forced or unfree choice is being made. Once an inducement is offered, the terms of the proposed transaction change and, from the perspective of the consenting agent, this now looks like a more attractive deal. The fact that the context in which the proposal looks more attractive is one of treatment does not bear directly on whether the choice is freely made.

The second principle does not see the offering of an inducement, in itself, as problematic relative to the requirement that consent should be informed. To repeat, if the offer of inducement is made in order to misdirect or mislead, that is plainly wrong. However, if we assume an inducement offered in good faith, the fact that such an offer is made in a treatment setting is no reason to question the adequacy of a resulting consent.

Accordingly, even if we should question the equity of offering inducements to patients in treatment settings, there do not seem to be any fresh issues of consent. Indeed, if the consent credentials of inducements are judged to be clean in research settings (where, without the inducement, there is simply a risk calculation to be made), it would be surprising if they were to be found wanting in treatment contexts (where there is already a risk/benefit calculation to be made).

To this, we might add a rather obvious rider. The context in which we feel most comfortable with inducements is that of commerce. If I am induced to enter into risky employment by the offer of 'danger' money or something of that kind, I might come to regret that decision. However, no one would suggest that my consent is tainted. In this respect, treatment and commerce are similar, for agents are already having to calculate the pros and cons of particular transactions and an inducement simply improves the pro side of the calculation. Even where agents are not already having to calculate in this way, as is the case with research, it seems to me that nothing material alters in relation to the adequacy of consent once an inducement is offered.

VI A Right to be Informed and Informed Consent

In the landmark decision of *Canterbury v Spence*,[53] the Court of Appeals of the District of Columbia observed that "[t]rue consent to what happens to one's self is the informed exercise of a choice, and that entails an opportunity to evaluate knowledgeably the options available and the risks attendant upon each'.[54] It was, thus, that the modern doctrine of informed consent was born. And, on this basis, it was held that it was no longer sufficient for physicians to follow their own lights, or the general practice of the profession, in deciding what information to give to patients about their treatment options and, in particular, the risks associated with a proposed course of treatment. Patients (subject to limited exceptions for emergency and for 'therapeutic privilege') have a right to know. The lead given by *Canterbury* was followed in other common law jurisdictions, notably by the Supreme Court of Canada in *Reibl v Hughes*[55] and by the High Court of Australia in *Rogers v Whitaker*,[56] as the common law world moved away from physician paternalism towards a patient-centred approach to the disclosure of medical options and risks.

Ruth Faden and Tom Beauchamp have famously told the story of how, in the US case law, consent as a defence to an action for battery evolved into an informed consent (notice of risk) requirement of negligence law.[57] However, even those who are sympathetic to this doctrinal evolution may wonder whether, for the purposes of informed consent, it is (a) being informed or (b) giving one's consent that is the vital factor. For example, in *Rogers v Whitaker*, the majority distanced itself from the US terminology as follows:

> In this context, nothing is to be gained by reiterating the expressions used in American authorities, such as 'the patient's right of self-determination' or even the oft-used and somewhat amorphous phrase 'informed consent'. The right of self-determination is an expression which is, perhaps, suitable to cases where the issue is whether a person has agreed to the general surgical procedure or treatment, but [it] is of little assistance in the balancing process that is involved in the determination of whether there has been a breach of the duty of disclosure. Likewise, the phrase 'informed consent' is apt to mislead as it suggests a test of the validity of a patient's consent.[58]

Similarly, the English courts, having declined to embrace either the language or the substance of the doctrine of informed consent in *Sidaway v Board of Governors*

[53] 464 F 2d 772 (DC Cir 1972).

[54] At 780.

[55] (1980) 114 DLR (3d) 1.

[56] (1992) 67 ALJR 47.

[57] Ruth Faden and Tom Beauchamp *A History and Theory of Informed Consent* (New York: Oxford University Press, 1986).

[58] (1992) 67 AJLR 47, 52 (Mason CJ, Brennan, Dawson, Toohey, and McHugh JJ).

of the Bethlem Royal Hospital and the Maudsley Hospital,[59] have signalled their doubts about the smoothness of this evolution.[60] What these judicial reservations alert us to is the possibility that, whilst the language of consent has been carried forward from the settled understanding that consent is a defence to battery, the doctrine of informed consent might not actually be concerned with whatever informational conditions are prerequisites of a valid consent.

In principle, there are two quite distinct questions as follows.[61] First, there is the question of how much information a person needs to have before he or she is sufficiently informed for the purpose of giving an authorizing consent. In a community of rights, an agent who purports to consent must certainly understand that consent has justificatory force in relation to the rights of agents; crucially, it must be understood that one is under no obligation to consent and that, if one consents, one will change the moral position. But, what else must an agent know and understand before the purported consent will be recognized as effective? Secondly, there is a question about the informational rights and obligations of agents. In what circumstances does an agent have a right to be informed and, conversely, in what circumstances does an agent have an obligation to inform another? How far do agents have a right to make informed decisions? How far do an agent's positive obligations to warn or inform extend? Not only are there these two distinct sets of questions, as a matter of principle, *it is quite clear that it is the second set that is prior*. For in a community of rights, consent functions as a dynamic relative to the established set of rights and obligations. In other words, until the background rights, including the background informational rights have been established, consent has no reference point. To repeat: in a community of rights, consent is integral to, and it operates in the setting of, the framework of rights.

In practice, however, particularly in clinical and research practice, the two questions get run together under the general rubric of informed consent. Thus, it takes something of an effort to force the questions apart and, in particular, to isolate the first question. Nevertheless, this is what we must endeavour to do.

We can proceed in the following stages: first, we can consider what, within a community of rights, might be judged to be the informational prerequisites for a valid consent; secondly, we can sketch the kind of background informational rights and responsibilities that we might find in such a community; thirdly, we can consider the position where the beneficiary of a consent is actually in breach

[59] [1985] 1 AC 871. Most recently, though, compare *Pearce v United Bristol Healthcare Trust* (1999) 48 BMLR 118 and *Chester v Afshar* [2004] UKHL 41; and see David Meyers '*Chester v Afshar*: Sayonara, Sub Silentio, *Sidaway*?' in Sheila AM McLean (ed) *First Do No Harm* (Aldershot: Ashgate, 2006) 255.

[60] For example, in *Sidaway* itself, see Lord Diplock at [1985] 1 AC 871, 894; and in *Re T (adult: refusal of medical treatment)* [1992] 4 All ER 649, at 663, Lord Donaldson MR says, very pointedly, that a doctor's failure to give such information as the law requires is a breach of duty that sounds in negligence and 'does not, as such, vitiate a consent or refusal'.

[61] Compare Manson and O'Neill (n 12 above) where this distinction, if not absolutely explicitly drawn, is surely implicit.

of his informational obligations relative to the agent who has apparently consented; and, fourthly, we can outline how, having separated out these matters, a community of rights might address concerns about overloading agents with information.

1. The informational prerequisites for consent

To say that an agent has consented without having relevant knowledge or understanding (without being adequately informed) is to flag up a problem that relates in some way to the agent's informational field, or to the agent's interpretation of data within that field, or to the beliefs formed by the agent by reference to the data within the informational field and the way in which such data is understood. For example, relevant data might be missing from the agent's particular informational field (in which event, the agent's consent is based on ignorance or a certain lack of awareness); or, where fraud or deception is involved, some of the data within the agent's informational field might be distorted (in which event, the agent's consent is based on misinformation). Or, where data is open to more than one interpretation, the particular way in which the data is interpreted might lead to a consent based on a 'misunderstanding'—for example, such a misunderstanding might be pleaded by persons who consent to a request from the hospital for retention of 'tissue' without appreciating that this term, as the hospital understands it, includes whole organs.[62] Or, again, where an agent, unaware that there are other options, consents to a particular treatment, T1, its consent is based on the erroneous belief that T1 is the only option.

Let us take it as read that we are dealing with an agent who understands that, where consent is given, this changes one's position relative to the background set of rights and responsibilities that apply across the community. In such a case, where we say that A's consent is (broadly speaking) under-informed or mis-informed, we are pointing to some deficiency that goes beyond an appreciation of the generic significance of giving one's consent. Now, where A is so under-informed or mis-informed, but not because of any blameworthy act or omission by B or C, the question of informed consent arises in a pure form; that is to say, the issue is simply about the informational prerequisites for an adequate consent.

Each consenting agent, as we have said, will act on the basis of certain operative beliefs which, in turn, draw on the agent's own particular informational field. However, each agent will have its own distinctive informational field. Some agents will have more extensive informational fields than others; some agents will have informational fields that are relatively intense at the site of the particular transaction, others will not; and so on. But no agent is omniscient; no agent will

[62] See Margaret Brazier 'Retained Organs: Ethics and Humanity' (2002) 22 Legal Studies 550, responding to John Harris 'Law and Regulation of Retained Organs: The Ethical Issues' (2002) 22 Legal Studies 527.

have a comprehensive and completely accurate informational field. In principle, therefore, any consenting agent might plead after the event that its informational field lacked some relevant item of data or that it included inaccurate data. How readily does such a plea translate into the proposition that the agent gave a consent without relevant knowledge and understanding, and that this was not a properly informed consent? In a community of rights, such a question will be seen as prompting two angles of inquiry, one concerning the *materiality* of the missing or inaccurate data, and the other concerning who bears the *responsibility* for inaccurate data or for the omission of material data from the consenting agent's informational field.

In principle, the item of data in question might have been *material* to the agent's decision to consent at more than one level. At weakest, the data might simply have raised a consideration that the agent would have wished to address. However, it would not have changed the agent's mind about consenting. At strongest, the data might have caused a reversal of the agent's decision: instead of consenting, the agent would have refused. And, in between these extremes, the data might not have caused the agent to withhold consent but it would have led to some qualifying condition (or reservation) being placed on the consent. Which of these senses of materiality should we adopt for our condition of relevant knowledge and understanding, and whose standpoint should we be guided by (that of the consenting agent, or a reasonable agent, or some other representative agent)?

Arguably, a community of rights would be drawn to a subjectivist approach; for, this seems to be the appropriate starting point when we consider that consent changes the protective cover that agents enjoy by virtue of the regime of rights. Moreover, as we have emphasized earlier in the chapter, the standpoint that matters is that of the agent who has ostensibly consented; after all, it is the consent that has been ostensibly given by this agent (not some other agent, real or representative) that is at issue. In practice, the agent is unlikely to plead a lack of informed consent unless, once aware of the data item, the agent would not have consented or would have given only a conditional consent. Nevertheless, it is arguable that a consenting agent acts without relevant knowledge or understanding if that agent's informational field lacks an item of data that the agent would judge (subjectively and sincerely) to be material in the sense that it at least raises a consideration that it would have wished to consider before making a decision as to consent.

This is not quite a licence to avoid the consequences of consents that one regrets, for we must also bring into the reckoning the question of who bears *responsibility* for the omitted (or incorrect) item. Assuming that the consenting agent's informational field is not deficient because of a failure by some other agent to discharge his or her informational responsibilities, the following guidelines may be suggested.

First, the consenting agent must bear the responsibility if it acts recklessly in relation to its own informational field. For example, if agent A is put on notice that, before consenting, it would be prudent to check out that 'x actually is the case' (as A assumes), then this surely must be A's risk if A proceeds to consent without double-checking that x is the case.

Secondly, it must also be the consenting agent who bears the risk if it fails to take reasonable care. Remember, we are hypothesizing a situation where the recipient of the consent has clean hands, where the background negative and positive informational obligations have been discharged.

Thirdly, we come to a genuinely hard case, one in which both agents to the transaction have acted reasonably and responsibly, yet the consent has been given in ignorance of material (present and potentially available) information.[63] Which side, the consenting agent or the recipient, should bear the risk and responsibility?

Such a case sets up a tension between two recurring regulative principles. On the one hand, it is fundamental to the thinking of a community of rights that we should strive to give effect to the agent's will; in other words, it is fundamental that we give due weight to a principle of fidelity to the consenting agent's will. On the other hand, agents cannot function without a degree of transactional security and it is important for practical purposes that the reasonable expectations of the recipient agent are given due weight—otherwise, in practice, there will be no reliance on what seem to be perfectly valid consents. We cannot give unqualified effect to subjectivism in relation to an informed consent without undermining the recipient's reasonable expectation. Arguably, in this light, to hold the reckless or careless consenting agent to the consent (albeit informationally deficient) is the better accommodation of these principles. However, where the consenting agent is neither reckless nor careless, there is reason to think that the fidelity principle reasserts itself. In such a hard case, where neither agent is the obvious risk-bearer, each community of rights and each legal regime will have to make its own good faith judgment as to the respective weights to be accorded to fidelity (for the sake of the consenting agent) and reasonable expectation (for the sake of the recipient of the consent). If we set aside future information (treating this as the consenting agent's risk), then the focus for any division of responsibility is information that is 'in' but inaccurately so or information that, although available, is 'not in'. A plausible default position for the hard case seems to be to hold: (a) that the consent does not meet the condition of an informed choice; but (b) because the recipient has acted in good faith, reliance on the consent is excused although not procedurally justified.[64] Having said this, it is worth repeating that this *is* a hard case; and that, faced with such powerful but competing regulative principles, the members

[63] Presumably, the consenting agent must bear the risk in relation to unknown future facts. Otherwise, if procedural justifications were vulnerable to the consenting agent changing its mind in the light of future facts, the recipient could not rely on the consent with any confidence at all.

[64] In some cases, where there has been reliance, there might be no practical difference between treating the recipient's acts as excused rather than procedurally justified. However, where there has been no reliance, there will be the possibility of reversing the transaction.

of a community of rights will feel the force of Justice Learned Hand's view that the spirit of free-thinking militates against being too sure that you are right.

2. Background informational rights and responsibilities

Where an agent complains about a failure of informed consent, the complaint might be that the consent was defective because the agent was not sufficiently informed. However, the complaint might be, not about consent as such, but that the agent's right to be informed was violated. How might the latter kind of complaint be grounded?

In a typical community of rights, the background regime of rights and duties will include negative obligations against fraud and misinformation as well as positive obligations to inform, such as the obligation of one (informed) agent to warn another (ignorant agent) of a hidden danger (paradigmatically, a life-threatening danger). The extent of such positive obligations will be guided by the twin principles that (a) agents should not be encouraged to free-ride on the information-seeking activities of others and (b) that no agent should be required to inform where this would represent a disproportionate burden relative to its own generic interests. These background informational obligations (both negative and positive), it will be understood, arise quite independently of consent—that is, the reason why these obligations are owed is not to increase the possibility that the act of consenting in particular will be informed but to increase the possibility that action in general will be taken on an informed basis. For example, the reason why there is a background duty to inform an agent that there is a fire ahead is not so that the agent, once warned, can give an informed *consent* to a transaction of some kind but simply so that the agent in question is equipped to act on an informed basis. It follows that these are obligations that agents owe to one another irrespective of whether the immediate context is one in which an agent is considering giving consent and irrespective of whether the information bears directly on an agent's decision whether or not to consent.

Having said this, the nature and extent of an agent's background positive informational obligations does vary from one context to another (as well as from one kind of relationship to another). Even in the case of the most general obligations, there is always a particular context that accounts for the agent having the positive obligation in question. Potentially, a particular context might bring into play a second layer of positive informational rights and obligations. For example, it is arguable that, in modern complex societies with high divisions of labour, suppliers of specialized goods or services have positive obligations to disclose the specialist features of those goods or services; suppliers know that their customers or clients will tend to rely on their specialist skill and judgment. Moreover, within these distinctive contexts, the features of particular transactions might bring into play a third layer of positive obligations—for example, obligations to ensure that vulnerable agents are as informed as non-vulnerable agents might be expected to be. Accordingly, when we refer to an agent's background informational rights and responsibilities, we are including all such rights and responsibilities as are in play, in the particular context, in the light of the background rule regime.

In this light, consider the medical context. Is it plausible to treat doctors as having a positive obligation to inform patients so that they might have a better understanding of the medical options available and the risks associated with particular interventions or courses of treatment? Although some positive informational obligations are of very general application (an agent does not need to be a structural engineer to warn about an unsafe bridge, or a fireman to warn about a fire hazard), the specification of obligations always depends on the context of who knows (or ought to know) what, when, and where (the obligation to warn has no purchase unless the context involves an agent with the relevant information concerning the hazard). It follows that, when we elaborate the positive informational obligations in the medical case, we do so in a particular health care context. One thing that is striking about this context is that the information in question will usually have an important bearing on the physical and psychological well-being of the patient; for one agent to the transaction, important generic interests are at stake. In *Rogers v Whitaker*, for example, the physician omitted to inform the patient that the procedure carried with it a very slight risk that she might lose her sight. The risk might have been slight but this was highly material information from the patient's standpoint and, to require the physician to disclose the risk, would impose no comparable cost on the doctor. More importantly, perhaps, the context is one of highly specialized knowledge and training. Doctors are experts relative to a particular kind of information—information that is not readily available or, at any rate, that is not readily comprehensible. In this light, it is unrealistic and unreasonable to argue that patients free-ride on doctors by looking to them for informed advice. It is true that some, if not all, patients might have trained as physicians and obtained the relevant information through their own unaided efforts. However, in societies that are organized around divisions of labour, specialization and various kinds of personal expertise, this seems not only inefficient in the extreme but, more to the point, contrary to the reasonable expectations of agents within such social settings. Accordingly, while patients might reasonably be expected to be self-reliant in gathering general information about the risks of surgery and the like, when the information lies deep in a particular field of medical expertise, there is no invitation to free-ride in requiring disclosure. Indeed, reflecting this approach, the law does not normally require doctors to disclose what are assumed to be generally available medical facts; rather, informed consent focuses on disclosure of specialized information, that is to say, information of the kind that is not readily accessible to lay agents.

Lest we are not yet convinced of the free-standing nature of a right to be informed, consider a case in which a patient decides *against* medical treatment. Here, there is no consent; in this sense informed consent is not an issue. Nevertheless, the patient, subsequently learning that the medical options were not fully disclosed and that there were options which should have been identified for consideration, now complains that his or her right to be informed has been breached. This surely is a perfectly intelligible claim. Regardless of whether the complaint can be made out on the facts, in principle, the patient has reason to complain—not because he or she gave a consent that was not sufficiently informed but because she was not sufficiently informed to contemplate giving a consent.[65]

What, then, of research contexts? Almost by definition, research trials involve some element of experimentation and risk; and, even if participants are not physically at risk—for example, as in a biobanking project[66]—this is still a specialized kind of undertaking and it cannot be assumed that participants will know precisely what is involved. In all such cases, therefore, it is plausible to treat participants as having a right to be informed. The nature of the research needs to be explained to prospective participants, not for the sake of improved cooperation, but as a matter of respect for the autonomy of agents.

In line with such thinking, Article 3.2 of the Clinical Trials Directive provides that a clinical trial may be undertaken only if (inter alia):

> (b) the trial subject... has had the opportunity, in a prior interview with the investigator..., to understand the objectives, risks and inconvenience of the trial, and the conditions under which it is to be conducted...

This gives some idea of the kind of information that, as a matter of right, the trial subject is entitled to have. Certainly, no one should participate in a clinical trial by acting on a false prospectus; but, beyond that, it is imperative that the researchers ensure that participants understand what benefits (if any) they might possibly obtain through participation and that they are clear about the risks (such as they are known). The question of how far researchers should go with their disclosure, the question of how much information should be given to prospective participants, is one to which we will return.

3. The effect of a breach of informational obligation

What is the position if B, the recipient of A's consent, is in breach of an informational obligation in relation to A? Essentially, there are two possibilities: (i) B is precluded from relying on A's consent as a justification for the act apparently authorized by A; or (ii) B is not so precluded but A has some kind of counter-claim against B. Or, of course, both preclusion and counter-claim might be applied.

[65] Compare the insightful analysis (and critique of English tort law) in Emily Jackson '"Informed Consent" to Medical Treatment and the Impotence of Tort' in Sheila AM McLean (ed) *First Do No Harm* (Aldershot: Ashgate, 2006) 273.

[66] See Alastair V Campbell 'The Ethical Challenges of Biobanks: Safeguarding Altruism and Trust' in Sheila AM McLean (ed) *First Do No Harm* (Aldershot: Ashgate, 2006) 203.

In order to determine how to respond to B's failure, a community of rights might be guided by two considerations, namely, the extent of B's culpability and the materiality of the failure relative to A's informational requirements.

Consider, first, the question of the materiality of the information to the consenting agent. If, as we have already suggested, a community of rights judges that a subjective approach is appropriate, this invites the following chain of reasoning. According to subjectivist guidelines, where A (the consenting agent) has taken care and regards the (missing or defective) information as material, the best that B can hope for is to be excused reliance on the consent. However, this only holds where B has clean hands. If (as in the kind of case that we are now considering) B is in breach of an informational responsibility to A, B will not have clean hands, and it seems to follow that B should not be excused. In other words, if we accept the subjectivist approach already outlined, B will be precluded from relying on A's apparent consent. B will have done wrong to A twice over, once by failing to discharge B's informational obligations and, as a corollary, by acting against A's rights in whatever way the consent would otherwise have covered.

Where B has intentionally breached his informational obligations, this might seem an appropriate outcome. For example, if B deliberately misleads A or intentionally withholds information that he knows would be material to A's decision, the argument that B, notwithstanding this deception, should enjoy the protection of A's consent is unattractive. However, if B has not acted intentionally in this way, it might seem disproportionate to penalize B for what is a less serious failure. We will recall that, in *Sidaway*, although there was an arguable informational failure by the medical team, there was never a thought that this might expose the defendants to an action for battery (or to criminal proceedings); the patient's consent was accepted as valid for this limited, but important, purpose. Yet, if the medical team negligently failed to discharge its informational obligations, the effect of the subjectivist approach is to deny it the shield of consent. In such a case, the medical team must answer not only for its informational wrongdoing but also for any other claim for wrongdoing to which it is now exposed. But, if we take the background set of rights seriously, this seems to be exactly as it should be.

We might resist this conclusion in one other way. It might seem that B's careless failure to discharge B's informational responsibilities to A is converted by A's consent into the equivalent of an intentional wrongdoing. However, this is not the case. In a case of surgery, or the like, B violates A's rights in two different ways: first, there is the violation of A's informational rights and, secondly, there is the violation of A's right to physical integrity. If A authentically consents to either act, B has a defence to the act in question. In our hypothetical, where there is no suggestion of A consenting to the first wrongful act, B is precluded, on the above analysis, from relying on A's apparent consent to the second wrongful act. However, this is not tantamount to treating B's carelessness in relation to A's informational rights as an intentional violation of A's rights. Rather, B's prima facie violation of A's right to physical integrity is always intentional; and, once B is disqualified from relying on A's consent, B is left to answer for the consequence of his intentional act.

The lesson to be taken from this analysis is clear: if B intends to rely on A's consent, then (i) B needs to have no reason to believe that A's consent is informationally deficient and (ii) B must take due care to discharge his or her informational responsibilities to A.

4. Informational overload

A community needs to be careful not to over-compensate for an historic tendency towards under-informing patients: as Onora O'Neill has remarked, '[g]enuine consent is not a matter of overwhelming patients with information'.[67] Let us suppose, then, that a community of rights is concerned that, in practice, its principled subjectivism is counter-productive, patients and research participants being overloaded with information as medical and research professionals seek to ensure that the consents they obtain are watertight. How might this dilemma be addressed?

It will be recalled that a recurring issue in a community of rights is how it sets the balance between fidelity to the consenting agent's will and the protection of the reasonable expectations of the beneficiaries of consent. One possibility, therefore, is for the community to revise the balance, possibly by weakening the subjectivist approach to materiality of information or by extending the cover available to the beneficiary. Let us suppose, however, that the community is not seeking a revision of this kind. Is there any other way out of the difficulty?

The starting point is with the framework regime of rights. Here, we need to be quite clear about the purpose of the right to be informed, or the right to make an informed choice. Arguably, what matters here is not so much the quantity of information given but the quality of the information. If the right is crafted in the light of this distinction, in general, clinicians and researchers will be able to discharge their informational responsibilities by presenting the matter not only in a way that is intelligible to most agents but also in a way that adverts to the considerations that most agents would judge to be material. Exceptions might need to be made for agents who present with exceptional informational requirements (for example, who are exceptionally risk-averse); but, in the standard case, agents would know that there was some information that was not disclosed to them and that would not be disclosed unless they asked for it. The purpose of withholding such information would not be to trick patients or prospective participants into making a decision desired by the medical team or the researchers but, quite

[67] Onora O'Neill 'Some Limits of Informed Consent' (2003) 29 Journal of Medical Ethics 6—a point that is repeated in Manson and O'Neill, n 12 above.

simply, to assist agents to make intelligent and defensible decisions.[68] Moreover, if agents did not quite trust the standard arrangements, it would be open to them to ask for full and complete information.[69]

To this, two caveats should be added. First, there is the important question of how agents would signal their preference for either the standard or the comprehensive information package. In a community of rights, (failure to exercise) an opt-out provision will be taken as a dubious signal of consent and, in general, it will be avoided.[70] Accordingly, rather than routinely assuming that agents accept the standard arrangement unless they indicate otherwise, procedures should present agents with the choice (each time or periodically, as appropriate) between the standard and the comprehensive information package—rather as motorists are presented with the choice between a basic and a comprehensive insurance package—no assumption being made until the choice has been exercised. Secondly, what if our understanding of the risks associated with the research or treatment is so primitive that, even with a comprehensive information package, there is a large question mark about the range of adverse effects? For example, in its report on nanomedicine, the European Group on Ethics in Science and New Technologies expresses doubts about the validity of informed consent procedures in a context of extreme uncertainty:

> The requirement for informed consent is of crucial importance in both medical research and health care. But both the lack of knowledge and the uncertainties that exist [with regard to the biomedical applications of nanotechnology] create problems for the attempts to provide adequate and understandable information and [to] obtain consent....[71]

Put bluntly, the puzzle is: how can we inform agents about risks of which we are entirely unaware? To which the answer perhaps is that we need to distinguish

[68] Compare the General Medical Council *Seeking Patients' Consent: The Ethical Considerations* (GMC, 1998) para 6:

> When providing information you must do your best to find out about patients' individual needs and priorities. For example, patients' beliefs, culture, occupation or other factors may have a bearing on the information they need in order to reach a decision. You should not make assumptions about patients' views, but discuss these matters with them, and ask them whether they have any concerns about the treatment or the risks it may involve. You should provide patients with appropriate information, which should include an explanation of any risks to which they may attach particular significance. Ask patients whether they have understood the information and whether they would like more before making a decision.

[69] The relationship between a community of rights and a culture of trust is not entirely straightforward: see Onora O'Neill *Autonomy and Trust in Bioethics* (Cambridge: Cambridge University Press, 2002) (the Gifford Lectures delivered at the University of Edinburgh, 2001); and Manson and O'Neill (n 12 above) ch 7.

[70] See Deryck Beyleveld and Roger Brownsword *Consent in the Law* (Oxford: Hart, 2007) 199–205.

[71] The European Group on Ethics in Science and New Technologies to the European Commission *Opinion on the Ethical Aspects of Nanomedicine* (Opinion No 21) (17 January 2007) para 5.7. Compare Lorraine Sheremata 'Nanotechnologies and the Ethical Conduct of Research Involving Human Subjects' in Geoffrey Hunt and Michael Mehta (eds) *Nanotechnology: Risk, Ethics and Law* (London: Earthscan, 2006) 247.

between two classes of case, namely: (i) those cases where we have sufficient knowledge and experience to indicate to agents that we have a range of risks on the radar; we might not be sure about individual susceptibility to these risks, and the like; but we are reasonably confident that what we have on the radar is the extent of the possible adverse effects; and (ii) those cases where we have such limited knowledge and experience that we cannot be confident that the potential risks that we have on the radar reflect the extent of the possible adverse effects. Those who are doing their level best to discharge their informational obligations can never do more than exercise their good faith judgment as to class of case they are dealing with. However, if they judge that a case falls within class (ii), then the warning concerning the limits of our knowledge and experience needs to be the first, not the last, thing that the prospectively consenting agent is told. Moreover, even if an agent has opted for the standard information package, this should not apply to class (ii) cases; in other words, the choice between a standard or a comprehensive information package should relate only to class (i) cases.

If the right to make an informed choice were to be regulated in this way, would there be a danger that an agent, having consented under the standard arrangements, might then legitimately complain that the consent was deficient as under-informed? We can be sure that, somewhere in the withheld information, there would be an item that the agent might seize on as subjectively material. If this were a risk, defensive practice would be adopted with doctors and researchers insisting on full and complete disclosure in every case. However, the regulatory regime should be set in such a way that any such risk is clearly neutralised. For, if the consenting agent has chosen to proceed without full disclosure, this implies an assumption of responsibility and the agent will be precluded from presenting the consent as under-informed. In other words, in such circumstances, the consent would protect the beneficiaries who, in good faith, have acted in reliance on it.

VI Conclusion

In this chapter, we have only scratched the surface of consent. There is a good deal more to say, for instance, about such matters as the freedom (unforced choice) threshold for consent, the way in which consent is signalled, the scope and interpretation of consent, and so on.[72] However, the key point is, quite simply, that what we make of this pervasive idea depends very much on where we stand in the bioethical triangle. And, characteristically, it is if we stand at the rights angle of the triangle that we will judge regulators most harshly if they fail to attend to the consent of rights-holding agents.

In a community of rights, consent is a matter of common concern. Against the backdrop of such a community, I have suggested that: (i) first-party consent

[72] These further issues are addressed in Deryck Beyleveld and Roger Brownsword (n 4 above).

at least gives the beneficiary of the consent an answer to the consenting party but not necessarily any more than that; (ii) third-party consent, direct authorization apart, is no kind of consent; (iii) threats, but not inducements, are incompatible with the agent making an unforced choice to consent; and (iv) we need to separate out the question of the informational threshold for consent from the question of background informational rights and responsibilities—in a community of rights, there might be a background right to be informed but there is no right to informed consent as such.

4

The Challenge of Regulatory Legitimacy III

I Introduction

Pluralistic communities—where fundamental values are disputed, or where there is disagreement as to the weight to be accorded to such values—are not designed for regulatory convenience. As the House of Commons Science and Technology Committee put the point in its controversial report on *Human Reproductive Technologies and the Law*:[1]

> We accept that [in] a society that is both multi-faith and largely secular, there is never going to be consensus on . . . the role of the state in reproductive decision-making. There are no demonstrably 'right' answers to the complex ethical, moral and political equations involved. . . . We recognise the difficulty of achieving consensus between protagonists in opposing camps. . . . We believe, however, that to be effective this Committee's conclusions should seek consensus, as far as it is possible to achieve.[2]

Under such conditions, unless regulatees are either not politically engaged or they are simply prepared to trust the judgments of regulators, the capacity of the regulatory system will be put to the test—or, at any rate, in the absence of happenstance consensus or convergence of views, this will be so. For where there are fundamental value differences and where disputants take their differences seriously, how are particular regulatory positions to be defended? Moreover, as regulatory regimes aspire to extend across national boundaries—as they increasingly do in relation to new technologies—claiming regional or even international jurisdiction, the problems posed by pluralistic communities seem even more intractable.[3]

[1] HC 7–1, Science and Technology Committee *Human Reproductive Technologies and the Law* (Fifth Report of Session 2004–05) (London: TSO, 24 March, 2005). Ironically, the report was judged newsworthy not simply for its permissive recommendations (especially concerning sex selection) but also for the fact that the committee, with its quest for consensus, was actually divided down the middle, 5 of the 11 members disagreeing with the report: see HC 491, Science and Technology Committee *Inquiry into Human Reproductive Technologies and the Law* (Eighth Special Report of Session 2004–05) (London: TSO, 29 March, 2005) Annex A.

[2] ibid para 46.

[3] Compare the excellent discussion in Aurora Plomer *The Law and Ethics of Medical Research—International Bioethics and Human Rights* (London: Cavendish, 2005) especially chs 1 and 2. See, also, Roger Brownsword 'What the World Needs Now: Techno-Regulation, Human Rights and Human Dignity' in Roger Brownsword (ed) *Human Rights* (vol IV of *Global Governance and the Quest for Justice*) (Oxford, Hart, 2004) 203.

The regulation of cloning is a case in point.[4] So far as human reproductive cloning is concerned, we have convergence: pluralism notwithstanding, it is agreed that cloning humans with reproductive intent is immoral (indeed, a crime against humanity, as the French have declared it) and that it should be prohibited. By contrast, we have deep pluralist divisions in relation to therapeutic cloning and the early stages of human embryonic stem cell research. Within nation states (the UK, for example) there are serious differences of view: some believe that this type of cloning is as immoral as reproductive cloning and that it should be prohibited; others believe that it is morally permissible and that it should be licensed, and possibly even encouraged, by regulators; and some, believing that we shirk our moral responsibilities to fellow humans if we do not pursue promising lines of research into killer diseases and disorders, might even argue that regulators should require such work to be undertaken. As we move beyond nation states to larger regulatory arenas, we find in both Europe and the United States a patchwork of regulatory positions and, at the United Nations, we find members struggling to find a suitably anodyne form of words that will accommodate their deepest differences—an unconvincing majority eventually calling for the prohibition of 'all forms of human cloning inasmuch as they are incompatible with human dignity and the protection of human life'.[5]

In the face of these difficulties, a turn to proceduralism might beckon.[6] That is to say, if regulators are not able to assuage their critics by appealing directly to the substantive legitimacy of their position, they might instead rely on the fairness of the procedures that led to the adoption of the position in question. As it were, if substantive due process will not work then regulators might resort to procedural due process. However, before resorting to such a second-best strategy, regulators might wish to assess the regulative potential of two principles that are widely accepted even in pluralistic communities. These are the principles, first, that we should do no harm to others;[7] and, secondly, that we should exercise precaution in the face of uncertain but potentially serious and irreversible risks.

[4] See, further, Roger Brownsword 'Stem Cells and Cloning: Where the Regulatory Consensus Fails' (2005) 39 New England Law Review 535.

[5] On 18 February 2005, the Legal Committee voted 71 in favour, 35 against, with 43 abstentions, to recommend to the General Assembly that members should be called on 'to prohibit all forms of human cloning inasmuch as they are incompatible with human dignity and the protection of human life' (UN press release GA/L/3271: <http://www.un.org/News/Press/docs/2005/gal3271.doc.htm>). On 8 March 2005, the General Assembly accepted this recommendation, 84 members voting in favour of the (non-binding) UN Declaration on Human Cloning, with 34 against and 37 abstentions (UN press release GA/10333: <http://www.un.org/News/Press/docs/2005/ga10333.doc.htm>).

[6] See Roger Brownsword 'Regulating Human Genetics: New Dilemmas for a New Millennium' (2004) 12 Medical Law Review 14; and Deryck Beyleveld and Roger Brownsword *Consent in the Law* (Oxford: Hart, 2007) ch 10.

[7] Compare the qualified libertarian approach of the Science and Technology Committee (n 1 above). Put shortly, the committee seeks to forge consensus around the principle that the state should not interfere with reproductive freedom provided that the exercise of such freedom occasions no demonstrable harm to others or to society.

The purpose of this chapter is fourfold. First, in Parts II and III, we take a harder look at the harm principle and the precautionary principle as candidate unproblematic regulative standards for pluralistic communities. Given the analysis of the previous chapter (where consent was shown to be a far from neutral principle), it will come as no surprise to find that what one makes of harm and precaution largely depends upon the point of the bioethical triangle that is taken as guiding. Secondly, in Part IV, we consider how the ideas of harm and precaution might be interpreted in a community of rights (leading to the thought that, in such a community, it might come to be accepted that the state legitimately exercises a precautionary stewardship). Thirdly, in Part V, nanotechnology is taken as a test-bed for the community's approach to risk (assessment and management) and to precautionary regulation. Finally, in Part VI, we return to proceduralism, considering, first, how it might function in a community of rights and then noting its limits where regulators face a divided ethical plurality.

II The Harm Principle

According to Article 4 of the UNESCO Universal Declaration on Bioethics and Human Rights:

> In applying and advancing scientific knowledge, medical practice and associated technologies, direct and indirect benefits to patients, research participants and other affected individuals should be maximized and any possible harm to individuals should be minimized.

In the latter part of this provision, we hear echoes of the ancient precept that we should do no harm to others (*primum non nocere*). Famously, too, it is the harm principle that is the fulcrum of John Stuart Mill's influential rule-utilitarian-inspired liberalism.[8] Thus, where my conduct is harmful to others, it falls in the public domain and there is a prima facie case for applying legal or moral coercion to restrain such conduct; but where my conduct is not harmful to others, it falls in the private domain and there is no prima facie case for applying legal or moral coercion to restrain such conduct—even if that conduct is judged to be harmful to me. Notoriously, however, attempts to ring-fence a private sphere by reference to whether our acts occasion any 'harm' to 'others' is problematic. However, the problem is not one that is simply unique to utilitarianism; the problem is that the concepts of 'harm' and 'others' are contested at all points of the bioethical triangle.[9]

[8] JS Mill 'On Liberty' in JS Mill *Utilitarianism* (London: Fontana Press, 1962) (edited by Baroness Mary Warnock).

[9] See, further, Roger Brownsword 'Cloning, Zoning and the Harm Principle' in Sheila AM McLean (ed) *First Do No Harm* (Aldershot: Ashgate, 2006) 527.

1. Utilitarianism

Following a utilitarian approach, 'harm' is largely equated with the stuff of disutility: that is to say, pain and suffering, distress, anxiety, the frustration of plans and non-satisfaction of preferences, and the like. As for 'others', quite simply, they are those beings who are capable of experiencing just this kind of pain and suffering.

So, for instance, if the harm principle, so understood, is applied to reproductive human cloning, utilitarians will support prohibition so long as the procedure is unsafe and, thus, capable of generating various types of disutility. Should reproductive cloning become a safe and reliable procedure, and should it prove to be less disruptive of familial relations than some fear, utilitarians might find that they are running out of reasons to maintain their opposition. Of course, those who (for non-utilitarian reasons) are distressed by reproductive human cloning will pose some awkward questions for utilitarian-minded regulators—in response to which, they might simply disregard such distress as irrational or, following the spirit of Mill, judge that the price of freedom is that the preferences of some will have to be overridden.

Applying the same approach to therapeutic cloning, utilitarians will see no objection to terminating the development of a 100-cell human embryo. At that stage of embryonic development, the prevailing wisdom is that there is no possibility of pain and suffering being experienced. The embryo, to be sure, is a potential other; but, at the relevant time, it is not yet in that category (it is not yet an other) and so it is not capable of being harmed.

2. Human Rights

In its most robust and distinctive form, human rights theory interprets 'harm' by reference to those particular interests that are protected by the set of human rights, including both negative and positive rights within this set, and viewing such rights under a will or choice theory.[10] As I have emphasized in Chapter 3, while consent can (and does) figure in other types of ethical thinking, it is the presupposition of will theory that gives informed consent its *integrated* role in human rights thinking, the rights-holder being able to authorize actions that would, consent apart, involve a violation of rights. It follows that, given this approach, it is human 'rights-holders' who are the relevant 'others'.

From such a perspective, human reproductive cloning is to be opposed where it threatens the well-being of rights-holders (as it might if cloning procedures issue in the birth of damaged children) or where the autonomy of rights-holders

[10] On the contrast between will (or choice) and interest theories of rights, see, eg, HLA Hart 'Bentham on Legal Rights', in AWB Simpson (ed) *Oxford Essays in Jurisprudence* (Second Series, Oxford: Clarendon Press, 1973) 171; and DN MacCormick 'Rights in Legislation' in PMS Hacker and J Raz (eds) Law, Morality, and Society (Oxford: Clarendon Press, 1977) 189.

is compromised. Highlighting this latter concern, Cass Sunstein invites us to engage in the following thought experiment:[11]

> Imagine a situation in which cloning was freely permitted—in which individuals could clone themselves, and in which people interested in children with a certain genetic endowment could assure themselves of that very endowment. If a family wanted a terrific athlete, it could obtain a genetic equivalent of, say, Michael Jordan; if a family wanted a terrific musician, it could obtain a genetic equivalent of, say, Bob Dylan; if a family wanted a terrific scientist, it could obtain a genetic equivalent of, say, Ian Wilmut; if it wanted a terrific philosopher, it could clone John Rawls. Why would this be objectionable? The reason is that people would be treating their children-to-be as means, with prearranged agendas, rather than as ends, to seek their own path.

In the human rights community, such a situation is thought to violate the principle that children have a right to be born with an open future (preserving their life-style autonomy).[12]

As for therapeutic cloning, while human rights theorists might disagree about the stage at which fetal or neonatal life attains rights-holding status (if at all), no will theorist would argue that a 100-cell human embryo is a *paradigmatic* rights-holder. For, there is, at this stage, a very long way to go before the embryo is capable of actively participating in a community of rights. Accordingly, in the absence of extreme precaution or arguments that are indicative of indirect risk to (unproblematic) rights-holders, the harm principle offers no reason to prohibit therapeutic cloning.

3. The Dignitarians

For dignitarians, 'harm' is understood as any act that compromises human dignity; and 'others' are understood individually, collectively, and inclusively as members of the community. So understood, the harm principle demands that human reproductive cloning should be prohibited because, even if a clonee is not harmed in any sense that would be recognized by utilitarian or human rights standards, this directly compromises human dignity.[13]

As for therapeutic cloning, the embryo is definitely an 'other', it is instrumentalized, possibly commodified and commercialized, and this is a procedure that is harmful—human dignity is violated.

The lesson is clear, and it can be stated summarily. Contrary to the Millian assertion, the harm principle does not give us a simple standard for the regulation

[11] Cass Sunstein 'Is There a Constitutional Right to Clone?' (2002) 53 Hastings Law Journal 987, at 1000.

[12] See, eg, Dena S Davis 'Genetic Dilemmas and the Child's Right to an Open Future' (1997) 28 Rutgers Law Journal 549, especially at 561–7 (arguing that a reflexive application of autonomy values will set limits to parents' reproductive autonomy); and Dena S Davis *Genetic Dilemmas* (New York: Routledge, 2001).

[13] Compare Donna Dickenson *Property in the Body* (Cambridge: Cambridge University Press, 2007) at 170 (for a tension between 'harm' as conceived by first world researchers and as conceived under the Tongan notion of human dignity).

of our interactions. What counts as 'harm', like who counts as an 'other', depends entirely on one's ethical perspective; and, in a pluralistic community, any attempt to build a regulatory consensus around this principle is liable to break down once the test cases get tougher.

III Precaution

Article 17 of the UNESCO Declaration on Bioethics and Human Rights, headed 'Protection of the environment, the biosphere and biodiversity', provides:

> Due regard is to be given to the interconnection between human beings and other forms of life, to the importance of appropriate access and utilization of [b]iological and genetic resources, to respect for traditional knowledge and to the role of human beings in the protection of the environment, the biosphere and biodiversity.

Article 20 then adds somewhat sparingly that '[a]ppropriate assessment and adequate management of risk related to medicine, life sciences and associated technologies should be promoted'. If Article 20 enshrines a very general and unspecified precautionary approach, Article 17 gives precaution a more particular application. In neither case, though, is precaution strongly prioritized.

By contrast, the development of the precautionary principle, particularly in the context of environmental protection law, prioritizes the need for sustainable development, and emphatically supports the polluter pays principle. As the Nuffield Council on Bioethics has expressed it:

> This is the rule that permits governments to impose restrictions on otherwise legitimate commercial activities, if there is a risk, even if not yet a scientifically demonstrated risk, of environmental damage.[14]

However, the precautionary principle is formulated in many different ways[15]—indeed, as its critics would have it, in far too many different ways. For example,

[14] Nuffield Council on Bioethics *Genetically Modified Crops: The Ethical and Social Issues* (London, May 1999) 162. For a more specific elaboration, see *Pfizer* [2002] ECR II–3305, at para 143: 'a preventive measure cannot properly be based on a purely hypothetical approach to risk, founded on mere conjecture which has not been scientifically verified'. So, mere conjecture and hypothesis will not suffice. But, a precautionary measure may apply where the risk 'has not yet been fully demonstrated' (para 146). The underlying science must be consistent with principles of 'excellence, transparency and independence' (para 172).

[15] See, eg, Robert Lee and Elen Stokes, 'Ecological Modernisation and the Precautionary Principle' in Jennifer Gunning and Søren Hom (eds) *Ethics, Law and Society* (vol 1, Aldershot: Ashgate, 2005) 103. For helpful recent overviews of the EC jurisprudence, see Veerle Heyvaert 'Guidance Without Constraint: Assessing the Impact of the Precautionary Principle on the European Community's Chemicals Policy' (2006) 6 The Yearbook of European Environmental Law 27, especially. 29–37, and 'Facing the Consequences of the Precautionary Principle in European Community Law' (2006) 31 European Law Review 185.

in a recent attack on the principle,[16] it is accused of being 'an overly-simplistic and under-defined concept that seeks to circumvent the hard choices that must be faced in making any risk management decision';[17] it is claimed that there are at least 19 different versions of the principle; and, quite understandably, it is argued that, in this light, the principle fails to offer a sound basis for a coherent regulatory framework.

Having said this, in most articulations of the precautionary principle, there are four key variables as follows:

(i) a degree of scientific uncertainty;
(ii) concerning some class, kind, or type of hazard or risk;
(iii) where the damage associated with the perceived hazard or risk is of a certain degree or character;
(iv) as a result of which some measure of precaution is advocated.

If we use the language of lawyers, we can say that the scientific uncertainty is such that we cannot be sure *beyond all reasonable doubt* that the relevant hazard or risk either does or does not exist. It follows that those who argue for precaution must maintain either (a) that the evidence of relevant hazard or risk is made out on *a balance of probabilities* or (b) that the evidence falls short of that standard. Where advocates of precaution can make out the case on a balance of probabilities, so that the risk is more likely than not, then even if this is not yet a scientifically demonstrated risk, it is still a plausible basis for precaution. Characteristically, however, the argument for precaution does not meet this threshold and advocates are making out their case from a much less compelling platform—either from the very weak position that it has not yet been shown beyond all reasonable doubt that there is no risk, or that there is some evidence of risk albeit short of the balance of probabilities threshold. However, whether the case for precaution assumes that the evidence lies above or below the balance of probabilities threshold, there is scope for endless argument about just how strong the evidence needs to be before precaution kicks in.

In relation to the second variable, whereas in some communities, especially in scientific communities, precaution tends to be focused on risks to health and environment, in other communities, precaution is thought to be appropriately applied additionally to a broad class of economic, social, and cultural risks.

[16] Gary E Marchant and Douglas J Sylvester 'Transnational Models for Regulation of Nanotechnology' (2006) 34 Journal of Law, Medicine and Ethics 714.

[17] ibid 722. In this remark, there are echoes of Marcia Angell's distinction between precautionary cynicism (which avoids distinguishing between reliable and unreliable evidence, between the likely and the unlikely, between the large danger and the small one, and so on) and engaged scepticism which tries to draw such distinctions: see Marcia Angell *Science on Trial: The Clash of Medical Evidence and the Law in the Breast Implant Case* (New York: WW Norton, 1997) especially at 158.

Then, there are questions about the degree or character of the damage associated with the perceived hazard or risk. In relation to environmental hazards, it is often stipulated that the damage threatened must be serious and irreversible,[18] as well as large-scale.[19] But, the first and the third of these stipulations, in particular, leave plenty of room for interpretation. Moreover, these leeways in the interpretation of the precautionary principle carry over if it is applied to non-environmental risks—for example, to the risks associated with stem cell-based therapies or germ-line gene therapy.

Finally, once the principle is engaged, it remains to specify the required response. If there is a relevant risk, how is it to be managed? Does precaution require outright prohibition or cessation, or is it sufficient to limit or adjust the activity or simply to monitor it? Again, the opportunities for finessing the principle are endless.[20]

Even if the variables within the precautionary principle could be stabilized, we should not forget the potential perversity of precaution, surely nowhere better exemplified than in the price paid by Samuel Butler's fictitious Erewhonians when they decided to destroy their machines for fear that they would supplant humans.[21] Modernizing this old lesson, Cass Sunstein has subjected the precautionary principle to a damning critique. Sunstein's point is that the taking of precautionary measures—or, at any rate, the taking of precautionary measures that involve giving up some activity—itself involves risk (sacrifice) and that this must be brought into what is otherwise a one-sided narrow screen calculation.[22] To appreciate the force of this point, we need only reflect on the choice between a safety-first (ex ante) regulatory strategy that delays the market authorization for what might prove to be life-saving medical products and a strategy that facilitates bringing products to market subject to ex post safety monitoring. More generally, as Adam Burgess concludes in his study of precautionary responses to the perceived hazards presented by mobile phones and cell phone towers, there is a worrying tendency to create risk shadows and then commit large resources to chasing them—thus, 'In the elusive quest to establish a risk-free existence, our autonomy,

[18] As in the famous Principle 15 of the Rio Declaration (June 1992) which requires parties to 'take precautionary measures to anticipate, prevent or minimize the causes of climate change and mitigate its adverse effects'. In this context, the declaration continues: 'Where there are threats of serious or irreversible damage, lack of full scientific certainty should not be used as a reason for postponing such measures'.

[19] See *EU Communication on the Precautionary Principle* (IP/OO.96) (February 2000).

[20] Compare Council for Science and Technology *Nanosciences and Nanotechnologies: A Review of Government's Progress on its Policy Commitments* (London, March 2007) paras 52 et seq (for the view that, while precaution does not entail a moratorium on the development of nanotechnology, the basic research should not be neglected). For similar emphasis on the importance of conducting the basic research, see the French National Consultative Ethics Committee for Health and Life Sciences, Opinion No 96 ('Ethical Issues Raised by Nanosciences, Nanotechnologies and Health', 2007) p 10.

[21] Samuel Butler *Erewhon* (London: Penguin Books, 1985: first published 1872).

[22] Cass Sunstein *Laws of Fear* (Cambridge: Cambridge University Press, 2005).

intelligence, and capacity for change and enlightenment stand in danger of being compromised and diminished'.[23]

The purpose of the current analysis, however, is not to repeat these many times rehearsed criticisms of the precautionary principle. Rather, the point to be emphasized here is that precaution plays differently depending upon where we are coming from in the bioethical triangle.

1. Utilitarianism

Generally, precaution testifies to a utilitarian concern about safety. However, unless there is a rule-utilitarian justification for adopting a strict precautionary approach in an identifiable class of situations, the precautionary calculation cannot be carried out in a one-sided way.[24] For the utilitarian, each option must be reviewed. If it is proposed that we should give up on certain lines of research, it is not enough to plead precaution or risk-aversion or distress avoidance. The utilitarian will want to know what the costs of precaution are (quite literally, how much it is costing to buy a bit more safety, and what benefits are being foregone); and the anticipated net result of the precautionary option will have to be superior to that of any alternative option.

If one were to apply precaution also to the *benefit* side of a utilitarian calculation, it might dampen our enthusiasm for those technologies that promise a great deal, not in the short term, but in the longer term. For example, in the *Harvard Onco-mouse* case,[25] the utilitarian-minded examiners thought it perfectly sensible to weigh in the moral balance (that they took to be required by Article 53(a) of the European Patent Convention) the distress occasioned to a genetically engineered mouse (the mouse being a test animal for cancer research). However, they were persuaded that the potential benefits to humans, relieved of a devastating human disease, outweighed the clear and present distress to the mice. If the *potential* benefits of the research could be equated with *actual* benefits, that might make the outcome more plausible; but one thing that we do know about research is that there are no guarantees that it will deliver its prospective benefit within the projected timeframe, indeed if ever. Accordingly, where we encounter hype and hope, as we frequently do in relation to modern

[23] Adam Burgess *Cellular Phones, Public Fears, and a Culture of Precaution* (Cambridge: Cambridge University Press, 2004) 281. But, the elusive quest continues: see, eg, Geoffrey Lean 'Wi-Fi: the Backlash' *The Independent on Sunday* 15 July 2007, p 14 (Haringey council resolving to adopt a precautionary approach to wi-fi technology in schools).

[24] Moreover, in societies where the trajectory is pro-technology, the precautionary principle is unlikely to be interpreted in a way that does more than slow down the pace of change: see the insightful analysis by Wolfgang van den Daele 'Legal Framework and Political Strategy in Dealing with the Risks of New Technology: the Two Faces of the Precautionary Principle' in Han Somsen (ed) *The Regulatory Challenge of Biotechnology* (Cheltenham: Edward Elgar, 2007) 118.

[25] OJ EPO 10/1992, 590.

technologies, a balanced precautionary approach within utilitarianism would have to discount for uncertainty on both sides of the risk/benefit calculation.

2. Human Rights

Because precaution relates to harm or damage, as conceived by a particular ethical viewpoint, when we adopt a human rights perspective, it is precaution for the sake of human rights that becomes focal. There are some tricky questions to be resolved here—classically, the question of how much precaution (qua due process) we should incorporate into the design of the criminal justice system lest we cause innocent persons to be arrested and detained, prosecuted, convicted, or punished.

For present purposes, suffice it to say that in a community of rights there might be an argument that we should exercise caution when dealing with human embryos (or human/non-human chimeras)[26] because we might be wrong in assuming that they are not bearers of rights;[27] or, again, it might be suggested that we need to be careful that treating human embryos (or chimeras) as a research tool does not change our attitudes so that we suffer a loss of respect for fellow rights-holders. How far we might run with these particular arguments is moot; but there is certainly a precautionary form of argument available, and waiting to be fully articulated, within human rights thinking. Shortly, we will discuss how such considerations might convince a community of rights that it needs to recognize the state as having a special responsibility for provisionally settling such matters—leading to a larger stewardship responsibility for the sustainability, physical and moral, of the community.

3. The Dignitarians

Dignitarians regard the compromising of human dignity as a self-standing reason for restraint—precaution does not enter into such an ethic in quite the same way. Crucially, dignitarianism (unless it is being operated disingenuously) is not interested in consequential calculation, whether of the likely costs and benefits (in the way that a utilitarian impact statement might be drafted) or of the effect on rights.[28] Dignitarianism, it cannot be emphasized too strongly, is a red light not an amber light ethic; its credo is that we should not proceed at all (where activities are judged categorically to compromise human dignity) rather than that we should

[26] Compare the interesting discussion in Françoise Baylis and Andrew Fenton, 'Chimera Research and Stem Cell Therapies for Human Neurodegenerative Disorders' (2007) 16 *Cambridge Quarterly of Healthcare Ethics* 195.

[27] Compare the analysis in Deryck Beyleveld and Roger Brownsword *Human Dignity in Bioethics and Biolaw* (Oxford: Oxford University Press, 2001) especially ch 6.

[28] For cultural conservativism masquerading as risk analysis, see again Wolfgang van den Daele (n 24 above).

proceed only with care. For dignitarians, the proposition that we should exercise precaution against the risk that biotechnology goes wrong misses the point; the point is that, if biotechnology goes right, human dignity is compromised.[29]

IV Precaution and Harm, Stewardship and Sustainability in a Community of Rights

In a community of rights, regulators will seek to prevent harm to rights-holders. However, the community needs a strategy for dealing with those cases where it is not entirely clear whether actions are harmful to rights-holders, whether the doubt concerns the status of those who are affected by the actions in question or whether it concerns the harmfulness of such actions. The community also needs to defend itself against insidious threats to its viability as a moral community and it needs a strategy that regulates against such a risk. Whether we choose to term the community's response as 'precautionary' is of no great moment; the point is that the community, having sensitized itself to such risks, needs to have a relevant risk-management strategy. We can tackle these issues by considering two precautionary dilemmas for the community and then the possible recognition of the state as having a legitimate role as steward for the community's sustainability.

1. Precaution and harm in a community of rights

Within a community of rights, precaution will be interpreted relative to the regime of rights. The risk to be guarded against is that rights are not respected. Such a community, as I have emphasized, is a reflective community. It is also a community that recognizes the limits of its own moral understanding. On the most fundamental issues of its moral orientation, the community is reasonably confident: it believes that, in orienting itself towards rights, and particularly those interests that are common to all agents, it is doing the right thing. However, a willingness to concede that it might be wrong is a defining characteristic of this community. Such an attitude invites a precautionary approach. In particular, what if the community has erred in drawing the line between those who are treated as rights-holders and those who are not? Or, what if the community miscalculates the indirect consequential impact of individual permitted acts in relation to the level of respect accorded to rights of members? We can comment briefly on these two precautionary dilemmas before identifying a deeper precautionary question that concerns the sustainability of the community itself.

[29] See Roger Brownsword 'Biotechnology and Rights: Where are We Coming From and Where are We Going?' in Mathias Klang and Andrew Murray (eds) *Human Rights in the Digital Age* (London: Cavendish GlassHouse, 2005) 219.

(a) *Who precisely are 'rights-holders' in general and 'relevant rights-holders' in particular?*

In the sad case of *Evans v Amicus Healthcare Ltd*,[30] Ms Evans sought to have access to her frozen embryos. These embryos had been created using Ms Evans's eggs and the sperm of her then partner, Mr Johnston. Alas, some time after the initial reproductive treatment, the couple had split up and Mr Johnston now declined to consent to the continuation of the treatment (even though the embryos were Ms Evans's only hope of having a child genetically connected to her). The case was largely determined (in Mr Johnston's favour) by the general provisions of the Human Fertilisation and Embryology Act 1990 and by the particular scope of the parties' consent. However, even if the 1990 Act spoke in favour of Mr Johnston's position, there was also the question of whether the legislation was compatible with the Human Rights Act 1998. Inter alia, this raised an issue about the status of an embryo as a possible rights-holder.

Responding to that issue, the Court of Appeal in *Evans* rejected the claim that Article 2 of the Convention (the right to life) is engaged in respect of an embryo. Thorpe and Sedley LJJ, in their joint judgment, said:

> In our domestic law it has been repeatedly held that a foetus prior to the moment of birth does not have independent rights or interests...Thus even more clearly can there be no independent rights or interests in stored embryos... [It is a fallacy to invoke] Article 2 in the present argument. Ms Evans' case is not about the right to life; it is about the right to bring life into being.[31]

There is, of course, a difference between (i) denying that an embryo is capable of having any rights (that it is not a rights-holder) and (ii) denying that an embryo (qua rights-holder) has a particular right (in this case the right to life). For any community of rights, the first question is an important aspect of the general exercise of drawing the line between rights-holders and others; it is both an inclusionary and an exclusionary exercise; and in the European community of rights, at least, it is clear that human embryos are not to be classed as rights-holders.[32]

The vexed question of who has rights is not just about embryos. The same question needs to be asked about fetuses and young children, non-human higher animals,

[30] [2003] EWHC 2161 (Fam), [2004] EWCA (Civ) 727.

[31] [2004] EWCA Civ 727, para 19. See, also, paras 106–7 (Arden LJ).

[32] Compare *Vo v France* (2005) 40 EHRR 12. There, the applicant challenged a decision of the Cour de Cassation in which the court refused to treat a doctor's unintentional termination of the applicant's six-month pregnancy as a criminal act and, thus, declined to treat the fetus as a life protected by the criminal law. The majority of the Strasbourg court held that the French decision was compatible with Article 2 of the Convention (concerning the right to life). According to the court, there was no consensus in Europe on the nature and status of the embryo and/or fetus. At best, it could be regarded as common ground between states that the embryo/fetus belonged to the human race. Its potential and capacity to become a person required protection in the name of *human dignity*, without making it a person with the right to life for the purposes of Article 2. In other words, rights-bearing humans must at least be born; for unborn humans, it is human dignity that does the protective work.

smart robots, and, in some future world, hybrids, cyborgs, and chimeras of various kinds. Each community of rights must debate such matters. Moreover, not only must it respond to the inclusionary question (who has rights?) but it must also determine its approach to those life forms that are to be excluded. What attitude does the community have to those who are judged not to qualify as rights-holders? Given the frailty of human reasoning, how precautionary should the community be? Is there a margin in which the benefit of doubt applies? If so, how wide is the margin to be?

In principle, the community might err in two ways in its classification. It might recognize false positives (incorrectly treating non-rights-holders as if they were rights-holders) or it might recognize false negatives (incorrectly treating rights-holders as if they were non-rights-holders). Neither error is cost free. However, the costs associated with false negative errors could scarcely be more serious. This being so, we might expect that precaution in a community of rights will build in a bias against making false negative errors.

(b) Indirect harm

Another difficult question for a community of rights is that concerning the indirect effects of acts that, in themselves, seem to involve only the interests of autonomous agents. To ban dwarf-throwing in French clubs or laser-shooting arcades in Germany or physician-assisted suicide in Europe and North America on the grounds that such activities, albeit the activities of consenting rights-holding agents, might negatively impact indirectly on the rights of other agents is to apply a broad precautionary mandate. The state's justification has the right shape but is this taking precaution too far?

As with the question of who has rights, the question of indirect harm invites errors, false positives (where we incorrectly assess that there is indirect harm), and false negatives (where we incorrectly assess that there is no indirect harm). Unlike the former question, however, it is not obvious which kind of error is the more serious one to make. To some extent, this depends upon the nature of the rights that are, respectively, directly restricted or indirectly violated. What we can say, however, is that the restriction definitely involves a prima facie violation of rights while the protection that we judge it provides might or might not be illusory.

The regulation of physician-assisted suicide is instructive. As is well known, in landmark judicial decisions on both sides of the Atlantic, prohibitions against physician-assisted suicide have been upheld.[33] For example, in *Washington v Glucksberg*,[34] it was the State of Washington's prohibition against assisted suicide

[33] See, in particular, *Washington v Glucksberg* 117 S Ct 2258 (1997), 138 L Ed 2d 772; *Re Rodriguez and Attorney General of British Columbia* (1993) 107 DLR 4th 342; and *R(on the application of Mrs Dianne Pretty v DPP and Secretary of State for the Home Department* [2001] UKHL 61; *Case of Pretty v United Kingdom* (2002) ECHR 2346/02, 29 April [2002] 35 Eur HR Rep 1.

[34] 117 S Ct 2258 (1997). 138 L Ed 2d 772.

that was challenged. After decisions swinging this way and that, the Supreme Court reversed the Ninth Circuit to leave the prohibition intact.

Yet, from a human rights standpoint, it is easy to argue that, in such test-case circumstances, no private wrong is done. It might be argued, for instance, that: (i) agents have a negative right against *unwilled* assistance with life termination; but (ii) where, as in these specimen cases, the right-holder consents to (indeed, requests) the assistance, the assisting agent does not violate this right; and hence (iii) assistance is permitted and involves no private wrong (at any rate, to the rights-holder). Alternatively, we might arrive at the same conclusion (the act of assistance involves no private wrong) by unpacking an agent's 'right to suicide'. By a parallel process of reasoning, we will also arrive at the conclusion that, given the agent's consent, active euthanasia involves no private wrong. Yet, in one test case after another, the highest courts in North America and Europe have rejected the pressure to relax the legal position in relation to assisted suicide; and, for most legal systems, the prohibition against active euthanasia is where the regulatory line is most clearly drawn in the sand.

The standard reason given by rights-committed legal regimes for their refusal to recognize the *public* lawfulness of assisted suicide or active euthanasia is that such recognition would potentially undermine the right to life of third parties, particularly of vulnerable third-party agents. From a human rights perspective, the general issue raised by the prohibitions imposed by such regimes against active euthanasia and assisted suicide can be put in the following terms: where (test-case) agent A is quite clearly consenting to agent B acting in a way that would otherwise be a violation of A's rights, why does this clear consent not take priority over the concern that we might have about the validity of ostensible consents given in the general run of cases? Where the state's public interest justification is that its prohibition is necessary and proportionate in order to secure respect for the rights of fellow agents in the community, does this pass muster?

First, we can accept that no rational legal regime can recognize consent as an ex post defence to a charge of unlawful killing. Quite simply, this would be a hostage to fortune.

Secondly, before a simple prohibition against euthanasia can be justified, it needs to be shown why a special procedure (to confirm ex ante that valid consents are in place) is not made available. If a state were to refuse to entertain a special regime with procedural safeguards, it could rightly be accused of being lazy;[35] and it might be open to the same kind of criticism if it fudged applications in an ad hoc way. It would also be rightly criticized as inconsistent where it already operated a special procedure permitting the life-terminating withdrawal of treatment and support from patients who are diagnosed as being in a persistent vegetative state.

[35] In *Glucksberg* 138 L Ed 2d 772, at 801, Justice O'Connor (likewise the minority in *Rodriguez*) allows for such a possibility.

Thirdly, accepting that the onus is on the state to justify not putting in place a special procedure for lawful active euthanasia, and accepting that an agent's will to live is no more important than an agent's will to die, what if the state pleads that it is not satisfied that even the best-intentioned special procedure will prove foolproof in practice? This is not an unreasonable doubt but, to complete its justification, the state must argue that respect for the rights of agents is better secured in a community where a special procedure is not recognized as opposed to one in which it is recognized. As Robert Nozick once said:

> [T]he statement that a particular piece of legislation makes some persons unfree to perform some acts they should not be unfree to perform (according to what is thought to be the optimal pattern of freedom and unfreedom), even if true, is not by itself a *conclusive* objection to the legislation. For it may be that no feasible and acceptable pattern of freedom and unfreedom is more optimal... than the one yielded by this legislation.[36]

At just this point, however, the justification runs into a haze of speculation and uncertainty. Who knows whether the pattern of regulation in, say, the Netherlands or Belgium (where special procedures are recognized) results in the frustration of fewer authentic wills than is the case in, say, the UK or Canada?[37] Moreover, I can see no way of rescuing the argument by invoking a default position that does not beg the question. Quite simply, there is no easy way to validate or invalidate the state's claim that the optimal pattern of freedom and unfreedom features a prohibition rather than a special procedure.

Fourthly, if this analysis is correct, and if a community is unable to resolve its differences because of these uncertainties, it falls to the state to make a provisional judgment and declare the public position accordingly. Thus, the state's justification opens by reference to the special need to secure the rights of all agents within the community; but, because this is a contested issue, it ends by appealing to its responsibility to provide a practical settlement of the matter.

Turning to the refusal to recognize consent as a defence to physician assisted suicide, it might be argued that the state has less cause for concern—it is, after all, acts of *assistance* rather than life-terminating acts that are at stake. However, this is to assume that there is a relatively robust line dividing mere acts of assistance from acts of life termination. In practice, however, especially where we are dealing with vulnerable agents, Chief Justice Rehnquist in *Glucksberg* might well be correct in alerting us to the dangers of fine distinctions and slippery slopes.[38]

36 Robert Nozick 'Coercion', in Peter Laslett, WG Runciman, and Quentin Skinner (eds) *Philosophy, Politics and Society* (4th Series Oxford: Basil Blackwell, 1972) 101, 126.

37 Compare Ronald Dworkin *Sovereign Virtue* (Cambridge, Mass: Harvard University Press, 2000) ch 14, especially at 470–2, who asks whether we can be confident that such empirical accounts as we have are (i) ethically clean (ie untainted by background ideological bias), (ii) methodologically sound, and (iii) applicable from one jurisdiction to another. For extended discussion of both the methodological and the comparability reservations, see Penney Lewis 'The Empirical Slippery Slope from Voluntary to Non-Voluntary Euthanasia' (2007) 35 Journal of Law, Medicine and Ethics 197.

38 138 L Ed 2d 772, at 795–6.

Certainly, we should not regulate less stringently for the validity of purported consents in the context of assistance with suicide. This being so, the problem again presents itself as one of finding the pattern of regulatory overview that least frustrates the legitimate will of agents (whether their will is in favour of, or against, assistance). If it is unclear what this pattern is, the state must again resort to its responsibility to take a public position provisionally settling moral differences.

2. Stewardship and sustainability in a community of rights

In the two precautionary instances that we have considered thus far, the uncertainty and risk is, so to speak, internal to the ongoing life of a community of rights. In one case, it is the status and recognition of rights-holders that is the issue; in the other, it is the indirect effects of acts. However, individual acts might jeopardize more than the rights of other members of the community. They might represent an indirect threat to the community itself. This is a theme that I will pursue pervasively in the second half of the book, but I can introduce the idea here.

A community of rights is both an aspirant *moral* community and, in particular, an aspirant moral community of *rights* (rather than of utility or the like). It follows that a threat to the sustainability of such a community might be a threat to its *moral* nature or a threat to the *rights* nature of its moral commitments. It is a threat of the former kind that is of present interest.

Let us suppose that the bar for an aspirant moral community (in the formal sense) is set relatively low. Let us suppose that it is agreed that no community may present itself as a moral community unless it holds its commitments sincerely and in good faith, it treats its standards as categorically binding and universalizable, some such standards at least are of an other-regarding nature, and there is an integrity, consistency, and coherence about its commitments as a whole. Relative to this standard, there is no difficulty in accepting that utilitarians, rights theorists, and dignitarians are moralists and that communities guided by such standards are moral communities. The intention is not to exclude any of the leading ethical constituencies; the formal account of the moral simply excludes self-interested and unprincipled positions that have no moral pretensions.

A community of rights, of course, is a distinctive kind of moral community. However, for the moment, let us stick with its character as an aspirant moral community. Like any such community, its sustainability is challenged under certain conditions. By this, I do not mean that it is challenged if there is a breakdown in the moral order such that there is far too much immoral conduct. What I mean is that it is challenged if the context for a moral way of life is threatened. There are, in other words, certain preconditions before the enterprise of a moral community makes any kind of sense. For example, if there were an abundance of resources available to a community, supply always far exceeding demand, it would make no sense to debate principles of distributive justice—because, under such conditions, the practical position would be one of 'to each according to his or her wants'. Similarly, if our biology had a protective and instantly regenerative capacity so that we could never be physically harmed, and if we were also immortal, it would make little sense to debate such matters as the right to life and the right to physical integrity. Particular moral debates presuppose a particular context; and I suggest that moral community, too, presupposes a certain kind of context.

What are the key features of such a context? Let me suggest two such features and their correlative conditions. One relates to the vulnerability of members of the community and the other relates to their perception of control, choice, and responsibility.

The first feature of a moral community, any moral community, is that members understand what it is to respect one another. They understand that each member has interests that are protected by the moral code; and they understand that, where other-regarding moral standards are breached, harm is occasioned. It follows that one condition of moral community is that members are vulnerable, that they bleed, that they are mortal, that they are not so thick-skinned that they cannot be humiliated, that they are not immune to being instrumentalized, and so on; in short, that they have interests that are capable of being adversely affected.

The second feature is that members view themselves as agents who are sufficiently in control of their actions to make their own choices and to be held to account for the choices that they make. Moral community, in other words, presupposes a degree of freedom and personal responsibility. For members of such communities, the burden of responsibility is significant but not crippling. Paradigmatically, members will strive to do the right thing; the choices that they make will reflect their best judgment of what doing the right thing is in particular circumstances; and, if called to account, their response will be that they judged, in good faith, that what they chose to do was the right thing to do.[39] It is this second feature that I propose we should designate as the precondition of human dignity (the dignity of human choice and responsibility).

If we focus on this second condition, then all aspirant moral communities, concerned for moral sustainability, need to be careful about actions or practices that challenge (directly or insidiously) the sense that members make and are responsible for their own choices. In the light of this, we can anticipate a number of anxieties (about possible corrosion of this condition of moral community) that might be prompted by the development of modern technologies. For example, those who are so concerned might point to genetic engineering (if and when we are able to engineer a particular genetic make-up that we know to be associated with particular aptitudes or abilities) and, similarly, to rapid recent developments in the

[39] It follows that, where members recognize the limitations of their own moral understanding, practice will focus on agent-morality rather than act-morality.

new brain sciences.[40] The question is whether such prospects and developments present a special threat to human dignity (now understood as one of the preconditions for moral community). I will return to the new brain sciences in the second half of the book, but how might the concern about genetic engineering be put?

Famously, Jürgen Habermas[41] has raised the possibility that genetic enhancement (or positive genetic engineering), if not fundamentally altering the extent to which humans have 'free will'[42] and the extent to which the predicates for human responsibility are met, nevertheless might affect our perception of such matters. The thought is that, to the extent that the idea of free will rests on a phenomenology of choice and responsibility, genetic modification could make a huge difference to the way in which we perceive ourselves, our 'achievements', and our 'failures'. If we come to see our genetic make-up as a programme that runs us, it will be tempting to think (against free will and responsibility) that we could not have acted otherwise; and, where our particular genetic make-up has been specified by others, if there is any responsibility left in the world, it seems to be with the specifiers rather than ourselves.[43] In other words, genetic enhancement threatens to alter the context by either undermining notions of free will and responsibility or by inviting the transfer of responsibility.

In our life and times, it is surely inconceivable that geneticists will understand enough about genetic pathways and interactions (both within the genome itself and with the natural and social environment) for selection or engineering of this kind to be achieved. Nevertheless, the thought that our particular dispositions and characteristics are strongly influenced by a genetic make-up over which we have no control already hints at an excuse or a degree of mitigation: if we act as we do because this is how we are genetically coded, then why should we be held responsible for our actions?[44] Moreover, in a future in which some enjoy the 'benefits' of genetic enhancement, those who have been less fortunate will argue that they should not be held responsible for 'wrongdoing' that can be attributed to their disadvantaged genetic inheritance.

[40] See Dai Rees and Steven Rose (eds) *The New Brain Sciences: Perils and Prospects* (Cambridge: Cambridge University Press, 2004).

[41] Jürgen Habermas *The Future of Human Nature* (Cambridge: Polity Press, 2003). See, also, Bill McKibben *Enough: Genetic Engineering and the End of Human Nature* (London: Bloomsbury, 2003).

[42] For a very helpful and accessible review of the impact of genetics and brain science on our thinking concerning free will and responsibility, see Peter Lipton 'Genetic and Generic Determinism: A New Threat to Free Will?' in Rees and Rose (n 40 above) 88.

[43] Similarly, see Ronald Dworkin *Sovereign Virtue* (Cambridge, Mass: Harvard University Press, 2000) 445.

[44] See, further, Nikolas Rose *The Politics of Life Itself* (Princeton, NJ: Princeton University Press, 2007) ch 8, especially 233–4, for discussion of the case of Stephen Mobley, a young man who was convicted of shooting the manager of a pizza store but who (unsuccessfully) pleaded a genetic inheritance by way of mitigation—Mobley's lawyers pointed to a four generation family history of violence, aggression, and behaviour disorder.

This is not to say that all expressions of modern biotechnology threaten the fabric of moral community. Far from it: green biotechnology presents no obvious threat to the viability of *moral* community and nor does therapeutic cloning, stem cell research, germ-line therapy, or the like. Even cytoplasmic hybrid embryos seem to be ethically clean on this score. Of course, such technologies might have a radical impact on the community (these are disruptive technologies), the life and times of the community might change, and some members might hanker after the good old days. However, so long as the community continues to function as a moral enterprise, its sustainability is not threatened in a relevant sense. Accordingly, if the state is to have a stewardship responsibility, in a community of rights, it cannot be treated as a licence for conservativism (with a small c); the state's responsibility is not to freeze the status quo but to monitor developments that might undermine the conditions that give its moral aspirations some sense and purpose. Such a responsibility and such conditions, as I have said, are matters to which I will return.

V Risk and Precautionary Regulation: the Case of Nanotechnology

In this part of the chapter, we can take our analysis forward, first, by sketching how a community of rights would read the idea of a risk profile and then by focusing on its precautionary approach to the regulation of a potentially hazardous technology. Biotechnology is an obvious test case; but so too is nanotechnology. And, having said a great deal about the former and very little about the latter, it is nanotechnology's turn to serve as the illustrative example.

1. Risk profile

Regulators need to tailor their interventions to the perceived risk profile presented by a particular technology. Is the relevant risk that the technology might go wrong or is it that it might be abused; or does the risk only really materialize if the technology works? Are we talking about low risk or high risk? Are we assuming that risk is stratified such that we need to consider, at one level, the hazards presented to the environment and to health; at another level, the economic impact of the technology; and, at yet other levels, the social, cultural, and moral hazards associated with the technology?[45] And, how does risk relate to the precautionary

[45] Generally, compare Paul Street 'Constructing Risks: GMOs, Biosafety and Environmental Decision-Making' in Han Somsen (ed) *The Regulatory Challenge of Biotechnology* (Cheltenham: Edward Elgar, 2007) 95; Graham Dutfield 'Should We Regulate Biotechnology Through the Patent System? The Case of Terminator Technology', ibid 203, especially at 208–9; and, in relation to nanotechnology, see Ronald Sandler and WD Kay, 'The National Nanotechnology Initiative and the Social Good' (2006) 34 Journal of Law, Medicine and Ethics, 675.

principle: is precaution something that should be built into risk assessment or is it exclusively a strategy for risk management?

In a community of rights, it would be understood that the elaboration of a risk profile for a particular technology should draw on the following considerations:

- the *kind* of harm (physical, environmental, social, economic, moral, political, and so on) to which the risk pertains[46]
- the *severity and scale* of the harm if the risk eventuates and
- the *probability* of the risk materializing.[47]

In practice, the judgments that we make depend on which of these considerations we take into account, how much weight we give to them, and which considerations we emphasize. So, for example, Martin Bauer is able to say that 'technically', nuclear technology is low-risk,[48] meaning that '[n]uclear power is characterized by high damage potential with relatively low probability'.[49] As for biotechnology, Bauer claims that the risks 'are still largely unknown'[50]—which, no doubt, is correct in relation to some kinds of harm; but, for those who oppose the technology on moral or religious grounds, the risks are already perfectly clear.

The efforts of UNESCO notwithstanding, there is a tendency to see risk in terms of physical and environmental safety only, to characterize the risk as low (rather than high) by reference to the probability of its eventuating, and to displace the precautionary principle from the stage of risk assessment (so that a particular technology is pronounced free from known hazard) leaving it as a tool of risk management with no risk to manage. Once the technology has been pronounced safe, or at any rate not demonstrably unsafe, the weight of 'expert' scientific opinion makes it difficult for dissenting voices to be heard and arguments concerning the protection of human rights are immediately, to use Sheldon Leader's evocative term, 'collateralised'.[51]

With regard to the risk profile presented by nanotechnology, we should note the complication that this is still an emerging technology where we suspect that

[46] See, eg, Sheila Jasanoff 'Product, Process, or Programme: Three Cultures and the Regulation of Biotechnology', in Martin Bauer (ed) *Resistance to New Technology* (Cambridge: Cambridge University Press, 1995) 311; and this question arises pervasively in Martin W Bauer and George Gaskell (eds) *Biotechnology – the Making of a Global Controversy* (Cambridge: Cambridge University Press, 2002).

[47] On these second and third considerations, see Martin Bauer 'Resistance to New Technology and its Effects on Nuclear Power, Information Technology and Biotechnology'(n 46 above) 1, especially at 8–11. See, also, the Nuffield Council on Bioethics *Genetically Modified Crops: the Ethical and Social Issues* (London, 1999) at 8: 'it is always possible, in principle, to distinguish between the two distinct questions of "how bad?" and "how likely?" That is, we can and should separate the reasons for regarding an outcome as evil from the likelihood of its occurrence'.

[48] Martin Bauer (n 47 above) at 8.

[49] ibid 19.

[50] ibid.

[51] Sheldon Leader 'Collateralism' in Roger Brownsword (ed) *Human Rights* (Oxford: Hart, 2004) 53. Broadly speaking, 'collateralism' captures a culture that tends towards specialized institutional interests being given a disproportionate weight where decisions calling for a balancing of considerations fall to be made.

there is a good deal that we do not know and cannot yet imagine. We find ourselves, so to speak, in a 'low-certainty, low-consensus' risk situation where the knowledge base is thin (meaning that there is low certainty about the nature and the extent of nanorisks) coupled with a low consensus as to how the risks should be framed, which methodologies should be adopted, which values prioritized, and so on.[52] In a recent Position Statement by the Quebec Commission on the Ethics of Science and Technology, this difficulty is put in the following terms:

> In terms of risk, two factors are worth considering: the probability that an event will occur and the nature and significance of damages resulting from the same event. These two factors are not always present in the case of nanotechnologies. They raise the questions of how to deal with scientific uncertainty, which in turn is related to the state of knowledge in this area as well as to ignorance about what could happen once a new technology is adopted.[53]

Such concerns are echoed by the European Group on Ethics in Science and New Technologies in its *Opinion on the Ethical Aspects of Nanomedicine*.[54] And, as we turn to the way in which a community of rights, with its particular reading of harm and precaution, might approach the regulation of nanotechnology, we will revisit both this Opinion and the work of the Quebec Commission.

2. Regulating nanotechnology

Put very simply, the term 'nanotechnology'[55] can be given a broad or a narrow meaning. In its broad meaning, it refers to any technology that operates within the stipulated range of the nanometric scale (the width of a human hair, it being recalled, measuring some 80,000 nanometres; or, if a human head, with a headful of hair, were a nanometre, the planet earth would be about one inch). The relevant range, in turn, might be specified in wider or narrower terms but the important point is that, on this broad reading, nanotechnology is simply a matter of size and scale. In effect, nanotechnology so understood is about the most sophisticated

[52] For the 'certainty-consensus' axis, see David Winickoff, Sheila Jasonoff, Lawrence Busch, Robin Grove-White, and Brian Wynne 'Adjudicating the GM Food Wars: Science, Risk, and Democracy in World Trade Law' (2005) 30 Yale Journal of International Law 81, 104–6. With particular reference to nanotechnology, see John Balbus, Richard Denison, Karen Florini, and Scott Walsh 'Getting Nanotechnology Right the First Time' in Geoffrey Hunt and Michael Mehta (eds) *Nanotechnology: Risk, Ethics and Law* (London: Earthscan, 2006) 130; and Roland Clift 'Risk Management and Regulation in an Emerging Technology', ibid at 140.

[53] Quebec Commission on the Ethics of Science and Technology *Ethics and Nanotechnologies: A Basis for Action* (Quebec, November 2006) p ii. For the background, see Michèle S Jean, Édith Deleury and Diane Duquet 'Early Assessment and Policy-Making' in Henk ten Have (ed) *Nanotechnologies, Ethics and Politics* (Paris: UNESCO, 2007) 205.

[54] The European Group on Ethics in Science and New Technologies to the European Commission *Opinion on the Ethical Aspects of Nanomedicine* (Opinion No 21) (17 January 2007).

[55] For a particularly authoritative review, see the Royal Society and the Royal Academy of Engineering *Nanoscience and Nanotechnologies: Opportunities and Uncertainties* (London: The Royal Society, 2004) (RS Policy document 19/04).

miniaturization yet developed. By contrast, in its narrower meaning, nanotechnology refers only to applications that exploit the special properties of materials that register on this part of the nanoscale. Taking this narrower view, we might define nanotechnology as 'the investigation and manipulation of material objects in the 1–100 nanometer range so as to explore novel properties and develop new devices and functionalities that essentially depend on the 1–100 nanometer range'.[56]

Although it is invisible without special microscopic equipment, in the nanoworld, materials do not always behave in ways that we might predict. In the nanoworld, seeing really is believing. Thus:

> Tiny particles of gold melt at temperatures several hundred degrees lower than a large nugget, and copper, which is normally a good conductor of electricity, can become resistant in thin layers in the presence of a magnetic field. Electrons... can simply jump (or tunnel) from one place to another, and molecules can attract each other at moderate distances.[57]

The fact that nanomaterials exhibit these unexpected properties promises many exciting applications, some of which are already in commercial production (such as clothing, sports equipment, screens and creams, wound dressings, and so on),[58] and with a huge enabling potential, or so it seems, in the fields of information and communication technology, biomedicine, energy, and environment.

Consider the potential of nanomedicine. According to some, nanomedicine 'has the potential to create a paradigm shift in the healthcare systems of tomorrow'.[59] Thus:

> Nanomedicine will be important to improve healthcare in all phases of the care process. New in vitro diagnostic tests will shift diagnosis to an earlier stage, hopefully before symptoms really develop and allow pre-emptive therapeutic measures, in vivo diagnosis

[56] Joachim Schummer 'Identifying Ethical Issues of Nanotechnologies' in Henk ten Have (ed) *Nanotechnologies, Ethics and Politics* (Paris: UNESCO, 2007) 79, at 81 (although, as Schummer observes, this definition is actually broad enough to cover 'all the classical natural science and engineering disciplines that investigate and manipulate materials or material objects' (ibid). Compare the official definition of the US National Nanotechnology Initiative: nanotechnology involves 'research and technology development at the atomic, molecular, or macromolecular levels, in the length scale of approximately 1 to 100 nm range, to provide a fundamental understanding of phenomena and materials at the nanoscale and to create and use structures, devices, and systems that have novel properties and functions because of their small and/or intermediate size', cited in *The Ethics and Politics of Nanotechnology* (Paris: UNESCO, 2006) at 5. Compare, also, K Eric Drexler 'Nanotechnology: From Feynman to Funding' in Geoffrey Hunt and Michael Mehta (eds) *Nanotechnology: Risk, Ethics and Law* (London: Earthscan, 2006) 25.

[57] Tom Standage (ed) *The Future of Technology* (London: Profile Books, 2005) 307.

[58] See *The Ethics and Politics of Nanotechnology* (Paris: UNESCO, 2006) 11–12. It is estimated that there are already more than 200 nanotechnology-based products in the consumer marketplace, see Ahson Wardak and Michael E Gorman 'Using Trading Zones and Life Cycle Analysis to Understand Nanotechnology Regulation' (2006) 34 Journal of Law, Medicine and Ethics 695.

[59] European Technology Platform *Nanomedicine: Nanotechnology for Health* (November 2006) para 1.1. But compare William P Cheshire Jr 'Doing Small Things Well: Translating Nanotechnology into Nanomedicine' in Nigel M de S Cameron and M Ellen Mitchell (eds) *Nanoscale* (Hoboken, NJ: Wiley, 2007) 315 and C Christopher Hook 'Nanotechnology and the Future of Medicine' in Cameron and Mitchell, op cit, 337.

will become more sensitive and precise thanks to new imaging techniques and nano-sized targeted agents. Therapy as well could be greatly improved in efficacy by new systems that allow targeted delivery of therapeutic agents to the diseased site, ideally avoiding conventional parenteral delivery. Regenerative medicine may provide a therapeutic solution to revitalise tissue or organs, which may make life-long medication unnecessary.[60]

Even if much of the research is blue-skies, and even if some of the envisioned nano-assisted therapies depend upon the progressive development of related lines of research, especially stem cell research, nanomedicine is sufficiently promising to attract significant funding and investment.[61]

In its report on nanomedicine, the European Group on Ethics in Science and New Technologies sketches a range of ethical questions concerning human rights and human dignity, justice and solidarity, the protection of the environment, and so on.[62] However, in the current state of the nano-art, it is questions of safety that seem to be paramount.[63] For example, 'how do we check that, because of their greater capacity to pass through biological systems... nanodevices designed for drug delivery would not induce negative side-effects for patients...?'[64] Bearing in mind that some nanohorses have already bolted, a community of rights will readily agree that we need to temper the promise of the technology with a degree of precaution.

Recalling the narrow definition of nanotechnology, it is the unknown properties of nanomaterials that present the greatest difficulty for regulators. If a carbon nanotube might be likened to graphite, but its structure resembles asbestos, then we need 'to find out whether these tubes behave like pencil lead or like a highly dangerous material'.[65] Hence, we find the Quebec Commission on the Ethics of Science and Technology emphasizing,

the importance of exercising precaution in the process of creating and developing medications and therapies with nanotechnology components. This precautionary approach encourages the pursuit of research and the documenting of potentially positive and negative effects of nanotechnology applications in the health sector, in order to make a better assessment of outcomes for patients and for the management of the health system in general.[66]

[60] ibid para 1.4.

[61] See the European Group on Ethics in Science and New Technologies to the European Commission *Opinion on the Ethical Aspects of Nanomedicine* (Opinion No 21) (17 January 2007) 42–3 and app I. And compare the French National Consultative Ethics Committee for Health and Life Sciences, Opinion No 96 ('Ethical Issues Raised by Nanosciences, Nanotechnologies and Health', 2007).

[62] European Group on Ethics in Science and New Technologies to the European Commission *Opinion on the Ethical Aspects of Nanomedicine* (Opinion No 21) (17 January 2007), 36. For further discussion, see Roger Brownsword 'Regulating Nanomedicine – the Smallest of Our Concerns?' (2008) 2 NanoEthics.

[63] See, eg, Geoffrey Hunt and Michael Mehta (eds) *Nanotechnology: Risk, Ethics and Law* (London: Earthscan, 2006) passim.

[64] ibid 38. See, also, ibid 54.

[65] Tom Standage (ed) *The Future of Technology* (London: Profile Books, 2005) 328.

[66] (n 53 above) vi.

Not surprisingly, the tone of the report on nanomedicine delivered by the European Group on Ethics in Science and New Technologies is not dissimilar. Adopting the precautionary principle as a general tool for risk management (although not in such a way as to skew a full and frank risk assessment), the group recommends that, in the light of the principle:

[t]he uncertainties and knowledge gaps associated with new nanotechnology-based diagnostics, therapies and preventive measures should be identified. These uncertainties need to be characterised and measures have to be developed in order to reduce them as far as possible.[67]

This is not to say that the precautionary principle should be applied disproportionately to create 'zero-risk' situations; rather, 'risk management actions should be aimed at identifying the 'acceptable risk' threshold with regard to the values at stake—and respect for the human body is undoubtedly one of the values deserving the highest legal protection'.[68]

In a community of rights, there will be concern about the potential harm that nanomaterials, nanodevices, and (especially) free nanoparticles and unfixed carbon nanotubes[69] might occasion to the conditions of physical well-being that are essential for flourishing agency. Agents are vulnerable; the physical environment might be at risk; agents who are willing to take a risk (for example, as a research participant or in relation to an experimental therapy) that concerns only their well-being should be free to do so; but, in general, care needs to be taken before nanoproducts are brought to market. On the other hand, the promise of nanosolutions will create a pressure for expedition, particularly if such nanoapplications are available elsewhere and seemingly safe. It is all very well enjoining regulators to set their sights on 'acceptable risk' (whatever this might mean where both the risk and the benefit assessments are so primitive); but, under conditions of intense uncertainty, with risks of one kind or another associated with each of the options, and with divided opinion in the community, the regulatory challenge—the challenge of knowing *when* to regulate, and then knowing *what* to regulate and *how*—is daunting.[70]

[67] The European Group on Ethics in Science and New Technologies to the European Commission *Opinion on the Ethical Aspects of Nanomedicine* (Opinion No 21) (17 January 2007) para 5.4.

[68] ibid para 4.2.3.

[69] See the recurrent concern about these hazards in the Royal Society and the Royal Academy of Engineering (n 55 above). Compare, also, C Vyvyan Howard and December SK Ikah 'Nanotechnology and Nanoparticle Toxicity: A Case for Precaution' in Geoffrey Hunt and Michael Mehta (eds) *Nanotechnology: Risk, Ethics and Law* (London: Earthscan, 2006) 154 (it will be noted that there is not the hint of a question-mark here: precaution, it is argued, certainly is required).

[70] See Michael D Mehta and Geoffrey Hunt 'What Makes Nanotechnology Special?' in Geoffrey Hunt and Michael Mehta (eds) *Nanotechnology: Risk, Ethics and Law* (London: Earthscan, 2006) 273, especially 275 et seq; Sonia E Miller 'Regulating Nanotechnology: A Vicious Circle' in Nigel M de S Cameron and M Ellen Mitchell (eds) *Nanoscale* (Hoboken, NJ: Wiley, 2007) 155; and Trudy A Phelps 'The European Approach to Nanoregulation' in Cameron and Mitchell, op cit, 189.

Quite rightly, the European Group advises that every step should be taken to encourage public participation and debate.[71] Moreover, the group appreciates that there is more to this than an exercise in public relations:

The participation of the public in all stages of the development of this innovative research sector is therefore important not only for the public acceptance of nanomedicine and nanotechnology, *but also for the adoption of a nanotechnology strategy where public concerns are approached and discussed from the beginning.*[72]

In a community of rights, this is exactly how public engagement has to be understood. As David Bazelon pointed out some years before technology went nano, although '[s]cientists *are* uniquely competent to address scientific/factual issues', and although 'science *is* elitist', it does not follow that scientists have a special competence in relation to values; indeed, when it comes to value choices, 'the opinions of scientists are entitled to no greater weight than those of the rest of us'.[73] Hence, experts should advise on their best guess as to the nature and probability of the apprehended risks but the public should be fully engaged in characterizing which risks are material, which risks are acceptable and, where there are conflicting rights involved, which priorities should be set. Echoing Bazelon's thinking, Ronald Sandler and WD Kay argue:[74]

[S]cience and industry experts have an important role to play.... They are well positioned to see what is possible, what is feasible, and what is required to achieve certain economic and technological ends. They thereby play a crucial informational role. But knowledge of what can and cannot be done, and of what is and is not required to do it, is quite different from knowledge of what ought and ought not to be done. What ends should be prioritised, how resources should be allocated in pursuit of those ends, and constraints on how those ends ought to be pursued are ethical and social questions to be addressed in the public sphere, not economic and technological ones to be worked out in boardrooms or laboratories.... So while scientists and industry leaders may be 'elite' in their knowledge of the science and business of nanotechnology, this status does not imply that they are 'elite' with respect to the [social and ethical] issues associated with nanotechnology...[75]

[71] Note 66 above, at para 4.4.2.2. For a valuable analysis of why public engagement might be important (for the sake of democracy, legitimacy, or better quality decisions) see DJ Fiorini 'Citizen Participation and Environmental Risk: A Survey of Institutional Mechanisms' (1990) 15 *Science, Technology and Human Values* 226; and, for an outstanding general discussion, see the Royal Society and the Royal Academy of Engineering, (n 55 above) ch. 7.

[72] ibid, emphasis added. Compare Council for Science and Technology *Nanosciences and Nanotechnologies: A Review of Government's Progress on its Policy Commitments* (London, March 2007) para 146. To similar effect, see Edna F Einsiedel and Linda Goldberg 'Dwarfing the Social? Nanotechnology Lessons from the Biotechnology Front' in Geoffrey Hunt and Michael Mehta (eds) *Nanotechnology: Risk, Ethics and Law* (London: Earthscan, 2006) 213.

[73] David L Bazelon 'Coping with Technology Through the Legal Process' (1977) 62 Cornell Law Review 817, 826–7.

[74] Ronald Sandler and WD Kay, 'The National Nanotechnology Initiative and the Social Good' (2006) 34 Journal of Law, Medicine and Ethics 675.

[75] ibid 679.

These sentiments resonate with the thinking in a report recently prepared for the Washington-based Project on Emerging Nanotechnologies,[76] according to which the public needs to be involved in two capacities: first, as citizens, members of the public are stakeholders in assessing the larger social and ethical risks associated with nanotechnology; and, secondly, as potential consumers of nanotechnology products, members of the public need to be able to make informed choices. Thus, picking up this latter point, we read:

> The tremendous potential of the technology will not develop without the public having a realistic view of the intended and unintended effects of NT. In its scope and diversity of applications, NT often has been compared with biotechnology. The lessons learned from biotechnology about the consequences of a poorly informed public should not be lost on those dealing with NT.[77]

Even if GM crops and nanomedicine are not quite comparable cases,[78] given the GM resistance in some parts of Europe, this surely makes a lot of sense. Moreover, this makes a lot of sense whether one approaches the matter from a utilitarian perspective, where the issue is about retaining public confidence and trust, or from a human rights perspective, where the issue is about due process and enfranchisement.[79]

If all ethical constituencies believe that the acceptable level and location of risk and the appropriate degree of precaution are best settled by a transparent deliberative process in which all voices, scientific as well as cultural, are heard, then does this point the way towards legitimate regulatory decision-making? The thought is that, even if the particular outcome is not quite in line with the preferences of a particular ethical constituency, at least regulators can point to the inclusive and fair process by which the outcome was reached. With this thought, we turn to the final part of the chapter.

[76] J Clarence Davies *Managing the Effects of Nanotechnology* (Washington: Woodrow Wilson International Center for Scholars, 2005), available at <http://www.wilsoncenter.org/events/docs/Effectsnanotechfinal.pdf> (last visited 30 August 2007).

[77] ibid at 29–30. Compare, Michael D Mehta 'From Biotechnology to Nanotechnology: What Can We Learn from Earlier Technologies?' in Geoffrey Hunt and Michael Mehta (eds) *Nanotechnology: Risk, Ethics and Law* (London: Earthscan, 2006) 121; and Julie Barnett, Anna Carr, and Roland Clift 'Going Public: Risk, Trust and Public Understanding of Nanotechnologies' ibid 196.

[78] See, further, Sandler and Kay (n 74 above) at 678. But compare David Winickoff, Sheila Jasonoff, Lawrence Busch, Robin Grove-White, and Brian Wynne (n 52 above) for the common 'low-certainty, low-consensus' characteristics of novel technologies.

[79] Compare the interesting proposal made by Veerle Heyvaert in 'Facing the Consequences of the Precautionary Principle in European Community Law' (2006) 31 European Law Review 185, at 204:

> Proposals for decisions within the precautionary zone [should be declared as such and then] subjected to heightened public access requirements, either through more extensive public consultation provisions, or even through the adoption of genuine deliberative mechanisms of decision-making. At the output side, precautionary decisions could come with strict review requirements, or with a limited fixed lifetime.

VI Procedural Legitimacy

Where, with any degree of frequency, regulators are unable to take up positions (not just in relation to nanotechnology or other technologies, but in relation to any matter where standards need to be set) that are judged to be ethically clean from all points of the ethical compass, this divides the community and, to some extent, destabilizes it. A tempting thought, therefore, is to rest the justificatory case not so much on the substantive position taken up by regulators but on the processes that they have employed to set the standards in question. If there has been a full and open public debate, with widespread public participation, and if the regulatory outcome is congruent with the judgments that are generally agreed to have crystallized from the debate, then does this not give regulators a complete answer to those who continue to reject the regulation as illegitimate?

Clearly, by its own admission, such a procedural justification does not give a *complete* answer to those who reject the standards set. A *complete* answer maintains that the right standards are being set by those who have the authority to set them and that, if certain procedures need to be followed, they have been correctly followed. A procedural justification, by conceding at once that no claim is made as to the rightness of the standard set, falls a long way short of a full justification. Nevertheless, it is a justification of sorts and what we make of it depends a great deal on whether we are viewing it in the context of a community of rights or in a pluralistic society that is home to more than one ethical constituency.

(a) Proceduralism in a community of rights

To repeat a by now familiar point, the members of a community of rights do not believe that they are morally omniscient. They do not believe that they know all the right answers. They realize, too, that, in practice, there will be some issues that divide the community; that there will be occasions when members not only disagree with one another, but (as members concede) not unreasonably disagree with one another; and that, if public standards are to be set, one might have to live with a regulatory position that one privately rejects. Nevertheless, the members of the community have an underlying unity that pulls them together. Their common aspiration is to conduct their affairs, both public and private, in a way that keeps faith with their ideal of a moral community in which members respect one another's rights. It follows that, in general, members will be disposed to accept a procedural justification on a contested question, not as a confirmation of the correctness of the standard set but as a reason for respecting the regulatory position that, for the time being at least, has been adopted. Indeed, where a community of rights accords the state a degree of stewardship, we might well expect there to be strong procedural requirements before such a jurisdiction is exercised.

However, even in a community of rights, a procedural justification will need to pass muster. In particular, members will need to be satisfied that the standard-setting process has not become detached from the community's substantive moral commitments—that is, members will need to be satisfied that the regulators have made a conscientious and good faith attempt to set a standard that is in line with their best understanding of the community's rights commitments.[80] Regulators do not have to claim that the standard set is right; but, before a procedural justification will be accepted, regulators must be demonstrably trying to do the right thing relative to the community's particular moral commitments. Provided that regulators survive this level of scrutiny, the key question concerns the adequacy of the procedures that are in place to facilitate public engagement. What kind of institutional design might be acceptable in a community of rights?

In a helpful paper, Denis Galligan points us in the right direction.[81] For two reasons, Galligan's discussion is particularly apposite: one is that he assumes that citizens have a *right* to participate (that participation is not to be favoured simply for instrumental reasons, or in the way that a utilitarian might rationalize it); and the other is that he frames his analysis specifically with reference to debates about the regulation of biotechnologies. According to Galligan:

> The ideal for any society is that laws and policies should be for the common good. Since we do not trust claims that there is an objective way of determining the common good on any matter, some mechanism has to be deployed for doing so. In democratic societies, the guiding principle is that the common good is forged from considering and accommodating the different interests and viewpoints within the society. The usual mechanism for making that determination consists in electing representatives and empowering them to decide matters. *Legitimacy is gained, not so much by the content of the outcomes, but from the fact that those who decide are elected by the people.*[82]

However, in complex and pluralistic societies, representative democracy is not enough: if decision-making is to advance the common good, it needs to be properly informed, decision-makers 'hearing and taking account of the different elements of civil society and their different viewpoints'[83] as well as being based on a sound understanding of the relevant science.

[80] See Deryck Beyleveld and Roger Brownsword *Law as a Moral Judgment* (London: Sweet and Maxwell, 1986) (reprinted Sheffield: Sheffield Academic Press, 1994) especially chs 7-9; and 'Principle, Proceduralism and Precaution in a Community of Rights' (2006) 19 Ratio Juris 141.

[81] Denis Galligan, 'Citizens' Rights and Participation in the Regulation of Biotechnology' in Francesco Francioni (ed) *Biotechnologies and International Human Rights* (Oxford: Hart, 2007) 335.

[82] ibid at 342, emphasis supplied.

[83] ibid., at 344. Compare David L Bazelon, (n 73 above) at 825:

> When the issues are controversial, any decision may fail to satisfy large portions of the community. But those who are dissatisfied with a particular decision will be more likely to acquiesce in it if they perceive that their views and interests were given a fair hearing. If the decision-maker has frankly laid the competing considerations on the table, so that the public knows the worst as well as the best, he is unlikely to find himself accused of high-handedness, deceit, or cover-up.

How, then, should procedures for public engagement be designed? Allowing that different levels of decision-making invite different designs, the general features to be designed in are as follows:

> (i) notice of the issue is widely displayed; (ii) the issue is fully defined; (iii) relevant scientific knowledge is made available in forms intelligible to the layman; (iv) relevant evidence and facts are made available; (v) an assessment of the consequences of the proposed course of action is carried out and made available; (vi) opportunities are provided for interested parties to present their cases, either orally or in writing; (vii) the reasons for decisions are given; (viii) the decision is based on the common good and is shown to be in the common good; (ix) the process respects relevant rights under international, European and national jurisdictions; (x) the reasons must show that all cases put forward have been considered and taken into account; (xi) the whole process is conducted in conditions of openness and transparency; (xii) subject only to defined situations of confidentiality.[84]

Without doubt, this articulates a formal model of processual integrity with which few would disagree. However, as Galligan recognizes, if regulators and regulatees are not fully signed up to the spirit of such procedures, or if regulators have been captured by powerful interests, and the like, constraints of this kind are unlikely to prevent decision-makers from offering up their own partial renditions of the common good.[85] In effect, regulators will hear only what they want to hear.[86]

In the ideal-typical instantiation of a community of rights, the process would not suffer from pathologies of this kind. By contrast, in a merely (and perhaps erratically) aspirant community of rights, there might be occasions when regulators or regulatees defect from their responsibilities; and this would be the time when the smartest of design solutions would be put to the test.[87] It follows that, in a community of rights, procedural legitimacy has a role to play. However, we should not make the mistake of thinking that the moral divisions that we find in a community of rights challenge regulators in just the way that they are challenged by ethical pluralism; and we should not suppose that proceduralism is clearly the answer that regulators are looking for in response to the legitimacy crisis that haunts them in communities that comprise a plurality of fundamentally divided ethical constituencies.

[84] Galligan (n 81 above) at 352–4.

[85] ibid 355–8.

[86] Seminally, see Julia Black 'Regulation as Facilitation: Negotiating the Genetic Revolution' in Roger Brownsword, WR Cornish, and Margaret Llewelyn (eds) *Law and Human Genetics: Regulating a Revolution* (Oxford: Hart, 1998) 29. For a fine illustrative example, see Robert Howse 'From Politics to Technocracy – And Back Again: The Fate of the Multilateral Trading Regime' (2002) 96 *American Journal of International Law* 94 (concerning the insider network at the WTO, how the line between insiders and outsiders shifts, and what is judged to be within the rules and what without); and, for a similar critique about trade insiders (backed by a larger Marxist ideological reading of legal institutions), see Jane Kelsey 'Legal Fetishism and the Contradictions of the GATS' in Douglas Lewis (ed) *International and Regional Organisations* (Oxford: Hart, 2006) 133.

[87] Compare Ian Ayres and John Braithwaite *Responsive Regulation* (Oxford: Oxford University Press, 1992).

(b) Proceduralism as a response to ethical plurality

The problem of legitimacy that we have been elaborating from Chapter 2 onwards is one of accommodating the fundamentally different moral viewpoints that are captured by the bioethical triangle. Each constituency demands that regulators should set the right standards but they are fundamentally divided as to the substantive test of rightness—and, to people who are committed to doing the right thing, it matters a great deal that the right thing is done.

As the cultural and ethical mix in societies intensifies, the legitimacy crisis becomes intolerable. There is no easy answer. However, a procedural approach has been sponsored by such influential theorists as John Rawls[88] and Jürgen Habermas,[89] these thinkers trumpeting the virtues of deliberative democracy, public reason, and the quest for an overlapping consensus at the commanding heights of the regime. The basic idea is very simple: if a society is to get away from trench warfare between the rival constituencies, the protagonists have to relax their positions and come to the table to talk their way to a reasonable accommodation.

Although this high theory of proceduralism comes with an impeccable pedigree, it seems a pretty unlikely story. Granted, the diagnosis is sound: for, in a context of pluralism, the problems of stability and authority are most acute when the law takes sides on opposed moral positions; and it is in just these circumstances that a legitimacy crisis is prompted. However, the proceduralist response (as the earlier Rawls might have expressed it) puts too great a strain on the parties. Quite simply, if the protagonists and pluralists are to bargain their way to a solution, where the only force is the Habermassian force of the better argument, then something very fundamental has to give. What the proceduralists ask of the disputants is not that they should give an inch or two but nothing less than that they should abandon their deepest (but incompatible) moral convictions—that is, those very beliefs that are the source of the instability, and which, if insisted upon, would fatally obstruct a consensual accommodation of all reasonable viewpoints, or of principles that could not be reasonably rejected.[90] This is quite a price

[88] John Rawls *Political Liberalism* (New York: Columbia University Press, 1993).

[89] Jürgen Habermas *Between Facts and Norms: Contributions to a Discourse Theory of Law and Democracy* (trans by William Rehg) (Cambridge Mass: MIT Press, 1996).

[90] Compare Scanlon's contractualist approach. In TM Scanlon 'The Aims and Authority of Moral Theory' (1992) 12 Oxford Journal of Legal Studies 1, at 5, Scanlon conceives of a moral wrong in the following terms: '[A]n act is morally wrong just in case it would be disallowed by any principles that no one could reasonably reject if they were seeking principles which could be the basis of informed, unforced general agreement'. Then at 11:

> According to my version of contractualism, for example, we have reason not to be cruel to people or to break our promises to them because such actions would not be allowed by principles that they could not reasonably reject.

Despite the multiple negatives in these formulations, the governing principles seem to be those that we could not reasonably reject if we hoped to achieve a consensus as to our governing principles. This is saying something more than that we are bound by reasonable principles; but, so long as the test hinges on disputants having a reasonable attitude (in the context of a desire to achieve consensus),

and the question is: why would it be rational for morally divided agents to accept such a procedural demand? For, it is surely an unstated premise of proceduralism that, given the right bargaining situation, it can be rational for persons to consent to being governed by a framework that might produce rules and decisions that go contrary to what those persons believe to be morally acceptable. On the face of it, the only (and quite exceptional) setting in which it might be rational to give ground in this way is where, from the viewpoint of each constituency, the consequences of accommodation better serve one's moral ideals than the consequences of standing firm. This is not a case of giving up one's beliefs so much as preferring to jump from the frying pan into the fire.

Where these exceptional conditions do not obtain then, while procedural integrity is important, it can only reach so far in a context of entrenched pluralism. If the outcome of the process is a regulatory decision that offends deeply held ethical convictions, procedural propriety (particularly the claim that all viewpoints were 'fully taken into consideration') cannot bear the burden of justification. For, as Frank Michelman[91] has convincingly pointed out, those of the relevant ethical conviction will not accept the process as legitimate unless certain outcomes are either vouchsafed or excluded by the terms of reference—and, where we are dealing with hard cases, this is simply too hard to do.[92]

In short, in a context of plurality, a procedural strategy will not overcome the legitimacy crisis unless (i) for each set of protagonists, (ii) relative to its own distinctive ethical lights, (iii) it is judged that the constituency's ethical commitments are better served by an adjustment of position and by reaching an accommodation with one another rather than by unreflectively standing one's ground. Where these conditions are not met, the persuasive force of proceduralism will be seriously diminished; and any attempt to defend a regulatory position by reference to the integrity of the process is liable to be rejected as defective.

VII Conclusion

The ethical plurality that sets the stage for the regulation of new technologies (including nanotechnology) brings together three key approaches: the consequential approach of the utilitarians; the rights-led approach of the human rights constituency; and the duty-driven approach of the dignitarian alliance. In this setting, the rhetoric of (no) harm to others and of precaution, like that of

it is not altogether clear precisely what or how much is being asked of parties, except that it is a great deal.

[91] Frank I Michelman 'Constitutional Legitimation for Political Acts' (2003) 66 MLR 1.

[92] See Roger Brownsword 'Regulating Human Genetics: New Dilemmas for a New Millennium' (2004) 12 Medical Law Review 14. Compare Kathy Bowrey *Law and Internet Cultures* (Cambridge: Cambridge University Press, 2005) ch 3.

consent, is not neutral. These terms take on their own particular significance (or insignificance) when viewed from a particular ethical viewpoint.

In a community of rights, there will be a well-developed process of public engagement that recognizes that members are entitled to participate in standard setting, in debates about the identification of acceptable levels and location of risk and precaution, and so on, *as a matter of right*; and that regulators have a responsibility to ensure that participation is properly informed. Such proceduralism will be consistently orientated to the community's commitment to rights.

In communities informed by other (utilitarian or dignitarian) ethics or by a plurality of ethics, proceduralism takes on a very different character. Crucially, in the latter, it will be in only very special circumstances that the protagonists will see the sense of adopting a procedural solution to their substantive differences. The force, alas, will not be with the parties and the legitimacy crisis will persist.

Stated summarily, in deeply divided communities, the challenge of regulatory legitimacy is chronic; there are no neutral safe havens (not consent, not harm to others, not even precaution); proceduralism has its limits; and where emergent technologies, such as nanotechnology, with uncertain risks and prospective benefits, invite a regulatory response, the legitimacy crisis becomes acute.

5

The Challenge of Regulatory Effectiveness

I Introduction

Broadly speaking, regulators are liable to be called to account in two fundamental ways. First, the question might be whether the objective or purpose associated with a particular regulatory intervention is appropriate or justifiable—that is to say, the question is whether regulators are trying to do the right thing. Secondly, even if it is conceded that regulators are trying to do the right thing, we might question whether they are setting about securing their regulatory objectives in the right kind of way. When we ask whether regulators are proceeding in 'the right kind of way', our question might be whether the intervention is likely to achieve its regulatory purposes—our question, in other words, is whether this particular intervention will work, whether it will be effective. Alternatively, our question might be more concerned with the legitimacy of the means adopted by the regulators: here, we do not doubt that the regulatory intervention will work, but we remain to be persuaded that it passes moral muster.[1] To be beyond reproach, therefore, a regulatory intervention must be backed by legitimate regulatory purposes, and the regulatory means employed must be both morally clean and effective.

In previous chapters, a good deal has been said about the first kind of question. I have suggested that where regulators seek to 'legitimate' their objectives, they might appeal to a broad range of ostensibly legitimating purposes (economic, medical, security, and so on) which they claim merit respect on the part of their regulatees. For example, it might be claimed by regulators that a bespoke regulatory framework for online contracting needs to be put in place in order to extend consumer choice and to open up new market opportunities for small businesses, or that a population-wide national DNA database needs to be established in order to detect criminals and to improve the level of public security. However, I have also suggested that, particularly in the case of modern biotechnology, regulators will often find that such legitimating reasons will not suffice; for regulators will also be pressed as to the (moral or ethical) 'legitimacy' of their purposes and

[1] In this chapter, the 'right kind of way' largely cues in questions of effectiveness. However, we might also want to query the legitimacy of the regulatory approach: compare Karen Yeung *Securing Compliance* (Oxford: Hart, 2004).

their particular positions.[2] So, for example, it might not be enough for regulators to present an intervention as one that promises to assist medical research (and, in due course, to deliver therapies for major human diseases); if the research in question is judged to violate human rights or to compromise human dignity, regulatees will seek to engage regulators as to the (moral or ethical) legitimacy of their actions. Once regulators are so engaged, I have suggested that in pluralistic ethical contexts (captured by what I have called the bioethical triangle), it is likely to be difficult to strike regulatory positions that satisfy each of the constituencies. Furthermore, I have suggested that these legitimacy problems will challenge regulators regardless of whether they offer a direct substantive justification (claiming that the regulatory position is compatible with human rights or human dignity, or whatever) or an indirect procedural justification (claiming that the fairness of the regulatory process immunizes the regulatory outcome against direct substantive challenge).

In the present chapter, we will turn away from questions of legitimation and legitimacy (relative to both ends and means). Instead, the focus will be on the second fundamental challenge to regulatory rationality, the challenge of regulatory effectiveness.

If we were to elaborate guidelines for the effective regulation of modern technologies, in principle, we might imagine three tiers of regulatory intelligence. At the first and most general level, there would be guidelines that would be applicable in all regulatory contexts, whether or not relating to modern technologies. At the second level, we would have guidelines that applied to the regulation of technologies (whatever the nature of those technologies). And, at the third level, we would have guidelines that applied only to a particular technology. This scheme would presuppose, and recognize, that while all regulatory spaces have some features in common, those regulatory spaces that centre on modern technologies have special features (such as rapid technological development and social change); and it would also allow for the possibility that, within the field of modern technologies, some individual technologies (and their concomitants) have particular characteristics that make the regulatory space even more distinctive. For example, Andrew Murray has argued that cyberspace is a distinctively complex and potentially chaotic regulatory space, where there is no clean and stable distinction between regulators and regulatees.[3] It follows, contends Murray, that regulators should act in ways that take account of 'the unique nature of the network environment' which, in turn, implies the 'need for a more cohesive, measured, prudent and non-interventionist approach'.[4] Similarly, Neil Gunningham has entered some significant caveats against the proposition that those (smart) approaches that

[2] I am treating an ostensibly 'legitimating' reason as any reason (other than force) to respect a regulatory intervention; and I am treating moral or ethical 'legitimacy' as a particular class of reason within the broad category of legitimating reasons. Generally, see ch 1.

[3] Andrew Murray *The Regulation of Cyberspace* (Abingdon: Routledge-Cavendish, 2007).

[4] ibid 54.

work in the context of environmental regulation can be transposed mechanically to the regulation of biotechnology.[5] Thus:

> [T]he political, social, economic and scientific contexts in which biotechnology and environmental regulation must operate are very different. For biotechnology, regulation must take account of high scientific uncertainty, high risks, a substantial imbalance of knowledge and power between the private sector and the state, diametrically opposed interests (and absolutely no consensus on either preferred outcomes or how best to achieve them), and in Europe at least, a breakdown of public trust.[6]

For a variety of reasons, we might suspect, too, that nanotechnology and neurotechnology present regulators with their own distinctive complexities.[7]

In the present chapter, we can review two important attempts to develop our regulatory intelligence, in both cases the particular context being information technology. First, we have the 20 basic principles for the guidance of regulators gathered together by Stuart Biegel at the conclusion of *Beyond Our Control?*;[8] and, secondly, we have the five starting points for regulators critically examined by Bert-Jaap Koops and his Tilburg co-authors in *Starting Points for ICT Regulation*.[9] Given that these basic principles and starting points have been articulated with reference to the regulation of information technology, we need to be careful about generalizing them to the regulation of technology, let alone to regulation in general. Nevertheless, some of the principles and starting points do invite a more general application.

The chapter has four parts. First, I make a few observations about the concept of regulatory effectiveness and its relationship with regulatory economy and efficiency. Secondly, I rehearse some salient features of our general regulatory intelligence, particularly underlining the risks of regulatory over-reach, of regulatory capture and of regulation having unintended (negative) consequences. Thirdly, I consider and reconstruct Biegel's 20 principles as a general guide to effective regulation. The key points here are that regulators should consider the necessity for making an intervention, that they need to be clear about their objectives and smart in their approach, and that the more that regulators are able to act with the grain of regulatees' values the more likely it is that their intervention will be effective. Finally, I consider how the ICT starting points, which Koops and his colleagues subject to a largely sceptical critique, might contribute to our understanding of regulatory effectiveness.

[5] Neil Gunningham 'Regulating Biotechnology: Lessons from Environmental Policy' in Han Somsen (ed) *The Regulatory Challenge of Biotechnology* (Cheltenham: Edward Elgar, 2007) 3.

[6] ibid 5.

[7] Compare Fabrice Jotterand 'The Politicization of Science and Technology: Its Implications for Nanotechnology' (2006) 34 Journal of Law, Medicine and Ethics 658, especially at 660.

[8] Stuart Biegel *Beyond Our Control? Confronting the Limits of Our Legal System in the Age of Cyberspace* (Cambridge, Mass: MIT Press, 2003).

[9] Bert-Jaap Koops, Miriam Lips, Corien Prins, and Maurice Schellekens *Starting Points for ICT Regulation: Deconstructing Prevalent Policy One-Liners* (The Hague: TMC Asser Press, 2006).

II Regulatory Effectiveness, Economy and Efficiency

According to Francis Fukuyama, 'pessimism about the inevitability of technological advance is wrong, and it could become a self-fulfilling prophecy if believed by too many people. For it is simply not the case that the speed and scope of technological development cannot be controlled'.[10] To be sure, in the absence of regulatory intervention, technology can advance at its own pace—at any rate, it can do so subject to any popular resistance (such as we have seen in Europe in relation to GM crops and GM food). Nevertheless, Fukuyama concedes that:

> [N]o regulatory regime is ever fully leak-proof, and if one selects a sufficiently long time frame, most technologies end up being developed eventually. But this misses the point of social regulation: no law is ever fully enforced. Every country makes murder a crime and attaches severe penalties to homicide, and yet murders nonetheless occur. The fact that they do has never been a reason for giving up on the law or on attempts to enforce it.[11]

It follows that, if we set the bar for regulatory effectiveness at the level of complete control (that is, complete achievement of the regulators' objectives), we will judge that virtually all regulatory interventions are ineffective. On the other hand, if we set the bar at a much lower level, we will find ourselves declaring that some regulatory intervention is effective when the ex post state of affairs merely represents an improvement (relative to the regulatory objectives) over the ex ante situation. Where, then, should we set the threshold for regulatory effectiveness? Should we judge that our homicide laws are effective only if they succeed in putting an end to murders, or if they significantly reduce the number of murders that otherwise would occur, or if they make any contribution, however small, to a reduction in the number of murders?

When the question is put this way, it invites the thought that perhaps we are asking the wrong question. Our cognitive interest is in regulatory effectiveness; but, instead of asking whether a particular regulatory intervention is or is not effective, perhaps we should ask how effective (or ineffective) that intervention is. After all, if we are able to compare the ex ante (pre-regulatory intervention) and the ex post (post-regulatory intervention) situations, we will see what difference the regulation has made—or, at any rate, if we make certain assumptions about the causal significance of the regulatory intervention, we can judge its effect (and, with that, its relative effectiveness).

There might also be a less obvious advantage in thinking about regulatory effectiveness in terms of such a spectrum of effect rather than in all or nothing terms. So long as we are thinking about an intervention that is designed to prevent the occurrence of certain conduct, we have a pretty clear idea as to the state

[10] Francis Fukuyama *Our Posthuman Future* (London: Profile Books, 2002) 188.
[11] ibid 189.

of affairs that would reflect complete regulatory effectiveness—namely, a state of affairs in which no conduct of the regulated kind occurs. However, if the intervention is designed to incentivize, encourage, and promote certain conduct (for example, in the way that the patent regime is intended to promote innovation), it is not so clear what would count as complete regulatory effectiveness. No doubt, regulators could identify a certain target level of activity to supply the effectiveness threshold (for example, so many small business contractors with a viable online enterprise, so much online consumption, and the like); but, if the regulatory view is that the more of the particular activity the better, an effectiveness ceiling is artificially imposed. Once again, then, we might do better to abandon a simple distinction between regulation that is effective and regulation that is ineffective and treat regulatory effectiveness always as a matter of degree.

Alongside a concern with regulatory effectiveness, new public management has given us a concern with regulatory economy and regulatory efficiency.[12] So, for example, clause 10(1) of the draft Human Tissue and Embryos Bill 2007 provides that the proposed new regulatory authority for Tissues and Embryos 'must carry out its functions effectively, efficiently and economically'. If *effectiveness* is the only consideration, there is no injunction for regulatory restraint. Hence, unless there is no pressure on regulatory resources, we should also consider whether regulation is as *economical* as it might be. Suppose, for example, that regulators, having decided that genetic discrimination by employers is as objectionable as racial or sexual discrimination, prohibit such discriminatory practices and establish a genetic discrimination unit (the GDU) to monitor employers and to enforce the prohibition. Let us suppose further, however, that employers generally see little advantage in genetic profiling of their employees (prospective and actual) and that, apart from a few exceptional cases, employers make no attempt to discriminate on the basis of genetic information.[13] With regulatees having little interest in flouting the regulation, the GDU might seem to be over-resourced. Accordingly, we might judge that, in the interests of regulatory economy, there should be a reduction in GDU resource. Indeed, we might judge that keeping the GDU lean and mean makes sense not only relative to considerations of economy but also to avoid the GDU using its surplus resource for unintended and possibly counter-productive purposes.

Once we have trimmed the regulatory resource to the point where any further cut will reduce the *effectiveness* of the regulatory intervention, we have taken regulatory *economy* as far as we should. However, this still leaves the consideration of regulatory *efficiency*, understood as the optimal gearing of regulatory input

[12] Generally, see Norman D Lewis *Choice and the Legal Order: Rising Above Politics* (London: Lexis Nexis, 1996); and, for a particularly clear account of the three Es, see Fidelma White and Kathryn Hollingsworth *Audit, Accountability and Government* (Oxford: Clarendon Press, 1999).

[13] For the famous Burlington Northern Santa Fe Railway Company case, see Stephen Fink '*EEOC v BNSF*: The Risks and Rewards of Genetic Exceptionalism' (2003) 42 Washburn Law Journal 525.

to effective regulatory output. To illustrate the import of regulatory efficiency, consider again the example of genetic discrimination by employers. However, let us suppose that the attitude of employers is exactly opposite to that previously hypothesized. Let us suppose, in other words, that employers have for some time been genetically profiling their employees (prospective and actual) and that they believe it is essential for the profitability of their businesses. In such a setting, the GDU, far from pushing at an open door, faces widespread and deep resistance to the regulatory prohibition against the practice of genetic discrimination that is already embedded. Given such resistance, regulators anticipate that it will take a major regulatory effort to turn things round. Facing this challenge, let us suppose that regulators commission projections as to the regulatory impact of various levels of regulatory resource. What the projections suggest is that a regulatory input of resource x (say, an annual budget of £10m for the GDU) will reduce genetic discrimination by 10 per cent, that a regulatory input of resource y (say, an annual budget of £15m for the GDU) will reduce genetic discrimination by 50 per cent, and that a regulatory input of resource z (say, an annual budget of £20m for the GDU) will reduce genetic discrimination by 55 per cent. On the basis of such projections, considerations of regulatory efficiency point to resource y. For, although this level of regulatory investment does not do as well in terms of regulatory effectiveness as higher levels of investment, the ratio of input to output is superior at this lower level.

By and large, once we enter the realm of regulatory economy and efficiency, we are leaving the real world behind. In the real world, regulatory intelligence is far less sophisticated. If we understood how to deliver effective regulation, we might be able to fine-tune it for economy and efficiency; but, in the present state of the art, this is something of a pipe-dream.[14]

III General Regulatory Intelligence

When we consider what makes for regulatory effectiveness, there is no point in reinventing the wheel. We do have some general regulatory intelligence. It is not as though observers of the regulatory process have detected no recurring patterns in (relatively speaking) regulatory failure and regulatory success.

For example, we can carry forward the principal insights of smart regulatory theory, namely that traditional (criminal law) interventions cannot be counted on to control in the way that regulators intend, that regulators have at their disposal a range of instruments that might be deployed to channel and control conduct, and that regulators would do well to seek out the particular combination of instruments that most effectively promotes their particular regulatory purposes.

[14] See, further, ch 11 where I consider whether there could be a coherent judicial review of an agency's performance relative to the criteria of effectiveness, economy, and efficiency.

While these insights are important in steering regulators away from interventions that are likely to be futile or even counter-productive, we are some way short of a comprehensive and reliable regulatory jurisprudence (with settled precedents) pointing to the particular combinations of instruments that are appropriate for particular cases.

Similarly, we can learn from responsive regulatory theory that, generally speaking, regulators should operate with a cooperative default approach (seeking out win-win relationships with their regulatees), that they do well to respond to non-compliance in a way that leaves room for escalating sanctions, for flexibility, and for sensitivity to the nature and character of particular regulatees, and that regulators should be geared to encourage structured self-regulation.[15] Such lessons, however, are not to be mechanically cashed in. As Ayres and Braithwaite caution:

> Responsive regulation is not a clearly defined program or a set of prescriptions concerning the best way to regulate. On the contrary, the best strategy is shown to depend on context, regulatory culture, and history. Responsiveness is rather an attitude that enables the blossoming of a wide variety of regulatory approaches... [16]

Again, when introducing their discussion of enforced self-regulation, the same authors caution:

> We do not present [the model of enforced self-regulation] as the best idea or even an innovation that is desirable in most circumstances. The contention of this book is that there is no such thing as an ahistorical optimal regulatory strategy. There are just different strategies that have a mix of strengths and weaknesses. The appropriateness of a particular strategy is contingent on the legal, constitutional, and cultural context and the history of its invocation.[17]

The claim of the best regulatory theorists, therefore, is not that there are off-the-shelf solutions for regulators. Rather, it is that regulation is a constant learning process. The history and experience of regulation does offer some lessons; but regulatory intelligence involves absorbing the lessons of today as much as those of yesterday.

Regulators with the right kind of attitude will also take note of the following familiar possibilities and problems:[18] (a) that regulators over-reach their authority or their practical competence; (b) that powerful regulatees, in effect, 'capture' (or corrupt) the agencies that are responsible for implementing the regulation; and (c) that, on some occasions, regulators can make things worse by intervening because the intervention produces unintended negative consequences. Each of these possibilities merits a few words by way of elaboration.

[15] Ian Ayres and John Braithwaite *Responsive Regulation* (Oxford: Oxford University Press, 1992).

[16] ibid 5.

[17] ibid 101.

[18] For the first of these possibilities, I am drawing on Stuart Biegel (n 8 above) ch 4 where he discusses the inherent limits of legal effectiveness.

(a) Regulatory over-reach

Regulatory over-reach can occur in several different ways; but, whatever the particular manifestation of over-reaching, the effect is that regulation does not have the intended effect.

First, at some level, because the politico-legal system is based on a social contract, regulators will lack public support where they push beyond the terms of the contract. Where this happens, and where the lack of public support is translated into popular resistance, the regulatory intervention in question will be ineffective. The use of marijuana as a recreational drug is the textbook example. Thus:

> The fact remains... that marijuana use continues to be illegal in most parts of the world, even as people continue to break these laws with apparent impunity. And there is no resolution in sight. The persistence of marijuana use remains a prime example of how our legal system is based on an implicit social contract, and how the laws on the books can cease to matter when a large percentage of people decide they want to do something that may not be acceptable under the law.[19]

Similarly, experience (especially in the United States) with regulatory prohibitions on alcohol suggests not only that legal interventions that overstep the mark will be ineffective but pregnant with corrupting and secondary criminalizing effects.

Secondly, laws tend to be less effective where they are operating in complex areas with many variables—drawing on experience in the United States, Biegel cites as examples attempts to equalize public-school funding, efforts to combat racism, and toxic tort litigation. We might also cite the difficulties that have been recently experienced by US courts where, in relation to peer-to-peer networks, they are faced with brokering a workable accommodation between the proprietary interests of media copyright holders, the general interest in the encouragement of inventive improvement (inter alia of media products), and the interests of researchers and consumers (some interests more fair than others) in accessing and using copyright-protected work.[20] Certainly, in the United Kingdom, courts are aware of the limits of their institutional competence and, in particular, they tend to steer clear of reviewing the resource allocation decisions made by public bodies. To give but one example: in *Marcic v Thames Water Utilities Limited*,[21] the House of Lords declined to support Mr Marcic (who suffered from repeated external sewer flooding at his home in Stanmore) when he sued Thames Water, the statutory sewage undertaker for the area, claiming inter alia that the defendant was liable

[19] Biegel (n 8 above) at 105. Compare, for the UK, the RSA Report, *Drugs – Facing Facts* (London, March 2007).

[20] For discussion, see eg Matthew Rimmer *Digital Copyright and the Consumer Revolution* (Cheltenham: Edward Elgar, 2007) ch 3.

[21] [2003] UKHL 66. For comment on *Marcic* and the equally restrictive decision in *Transco plc v Stockport MBC* [2003] UKHL 61, see Maria Lee 'Private Nuisance in the House of Lords: Back to Basics' (2005) 15 KCLJ 417.

under the common law tort of nuisance.[22] Although the speeches emphasize the closed nature of the statutory regime—with a channel for complaints going to the Director General of Water Services, the industry regulator—the House is plainly reluctant to encourage the use of the common law in general, and the law of nuisance in particular, as a means to put pressure on public service providers or public regulators. For if a court were to back a claim such as that made by Mr Marcic, not only might this unfairly reward the litigious (who are not necessarily the most eligible for relief),[23] it would set in motion unpredictable redistributive effects.[24] In the event, prompted by widespread floods in October 2000, the director agreed additional funding for remedial works with Thames Water and, at the same time, made some allowance for the costs incurred by the latter in setting sewerage charges—and, happily, one of the results of this process was that, in 2003, remedial work was carried out for the benefit of 10 properties in Stanmore including that occupied by Mr Marcic.

Thirdly, regulatory over-reach is quite likely to occur when the issues and the boundaries of the problem are not localized (in the sense that the source of the problem is located beyond the would-be regulating state's geographical boundaries). Notoriously, the development of cyberspace is a particularly vivid example of the limits to effective regulation where national legal systems no longer map in a straightforward way on to particular regulatory spaces.[25] Whilst authoritarian states can exert some control over their citizens' access to internet sites, this is much more difficult in liberal democracies.[26] This is a matter to which we will return in Chapter 7.

(b) Regulatory capture (and corruption)

In *Corporate Crime in the Pharmaceutical Industry*,[27] John Braithwaite paints a sobering picture of industry-wide declarations of 'questionable payments'. This is not the view of a nihilist, simply a realistic assessment of how business is actually done and how far regulators can go in controlling bribery and corruption. We do not, however, need to resort to such obviously pathological relationships between regulators and regulatees to see how (vulnerable) regulatory agencies can be captured and dominated by powerful regulatees.

[22] Mr Marcic also pleaded, unsuccessfully, a Human Rights Act point; but this is not directly of relevance to the present discussion.

[23] Some householders, for example, experienced *internal* fouling and flooding.

[24] See especially Lord Hoffmann's judgment [2003] UKHL 66, at paras 63 and 64.

[25] Seminally, see David R Johnson and David Post 'Law and Borders – The Rise of Law in Cyberspace' (1996) 48 Stanford Law Review 1367.

[26] Compare Ronald J Deibert and Nart Villeneuve 'Firewalls and Power: An Overview of Global State Censorship of the Internet' in Mathias Klang and Andrew Murray (eds) *Human Rights in the Digital Age* (London: Cavendish, 2005) 111. Even in authoritarian states, there can be no certainty about the reaction of other states, see Andrew Murray *The Regulation of Cyberspace* (Abingdon: Routledge-Cavendish, 2007) especially at 52–3.

[27] John Braithwaite *Corporate Crime in the Pharmaceutical Industry* (London: Routledge and Kegan Paul, 1984) ch 2.

Consider the common case of a regulatory agency that is charged with monitoring the various medicines and therapies that are available both in the public health system and in the private marketplace. The mission of the agency is to supervize and license these health care products and services, ensuring that patients and consumers (a) are properly informed and (b) are not exposed to undeclared or unreasonable risks. Braithwaite offers many examples of the way in which dangerous drugs (including Thalidomide) have been able to slip through the regulatory net and cause grievous harm to patients and consumers; and in *Dispensing with the Truth*,[28] Alicia Mundy presents an extended account of how the Fen-Phen diet drug found its way into the marketplace where it took a heavy toll on its users.

According to Mundy, the personal tragedies brought about by use of Fen-Phen might have been averted had American Home Products (through its Wyeth-Ayerst division) not been so economical with the truth in relation to the risks associated with the drug and had the prevailing culture at the regulatory agency (the FDA) been less concerned with assisting the pharmaceutical companies to bring their products to market and more concerned with product safety. Once the lawyers were able to make the right connections between the knowledge of the producers of Fen-Phen, the properties of the drug, and the damage done to the complainants, AHP had little choice but to make massive compensatory settlements with individual and mass tort claimants. Generally speaking, the tort system comes out of Mundy's account rather well and public regulation rather badly. By and large, individual tort litigators shine through as honest and independent operators with honourable intentions. However, so far as the FDA is concerned we have a familiar tale of regulatory capture: put crudely, the agency is either not willing or not able to distance itself from the interests of the pharmaceutical companies (resulting in a failure to take a hard look at the companies' claims) and this arises, in part, from the influence that the companies exert directly over the agency and, in part, from the indirect influence that is exerted via the political branch over, inter alia, resourcing for the agency.

The form of the Fen-Phen story is by no means unique. Indeed, the story of the COX-2 inhibitor, Vioxx, that has unfolded in courts and claims on both sides of the Atlantic, has a very familiar ring to it.[29] But, it is not just dangerous drugs that can slip past the regulatory sentries. There are many instances in which the task of monitoring a product or a state of affairs that is a matter of concern to public health is charged to a public agency, but where a hazard gets through the public health net and, having caused personal injury or damage, it is left to the tort

[28] *Dispensing with the Truth* (New York: St Martin's Press, 2001).

[29] Maxine Frith 'Exposed: How Drugs Giant Pushed Vioxx Painkiller' *The Independent* 22 August 2005, p 1; James Burleigh 'Vioxx Firm May Settle with Drug Claimants' *The Independent* 27 August 2005, p 28; and see, also, David Prosser 'Class Action Offers Hope in the Legal Battle against Goliath' *The Independent* 27 August 2005 'Save and Spend', p 3.

system to sound the alarm bells. That the tort system played a key role in cleaning up after BSE, tobacco, asbestos, thalidomide, and the like, seems undeniable.

Nevertheless, we should not place too much faith in tort. We need only recall the oft-rehearsed limitations that afflict the general effectiveness of private law actions.[30] Potential claimants will often be unaware of their legal position and they will be deterred from inquiring because of the fear of costs; one-shot individual litigants will do much less well than repeat-players;[31] one-off claims, unless they are class claims, might deliver a remedy for the particular claimant but they do little to remedy a more general problem; and the doctrinal hurdles put in front of claimants are serious—even if the adoption of product liability regimes removes the need for the claimant to prove a lack of reasonable care, here and elsewhere there are causation requirements that are notoriously problematic where there is an asymmetry of information between the parties.[32] Not surprisingly, then, the studies consistently indicate that there is a significant under-use of legal measures that are designed to protect more vulnerable persons against exploitation, discrimination, and deception whether in the workplace, in the housing sector, in the consumer marketplace, or even in their own homes.[33] In some cases, the parties concerned have alternative (sometimes more satisfactory) ways of dealing with their disputes and grievances; but, in many instances, the victims of wrongdoing who might be expected to come forward to take legal action simply do not do so.

(c) Unintended consequences

Sometimes, regulatory interventions not only fail to achieve the desired effect, they generate undesired and unintended negative consequences, or they are actually self-defeating.[34] As we have seen already, the war on drugs (like prohibition before it) has not only failed to prevent the use of cannabis (and many other psychoactive substances) for recreational purposes, it has created a thriving black market and, in turn, created a huge volume of connected property

[30] Compare, eg, Stuart Biegel *Beyond Our Control?* (Cambridge, Mass: MIT Press, 2003) ch 4; and Mauro Cappelletti 'Alternative Dispute Resolution Processes Within the Framework of the World-Wide Access-to-Justice Movement' (1993) 56 MLR 282.

[31] Famously, see M Galanter 'Why the "Haves" Come Out Ahead: Speculation on the Limits of Legal Change' (1974) 9 Law and Society Review 95.

[32] The much-discussed relaxation of standard causation principles in *Fairchild v Glenhaven Funeral Services* [2002] 3 WLR 89, does not assist claimants who need the cooperation of better informed defendants if the right causal link is to be established.

[33] No doubt, there are many appropriate references. A good place to start is Vilhelm Aubert 'Some Social Functions of Legislation' (1966) 10 *Acta Sociologica* 99; and, generally, see Bob Roshier and Harvey Teff *Law and Society in England* (London: Tavistock, 1980).

[34] Compare Cass R Sunstein 'Paradoxes of the Regulatory State' (1990) 57 University of Chicago Law Review 407—for example, the introduction of a minimum wage will be self-defeating if it means that there are fewer employment opportunities for low-paid workers.

crime.[35] In a report[36] recently prepared for the House of Commons Committee on Science and Technology, the scale of the problem is summarized in the following terms:

The United Nations suggests that the international drug market is worth around $430 billion. Of this the UK market is estimated at around £6.6 billion. The drug related economic costs to the UK can be broken down into direct costs on tackling drugs (£1.2 billion), the associated cost of drug related crime (estimated to be £10.5 billion for England and Wales), the cost to industry (£800 million) and the cost to the NHS (£234 million). Of the £1.5 billion that the government pledges annually to tackling the drugs problem, around 75% of the budget is spent on enforcing the drugs laws, with 12% spent on education and 13% on treatment in 1998.[37]

As a result, the distribution of resources in the UK criminal justice system is now seriously distorted by the need to address not just a range of serious drug offences (in particular, trafficking and supplying) but also the satellite criminality that probably accounts for about half of all crimes committed. With the prospect of drugs being used for cognition and performance enhancement moving rapidly up the agenda,[38] regulators clearly need to be mindful of the recent history of their disastrous handling of recreational drug use.

To take another cautionary tale: in *Genes and Insurance*,[39] Marcus Radetzki, Marian Radetzki, and Niklas Juth argue against regulatory regimes that prohibit insurance companies from either requiring genetic tests to be taken or, where test information is already available, requiring disclosure of the results (so-called 'total regulation'). The authors' principal contention is that such regimes are unlikely to have the intended effect of shielding those whose genetic make-up would otherwise disadvantage them in the insurance market; and, indeed, the consequences of adopting such regulatory approaches might be so counter-productive that the market itself collapses when it can no longer bear the weight of its high-risk burden.

[35] See, eg, Deborah Brown, Mark Mason, and Rachel Murphy 'Drug Supply and Trafficking: An Overview' (2003) 42 Howard Journal of Criminal Justice 324; Department of Health *United Kingdom Drug Situation: Annual Report to the European Monitoring Centre for Drugs and Drug Addiction* (2005); and, more widely, see EMCDDA (European Monitoring Centre for Drugs and Drug Addiction) *The State of the Drugs Problem in Europe* (Annual Report 2005) (Lisbon, Portugal).

[36] Ruth Levitt, Edward Nason, Michael Hallsworth *The Evidence Base for Classification of Drugs* (Santa Monica, CA: the RAND Corporation, 2006).

[37] ibid 1.8, para 31.

[38] See, eg, Alexandra Frean and Patrick Foster 'Cheating Students Turn to 'Smart Drugs' for Edge in Exams' *The Times* 23 June 2007, 16–17. For the principal regulatory options and their likely impact, see Robin Room 'Social Policy and Psychoactive Substances' in David Nutt, Trevor W Robbins, Gerald W. Stimson, Martin Ince, and Andrew Jackson (eds) *Drugs and the Future* (London: Academic Press, 2007) 337; and, for an evaluation from a rights perspective, see Richard Ashcroft, Alastair V Campbell, and Ben Capps 'Ethical Aspects of Developments in Neuroscience and Drug Addiction' ibid 439.

[39] *Genes and Insurance* (Cambridge: Cambridge University Press, 2003).

Let us assume that the intended purpose of such regimes is to prevent insurance companies from discriminating against applicants whose genetic profile shows up as a bad risk and, concomitantly, to protect such applicants against being priced out of, or excluded altogether from, vital insurance or insurance-financed services. In this way, the intention underlying such regulation is that the private insurance market should mimic solidarity-based social insurance. Yet, as the authors observe, the regulators seek to do this at just the time that social insurance is being dismantled. Not only this, this particular regulatory approach is adopted in the face of burgeoning information about the human genome and in a context of globalization. Putting these pieces together, the authors argue that regulatory prohibition simply will not work.

To understand why there is a problem with such regulatory regimes, we need to recall a truism about disclosure in contracting situations. In many contractual negotiations (including negotiations for insurance), there is an asymmetry of information. The asymmetry might favour the buyer or the provider. If the former, then the rational-economic buyer will disclose the information in question if the effect of disclosure will be to reduce the price. However, if the effect of disclosure will be to increase the price, the rational-economic buyer will not disclose. Now, imagine the position of an applicant for insurance who has information (asymmetrically) about his own genetic make-up. If disclosure of that information will exert a downward pressure on the premium, the information will be disclosed; but if disclosure would exert an upward pressure, the applicant would not usually wish to disclose. The intended effect of total regulation is to permit the latter kind of applicant to withhold the information and, thus, to enjoy what is in effect a discounted premium (as well as avoiding whatever collateral disadvantages might flow from putting this information into circulation). However, the secondary effect of total regulation is that low-risk applicants, who are willing to disclose, are either not permitted to do so or are not able to profit from doing so. In consequence, lower-risk applicants (unwillingly) subsidize those who are higher-risk and, with this, there is a danger that the pool will be destabilized through the process of 'adverse selection'.

In the first instance, the stability of an insurance pool (comprising both high-risk and low-risk insured parties) subject to a regime of total regulation depends on the attitudes of the three key stakeholders. Those who are high-risk parties will normally wish to sustain the pool on total regulation terms (because it is to their economic advantage to do so); those who are low-risk will wish to revise the regulatory terms on which the pool operates so that premiums or contributions paid by individuals more faithfully reflect real risk profiles or, failing this, they will wish to exit the pool in order to join a pool with more favourable terms; and, depending upon a number of economic variables, the insurance companies might or might not prefer the pool to be run under total regulation terms or on terms that allow for premiums to be set on sophisticated differential terms. Given this, although there might be some occasional abuses of a total regulation scheme by those who know that they are high-risk, the major impulse for change (and the most likely source of destabilization) will come from low-risk stakeholders who would prefer to participate in a pool where premiums are adjusted in line with disclosed risk profiles.[40]

Whilst the authors' thesis that total regulation invites adverse selection is certainly plausible, whether or not low-risk stakeholders actually leave the pool depends upon a number of variables about which we can be rather less certain. For example, the dynamics of this situation depend upon how much genetic information we have and just how informative such information actually is for insurance purposes;[41] the availability of, and ease of access to, alternative insurance pools that operate in accordance with standard rules for disclosure; the degree of inertia, caution, longer-term calculation, or loyalty displayed by low-risk parties in sticking with their existing pools; whether insurers who operate in total regulation schemes *and who have an interest in sustaining such schemes*, are able either to impose costs against exit that deter low-risk members from leaving or to devise incentives for staying within the pool; and so on. Having said this, it seems reasonable to assume that, other things being equal, low-risk members will take their business away from insurance pools that are subject to total regulation. As a pool progressively becomes a club for high-risk members, premiums necessarily will rise—and, indeed, as insurers understand what is happening to the pool, they might well inflate premiums in anticipation of the higher risks that they now realize they are covering. With membership becoming more expensive, even high-risk insured parties might have to drop out; and, in due course, dwindling membership might threaten the viability of the scheme so that the few remaining members are treated as uninsurable.

Good intentions, it seems, are no guarantee of good regulatory results. As we said in the introductory chapter, even if regulators do not yet know all the right moves, at least they can try to avoid some of the more stupid ones.

IV Biegel's Basic Principles

In the concluding chapter of *Beyond Our Control?*, Stuart Biegel gathers together 20 basic principles that he suggests might be used as guidelines to inform the

[40] In identifying low-risk parties as the key source of instability, I am conscious that I am departing from what I take to be the orthodox view that it will be unconscionable profit-taking by high-risk insureds that is the real problem. However, there are various ways that insurers can limit their exposure to this kind of opportunism and, with the appropriate safeguards in place, the real problem then lies with low-risk parties. For an appreciation of both high-risk and low-risk sources of difficulty, see Ronald Dworkin *Sovereign Virtue* (Cambridge, Mass: Harvard University Press, 2000) ch 13.

[41] Compare Onora O'Neill 'Insurance and Genetics: The Current State of Play' in Roger Brownsword, WR Cornish, and Margaret Llewelyn (eds) *Law and Human Genetics: Regulating a Revolution* (Oxford: Hart, 1998) 124.

regulation of cyberspace.[42] Some of the principles straddle both matters of legitimacy and effectiveness. For instance, the third principle reads:

> In order to ensure that the Internet retains its ability to serve as a dramatic and unique marketplace of ideas, it is essential that would-be regulators continue to respect the autonomy of individuals and groups in the online world.[43]

For the most part, however, the focus of the principles is on regulatory effectiveness; and our interest in Beigel's principles is not simply with regard to the effective regulation of cybertechnology but, more generally, with regard to the regulation of modern technologies.

Having said this, we cannot ignore the fact that some of the principles are specifically tied to the regulation of cyberactivities. For example, the eighth principle is particularly concerned with one of the starting points identified by the Tilburg group,[44] namely that what holds offline should also hold online. Here, Biegel qualifies whatever conventional wisdom this starting point expresses by proposing that (i) before regulators intervene in relation to some online activity, they should consider how unique the particular setting and specific behaviour is; and (ii) in some cases, the online features (such as speed, scale, and anonymity) might require a different approach to that adopted for the offline analogue. If we were to try to generalize this principle, we would need to substitute technologically assisted activities for online activities and technology-free activities for offline activities—such that we might then employ the principle in relation, for instance, to the use of reproductive technologies and their natural reproductive analogues.[45] However, while we are looking for whatever regulatory lessons we can learn in relation to modern technologies, we should not distort the guidance by neglecting the possibility that some regulatory principles are specific to a particular technology. With these caveats in mind, we can attempt to elaborate and reconstruct Biegel's principles so that they speak to the question of regulatory effectiveness.

Allowing for some repetition and overlapping, the principal regulatory guidelines to be derived from Biegel's set are as follows.[46]

1. (1, 8, 20) Before acting, regulators should consider whether a fresh regulatory intervention is necessary or desirable. Whilst regulators should not assume that the status quo is inviolable, neither should they assume that an

[42] Stuart Biegel *Beyond Our Control? Confronting the Limits of Our Legal System in the Age of Cyberspace* (Cambridge, Mass: MIT Press, 2003) 359–64.

[43] ibid 360. For a powerful illustration of the interaction between legitimacy (in the form of a concern not to stifle technological ingenuity) and effectiveness (a resulting light touch regulatory approach), see Jonathan Zittrain 'A History of Online Gatekeeping' (2006) 19 Harvard Journal of Law and Technology 253.

[44] See n 9 above.

[45] Compare Emily Jackson 'Conception and the Irrelevance of the Welfare Principle' (2002) 65 Modern Law Review 176 for a critique of this kind (albeit with regard to legitimacy rather than effectiveness).

[46] The numbers in round brackets tie back to the original numbering in Biegel.

intervention is always the right option. Intervention might be wasteful in using disproportionate resources to produce a marginal improvement (violating principles of regulatory economy and/or efficiency); or it might be futile; or, in some cases, it might make things worse, either directly or through indirect unintended effects.

2. (6) Where regulators decide that a regulatory intervention is appropriate, they should be clear about their objectives.
3. (3, 7, 9, 17, 18) Wherever possible, in setting their objectives, regulators should strive to build on a consensus (regulate with the grain). Thus:

   > [A] proposed regulatory approach may not be possible unless those that have the ability to resist agree to go along with the plan. And the list of such persons and entities would include not just the powers-that-be, but also [in the case of online activities] Internet advocacy groups, virtual communities, and individual Netizens.[47]

   Moreover, regulators should avoid acting ultra vires relative to the terms of the implicit social contract; and, where individual autonomy is valued, regulators should be mindful of the importance of individual freedom and choice.
4. (2, 13, 14) Regulators should consider the full range of regulatory instruments, from law-like interventions to strategies of self-regulation to code-based approaches. As Biegel puts it:

   > When addressing a particular problem area, [regulators should] consider the entire range of regulatory approaches, including litigation, legislation, policy changes, administrative agency activity, international cooperation, architectural changes, private ordering, and self-regulation. In cyberspace, it is reasonable to assume that a creative combination of approaches will be more effective than any single regulatory strategy.[48]

   Here, we have distinct echoes of Lawrence Lessig's seminal work on the four key regulatory modalities coupled with the lessons of smart regulatory theory.[49]
5. (2, 19) Regulators should also consider the optimal combination of regulatory instruments. Where problems are particularly intractable, there is no quick fix and regulators should 'identify combinations of approaches that may serve to move things in the right direction'.[50]
6. (15, 16) Where regulators adopt a law-like approach, the standards should be 'clear, direct, and understandable'[51] and their requirements should be realistic.[52]

[47] Stuart Biegel *Beyond Our Control? Confronting the Limits of Our Legal System in the Age of Cyberspace* (Cambridge, Mass: MIT Press, 2003) 361.

[48] ibid 360.

[49] See ch 1.

[50] Stuart Biegel *Beyond Our Control? Confronting the Limits of Our Legal System in the Age of Cyberspace* (Cambridge, Mass: MIT Press, 2003) 363.

[51] ibid 362.

[52] Compare the classic discussion in Lon L Fuller *The Morality of Law* (New Haven: Yale University Press, 1969).

7. (10, 11, 12) Where the activity reaches beyond national boundaries, regulators should first consider the impact of a national legal intervention; and, if such an intervention seems inadequate, they should seek to act at the appropriate global or regional level.
8. (9) Where a regulatory intervention is not self-enforcing, regulators should be sensitive to the strains that they might be putting on their enforcement resources.

Before we move on to the Tilburg commentary, in an attempt further to distil the regulatory intelligence to be drawn from our reconstruction of Biegel's guidance, we might highlight the following three matters.

First, there are some important reminders here about the risks of over-reaching and ignoring the possibility of unintended effects. These risks are familiar; but regulators whose targets are of a technological nature cannot afford to let familiarity breed contempt.

Secondly, there is the simple but crucial insight that regulators tend to do better when they act with the backing of regulatees (with a consensus rather than without it).[53] Regulatees who truly internalize the regulations and their purpose will outperform regulatees who mechanically apply the prescribed standards—'[r]egulations', as John Braithwaite pointedly remarks, 'can enforce minimum standards, but they cannot enforce common sense and social responsibility'.[54] Having said that, the more serious concerns arise in relation to regulatees who not only have not internalized the spirit of the regulations but also are not disposed to comply (or even disposed not to comply). However, before we can make the most of this insight, we need to understand much more about the roots of regulatee resistance, whether it be economic, cultural, professional, or moral in nature.

One of the key factors that will determine the penetration of a law is whether there is any economic resistance: quite simply, if regulatees act like rational economic actors, they will tend to view law as a tax on certain kinds of conduct. If non-compliance is the better economic option, the logic for such regulatees is to disobey and (sometimes) pay. For instance, in the days when Sunday trading was illegal, it made good business sense for large-scale DIY enterprises to open their doors on Sundays and occasionally pay a £2,000 fine. If Sunday trading had damaged the reputation of these businesses, this would have had to have been factored into the economic calculation; but, generally, the public supported the vanguard Sunday traders, and so there was no such risk. Putting the point rather generally, we can say that, where business people believe that compliance makes

[53] The idea that regulators do best when they 'work with the grain' is emphasized in Iredell Jenkins *Social Order and the Limits of Law* (Princeton, NJ: Princeton University Press, 1980); see, also, Phillipe Sands *Lawless World* (London: Penguin, 2005) at 56, for the eminently generalizable piece of regulatory wisdom that 'there exists in diplomatic circles a strongly held view that if a treaty cannot be adopted by consensus its long-term prospects are crippled'.

[54] John Braithwaite *Corporate Crime in the Pharmaceutical Industry* (London: Routledge and Kegan Paul, 1984) 137.

economic sense, they will comply; but, where compliance does not make economic sense, they will be less ready to comply.[55]

Another key element of resistance is often to be found in the culture of target regulatees, whether popular or professional, occupational or business. For example, if popular culture treats file-sharing of one kind or another as a fair use, copyright and contract rules notwithstanding, then the law will be remarkably difficult to enforce. In such a context, as Jessica Litman has remarked: 'If a law is bad enough, even its proponents might be willing to abandon it in favour of a different law that seems more legitimate to the people it is intended to command'.[56] Regulators also need to reckon with the attitudes of the professions: professional bodies (particularly the legal and the medical professions) tend to be extremely jealous of their autonomy and, not unreasonably, think that they know their own businesses best. Attempts to regulate the professions in a way that runs across the grain of professional culture will almost certainly be ineffective. Similarly, where there is a certain occupational culture ('cop culture', the culture of getting the policing job done, itself is the best example), regulators will meet with resistance where they try to legislate across the received norms of that culture. And, of course, so long as the culture of business is to maximize profits, attempts by regulators to encourage corporate social responsibility will tend to be more effective where they channel businesses towards win-win practices.[57]

Nor should we forget the resistance of individuals exercising an interest in matters of life and death. Diane Blood's campaign to have access to her deceased husband's sperm so that she could start the family that she and her husband had planned is a story that has been told many times.[58] Like the stories of the Hashmi and Whitaker families whom we meet in the next chapter it is a story that tells us something about the persistence of determined individuals, the limited resources of regulatory bodies when issues are litigated, and the way in which public sympathy for reasonable campaigns can be mobilized.[59]

The lessons of *Blood* are reflected in the Human Fertilisation and Embryology Authority's report on sex selection.[60] On the face of it, British public opinion

[55] To a considerable extent, rational economic man operates on both sides of the regulatory fence—for example, in both the licit and the illicit drugs market. Compare Nichola Dorn, Tom Bucke, and Chris Goulden 'Traffick, Transit and Transaction: A Conceptual Framework for Action Against Drug Supply' (2003) 42 Howard Journal of Criminal Justice 348, at 363, according to whom, it seems likely that 'only interventions causing traffickers to perceive a significant risk of capture leading to imprisonment have a worthwhile deterrent effect, lower-impact interventions providing for traffickers no more than the expected "costs of doing business"'.

[56] Jessica Litman *Digital Copyright* (New York: Prometheus Books, 2001) 195.

[57] See John Parkinson 'Corporate Governance and the Regulation of Business Behaviour' in Sorcha MacLeod (ed) *Corporate Governance* (Oxford: Hart, 2006) 1.

[58] See, eg, John N Adams and Roger Brownsword *Understanding Law* (4th edn, London: Sweet and Maxwell, 2006) 112.

[59] For the litigation, see *R v Human Fertilisation and Embryology Authority, ex parte Blood* [1997] 2 All ER 687. For comment, see Derek Morgan and Robert G Lee 'In the Name of the Father? *Ex parte Blood*: Dealing with Novelty and Anomaly' (1997) 60 MLR 840.

[60] *Sex Selection: Options for Regulation* (November 12, 2003).

runs strongly against access to sex selection techniques for social purposes;[61] but the authority recognizes that determined couples will seek out the required services in jurisdictions that lie beyond its regulatory reach.[62] For sure, we can anticipate that global markets for reproductive services coupled with determined purchasers will add up to sales. Moreover, if the media is able to mobilize support for a woman having access to her deceased husband's sperm so that she can have his children would it be so difficult to mobilize public support for a couple who already have a houseful of girls and who would now like a boy? The authority's survey of public opinion suggests that there is little sympathy for such a couple; but it would be extremely surprising if the questions, framed in a different way, would not elicit a different response or if such a cause (for the sake of a balanced family) could not be spun as eminently reasonable in a carefully cultivated context.

Occasionally, resistance to the law is required as a matter of conscience—witness, for example, the peace tax protesters; physicians who ignore what they see as unconscionable legal restrictions; members of religious groups who defy a legally supported dress code, and the like. Such persons are probably the exception rather than the rule; but where the law is up against a case of genuine conscientious objection, then it is truly up against it.

Thirdly, although Biegel's guidelines go a long way towards keeping regulators on the right tracks, they do not speak directly to the question of how regulators might handle the problem of regulatory sustainability (the challenge of regulatory connection). Given that information technology, like most modern technologies, presents regulators with this problem, this is a little surprising. However, it is picked up in one of the Tilburg starting points and the challenge of regulatory connection is the focus for Chapter 6.

V Five Starting Points for Regulators

In *Starting Points for ICT Regulation*,[63] Bert-Jaap Koops and his co-authors take a hard look at five supposed self-selecting starting points for the regulation of ICT.

[61] In her Chair's Foreword to the report (n 60 above), Suzi Leather says that the 'strength of opposition to sex selection for any but the most serious of medical reasons ... is unmistakable'. For example, 82 per cent of respondents to the consultation questionnaire *disagreed* with the statement 'The use of sperm sorting should be permitted in sex selection for non-medical reasons'; 82.85 per cent *disagreed* with the statement 'The use of PGD should be permitted for selecting the sex of offspring for non-medical reasons'; 82.68 per cent *disagreed* with the statement 'Sex selection (by either sperm sorting or PGD) should be permitted for non-medical reasons when a family has at least two children of one sex and none of the other sex' [ie sex selection for family balancing reasons]; and 85.06 per cent *disagreed* with the statement 'Sex selection (by either sperm sorting or PGD) should be permitted for non-medical reasons other than family balancing'.

[62] ibid para 130.

[63] Bert-Jaap Koops, Miriam Lips, Corien Prins, and Maurice Schellekens (eds) *Starting Points for ICT Regulation – Deconstructing Prevalent Policy One-Liners* (The Hague: TMC Asser Press, 2006).

The starting points in question are: (i) that what holds offline should also hold online; (ii) that regulation should be 'technology neutral'; (iii) that self-regulation should be the preferred regulatory option; (iv) that regulation should be undertaken at an international level; and (v) that, where we have the technology, code-based approaches should be adopted by regulators.

Although the Tilburg team's interest in these starting points is both broader and less explicitly specified than our own (which is whether they might serve as guidelines for effective regulation), the emerging view is that regulators are unlikely to find any short-cuts to success in this list. Rather, the judgment of the Tilburg team is that the relevance and applicability of the starting points is highly context specific even within the narrow setting of ICT. Moreover, in a concluding review, Schellekens, Koops, and Prins remark:

> Still, one thing is blatantly absent and that is content . . . the starting points are procedural guidelines; they point to a method, but are empty as to what substantive direction regulatory decisions might take. Values are absent, and if there is one thing that is characteristic of regulation, it is that regulation is normative: it tells society which direction to take, it tells citizens, governments, consumers, and businesses alike what to do and what to leave undone. A checklist for e-regulation that fails to contain any indication of the direction that the information society is to take is a poor instrument for regulation developers.[64]

This is a point well made. Even if regulators understood precisely how to intervene in order to steer the information society in a particular direction, there would be the prior question of regulatory legitimation and, in particular, whether regulators could hold their line against challenges to the legitimacy of their preferred direction. In this light, we should remind ourselves that the appropriateness of the so-called 'starting points' that we are about to consider only becomes relevant once the regulatory purpose has been established.

(i) 'What holds off-line, also holds on-line'

The idea that 'what holds off-line, also holds on-line' has been proclaimed on many occasions—for example, at the EU Ministerial Conference, held in Bonn in July 1997, where it was agreed inter alia that 'general legal frameworks should be applied on-line as they are off-line';[65] and in the e-principles adopted by the UK Government, we read that '[the] effects of the off-line and on-line regulatory environments, including the criminal and civil law, should be as similar as possible'.[66]

[64] Maurice Schellekens, Bert-Jaap Koops, and Corien Prins 'Conclusion' (n 63 above) 229, at 237–8.

[65] Bonn Ministerial Declaration, Recommendation 22.

[66] <http://archive.cabinetoffice.gov.uk/e-envoy/guidelines-eprinciples/$file/>. For the guidance of policy makers, eight principles are specified as follows: (i) always establish the policy consequences for e-commerce; (ii) avoid undue burdens on e-commerce; (iii) consider self and co-regulatory options; (iv) consult fully on e-commerce implications; (v) regulation should be technology neutral in its effects; (vi) check that your proposals are enforceable in an electronic age; (vii) take account of

Insofar as this principle asserts that online activities are not exempt from regulation, or that the offline rules should be applied to their online analogues, it has little or nothing to do with regulatory effectiveness—or, at any rate, it does not point the way to effective regulation of online activities unless the offline rules are exemplars of effectiveness (which we can take to be unlikely). However, if we read the principle as echoing Biegel by reminding regulators to look first to existing law, then we have a sound principle of regulatory *economy*. After all, there might be no need to reinvent the law of contract to cover e-commerce; it is enough if regulators make it clear that transactions carried out in online environments (making use of digital messages, electronic signatures, and the like) are as valid and enforceable as offline contracts.[67] Similarly, regulators do not need to reinvent the criminal laws of theft and deception to penalize fraudsters who use eBay to deprive unsuspecting purchasers of their money; and, again, the law of copyright might carry across with some minor tweaking to regulate multimedia digital products.[68] To repeat, however, this is a principle that speaks to regulatory economy rather than regulatory effectiveness; for it might well be that the body of contract, copyright, and criminal law that is carried across to the online world is not particularly fit for its traditional offline purposes—in which case, it would be a serious mistake to advocate that what holds offline (namely a largely ineffective body of regulation) should also hold (equally ineffectively) online.

(ii) Technological neutrality

Regulators are frequently pressed to observe the principle of technological neutrality. Moreover, this principle is often expressed in the same breath as the previous principle; and, indeed, this is so in both the Bonn Declaration and the e-principles mentioned above.[69] This hints at some confusion as the two principles are elided. In a searching analysis of the matter, Bert-Jaap Koops isolates three distinct meanings of the principle of technological neutrality:

> From the perspective of the goal of regulation, the statement stresses that, in principle, the effects of ICT should be regulated, but not the technology itself; it may thus serve as a means to achieve equivalence between off-line and on-line regulation. From the perspective of technology development, the statement stresses that, in principle, regulation should not have a negative effect on the development of technology and should not unduly discriminate between technologies. From the perspective of legislative technique, the starting point

the global market place—the EU and international angle; and (viii) consider the implications for e-government. The injunction to harmonize offline and online regulatory environments appears under the fifth principle (technological neutrality).

[67] Compare Roger Brownsword and Geraint Howells 'When Surfers Start to Shop: Internet Commerce and Contract Law' (1999) 19 Legal Studies 287.

[68] See Tanya Aplin *Copyright Law in the Digital Society* (Oxford: Hart, 2005).

[69] See n 65 and 66 above.

stresses that legislation should abstract away from concrete technologies to the extent that it is sufficiently sustainable and at the same time provides sufficient legal certainty.[70]

Picking up on the third use (from the perspective of legislative technique), Koops points out that, while this is not a new insight, 'it may be useful to stress that, in ICT regulation, particular attention must be given to the sustainability of laws that target technology, because there is a greater risk than usual that changes in the subject matter may soon make the law obsolete'.[71] The challenge, however, as Koops perceptively observes, is to find the optimal trade-off between, on the one side, the certainty, clarity, and precision of legal instruments and, on the other side, the flexibility that allows for adjustment and sustainability. Thus:

> The starting point that regulation should be technology-neutral can be seen as reflecting this trade-off. Legislation should abstract away from concrete technologies to the extent that it is sufficiently sustainable and at the same time provide sufficient legal certainty. Depending on a number of criteria, such as the goal of the regulation at issue, the nature and turbulence of the technology at stake, the urgency of providing legal certainty, and the scope for interpreting the regulation, there are several ways to deal with this trade-off. Through multi-level legislation, open-ended formulations, and a mixed approach of abstract and concrete rules that are periodically evaluated, adequate legal certainty with respect to current technologies may be ensured, while at the same time sufficient scope is given for future technological developments. Further safeguards for sustainability can be established by leaving ample scope for interpreting the law in a functional way and providing clear guidance as to the aims and rationale of the regulation.[72]

In the next chapter, we will return to the challenge of maintaining regulatory connection (sustainability). At this juncture, suffice it to say that, even if all concerned with the regulatory enterprise attend to Koops's discussion and strive to make an intelligent trade-off between the specificity of regulatory standards and their sustainability, the injunction to adopt a 'technologically neutral' approach will not greatly assist them—and it certainly will not guarantee that their regulatory interventions are all that they should be, for the challenge of connection is as much about regulatory legitimacy as it is about regulatory economy and effectiveness.

(iii) Self-regulation

In the early days of e-commerce, the idea that regulators should encourage online stakeholders to self-regulate their activities was a familiar one. For example, this was a prominent theme in the White House's Framework for Global Electronic Commerce where it was stated, inter alia, that 'governments should encourage

70 Bert-Jaap Koops 'Should ICT Regulation be Technology-Neutral?' op cit (n 63 above) 77 at 107.

71 ibid.

72 ibid 107–8.

industry self-regulation wherever appropriate and support the efforts of private sector organizations to develop mechanisms to facilitate the successful operation of the Internet'.[73] Moreover, one might point to some spectacular examples of relatively successful self-regulating activity, most notably perhaps the Uniform Domain Name Dispute Resolution Policy developed by ICANN in 1999. To be sure, the policy has its critics,[74] but when we bear in mind the global reach of this regulatory initiative, it speaks to the potential that self-regulation has for getting things done.

Having said this, there is a fundamental objection to adopting a self-regulated approach. Put bluntly, the objection is that self-regulation is a licence for self-interested regulatory activity. Thus, if we leave it to industry or the professions to self-regulate, they will tend to act in whichever way seems to suit their own interests, setting only such regulatory standards as they are happy to comply with and enforcing their standards only so long as the business or professional case for enforcement is made out. Accordingly, so the objection goes, we invite problems with both regulatory legitimacy and regulatory effectiveness if we leave it to self-regulation. Moreover, any attempt to correct for one problem will exacerbate the other; for, if we try to modify self-regulatory standards to bring them more into line with the public interest, we are likely to increase regulatee resistance and, if we try to make it easier for regulatees to comply, we are likely to mandate standards that are less well aligned with the public interest. Echoing this Catch 22, the Tilburg authors comment:

> [A] convincing case for self-regulation can only be made if the relevant parties to the self-imposed rules or standards formulate organizational compliance measures with inherently binding provisions, for example, in operational policies. But... unwilling actors must also be taken into account ....That is to say, self-regulation works well with willing actors, but as long as a certain part of the market has an interest in not complying, self-regulation alone cannot do the trick. In the end, the effectiveness of self-regulation largely depends on the internal discipline of the organization or group of actors.[75]

Faced with these inter-related difficulties of effectiveness and legitimacy, the Tilburg team concludes that it is a mistake to treat self-regulation as the

[73] The White House *A Framework for Global Electronic Commerce*, 1 July 1997, <http://www.technology.gov/digeconomy/framewrk.htm>. Five principles are specified in this framework, as follows: (i) the private sector should lead; (ii) governments should avoid undue restrictions on electronic commerce; (iii) where governmental involvement is needed, its aim should be to support and enforce a predictable, minimalist, consistent and simple legal environment for commerce; (iv) governments should recognize the unique qualities of the Internet [viz its decentralized nature and its tradition of bottom-up governance]; and (v) electronic commerce over the internet should be facilitated on a global basis. The plea for self-regulation is made under the first of the principles.

[74] See, especially, Michael Froomkin 'Wrong Turn in Cyberspace: Using ICANN to Route Around the APA and the Constitution' (2000) 50 Duke Law Journal 17.

[75] Bert-Jaap Koops, Miriam Lips, Sjaak Nouwt, Corien Prins, and Maurice Schellekens 'Should Self-Regulation be the Starting Point?' in Bert-Jaap Koops, Miriam Lips, Corien Prins, and Maurice Schellekens (eds) *Starting Points for ICT Regulation – Deconstructing Prevalent Policy One-Liners* (The Hague: TMC Asser Press, 2006) 109, at 137–8.

default position. On the contrary, the starting point should carry quite the opposite emphasis—hence, the starting point should be that government regulates as far as this is required in order to protect fundamental (human rights) values, vulnerable citizens, and those interested parties who might be unfairly excluded by self-regulating groups;[76] having secured the regulatory space in this way, co-regulation is an option to be explored. Again, however, this is not a starting point that leads anywhere very quickly: for 'it says little about when and how what forms of co-regulation are to be chosen'.[77]

(iv) International cooperation

According to Recommendation 46 of the Bonn Ministerial Conference Declaration, 'Ministers agree to work together towards global principles on the free flow of information whilst protecting the fundamental right to privacy and personal and business data, building on the work undertaken by the EU, the Council of Europe, the OECD, and the UN'.[78] Is international cooperation and global harmonization of regulatory standards the key to regulatory effectiveness?

In one sense, there is a very straightforward answer to this question. Quite simply, where a particular regulatory project is explicitly global in its nature, it necessarily presupposes an international approach. For instance, if the regulatory project is to instate a global online marketplace, the regulatory framework for that marketplace must be global.[79] Generalizing this point, Corien Prins contends that:

> [A]n appeal to national sovereignty seems less appropriate where it concerns issues related to economic interests (e-commerce, e-signatures, and intellectual property rights). Here the argument of transboundary effects of electronic communication could justify that

[76] Arguably, the governance framework for the UK Biobank, although elaborated by an independent expert group, betrays some such characteristics, see Roger Brownsword 'Biobank Governance: Property, Privacy, and Consent' in Christian Lenk, Nils Hoppe, and Roberto Andorno (eds) *Ethics and Law of Intellectual Property: Current Problems in Politics, Science and Technology* (Aldershot, Ashgate, 2007) 11.

[77] Bert-Jaap Koops, Miriam Lips, Sjaak Nouwt, Corien Prins, and Maurice Schellekens 'Should Self-Regulation be the Starting Point?' in Bert-Jaap Koops, Miriam Lips, Corien Prins, and Maurice Schellekens (eds) *Starting Points for ICT Regulation –Deconstructing Prevalent Policy One-Liners* (The Hague: TMC Asser Press, 2006) 109, at 149. Nevertheless, broadly speaking, this is the approach advocated for the regulation of *nanotechnology* in Glenn Harlan Reynolds 'Nanotechnology and Regulatory Policy: Three Futures' (2003) 17 Harvard Journal of Law and Technology 179.

[78] Koops et al (n 77 above) cited at 155.

[79] See, eg, the fifth principle of The White House *A Framework for Global Electronic Commerce*, 1 July 1997 (n 73 above) under which we read:

> The Internet is emerging as a global marketplace. The legal framework supporting commercial transactions on the Internet should be governed by consistent principles across state, national, and international borders that lead to predictable results regardless of the jurisdiction in which a particular buyer or seller resides.

regulation can no longer be addressed at a national level, but must be dealt with at an international level.[80]

When we switch the regulatory focus from commerce to culture, the case for internationalism is less obvious. Nevertheless, if the project is about spreading what are judged to be cosmopolitan values (such as in support of human rights, or against online child pornography), then an international approach is called for. In other words, if the regulatory project is effectively international, then regulatory effectiveness implies an international approach. However, is there more to international cooperation than this?

The case of cybercrime enables us to see both the positive and the negative aspects of internationalism. On the positive side, we might say that the online world needs to be protected against the kind of damage that can be inflicted by the spread of 'viruses' and the like.[81] The fact that the source of the virus can be anywhere in the online world needs to be reflected in offline criminal practice. So, for example, when the author of the so-called 'Love Bug' virus was able to take sanctuary in the Philippines, this exposed a weakness in the regulatory environment. Accordingly, so the case goes, it makes sense to promote international cooperation in just the way that the Council of Europe does in its Convention on Cybercrime.[82] Turning to the negative side of internationalism, however, we might jib at a regulatory approach that tries to dictate local standards where there is serious resistance to the imposed global norm. In practice, the international community is in no position to impose its views on hate speech on the United States, or its views on freedom of expression on China; but imagine that the situation was more or less reversed, with the United States seeking to impose its cultural commitments on the rest of the world—as, indeed, it sought to do at the United Nations in relation to its desired global prohibition on therapeutic cloning.[83] In such circumstances, we would anticipate problems of both regulatory legitimacy and regulatory effectiveness—and these are problems that we revisit in Chapter 7 when we focus on the challenge of regulatory cosmopolitanism.

[80] Corien Prins 'Should ICT be Undertaken at an International Level?' in Bert-Jaap Koops, Miriam Lips, Corien Prins, and Maurice Schellekens (eds) *Starting Points for ICT Regulation – Deconstructing Prevalent Policy One-Liners* (The Hague: TMC Asser Press, 2006) 151, at 191.

[81] Compare Jonathan Zittrain 'The Generative Internet' (2006) 119 Harvard Law Review 1974. Although note Mathias Klang *Disruptive Technology* (Göteborg: Göteborg University, 2006) where some reservations are entered against demonising virus senders. Of course, it is well known that the intentions of 'virus' senders are not always malign; but Klang makes the additional point that the blanket criminalization of virus sending might cut across legitimate expression of political protest. For a recent programmatic initiative, see International Telecommunication Union, *ITU Global Cybersecurity Agenda [GCA]: A Framework for International Cooperation in Cybersecurity* (Geneva, October 2007).

[82] Budapest, 23 November 2001. For discussion of the jurisdictional aspects of the convention, see Henrik WK Kaspersen 'Jurisdiction in the Cybercrime Convention' in Bert-Jaap Koops and Susan W Brenner (eds) *Cybercrime and Jurisdiction* (The Hague: TMC Asser Press, 2006) 9.

[83] See ch 2.

In her concluding remarks, Prins, having reminded readers that 'the interplay between ICT developments and international regulation is highly complex',[84] gathers together some important threads in her discussion in the following way:

> Although the Internet may be a global phenomenon, the assumptions regarding the meaning, use, and limitations of this in principle unbounded network vary between countries, regions and individuals and are as such determined by 'borders'. The rich diversity of assumptions reflects historical, cultural, and economic realities that have evolved over many decades and do not disappear overnight. For this reason, it is unrealistic to think that irreconcilable differences resulting from these realities can be abrogated by international negotiation. Achieving regulatory models for the Internet requires recognition of the variety of historical, cultural and economic realities. Hence in dealing with ICT rule-making at an international level, the question is how social, cultural, economic, and individual identity and diversity can be balanced with the obvious advantages of harmonization...[85]

In sum, then, while some regulatory projects might, in and of themselves, necessitate an international approach, the drive for harmonized global regulation is unlikely to be effective (nor perceived to be legitimate) where it seeks to steamroller over local culture and difference. Clearly, there is unfinished business here and, as I have said, these are matters to which we will return.

(v) A code-based approach

The idea that regulators might usefully explore self-regulatory or international approaches is hardly new; and it is not uniquely prompted by the development of modern technologies, let alone information technology. However, the idea that regulators might turn to code-based strategies has been very much associated with the development of IT software and hardware. According to Biegel, code-based regulatory approaches are perhaps the 'single most powerful regulatory strategy available'[86] in relation to online activities; and, of course, Lessig has famously identified code as having the potential to become a perfect method of control. If regulatory effectiveness is what we want, and if effectiveness is all that we care about, then a code-based approach might be the answer.

For the Tilburg team,[87] there are reasons to be sceptical about the view that code is the cure to our regulatory difficulties. On the one hand, it is not clear that the technology can yet match the subtlety of traditional regulatory standards

[84] Corien Prins (n 80 above) at 200.

[85] ibid.

[86] Stuart Biegel *Beyond Our Control? Confronting the Limits of Our Legal System in the Age of Cyberspace* (Cambridge, Mass: MIT Press, 2003) 362.

[87] See Simone van der Hof and Kees Stuurman 'Code as Law?' in Bert-Jaap Koops, Miriam Lips, Corien Prins, and Maurice Schellekens (eds) *Starting Points for ICT Regulation – Deconstructing Prevalent Policy One-Liners* (The Hague: TMC Asser Press, 2006) 203; and Maurice Schellekens, Bert-Jaap Koops, and Corien Prins 'Conclusion', ibid 229.

(with their exceptions and built-in flexibility); code, at present, is too blunt an instrument.[88] There are also, of course, those who, subscribing to the maxim 'where there's a will there's a way', believe that counter-technologies will always defeat the regulatory code.[89] On the other hand, if code were able to match the normative sophistication of traditional regulatory standards and if it were to be counter-technology proof, there would be serious concerns about its legitimacy. Given that the legitimacy of a code-based approach—central to what I am calling the West Coast style of regulation—occupies most of the second part of this book, for the time being, we can let the matter rest here.

VI Conclusion

Unless regulation has a purely symbolic purpose, unless it is simply designed to appease certain constituencies and to lower blood pressure, a regulatory intervention will be fit for its purpose only if it channels conduct in the intended way. However, we need to recognize that the channelling power of law is limited. 'It is not entirely clear', remarks Yochai Benkler, in an understated way, 'that law can unilaterally turn back a trend that combines powerful technological, social, and economic drivers'.[90] Regulation needs to positively make a difference and the difference that it makes needs to be positive. Yet, what is it that holds the key to regulatory effectiveness?

Fairly clearly, one of the keys to regulatory effectiveness is to build on a consensus that backs the regulatory position coupled with a disposition on the part of regulatees to comply with and to support the intervention. In such circumstances, the intervention might not make a great deal of difference but the difference it makes is positive. Regulators should have learned by now that the declaration and prosecution of 'wars' that do not command public support is bound to end in tears.

For regulators who have taken it to heart that consensus and compliance go hand in hand, there is still the difficulty of dealing with ethical pluralism. Under such conditions, consensus is difficult to obtain. Hence, if regulators seek to prevent actions that a significant number of regulatees think are legitimate, there will be resistance that impedes regulatory effectiveness; but, if regulators respond by taking a more permissive approach, they are liable to offend another group of regulatees and resistance will simply be shifted from one place to another. Regulators can do their best by taking a smart, responsive, and imaginative approach; but,

[88] Compare Andrew Murray *The Regulation of Cyberspace* (Abingdon: Routledge-Cavendish, 2007) 40: '[design-based solutions] cannot match the plasticity of socially mediated solutions in the short-to-medium term'. See, further, ch 11.

[89] See, eg, Charles Fried 'Perfect Freedom, Perfect Control' (2000) 114 Harvard Law Review 606.

[90] Yochai Benkler *The Wealth of Networks* (New Haven: Yale University Press, 2006) 471. If we need flesh to put on these bones, compare Zittrain (n 43 above).

in these difficult conditions, the expectation of effective regulation should not be pitched very high.

Where the technology moves beyond the boundaries of national legal systems, regulators confront a double difficulty. First, the nature of the ethical plurality is likely to be even more contested; it is not a case, at all, of the more the merrier. Secondly, the capacity of regulators to control for extra-territorial action is limited. In a world that is divided by economic, cultural, and religious differences, national regulators simply cannot count on cooperation beyond their borders.

Over and above these difficulties, there is also the fact that we are dealing here with rapidly changing technologies. New technologies emerge before regulators see them coming; and established technologies move on. This gives rise to the challenge of regulatory connection; and this is the particular matter to which we now turn.

6

The Challenge of Regulatory Connection

I Introduction

In the previous chapter, I remarked that Stuart Biegel's guidelines to regulators do not speak to the problem of regulatory connection. Yet, this is surely one of the distinctive challenges presented to regulators by rapidly developing modern technologies; and there is no reason to think that, in this respect, information technology is atypical or exempt. In fact, it was in the context of the development of the internet that John Perry Barlow declared, in the most graphic of terms, that the problem of regulatory disconnection is both acute and chronic:

> Law adapts by continuous increments and at a pace second only to geology in its stateliness. Technology advances in ... lunging jerks, like the punctuation of biological evolution grotesquely accelerated. Real world conditions will continue to change at a blinding pace, and the law will get further behind, more profoundly confused. This mismatch is permanent.[1]

If Barlow is correct, if the mismatch is permanent, this gives rise to a regulatory crisis because regulatees simply will not know where they stand. This violates one of the fundamental principles of the Rule of Law, namely, that regulators should make it clear to regulatees what the regulatory position is.[2] Faced with such uncertainty, how are regulatees to interpret the regulatory void? Should they assume that their desired acts are permitted or, in the absence of clear authorization, should they treat their acts as prohibited?

Where there is such a mismatch, where the law is no longer fully connected to the technology, judicial interpreters, too, face a choice: either, they can interpret and apply the law as declared on the face of the legislation; or, they can seek to reconnect the law to the technology by adopting a creative approach. Neither choice is unproblematic. If interpreters take the former approach, recognizing that the law no longer covers the technology, this satisfies a straightforward reading of

[1] John Perry Barlow, 'The Economy of Ideas: Selling Wine Without Bottles on the Global Net' available at <http://www.eff.org/~barlow/EconomyOfIdeas.html>, and extracted in Yee Fen Lim *Cyberspace Law* (Oxford: Oxford University Press, 2002) 398, at 402.

[2] Seminally, see Lon Fuller *The Morality of Law* (New Haven: Yale University Press, 1969); and Judith N Shklar *Legalism* (Cambridge, Mass: Harvard University Press, 1964).

the Rule of Law principle of congruence[3] but it leaves a regulatory void until the legislature is able to take steps to repair and reconnect the law. However, if interpreters take the latter (creative) approach, not only might the repair be a temporary one (postponing the time when the regulation has to be properly fixed), the principle of congruence seems to be observed in the breach.

My discussion in this chapter is in two principal parts. In the first part, after making some general remarks about the problem of disconnection (and the process of re-connection), I introduce three key distinctions: one between 'descriptive' and 'normative' disconnection, a second between 'productive' and 'unproductive' disconnection, and a third between 'intelligent' and 'unintelligent' purposive re-connection. In the second part, I review the way in which the English courts have recently responded to disconnection—with particular reference to the rapidly developing technologies of cell nuclear replacement (CNR), pre-implantation genetic diagnosis (PGD), and pre-implantation tissue-typing (PTT)—by seeking to reconnect the regulatory framework (namely, the Human Fertilisation and Embryology Act 1990). Essentially, the difficulty is twofold: first, embryology has moved on rapidly since the regulatory scheme was put in place;[4] and, secondly, the mismatch between the law and the technology presents an opening for legal challenge to be taken up by those who (for dignitarian reasons) are ethically opposed to the use of human embryos for research.[5] My basic point is that, where interpreters face a case that is not straightforwardly one of unproductive descriptive disconnection, there is a danger that reconnnection effected through purposive interpretation might not only fall foul of the principle of congruence but also hinder the need for a reconsideration of the law.

II Disconnection

In this part of the chapter, I start by making some general remarks about the pervasive problem of disconnection and then I introduce the three organizing distinctions to which I have already referred—that is, the distinctions between 'descriptive' and 'normative' disconnection, 'productive' and 'unproductive' disconnection, and 'intelligent' and 'unintelligent' purposive reconnection.

[3] That is, the principle that the administration of the law should be congruent with the rules as promulgated; see Lon Fuller *The Morality of Law* (New Haven: Yale University Press, 1969) especially at 209–10.

[4] See Department of Health *Review of the Human Fertilisation and Embryology Act* (Cm 6989, December 2006) para 2.10.

[5] See, eg, Roger Brownsword 'Bioethics Today, Bioethics Tomorrow: Stem Cell Research and the "Dignitarian Alliance"' (2003) 17 Notre Dame Journal of Law, Ethics and Public Policy 15; and 'Stem Cells and Cloning: Where the Regulatory Consensus Fails' (2005) 39 New England Law Review 535.

(i) The nature of the problem

Whether one looks at the regulation of information technology or the regulation of biotechnology[6]—or, for that matter, at the future regulation of nanotechnology[7] or the new brain sciences[8]—there seems to be ample support for Barlow's thesis. Indeed, it is arguable that the pace of technological development, already too fast for the law, is accelerating. Whilst this is not an easy matter to measure,[9] there are at least two respects in which modern information technology, in addition to being significant in its own right, plays a key enabling role relative to other technologies—facilitating basic research in biotechnology (spectacularly so in the case of sequencing the human genome) as well as the commercial exploitation of the products of other technologies. As I suggested in Chapter 1, whether or not this amounts to a further technological 'revolution' is hardly worth arguing about. If the wheels of technology are spinning faster, this suggests that Barlow's prognosis is correct—legal provisions will lag further and further behind the technology in question.

Technology is capable of leaving the law behind at any phase of the regulatory cycle—before regulators have anything resembling an agreed position, before the terms of the regulation are finalized, and once the regulatory scheme is in place. For example, a new technology might emerge very quickly, catching regulators (at any rate, national legislators) cold; or it might be that a controversial new technology (nanotechnology perhaps being a case in point) develops and circulates long before regulators are able to agree upon the terms of their regulatory intervention. While regulators are getting up to speed, or pondering their options and settling their differences, the technology moves ahead, operating in what for the time being at least amounts to a regulatory void.[10] Sometimes a new and unanticipated technological development can appear to disrupt the negotiation of a more general regulatory instrument. In Europe, this happened when the rapid development of the internet overtook the drafting of the Directive on Distance Contracts;[11] and it happened again when the drafting of the Directive on the Legal

[6] Compare Robert G Lee and Derek Morgan 'Regulating Risk Society: Stigmata Cases, Scientific Citizenship and Biomedical Diplomacy' (2001) 23 Sydney Law Review 297 at 305:

> Increasingly, developments will be funded, findings unveiled, possibilities mooted, results replicated and then (and only then) regulatory responses sought. Previous structures of cooperative and corporatist workings may fall under the competitive pressures of a global market. Regulation within domestic markets will become more problematic as providers of services can engage in regulatory arbitrage and operate from their chosen base in an increasingly global market.

[7] See Glenn Harlan Reynolds 'Nanotechnology and Regulatory Policy: Three Futures' (2003) 17 Harvard Journal of Law and Technology 179.

[8] See, eg, Dai Rees and Steven Rose (eds) *The New Brain Sciences: Perils and Prospects* (Cambridge: Cambridge University Press, 2004). For the state of the neuro art, see David Nutt, Trevor W Robbins, Gerald W Stimson, Martin Ince, and Andrew Jackson (eds) *Drugs and the Future* (London: Academic Press, 2007).

[9] Compare the thoughtful remarks in Monroe E Price 'The Newness of New Technology' (2001) 22 Cardozo Law Review 1885.

[10] Cloning is perhaps a case in point: see Richard A Merrill and Bryan J Rose 'FDA Regulation of Human Cloning: Usurpation or Statesmanship?' (2001) 15 Harvard Journal of Law and Technology 85.

[11] Directive 97/7/EC [1997] OJ L144.

Protection of Biotechnological Inventions[12] was overtaken (and all but extinguished) by developments concerning the identification and isolation of human gene sequences.

Even (or especially) when regulatory frameworks have been put in place, they enjoy no immunity against technological change. Consider, for example, the legislation that is central to the discussion in this chapter, namely, the Human Fertilisation and Embryology Act 1990. As already indicated, this regulatory framework has been overtaken by developments in embryology (in particular, the ability to carry out genetic engineering in eggs which are then stimulated without fertilization rather than in embryos).[13] Similarly, modern information technology has outstripped a straightforward reading of legislation such as the Protection of Children Act 1978[14] and the Video Recordings Act 1984;[15] and, in another island community, that of Hawaii, the local peeping-tom laws were found wanting when 'Tyler Takehara, a voyeur who shot video up the skirts of unsuspecting women at [a shopping mall] in Honolulu . . . managed to escape conviction because of a legal loophole—at the time, Hawai'i law prohibited only the installation of tiny cameras in private places, such as bathrooms'.[16] Famously, the mismatch created by rapidly developing information technology (specifically that between European data protection law[17] and computing) has been vividly highlighted by Peter Swire and Robert Litan:[18]

In both the United States and Europe, debates are being driven by fears that computers pose a threat to privacy. That is, computers are *the key reason* for data protection rules. But

[12] Directive 98/44/EC.

[13] See, eg, House of Commons Science and Technology Committee *Human Reproductive Technologies and the Law* (Fifth Report of Session 200–405) vol 1 (London: Stationery Office, 2005) ch 4. Early in the report, the committee recalls that, some three years earlier, it had 'concluded that it was necessary to "reconnect the Act with modern science"' (ibid para 2).

[14] Under the Act, it is an offence, inter alia, to take, distribute, or show indecent 'photographs' of children, or to possess such 'photographs' with a view to their being distributed or shown by oneself or others. But, what is a 'photograph'? Does it, for example, include indecent images (scanned from conventional photographs) that are stored on a computer hard disc, and that are available via the internet to be shown on a monitor screen but that are never actually printed out (see *R v Fellows and Arnold* [1997] 2 All ER 548); or images recorded directly onto a disc by a digital camera before being transferred to a computer and viewed on screen? For discussion, see Lilian Edwards 'Pornography and the Internet' in Lilian Edwards and Charlotte Waelde (eds) *Law and the Internet* (2nd edn, Oxford: Hart, 2000) 275, at 283 et seq; and Ian J Lloyd *Information Technology Law* (3rd edn, London: Butterworths, 2000) 276–9.

[15] This Act targets so-called 'video nasties'. In *Meechie v Multi-Media Marketing* 94 LGR 474, there was a question whether a video product, front-ended by a game successful completion of which prompted the display of a series of erotic images, fell within the terms of the legislation. In particular, was this product (with its series of images) a 'video work' as defined by section 1 of the Act (where 'a moving picture' was contemplated); and was the product a video game so as to come within the exempting provisions of section 2? See Ian J Lloyd *Information Technology Law* (3rd edn, London: Butterworths, 2000) 279–81.

[16] Aimee Jodoi Lum 'Don't Smile, Your Image has just been Recorded on a Camera-Phone: The Need for Privacy in the Public Sphere' (2005) 27 University of Hawaii Law Review 377, at 398. Even the Takehara case does not reflect state-of-the-art video voyeurism: Lum highlights the use of camera-enabled mobile phones, coupled with posting of the shots on the internet.

[17] As in the Directive on Data Protection, Directive 95/46/EC, [1995] OJ L281/31.

[18] On the latter, see the seminal analysis in Peter P Swire and Robert E Litan *None of Your Business: World Data Flows, Electronic Commerce and the European Privacy Directive* (Washington DC: Brookings Institution Press, 1998).

changing computer technology also makes the Directive's rules seem badly matched to the reality of information flows.

The Directive's approach is designed for the regulation of mainframe computers in which one expects a relatively small number of hierarchical systems. Information technology, however, has shifted radically to new configurations such as client-server systems and the Internet. Today there is a much larger number of systems organized into distributed networks rather than simple hierarchies. The data protection regime designed for mainframes performs much less well when applied to the many and the distributed.

The language of the Directive evokes its mainframe, top-down assumptions. Consider the terms 'controller' and 'data subject.' A controller is at the top of the hierarchy, the person in command of a unified computer system. One expects a 'controller' to have many minions, who carry out commands. A data subject is clearly much less powerful—acted upon and subject to manipulation by one who controls.

This language is far less apt in a world of personal computers and the Internet. The entity running a Web site is often an individual or a small company—hardly worthy of the term 'controller'. The persons browsing may be equipped with a large variety of tools for protecting their privacy. For instance, they might be able to browse anonymously, use software to disable a site's 'cookies', or submit false information on any forms that the site employs. Such people are no longer passive and powerless. They instead may be more sophisticated than the operators of the Web site and will often be employed by major corporations.[19]

As the authors go on to suggest, data protection regimes are designed for large visible 'elephants' rather than highly mobile 'mice' that scurry hither and thither.[20] And, so it is more generally: the regulatory jungle is a shifting scene, what we see today might be gone by tomorrow, constantly challenging the accuracy and focus of the regulatory gaze.[21]

[19] ibid 50–1.

[20] ibid 200 et seq. Europe sought to catch up with the 'mice' by enacting Directive 2002/58/EC (the Directive on privacy and electronic communications). But, even then, the world of technology does not stand still. See, eg, the discussion in Daniel B Garrie and Rebecca Wong 'Regulating Voice Over Internet Protocol: An EU/US Comparative Approach' (2007) 22 American University International Law Review 549, at 580, where it is concluded that 'as technology is evolving with respect to VoIP and oral Internet communications [the regulatory position] is becoming progressively greyer . . . '.

[21] Compare Kirstie Ball, David Lyon, David Murakami Wood, Clive Norris, and Charles Raab *A Report on the Surveillance Society* (September 2006), para 44.9:

Neither the data protection principles nor the fragmented condition of regulatory machinery and instruments seem fully capable of meeting challenges that are likely to be posed in the future from public, private and combined sources. The advent of many new information and communication technologies . . . , including the Internet and mobile telematics, and the coming environment of AmI and ubiquitous computing that integrates many and varied surveillance devices, puts a question-mark over the efficacy of regulatory concepts and instruments that originated to handle issues in the age of the mainframe computer, *or even of the laptop, the mobile telephone, and the Internet.* (emphasis added)

For a similar point, concerning current data protection regulation and upcoming profiling data sets, see Mireille Hildebrandt 'A Vision of Ambient Law' in Roger Brownsword and Karen Yeung (eds) *Regulating Technologies* (Oxford: Hart, 2008).

If we are concerned only about congruence, then we might accept that regulators will constantly have to play catch-up with modern technologies and that it is the role of interpreters to identify cases of disconnection before remitting them to the regulators for repair. However, if we aspire towards a smarter style of regulation, then catch-up might not appeal as the optimal way of dealing with the mismatch between the regulation-in-the-books and the latest technology in action. It will seem trite that strategies should be adopted or developed that improve the chances of the regulation staying connected. Alas, it is far from clear how this is best achieved. How is regulatory connection to be maintained? The obvious move is to rely on regulatory responses that are geared for flexibility and adaptability—for example, on 'technology neutral' drafting, on 'soft' law, on open-ended standards,[22] on purposive interpretation, and the like.[23] The obvious drawback, though, is that the less hard-wired the law, the less calculable and consistent it will tend to be; and, particularly in relation to criminal process and the criminal law, there are important due process considerations militating against an over-broad casting of police powers[24] and the application of penalties without fair warning.[25] How are we to strike the right balance between calculability and flexibility?

In the final chapter of the book, I will return to the question of the trade-offs that are implicated in addressing the challenge of regulatory connection. However, in the present chapter, after I have elaborated three key distinctions, my focus is simply on purposive interpretation as a response to the problem of disconnection.

(ii) Three key distinctions

In an attempt to tighten our grip on both understanding and responding to the problem of disconnection, I suggest that we should be guided by the following

[22] Compare Mike Feintuck *Media Regulation, Public Interest and the Law* (Edinburgh: Edinburgh University Press, 1999) at 201 (proposing a flexible discretion for media regulators guided by the overriding objective of supporting 'the maintenance of availability to all of a wide and high-quality range of media products (as a pre-requisite of citizenship)'). In the context of this chapter, Feintuck's coupling of flexibility with an overarching citizenship approach is particularly appropriate.

[23] Compare Christopher Slobogin 'Technologically-Assisted Physical Surveillance: The American Bar Association's Tentative Draft Standards' (1997) 10 Harvard Journal of Law and Technology 383, at 425 (for the view that the pace of technological development renders regulation obsolete) and 426 (for the, predictable, response that guidelines have a better chance than rules of staying connected).

[24] Compare *Olmstead v US* (1928) 277 US 438 (especially Justice Holmes's dissent). For discussion in the context of the problem of connection, see Lawrence Lessig *Code and Other Laws of Cyberspace* (New York: Basic Books, 1999) ch 9.

[25] Seminally, see *McBoyle v US* (1930) US 25, at 27 (Justice Holmes). For a nice illustration of the difficulties of forcing a square peg (the facts associated with the new technology) into a round hole (existing criminal law offences), see Alisdair A Gillespie 'Child Protection on the Internet – Challenges for Criminal Law' (2002) 14 CFLQ 411; the particular problem of the 'grooming' of children was addressed by s 15 of the Sexual Offences Act 2003.

three sets of distinctions. The first (descriptive and normative disconnection) relates to the type or nature of disconnection, the second (productive and unproductive disconnection) to whether disconnection is functional, and the third (intelligent and unintelligent purposive re-connection) to how interpreters might respond to cases of disconnection.

(a) 'Descriptive' and 'normative' disconnection

Disconnection will often arise from a lack of correspondence or fit; but it might also arise from a disturbance to the regulatory compact. In the former case, 'descriptive disconnection' as I will term it, the problem is that the covering descriptions employed by the regulation no longer correspond to the technology or to the various technology-related practices that are intended targets for the regulation. In the latter case, 'normative disconnection' as I will term it, the problem is that the technology and its applications raise doubts as to the value compact that underlies the regulatory scheme—for example, because a known technology is now being applied for a different and questionable purpose or because a new technology raises questions of principle or policy that are not clearly settled by the regulatory scheme. In the former case, it is as though we compare a snapshot that the regulators took of a technology and related practices as they once were with the way that the successor technologies and practices now are; the mismatch is one of descriptive fit. In the latter case, it as though we compare the values that once informed the regulators' judgment with the values and their application that now seem to be relevant; the mismatch is one of moral fit. In both cases, the credibility of the regulatory framework is compromised and remedial steps (but not necessarily by way of interpretive reconnection) are required.

(b) 'Productive' and 'unproductive' disconnection

One technique for maintaining connection is to interpret the relevant regulation in a purposive way, treating the guiding spirit and intent of the legislation as more important than its letter.[26] Where regulation is drafted in technology neutral terms (for example, 'any means of transport', 'any means of communication', 'any means of human reproduction', or the like), a literal interpretation will keep the law connected to the technology. However, where the drafting is more technology-specific, and where current technology has outrun its covering regulatory framework, a literal interpretation will inevitably lead to the conclusion that the law and the technology are no longer connected.

Where disconnection is declared, it might be viewed as unproductive or productive. By 'unproductive disconnection', I mean that, where the new technology

[26] Another technique is to facilitate dynamic development in the common law by employing general duties. See, eg, Roger Brownsword, 'An Interest in Human Dignity as the Basis for Genomic Torts' (2003) 42 Washburn Law Journal 413. See, too, Lum (n 16 above).

is clearly within the spirit and intent of the regulatory framework (whether that intent is to prohibit or to permit the technology—although usually the latter), it is an unproductive use of regulatory resource to have to translate the unproblematic regulatory intent into the regulatory letter (for the avoidance of doubt).[27] This clearly breaches the ideal of regulatory economy. By contrast, 'productive disconnection' presupposes that there is a genuine question about whether (and, if so, where) the new technology falls within the spirit and intent of the regulatory scheme. On this view, it is entirely appropriate that regulatory resource should be committed to further debate and decision concerning the new technology. Where interpreters take a flexible purposive approach, this is surely an intelligent response to what would otherwise be unproductive disconnection. However, a similar approach in the face of productive disconnection is less compelling; for, here, purposive interpretation papers over a problem that really needs to be addressed by regulators.

(c) 'Intelligent' and 'unintelligent' purposive re-connection

It is implicit in the first two sets of distinctions that an intelligent interpretive response will presuppose a correct analysis of the kind of disconnection at issue. Interpreters need to be sensitive to both the descriptive and the normative types of disconnection and, concomitantly, the distinction between productive and unproductive disconnection. Accordingly, where a case of descriptive disconnection shows up, interpreters should not ignore it; but, neither should they rush in a reconnecting cure without considering whether this is an opportunity for productive disconnection and, in particular, whether this is the occasion for taking time out to reassess the regulatory compact. Where descriptive disconnection is a signal for normative disconnection, interpreters do us no favours if they cover over the latter for the sake of restoring descriptive connection.

Putting this in terms of intelligent and unintelligent purposive reconnection, interpreters do the intelligent thing if they employ a purposive approach to reconnect in the case of unproductive descriptive disconnection; but they do not act intelligently if they take a purposive approach to reconnect when, in fact, the disconnection (whether descriptive or normative) is productive and invites more general debate.

If we value congruence (as an aspect of the Rule of Law), then there is no reason to exclude intelligent purposivism. Far from it. Even Lon Fuller would endorse smart reconnection; for his idea of fidelity to the law, albeit not confronted by technological developments of the kind being broached in the current century, certainly encompassed such forms of interpretive intelligence.[28]

[27] Compare *Grant v Southwestern and County Properties Ltd* [1975] ch 185, where Walton J concluded that a tape recording was a 'document' within the meaning of the Rules of the Supreme Court because a tape recording, like a document, furnished information.

[28] Lon L Fuller, 'Positivism and Fidelity to Law – A Reply to Professor Hart (1957–58) 71 Harvard Law Review 630.

III From Disconnection to Re-connection

Having sketched the general nature of the problem and put in place some analytical tools, we can turn to two test cases in the recent English jurisprudence—the *Pro-Life Alliance* case[29] and *Comment on Reproductive Ethics*[30] (the CORE case, also referred to as *Quintavalle*).

The pattern of each of these cases is broadly similar. Embryology and its associated techniques have moved on since 1990 when the framework legislation, the Human Fertilisation and Embryology Act, was enacted. In the former case, the new development was the dramatic breakthrough made with cell nuclear replacement (CNR) and, in the latter, it was the development of pre-implantation diagnostic (PGD) techniques coupled with procedures for pre-implantation tissue-typing (PTT). In both cases, the legislative language, quite understandably, does not readily cover these developments. In the former case, this is because the Act appears to define an embryo in a way that assumes that it is the product of a process of fertilization;[31] and, in the latter, it is because the Act, insofar as it permits embryos to be screened, seems to do so on the basis that this will facilitate a successful pregnancy rather than eliminating embryos that carry a genetic marker for a particular disorder let alone identifying an embryo that will be a tissue-match for an identified individual.

In both cases, the High Court took a fairly literal approach to the Act (thus holding that the Act was now disconnected from the technology) only to be reversed by the Court of Appeal; and, in both cases, the House of Lords unanimously affirmed the decisions made by the Court of Appeal. However, the effect of treating the Act as disconnected was not identical in the two cases. In the *Pro-Life Alliance* case, if CNR embryos fell outwith the jurisdiction of the regulatory authority, and if they were not otherwise covered by the Act, then the residual regulatory position seemed to be that research on CNR embryos (including reproductive cloning) was unconditionally permitted. In the CORE case, if PGD and PTT fell within the jurisdiction of the regulatory authority but outwith its licensing powers, then such procedures were not permitted. If the result of disconnection in the former case was to generate a moral panic and a rush to prohibition (lest the UK should become a haven for aspiring human reproductive cloners),[32] in the latter it was to generate pressure to permit these newly developed techniques to be applied (lest the life of a young boy should be lost).

[29] *R v Secretary of State for Health ex parte Quintavalle (on behalf of Pro-Life Alliance)* [2001] EWHC 918 (Admin) (Crane J), [2002] EWCA Civ 29, [2003] UKHL 13.

[30] *R (Quintavalle on behalf of Comment on Reproductive Ethics) v Human Fertilisation and Embryology Authority* [2002] EWHC 2785 (Admin), [2003] EWCA 667, [2005] UKHL 28.

[31] Human Fertilisation and Embryology Act 1990, s 1(1).

[32] See the Human Reproductive Cloning Act 2001. The Bill was introduced just six days after the High Court decision and it became law about two weeks later.

We can deal with these cases and the issues to which they give rise in the following four stages: (i) responding to descriptive disconnection (in the *Pro-Life Alliance* case); (ii) purposive interpretation as practised in the two cases; (iii) responding to (arguable) normative disconnection (in the CORE case); and (iv) the requirements of intelligent purposivism.

(i) Responding to descriptive disconnection

When the Human Fertilisation and Embryology Act was enacted, the science as it stood encouraged Parliamentarians to make two relevant assumptions. One assumption was that a human embryo would necessarily be the product of a process of fertilization (of a human egg by human sperm); and the second was that, if there was to be cell nuclear replacement for the purposes of cloning, then it would involve manipulation of an *embryo* (rather than replacement of the nucleus of an *egg*).[33] In line with the first of these assumptions, section 1(1) of the Act provides:

'In this Act, except where otherwise stated—

(a) embryo means a live human embryo where fertilisation is complete, and

(b) references to an embryo include an egg in the process of fertilisation, and, for this purpose, fertilisation is not complete until the appearance of a two cell zygote.'

In line with the second assumption, section 3(3)(d) of the Act provides that no licence may authorize 'replacing a nucleus of a cell of an embryo with a nucleus taken from a cell of any person, embryo or subsequent development of an embryo'.

However, as embryologists developed processes for engineering eggs and then stimulating eggs to divide and develop into embryonic clusters, two nice questions of legal interpretation arose. One question was whether the 1990 Act applied to such embryonic clusters (to what were the functional equivalents of embryos produced by fertilisation); and the other was how the prohibition in section 3(3)(d) related to such developments. In the *Pro-Life Alliance* case, these two questions were put to the test.

At first instance, Crane J, taking a literal approach, held that the Act applied only to human embryos produced by a process involving fertilization. However, the Court of Appeal and the House of Lords, taking a more purposive approach, arrived at the different view that such embryos, albeit not produced by fertilization but by CNR and stimulation, fell within the terms of section 1(1). Moreover, it was also the view of the Court of Appeal and the House of Lords that the prohibition against CNR in an embryo, as provided for by section 3(3)(d), did not cover CNR in an egg. This led to the convenient conclusion that the Act did not leave a worrying loophole in relation to human reproductive cloning—although,

[33] According to Department of Health *Review of the Human Fertilisation and Embryology Act* (Cm 6989, December 2006) 2.77, the aim of the restriction was 'to prevent the possibility of *reproductive* cloning'.

ironically, by the time that the appeal courts had finally confirmed this, Parliament had rushed through legislation to create a new criminal offence to cover the maverick cloners.[34]

To deal, first, with the interpretation of section 1(1): in order to achieve a semblance of congruence, the appeal courts effectively read into the definition section the additional phrase '[if it is produced by fertilization]'. With the benefit of this addition, section 1(1)(a) defined an embryo in terms of 'a live human embryo where [if it is produced by fertilization] fertilisation is complete'. So transformed, section 1(1) simply specified what counted as an embryo for the purposes of the Act where the embryo in question happened to be the product of fertilization. However, this was no longer an exhaustive definition; for section 1(1) did not presume to exclude the possibility that an embryo might be produced by some process other than fertilization—indeed, by just such a process as that of CNR and stimulation that became headline news almost a decade after section 1(1) was drafted. Clearly, such a creative reading of the section is driven by considerations other than the ordinary meaning of the text and the deeper question is whether it is backed by intelligent purposivism.

Delivering the leading judgment, Lord Bingham asserts that the references to fertilization in section 1(1) cannot have been intended to signal a material distinction between 'live human embryos produced by fertilisation of a female egg and live human embryos produced without such fertilisation'; for, 'Parliament was unaware that the latter alternative was physically possible'.[35] Rather, continues Lord Bingham:

> [t]he crucial point... is that this was an Act passed for the protection of live human embryos created outside the human body. The essential thrust of section 1(1)(a) was directed to such embryos, not the manner of their creation, which Parliament (entirely understandably on the then current state of scientific knowledge) took for granted.[36]

Let us suppose that this is a plausible reconstruction of the regulatory intentions of Parliament—that is to say, let us suppose that it is plausible to treat Parliament as intending to regulate live human embryos, whether such embryos were produced by fertilisation or by some other technique, not yet contemplated and, necessarily, yet to be developed. We might even go as far as Lord Millett and say that any other reading would 'not only defeat the evident purpose of Parliament... but would produce an incoherent and irrational regulatory code'.[37] And, more generally, we might agree that, while such an irrational code 'could be the inevitable result of legislation enacted at the time of rapid technological development, a construction which leads to this result should not be adopted where it can be avoided'.[38]

[34] The Human Reproductive Cloning Act 2001.

[35] *R v Secretary of State for Health ex parte Quintavalle (on behalf of Pro-Life Alliance)* [2003] UKHL 13, para 14.

[36] ibid.

[37] Para 49. [38] ibid.

Fine. But, now, what would such an approach suggest about the application of section 3(3)(d)? Clearly, it implies that no licence may authorize cell nuclear replacement in a human embryo, whether that embryo is produced by sperm-fertilization of an egg or by a technique other than fertilization (such as CNR). The question dramatically raised by the *Pro-Life Alliance* case, however is whether a licence may authorize cell nuclear replacement in a human egg when, as we have just inferred, no licence may authorize cell nuclear replacement in a human embryo that itself has been developed by CNR techniques. If Parliamentarians in 1990 saw fit to prohibit cloning at the embryonic stage, would they not also intend to prohibit cloning at the earlier egg stage? Copying across Lord Bingham's language as applied to section 1(1), we would say that the essential thrust of section 3(3)(d) was directed to cloning, not the particular technique of cloning, which Parliament (entirely understandably on the then current state of scientific knowledge) took for granted as involving *embryonic* manipulation. Yet, quite to the contrary, Lord Bingham reads section 3(3)(d) as having a very restricted ambit, literally to cell nuclear replacement in the human embryo and to nothing else.[39]

The conjunction of the broad approach to section 1(1) with the narrow approach to section 3(3)(d) is highlighted by one of Lord Steyn's remarks on the latter point. Referring back to the similar approach taken by the Court of Appeal, Lord Steyn says:

> The Master of the Rolls observed that he could see no basis for arguing that an unfertilised egg, prior to the insertion of the nucleus by the cell nuclear replacement process, is required to be treated under the Act as if it is an embryo: para 51. I agree.[40]

However, this only serves to highlight the layering of the interpretive tensions. On a literal reading of the provisions, a CNR embryo is not an embryo produced by fertilization (so section 1(1) decrees that the Act has no application to CNR embryos); and an egg is not an embryo (so the prohibition in section 3(3)(d) does not apply to CNR manipulation of an egg). The first tension is that it is wholly unclear why the appeal courts adopt the latter literalism but not the former. Why say (literally) that an egg is not an embryo (for the purposes of section 3(3)(d)) but (non-literally) that a stimulated CNR egg can count as an embryo (for the purposes of section 1(1))? A second tension crystallizes when we consider how the failure to anticipate developments in embryology impacts on the interpretation. In the one case, Parliamentarians are excused from not anticipating such developments; in the other case they are not. In the one case, the gist of what Parliament intended to cover is relied on; in the other case (the intention to ban cloning), it is not even allowed to make an entry.

One more point needs to be made. As we have said, by the time that the appeal courts heard the appeal, Parliament had already responded to a possible loophole in the legislation by prohibiting reproductive human cloning. How far we can assume continuity between the intentions of the legislators in 1990 and 2001 is

[39] Para 18. [40] Para 28.

moot. However, it is certainly arguable that the legislators of 1990 intended to prohibit any activities that resembled what we now take to be human reproductive cloning.[41] If so, the fine-grained question under section 3(3)(d) was whether the Act, by implication, prohibited both reproductive and therapeutic human cloning. To respond that an egg is not an embryo hardly does justice to the issue. Of course, Lord Bingham is right in recognizing 'the difficulty of legislating against a background of fast-moving medical and scientific development',[42] and he might have gone on to note the difficulties that are created for the courts when 'Parliament has to frame legislation apt to apply to developments at the advanced cutting edge of science'.[43] Even so, we might wonder whether the courts might rise more convincingly to the challenge of regulatory connection than we find in the *Pro-Life Alliance* appeals.

(ii) Purposivism in the courts

In both the *Pro-Life Alliance* and the CORE appeals, it is Lord Wilberforce's speech in *Royal College of Nursing of the United Kingdom v Department of Health and Social Security*[44] that is taken as seminal. According to his Lordship:

> In interpreting an Act of Parliament, it is proper, and indeed necessary, to have regard to the state of affairs existing, and known by Parliament to be existing, at the time. It is a fair presumption that Parliament's policy or intention is directed to that state of affairs.... [W]hen a new state of affairs, or a fresh set of facts bearing on policy, comes into existence, the courts have to consider whether they fall within the Parliamentary intention. They may be held to do so, if they fall within the same genus of facts as those to which the expressed policy has been formulated... [or] if there can be detected a clear purpose in the legislation which can only be fulfilled if the extension is made. How liberally these principles may be applied must depend upon the nature of the enactment, and the strictness or otherwise of the words in which it has been expressed. The courts should be less willing to extend expressed meanings if it is clear that the Act in question was designed to be restrictive or circumscribed in its operation rather than liberal or permissive. They will be much less willing to do so where the subject matter is different in kind or dimension from that for which the legislation was passed.[45]

Lord Wilberforce continued by emphasizing that what judges categorically must not do is to gap-fill and second-guess Parliament's intention. But, of course, what constitutes gap-filling and second-guessing largely hinges on whether the present case can be subsumed under the same genus or the covering policy,

[41] See Department of Health *Review of the Human Fertilisation and Embryology Act* (Cm 6989, December 2006) para 2.77.
[42] [2003] UKHL 13, para 12.
[43] ibid.
[44] [1981] AC 800.
[45] ibid 822.

which in turn depends on whether the court judges that a liberal or restrictive approach is called for.

Whether or not a liberal or a restrictive approach is deemed appropriate depends largely on how the courts read the regulatory tilt.[46] By this, I mean the tilt of the interpretive default position where regulation is silent or unclear on a particular point. Whereas a liberal tilt assumes that permission is the default position, a restrictive tilt assumes that prohibition is the default position. Whereas a liberal regulatory tilt interprets silence as an indication of an intention to permit rather than to prohibit, a restrictive regulatory tilt interprets silence as an indication of an intention to prohibit rather than to permit. And, whereas a liberal regulatory tilt resolves ambiguity, or the like, in favour of permission, a restrictive regulatory tilt resolves it in favour of prohibition. The reasons that prompt particular courts to adopt one or other of these default positions merits further examination; but, for the purposes of this chapter it suffices to remark that, in our specimen cases, it is the lower courts that adopt a restrictive regulatory tilt and the appeal courts that adopt a more liberal default position.

In both cases, without saying so explicitly, the higher courts distil from Lord Wilberforce's guidance the eminently plausible principle that cases involving like technology (like techniques or like products) should be treated alike (and unlike cases differently). In the *Pro-Life Alliance* case, the functional equivalence between an embryo produced by fertilization and one produced by CNR, persuades the appeal courts that, if research on the former may be licensed, then the same must be so with the latter. As Lord Steyn argued, if there is no good reason 'why an embryo produced otherwise than by fertilisation should not have the same status as an embryo created by fertilisation ... [this is] a classic case where the new scientific development [falls] within what Lord Wilberforce called "the same genus of facts"'.[47] In the CORE case, the Court of Appeal reasons in a parallel way. According to the Court, if the regulatory authority could license a PGD biopsy on an eight-cell embryo to screen for a serious disease then why should it not also license a tissue-match test on the biopsied material? In other words, if there is no good reason for distinguishing between one biopsy on an embryo and another, then as Mance LJ put it, the cases fall 'within the same genus (even if not the same species) of facts as those to which the expressed statutory policy has been formulated'.[48]

It is trite, of course, that the principle of treating like cases alike lacks a sense of direction until we specify a criterion of likeness. For courts committed to a purposive style of interpretation, it is striking that the favoured criterion of technological comparability is not more heavily qualified by a consideration of the purposes to which the technology is to be applied. Moreover, it should not

[46] See ch 1.

[47] [2003] UKHL 13, para 26.

[48] *R (Quintavalle on behalf of Comment on Reproductive Ethics) v Human Fertilisation and Embryology Authority* [2003] EWCA 667, para 144.

be supposed that 'technology-neutral' drafting is comparable to purpose-neutral interpretation. Let us suppose that, instead of the questions raised, the issue had focused on whether the first steps towards human reproductive cloning were to be treated in the same permissive way as the first steps towards therapeutic cloning. Do we seriously imagine that a court would hold that these are like cases because the technology involved is similar (in fact, identical)? I think not—and the reason for distinguishing between the two technological processes is that they are directed at very different purposes. However, if the purpose to which a technology is directed is relevant in the case of cloning, it must be relevant too in the case of other biotechnologies. Viewed in this way, how convincing are the claims made in the *Pro-Life Alliance* and CORE appeals that the technologies are within the same genus?

Once we focus on the purpose behind the technology, we can detect an important difference between an embryo produced by fertilization and one produced by CNR and stimulation. Broadly speaking, whilst in the former case the embryo is created for reproductive purposes (for the purpose of assisting a woman to have a child), in the latter case the embryo is created for the purposes of research and medical treatment. Granted, many supernumerary fertilized embryos are used for research and a handful of fertilized embryos are created specifically for research. However, in both cases, the background context is dominated by reproductive purposes. With CNR embryos, the purpose and context is very different. This is not to say that the creation and use of CNR-embryos as research tools to develop therapies for some of the most serious killer diseases is not appropriate nor that such research purposes are not worthy. The point is a much more modest one. It is merely that a purpose-free comparison of one type of embryo with the other moves too quickly to the conclusion that these are like cases.[49]

(iii) Responding to (arguable) normative disconnection (in the CORE case)

The background to the CORE case, to *Quintavalle*,[50] can be stated shortly. In February 2002, the Human Fertilisation and Embryology Authority granted

[49] Subsequently, the government declared its intention to bring 'all human embryos outside the body, regardless of the manner of their creation, . . . within the scope of regulation' (that is to say, within the jurisdiction of the regulatory authority): see Department of Health *Review of the Human Fertilisation and Embryology Act* (Cm 6989, December 2006) para 2.11. In line with this declaration of intention, clause 14(2) of the draft Human Tissue and Embryos Bill 2007 defines an embryo broadly as 'a live human embryo' not including 'an inter-species embryo'. Having already isolated one kind of research tool (the inter-species embryo), the Bill (in clause 16(5)) then distinguishes between permitted and non-permitted embryos for reproductive purposes, fertilization of a permitted egg by permitted sperm being one of the defining conditions of a permitted embryo. Even though we might complain that, with at least three different types of embryo recognized in the Bill, this is more than transparency or clarity can take, it confirms that one type of embryo is not necessarily to be treated as like another.

[50] [2005] UKHL 28.

a licence that would permit both PGD and PTT in relation to Mr and Mrs Hashmi's embryos. The purpose of such dual screening was to identify an embryo that would be suitable for implantation, being free of the beta thalassaemia gene that runs in the family as well as being a tissue match with young Zain Hashmi who suffers from the disease. All being well, Mrs Hashmi would carry one such embryo through to term and the newly born child would be fit to serve as a (cord blood or bone marrow) donor for the benefit of Zain. However, the Hashmi's project was stopped in its tracks when legal proceedings were brought by Comment on Reproductive Ethics challenging the power of the authority to grant such a licence.

At first instance, Maurice Kay J ruled that the authority had acted beyond its licensing powers;[51] but his decision was reversed by a unanimous Court of Appeal[52] and the latter decision was confirmed by a unanimous House of Lords. With the legal position thus clarified, the way was clear for the Hashmis to continue with their attempts to create a so-called 'saviour sibling' for Zain. We can track this highly publicized case through both the Court of Appeal and the House of Lords.

Court of Appeal

If the reasoning in the *Pro-Life Alliance* case seems insensitive to the purpose to which the technology is put, it is even more conspicuously true of the Court of Appeal's reasoning in the CORE case. The focal question there was whether the dual screening required by the Hashmi family could be subsumed under the statutory provisions which empower the authority to license the checking of embryos. It was common ground that such a licence would be valid provided that (i) the activity is judged 'to be necessary or desirable for the purpose of providing treatment services'[53] (that is, services provided 'for the purpose of assisting women to carry children')[54] and (ii) the purpose of the checking is 'to secure that embryos are in a suitable condition to be placed in a woman or to determine whether embryos are suitable for that purpose'.[55]

The idea of the suitability of an embryo for its purpose could be taken in more than one way. At narrowest, such suitability refers to the embryo being free from serious congenital disease. Thus, relatively uncontroversially, Lord Phillips MR says, where 'the object of the treatment is to enable a woman to bear a child confident that it will not carry a hereditary defect, an embryo will only be suitable for

[51] *R (Quintavalle on behalf of Comment on Reproductive Ethics) v Human Fertilisation and Embryology Authority* [2002] EWHC 2785 (Admin).

[52] [2003] EWCA Civ 667 (Lord Phillips MR, Schiemann and Mance LJJ). On which, see Roger Brownsword 'Reproductive Opportunities and Regulatory Challenges' (2004) 67 Modern Law Review 304.

[53] Schedule 2, 1(3).

[54] Section 2(1).

[55] Schedule 2, 1(1)(d).

the purpose of being placed within her if it is free of that defect'.[56] However, if suitability is equated far more broadly (and contingently) with fitness for such purposes as the parents may specify, the specified purpose may be simply to have a healthy child, or to have a child of a certain sex, or to have a child enhanced in some way, or (as the Hashmis wanted) to have a child to act as a source of live-saving cord-blood or bone marrow for transplantation to another child. The biopsy procedure may be similar in many of these cases but the purposes of the screening vary significantly—and, as with cloning, it is inconceivable that a court would allow the licensing of 'designer babies' on the ground that the technology involved is comparable to technologies that are already permitted under licence. Yet, in the CORE case, neither Lord Phillips MR nor Schiemann LJ squarely addresses this matter.[57] It is left to Mance LJ to air the troubling question.

Having followed Lord Phillips in accepting that PGD falls within the ambit of the legislation, Mance LJ turns to the question of whether tissue-typing also falls within the legislative scheme as a matter for the discretion of the authority:

> [T]he present circumstances lie conceptually between the two poles of 'good medical reasons' for tests... and testing for 'purely social reasons'.... However they lie far closer in spirit in my view to the former pole than to the latter. There are here good reasons for screening any embryo, although they do not relate to any future child's health. The concerns to which the HFEA's decision and the licence for Mr and Mrs Hashmi are directed are anything but 'purely social', relating as they do to the health of a sibling and the well-being of the whole family.[58]

Yet, the question of whether the purpose is medical or social is not the end of the matter. Assuming that the purpose is medical, we should ask whether tissue-matching satisfies the standard test for a medical intervention. Is the intervention authorized by a relevant consent (actual or anticipated); or, if consent is not the appropriate requirement, is the intervention justified as advancing the best

[56] Note 52 above, para 44.

[57] Relative to his test of the confidence of the pregnant woman, Lord Phillips declares that the tissue-match is as important as the absence of the thalassaemia gene. He concludes (at para 50):

> IVF treatment can help women to bear children when they are unable to do so by the normal process of fertilisation. Screening of embryos before implantation enables a choice to be made as to the characteristics of the child to be born with the assistance of the treatment. Whether and for what purposes such a choice should be permitted raises difficult ethical questions. My conclusion is that Parliament has placed that choice in the hands of the HFEA.

For Schiemann LJ, any concern that approving the tissue-typing procedure would mean that 'licensing activities for the purpose of social selection is an unavoidable consequence' (para 98) was covered by leaving the decision to the HFEA. This would, at least, mean that parents would not have a right to demand such treatment. However, the Whitakers, whose tissue-typing application was turned down by the HFEA in summer 2002, circumvented the control by travelling to the USA for the test. For the subsequent birth of the Whitakers' donor child and its implication, see, eg, Sarah Boseley 'As Age of the Saviour Sibling Dawns, Pressure Mounts Inexorably to Change Embryo Rules' *The Guardian* 20 June 2003, p 3.

[58] ibid para 135.

interests of the relevant person? Plainly, these questions leave plenty of room for disagreement.

The House of Lords

The House of Lords starts in the right way, emphasizing that the question for the court is not whether it favours a conservative or a liberal approach to such questions as the use of PGD for sex selection or access to PGD and PTT for the production of saviour siblings. Rather, the question is whether the allocation of responsibility set up by the 1990 legislation envisaged that the authority should be empowered to deal with such matters or whether it put them off limits. In other words, it is to settling matters of institutional design rather than the merits of designer children, or the like, that the interpretive efforts of the House are largely directed.

With the general issue very clearly in focus, the House also has the gist of the challengers' claim clearly in focus. It is put very crisply by Lord Brown in the following terms:

> [T]he appellant's argument [is] that PGD screening is one thing, and properly licensable under the 1990 Act, tissue typing a completely different concept and impermissible. It is one thing to enable a woman to conceive and bear a child which will itself be free of genetic abnormality; quite another to bear a child specifically selected for the purpose of treating someone else. One can read into the statutory purpose..., that of 'assisting women to carry children', the notion of healthy children—only a genetically healthy embryo being 'suitable'.... To read into [that statutory purpose], however, the notion that the child will be a suitable future donor for the health of another would be to stretch the statutory language too far.[59]

Notwithstanding such clarity of focus in relation to both the general question and the challengers' contention, it is arguable that the House gets things badly out of focus when it seeks to interpret the said statutory language.

In argument before the House, the critical interpretive question becomes what one makes of Schedule 2, paragraph 1 of the 1990 Act when it provides that, in the course of providing treatment services (treatment services being equated, broadly speaking, with medical services that are designed to assist women to carry children),[60] the authority may license '(d) practices designed to secure that embryos are in a suitable condition to be placed in a woman or to determine whether embryos are suitable for that purpose'. This opaque drafting invites the following two questions:

(i) in what sense might reproductive service providers be checking to ensure that an embryo is 'in a suitable condition' for implantation; and

(ii) in what sense might reproductive service providers be checking to determine whether an embryo is, in the statutory language, 'suitable for that purpose'?

[59] [2005] UKHL 28, para 51.

[60] Section 2(1) of the HFE Act.

The answer to the first question is tolerably clear. Or, at any rate, it is not difficult to think of activities that fit the statutory description—for example, checking the condition of an embryo that, having been frozen and stored, is now unfrozen with a view to implantation. However, the answer to the second question is much less clear. Assuming that the activity is not concerned with checking the condition of the embryo, it seems that the check here is, as it were, for fitness for purpose rather than as to basic implantable quality. But, the fundamental question remains: relative to which or whose purposes is an embryo to be judged fit—or, to which or whose purpose does the phrase 'that purpose' refer?

In response to this question, both the Court of Appeal and the House of Lords took the relevant reference point to be that of the woman to whom treatment services are being supplied. In other words, it is *the particular reproductive purposes of the particular client woman* that are treated as the governing reference point.[61] On this view, the range of licensable activities covers checking the suitability of the embryo relative to the particular purposes (*whatever those purposes*) of the particular woman in question. How did the House account for this quite extraordinary reading of the legislation?

The central feature of Lord Hoffmann's leading speech (supported by Lord Brown) is to make and to reiterate the point that the word 'suitable' is an adjective that is context-sensitive, that it 'is an empty vessel which is filled with meaning by context and background'.[62] So, for instance, as Lord Scott apparently put it in argument, 'a suitable hat for Royal Ascot is different from a suitable hat for the Banbury cattle market'.[63] No doubt, this is the case. However, it is not the word 'suitable' that is the key to cracking the legislative code. Rather, the key is the phrase 'that purpose'. *If* 'that purpose' translates as 'whatever reproductive purpose the particular woman specifies' then suitability is indeed an empty vessel waiting to be filled by the particular context and background—namely, the particular context and background supplied by the particular reproductive purposes declared by the particular woman; and it might well be the case that the racing aristocracy at Ascot might have rather different criteria of suitability (both in relation to their hats and their offspring) from the country folk in Banbury let alone the Hashmis from Leeds. On the other hand, if 'that purpose' refers generically to assisting women to have children (or healthy children), the context and background for suitability is already set; and for the women of Ascot, Banbury, and Leeds alike, the criteria are the same. It follows that the judgment handed down by the House passes legal muster only if it convincingly explains why 'that purpose' is to be

[61] See [2005] UKHL 28, at para 49 where Lord Brown neatly summarizes the three interpretations. These are that embryonic screening is permitted: (i) solely in order to ensure that 'the woman can carry the child successfully to full term'; (ii) not only in order to ensure that the woman can carry the child successfully to full term, but also 'to eliminate gene and chromosome defects such as may affect that child'; or (iii) in order to provide 'information about the characteristics of the embryo which is relevant to the woman's decision whether or not to carry the child'.

[62] ibid para 33.

[63] ibid para 14.

read in the former (woman specific) way rather than the latter (generic) way. Effectively, three arguments are directed against the latter interpretation.

First, once it is conceded that the authority may license PGD not only to check the viability of an embryo (as Maurice Kay J held) but also to check its health prospects (as the challengers eventually conceded), it would be difficult to draw a line between those serious conditions for which PGD may be authorized and those less serious conditions that would fall beyond the authority's licensing remit. Echoing Lord Hoffmann's reservations,[64] Lord Brown says:

> The fact is that once the concession is made... that PGD itself is licensable to produce not just a viable foetus but a genetically healthy child, there can be no logical basis for construing the authority's power to end at this point. PGD with a view to producing a healthy child assists a woman to carry a child only in the sense that it helps her decide whether the embryo is 'suitable' and whether she will bear the child.[65]

But, to the contrary, once the concession is made, while there is a margin of interpretive doubt about the bounds of health (as in a healthy child), this does not entail that a generic reading of 'that purpose' must be abandoned. What this concession signifies is simply that the terms of the generic reading must be qualified so that the purpose in question is not simply to help women to have children but to do so in a way that avoids implanting an embryo that carries a serious disease. As Lord Brown said when rehearsing the gist of the challenge, '[i]t is one thing to enable a woman to conceive and bear a child which will itself be free of genetic abnormality; quite another to bear a child specifically selected for the purpose of treating someone else'.[66] And, similarly, it is one thing to modify the generic purpose as indicated and quite another to claim that this entails accepting that the governing purpose is supplied by whatever particular purpose the particular woman specifies.

Secondly, if the only purpose for which embryos may be screened is to avoid an implantation that cannot result in the birth of a genetically healthy child, then this would seem to mean that it would not be lawful for the authority to license PGD to check an embryo where a mix up of some sort is suspected. However, there is nothing in this point. If it is agreed that the legislation must allow for PGD to be used to confirm that the embryo to be implanted is that of the couple in question then it is easy enough to modify the generic purpose. To read 'that purpose' as covering such cases in no way assists the argument that 'that purpose' hinges on the particular reproductive purposes of the particular woman.

Thirdly, Lord Hoffmann argues that the absence from the legislation of any reference to the use of PGD for sex selection is a telling indicator of the legislative intention to confer upon the authority very broad licensing powers. 'It is hard to imagine', suggests Lord Hoffmann, 'that the reason why the Act said nothing on the subject was because Parliament thought it was clearly prohibited by the

[64] ibid para 27. [65] ibid para 62. [66] ibid para 51.

use of the word 'suitable' or because it wanted to leave the question over for later primary legislation'.[67] Indeed, this is so: it surely is implausible to suppose that Parliament thought that the word 'suitable' would signal that PGD for sex selection was prohibited. However, it is entirely plausible to suppose that Parliament thought that 'that purpose', by referring back to the general generic objectives of the legislation, signalled that PGD for sex selection was off limits. On this analysis, the regulatory tilt[68] is against conferring this discretion on the authority; and, if PGD for sex selection is to be licensable, it needs to be explicitly so declared by Parliament.

Whatever we make of the merits of their Lordships' reasoning, the upshot of their decision, as Lord Hoffmann freely admits, is that the legislative scheme is to be understood as conferring on the authority a much wider licensing remit than previously appreciated. As the challengers put it, and as Lord Hoffmann accepted, 'once one allowed the mother's choice to be a legitimate ground for selection, one could not stop short of allowing it to be based upon such frivolous reasons as eye or hair colour as well as more sinister eugenic practices'.[69] Yet, the House was not deterred. If particular women came along with preposterous reproductive purposes, the authority would be expected not to license such activities; and, failing that, the Secretary of State would intervene by invoking the regulatory powers reserved under section 3(3)(c) of the Act.

What *Quintavalle* boils down to, therefore, is a choice between two institutional designs. One design is that favoured by the House, under which the authority has a broad discretion to deal with a wide range of controversial reproductive choices subject to parliamentary reserve powers; the other design is one that confers upon the authority a limited licensing discretion with Parliament having to authorize expressly each significant extension of the authority's remit. The House does not take us into the kind of debate that might stake out the relevant considerations that bear on making a rational choice between these alternatives. If it were not for the fact that the government cut across the process by reviewing the legislation and bringing forward proposals that are relatively restrictive in relation to the use of PGD, we might have thought that *Quintavalle* presaged a period during which the authority would be invited to flex its full licensing powers.[70]

(iv) The requirements of intelligent purposivism

In the *Pro-Life Alliance* case, the development of CNR occasions a descriptive disconnection with the terms in which section 1(1) of the Act is drafted. In the

[67] [2005] UKHL 28, para 29.

[68] Compare Roger Brownsword 'Regulating Human Genetics: New Dilemmas for a New Millennium' (2004) 12 Medical Law Review 14, at 17–18.

[69] [2005] UKHL 28, para 25.

[70] Compare Department of Health *Review of the Human Fertilisation and Embryology Act* (Cm 6989, December 2006) paras 2.41–2.43 (screening and selection of embryos).

CORE case, there is no straightforward descriptive disconnection, but the development of PGD, and its extension to PGD plus PTT, arguably generates a normative disconnection (with Schedule 2, paragraph 1(d) becoming the focal point of interpretation). In both cases, the appeal courts make a reconnection by taking a purposive approach. However, whether or not such purposivism is intelligent is another matter. If the disconnection disclosed in these appeals was productive, it was not intelligent to try to re-connect the law without the issues involved being debated in the right way and in the right place. The crucial question, therefore, is whether we regard the disconnection highlighted by these cases as productive or unproductive. Was the job for the courts simply a routine matter of running repairs (a case of taking the car to the garage rather than recalling it to the manufacturers)? Or were these cases where a fundamental overhaul was necessitated; and, if so, which institution has the competence and legitimacy to carry out such a task?

The regulatory framework established in 1990 put in place three levels of control.[71] First, some activities, such as those covered by section 3(3)(d), are categorically prohibited. Without fresh legislation, these prohibitions cannot be lifted. Secondly, some activities may be prohibited by the Secretary of State acting under delegated powers (reference has been made above to the reserve powers in section 3(3)(c)). Thirdly, where activities are neither prohibited nor unreservedly permitted, the regulatory authority has the power to grant licences. By implication, there is a fourth category, one of non-control, where the activity falls outside the ambit of the legislation and is simply permitted. In the light of this framework, an intelligent interpreter should ask, first, whether the activity in question fits better with those activities that are subject to control rather than those that are simply permitted; and, secondly, if the activity is controlled, whether it fits better with those activities that are categorically prohibited or with those that are licensable by the regulatory Authority (always bearing in mind the Secretary of State's reserve powers).

Applying such an approach, in the *Pro-Life Alliance* case, the question is what we make of the creation and use of CNR embryos. First, are such 'embryos' subject to control? For two reasons, there are grounds for thinking that the spirit of the regulatory scheme extends to the creation and use of CNR embryos.[72] One reason is that a CNR embryo is a potential human being; and the other is that it is being designed and used as a tool for research. Given that, in the lead-up to the 1990 legislation, there was a great deal of nervousness about permitting human embryos to be used for research purposes, it is plausible to reason that the Act applies to CNR embryos—and, to this extent, the appeal courts are right in suggesting that the Parliamentarians of 1990 would not have drawn a

[71] See [2003] UKHL 13, para 4.

[72] Compare the argument in Deryck Beyleveld and Shaun D Pattinson 'Globalisation and Human Dignity: Some Effects and Implications for the Creation and Use of Human Embryos' in Roger Brownsword (ed) *Human Rights* (Oxford: Hart, 2004) 185.

distinction between an embryo produced by fertilization and one produced without fertilization. This leads to the second question, namely: if CNR embryos are covered by the Act, is their creation to be treated as categorically prohibited (by analogy with the prohibition in section 3(3)(d)) or as licensable in the ordinary way? Given that CNR techniques pave the way to embryonic stem cell research and the promise of a therapeutic revolution, it scarcely suffices to dispose of the legal question by insisting that an embryo is not an egg. As it happened, as the *Pro-Life Alliance* case was going through the courts, there was already a major debate about stem cell research underway in Parliament;[73] and so it was perhaps not imperative that the courts seized on the regulatory disconnection as an opportunity to launch a debate about the regulatory position. However, it is arguable that the *Pro-Life Alliance* case presented an opportunity for productive disconnection and that an intelligent purposive approach would have seized the moment.

Turning to the CORE case, there was a question about whether PGD and PTT are controlled activities. However, by the time that the case had reached the appeal courts, it was pretty clear that this kind of activity fell within the ambit of the legislation. The essential question for the appeal courts, therefore, was whether PGD and PTT are activities of a kind that may be licensed by the regulatory authority or whether they are categorically prohibited. In 1990, regulators approved the possibility of human embryos being created for reproductive purposes and, exceptionally, such embryos being created for research purposes where those purposes related to reproduction. So long as newly developed techniques, such as PGD, relate to the facilitation of successful reproduction, it is arguable that they come within the spirit and intent of the legislation—and an intelligent purposivism would ease the way accordingly. However, where PGD is not simply designed to facilitate reproduction but to facilitate the production of children who are free of certain disorders, the normative frame of reference changes. And, when we contemplate the use of PGD in conjunction with PTT to facilitate the production of a child who is not only free of a certain disorder but also a tissue-match with a third-party beneficiary, the normative frame of reference changes again. Reproduction simpliciter is one thing; the production of 'healthy' children is something else; and the production of children who are bearers of therapeutic products for third-party beneficiaries is something else again. This, I repeat, is not to argue that the technologies of PGD and PTT should not be so exploited. It is simply to say that the normative frame of reference for the issues debated in 1990 has changed; and that there is a need for further debate. Accordingly, intelligent purposivism would recognize that this is an occasion for productive disconnection.

Now, in defence of the appeal courts in the CORE case, it might be argued that the result of their decision is not to close off debate but to remit the question

[73] Roger Brownsword 'Stem Cells, Superman, and the Report of the Select Committee' (2002) 65 Modern Law Review 568.

to the regulatory authority for case-by-case determination. Yet, is this the right response? Is this what intelligent purposivism indicates? One problem with returning the issue to the regulatory authority for its case-by-case decision is that this prolongs the uncertainty (but, of course, one might say, rightly so). More importantly, it exposes the authority to the charge, from one side, of being unaccountable, and from the other, of lacking independence.[74] The other option is to return the issue to Parliament, leaving it to politicians to decide whether PGD and PTT should be categorically prohibited or left to the licensing discretion of the regulatory authority. This option, too, would involve some delay in settling the regulatory position but at least it would be made by accountable regulators.

We could continue to debate whether or not the decision in *Quintavalle* exemplifies intelligent purposivism. However, the show has moved on. The Department of Health, having consulted widely, has published its review of the 1990 Act; and the draft Human Tissue and Embryos Bill 2007 has undergone pre-legislative scrutiny by a committee drawn from both Houses of Parliament.[75] Even if the appeal courts are reluctant to recognize a case of productive disconnection, the politicians it seems are more than ready to revisit the regulation of the reproductive revolution.

IV Conclusion

New technologies present more than one kind of threat to the Rule of Law. In the case of modern biotechnology, the obvious difficulty, as I have explained in the earlier chapters of this book, is accommodating the ethical pluralism that is characteristic of many modern societies. However, in this chapter, I have focused on a challenge of what, at first blush, seems to be a more technical kind, namely how regulatory frameworks might stay connected to technologies that develop in ways that regulators have not contemplated. And, in particular, I have considered how a purposive approach to interpretation might help or hinder Rule of Law values.

In general, my claim is that intelligent purposive interpretation is in line with the value of congruence that is central to the ideal of the Rule of Law. Although such an approach might deviate from the literal meaning of the regulation, it does not threaten congruence so long as it remains within the spirit and intent of the regulation. When confronted by a case of disconnection, interpreters should

[74] In this light, we might be less than reassured by the government's claim that the HFEA 'now provides an invaluable safeguard...by ensuring that genetic advances in reproduction are used only for serious medical purposes and only in a responsible and appropriate way', see Department of Health *Our Inheritance, Our Future* (Cm 5791, June 2003) para 6.10.

[75] House of Lords and House of Commons Joint Committee on the Human Tissue and Embryos (Draft) Bill *Human Tissue and Embryos (Draft) Bill*, HL Paper 169–I, HC Paper 630–I (London: The Stationery Office,1 August 2007). The Joint Committee supports the government's attempt to broaden the definition of an embryo (that would fall within the jurisdiction of the regulatory agency) and favours relaxing the 'saviour sibling' draft provisions to bring them, broadly speaking, into line with the HFEA's current practice.

not resort to a purposive approach in order to reconnect at all costs—for the costs might include that of congruence. Rather, interpreters should bear in mind that a narrow concern with regulatory economy might prove to be a false economy; instead, they should consider more broadly whether disconnection is productive and, in fact, an opportunity for regulators to clarify their intentions or re-open a debate that will draw out the legitimate bounds of the regulation.

Applying such standards to the *Pro-Life Alliance* case and to the CORE (*Quintavalle*) case, it is arguable that the appeal courts moved too quickly to reconnect the Human Fertilisation and Embryology Act 1990 to the developing technologies of CNR, PGD, and PTT. To be sure, it is easy to be wise after the event; but the fact that the important questions of principle raised by these cases are now being addressed in Parliament confirms that the debates (and regulation) of 1990 do not readily reach through to the technology of the early 21st century—a technology that is giving a new meaning to the reproductive revolution.[76] If we are not sure whether this technology is a good or a bad thing, then disconnection leading to further public debate is certainly no bad thing.

[76] For early-warning signs, see eg, Margaret Brazier 'Regulating the Reproduction Business' (1999) 7 Medical Law Review 166.

7

The Challenge of Regulatory Cosmopolitanism

I Introduction

In his eloquent interpretation of the cosmopolitan project, a project that aspires to do justice to the twin ideals of universal concern and respect for legitimate difference, Kwame Anthony Appiah makes no apology for the complex and challenging nature of this aspiration:

> [T]here are two strands that intertwine in the notion of cosmopolitanism. One is the idea that we have obligations to others, obligations that stretch beyond those to whom we are related by the ties of kith and kind, or even the more formal ties of a shared citizenship. The other is that we take seriously the value not just of human life but of particular human lives, which means taking an interest in the practices and beliefs that lend them significance. People are different, the cosmopolitan knows, and there is much to learn from our differences. Because there are so many human possibilities worth exploring, we neither expect nor desire that every person or every society should converge on a single mode of life. Whatever our obligations are to others (or theirs to us) they often have the right to go their own way....[T]here will be times when these two ideals—universal concern and respect for legitimate difference—clash.[1]

In a similar vein, we might recall that Article 12 of the UNESCO Universal Declaration on Bioethics and Human Rights emphasizes that, in the spirit of universal concern, there needs to be respect for 'human dignity, human rights and fundamental freedoms' but that, at the same time and as a matter of respecting legitimate difference, '[t]he importance of cultural diversity and pluralism should be given due regard'.[2] There is a sense, Appiah aptly remarks, 'in which

[1] Kwame Anthony Appiah *Cosmopolitanism* (London: Penguin, Allen Lane, 2006) xv. For a complementary analysis, with a particular emphasis on the plurality and plasticity of individual identity (as well as the political advantages in highlighting these features), see Amartya Sen *Identity and Violence: The Illusion of Destiny* (London: Penguin, Allen Lane, 2006). According to Sen (at 182):

> If a person can have only one identity, then the choice between the national and the global becomes an 'all or nothing' contest. And so does the contest between any global sense of belonging we may have and the local loyalties that may also move us. But to see the problem in these stark and exclusive terms reflects a profound misunderstanding of the nature of human identity, in particular its inescapable plurality.

[2] See ch 2 above.

cosmopolitanism is the name not of the solution but of the challenge'.[3] For regulators—whether local, regional, or international—who operate in a world where the tendencies towards globalization are accelerated by new technologies, the challenge represented by cosmopolitanism is daunting.

Regulatory cosmopolitanism represents a multi-faceted challenge of both principle and practice.[4] As a matter of principle, the essential challenge (a challenge of regulatory legitimacy) is this: on the one hand, the ideal of universal concern demands that there should be no under-interpretation of fundamental values;[5] on the other hand, the ideal of respect for legitimate difference demands that there should be no international over-reaching—even if cultural diversity is not a good in itself, permissible local difference should be treated with respect. As a matter of practice, the challenge is to find effective ways to secure compliance with international or regional regulatory articulations of fundamental values while empowering national regulators who strive to seek compliance with local standards.[6]

In this chapter, we can complete our discussion of the regulatory challenges presented by modern technologies by considering some particular puzzles for regulatory cosmopolitanism. I am conscious that this will barely scratch the surface of a topic that merits a book in its own right. Nevertheless, for present purposes, discussion of three test cases must suffice. The first two cases (discussed in Parts II and III) largely concern matters of principle, the third (discussed in Part IV) concerns matters of practice.

The first test case focuses on the interpretation of the moral exclusion (against patentability) that is characteristic of European patent regimes, both regionally and locally.[7] Prior to the emergence of modern biotechnology, the morality exclusion was rarely activated; and the jurisprudence relating to its interpretation was virtually non-existent. However, once applications were made to patent offices for the protection of inventive work in modern genetics, the question of moral exclusion assumed a dramatically fresh importance. With Europe seriously divided as to the ethics of conducting research in genetics and, concomitantly, lacking a common view as to the patentability of such work, the challenge for the regional patent office is to articulate a pan-European standard while allowing room for legitimate local exception.

[3] Appiah (n 1 above) at xv.

[4] Generally, compare Bronwen Morgan and Karen Yeung *An Introduction to Law and Regulation* (Cambridge: Cambridge University Press, 2007) ch 6.

[5] Compare Roger Brownsword 'Ethical Pluralism and the Regulation of Modern Biotechnology' in Francesco Francioni (ed) *Biotechnologies and International Human Rights* (Oxford: Hart, 2007) 45.

[6] We should be troubled by the view that the international community is doing rather better at globalizing free trade than it is at globalizing justice and human rights: see, eg, Anne-Marie Slaughter, 'Judicial Globalization' (2000) 40 Virginia Journal of International Law 1103.

[7] For the regional exclusions, see Article 53(a) of the European Patent Convention and Article 6(1) of Directive 98/44/EC (on the legal protection of biotechnological inventions).

The second test case also concerns local moral exclusion but, this time, against the principle of market access that is enshrined in regional and international free trade agreements. Suppose, for example, that a country takes moral exception to GM crops or to online gambling. Are these the kind of goods or services to which a local community may legitimately close its markets? Is this a case of legitimate local difference that merits respect? Here, the challenge is to determine which concessions to local culture are required as a matter of regulatory legitimacy but without undermining the effective facilitation of international commerce.

Whereas the first two cases presuppose a process of global consensus-building around general rules and special exceptions, the third case involves a more direct assertion of power by the local community. This is the case of a nation state endeavouring to enforce its own local standards, particularly where the effectiveness of its own local regulation threatens to be undermined by the technology of the internet, a technology that knows no physical borders.

II Patentability and Moral Exclusion

In the European Union, debates leading to the Directive on the Legal Protection of Biotechnological Inventions[8] stretch back to 1988. Central to those debates (as in parallel debates at the European Patent Office, operating under the European Patent Convention) has been the question of whether the processes and products of modern biotechnology should be treated as patentable. While, on the one side, the interests of the biotechnology industry (aided by the generally scientific and technical approach of the patent community) have argued for a permissive approach, on the other side, the interests of various constituencies concerned about such matters as human dignity and the commercialization of life, animal welfare, and environmental harm have argued for restriction.[9]

The resulting regulatory framework responds to these competing interests in two ways. First, in general, biotechnology is to be treated no differently from any other inventive science that comes forward with patent claims. Thus, provided that the particular claim relates to an invention (with a declared industrial application) rather than to a mere discovery, genetically engineered products—even those incorporating human gene sequences—will satisfy the technical criteria of patentability. Similarly, there are to be no new *general* tests of exclusion for biotechnological inventions: the standard exclusions from patentability, concerning in particular morality, *ordre public*, essentially biological processes for the production of plants or animals, and plant and animal varieties, will apply. To this

[8] Directive 98/44/EC; [1998] OJ L213.

[9] For discussion of these issues under the European Patent Convention, see Deryck Beyleveld and Roger Brownsword *Mice, Morality, and Patents* (London: Common Law Institute of Intellectual Property, 1993). Generally, see Sigrid Sterckx (ed) *Biotechnology, Patents and Morality* (Aldershot, Ashgate, 1997).

extent, a level playing field is maintained for biotechnology. Secondly, however, the concerns of those who have opposed the opening of the patent system to modern biotechnology are reflected in a number of specific exclusions[10]—including exclusions relating to cloning and germ-line modifications in humans as well as transgenic animals.[11]

Taking a larger view, what is striking about the principal regimes of patent law in Europe, unlike in some other patent jurisdictions (for example, in North America), is their inclusion of an *explicit* provision against granting a patent where (roughly speaking) this would be contrary to morality.[12] In practice, of course, moral considerations can, and sometimes do, covertly influence the way that ostensibly technical notions, such as 'utility' or 'inventive step', are interpreted and applied. For the sake of argument, however, let us assume that there is a clean choice between a patent regime designed to make immorality a specific ground for exclusion from patentability and a regime that is designed to make patentability entirely independent of moral considerations. The general impression given by European patent practitioners is either (i) that the latter is preferable to the former, the morality exclusion of the former constituting an unhelpful interference with the operation of the patent process, or (ii) that the former is tolerable so long as the exclusion is applied only in the most extreme circumstances, where the granting of a patent would be inconceivable or utterly abhorrent, or something equivalently shocking. In this part of the chapter, I will check the strength of these positions in the light of the approaches represented by the bioethical triangle,[13] after which I will indicate how such matters might be approached in a regulatory zone where there is both regional and local commitment of the kind associated with a community of rights.

(i) The claim that a patent regime should not include a morality exclusion

For a utilitarian, it is far from obvious that a patent regime should include a morality exclusion. Utilitarians do not recognize categorically binding moral principles in the way that is characteristic of deontological approaches; and there might well be disutilities associated with morality exclusions if they discourage inventors from putting their inventive work in the public sphere and/or if they consume significant resource at patent offices. On the other hand, if a morality check increases public confidence in patent systems, and if such a check is more efficient and effective

[10] For French resistance to the Directive, see Donna Dickenson *Property in the Body* (Cambridge: Cambridge University Press, 2007) ch 5.

[11] This particular exclusion following the lead given at the European Patent Office in the Harvard Onco-mouse case [1990] 1 EPOR 4 (original examination); [1990] 7 EPOR 501 (Board of Appeal): OJ EPO 10/1992, 590 (re-examination).

[12] See Article 53(a) of the European Patent Convention and Article 6 of Directive 98/44/EC on the Legal Protection of Biotechnological Inventions.

[13] As in ch 2.

when placed in the patent regime rather than outside it (as, say, in the political or wider legal regime), then a morality exclusion might have some utility. Indeed, Norway has taken the lead here (not necessarily, it should be said, for utilitarian reasons) by setting up a specialist ethics advisory committee within the local patent office.[14]

Although patent practitioners seem to be convinced that a morality exclusion is counter-productive, the analogy with morality (and public policy) exclusions in regimes of contract law might give the utilitarian pause. The law of contract, like patent law, is an option presented by mature legal systems. Parties to transactions are not required to engage the law of contract; it is permissible and perfectly possible for markets to operate outside the law of contract (as indeed eBay sought to operate initially).[15] Similarly, inventors are not required to apply for patent protection or (at any rate, not usually) to declare their inventive knowledge; it is permissible and often possible for inventors to protect their knowledge by other means. The analogy goes further; it is a truism that certainty, calculability, and security are essential for the law of contract, just as these are desiderata for patent law. Yet, in the case of the law of contract, regimes provide as standard that transactions having immoral purposes shall not be recognized and enforced. In other words, the law of contract, geared for certainty every bit as much as patent law, takes it as read that regimes should include what is in effect a morality exclusion. This does not clinch the argument for a morality exclusion in patent law, but utilitarians, presented with this analogy, might hesitate before knocking out morality exclusions.

The Belgian patent regime explicitly excludes patents on inventions that are inconsistent with respect for human rights. Where states are already committed to human rights instruments, such as the European Convention on Human Rights, such an exclusionary provision is surely no more than the logic of their commitments.[16] Where states are not so committed, proponents of human rights will argue that patent regimes (like any other legal regime) must be subject to compatibility with human rights. Thus, the view from this corner is not simply that patent regimes should include a morality exclusion but, more specifically, that they should be human rights compliant.

From such a human rights perspective, the European Court of Justice erred badly in its response to the Netherlands' challenge to the Directive on the Legal Protection of Biotechnological Inventions (Directive 98/44/EC).[17] One of the

[14] Although it should be observed that, thus far, the Norwegian Patent Office has not referred any applications to the ethics advisory committee and a review is underway to clarify the relationship between the Patent Office and the committee.

[15] Generally, see Roger Brownsword *Contract Law: Themes for the Twenty-First Century* (2nd edn, Oxford: Oxford University Press, 2006) especially ch 1.

[16] Compare the argument in Deryck Beyleveld and Roger Brownsword *Mice, Morality and Patents* (London: Common Law Institute of Intellectual Property, 1993).

[17] Case C–377/98. For commentary, see Deryck Beyleveld and Roger Brownsword 'Is Patent Law Part of the EC Legal Order? A Critical Commentary on the Interpretation of Article 6(1) of Directive 98/44/EC in Case C–377/98' (2002) Intellectual Property Quarterly 97.

claims advanced by the Netherlands was that the directive is morally deficient in that it fails to do enough to ensure that, where biological samples are taken, the donors give a full, free and informed consent—crucially, whether provision is made to ensure that donors consent all the way through to possible patenting and commercial exploitation. The ECJ could have given a perfectly plausible response to this element of the Netherlands' challenge by pointing to the way in which recital 26 of the directive underlines the importance of informed consent.[18] Far from relying on a robust interpretation of recital 26, however, the ECJ effectively said that such a matter was not one for the patent regime. In other words, the ECJ sought to disconnect patent law from the ethics of patenting (even where the ethics at issue involved fundamental human rights values). On this approach, patent courts are technical courts, courts of law not morals, and if there is an issue about informed consent it needs to be remitted elsewhere for debate and decision.

For the dignitarians, the protracted campaign to entrench respect for human dignity in the EC patent directive eventually bore fruit.[19] The morality exclusion in Article 6 is in two parts. First, Article 6(1) provides:

> Inventions shall be considered unpatentable where their commercial exploitation would be contrary to *ordre public* or morality; however, exploitation shall not be deemed to be so contrary merely because it is prohibited by law or regulation.

Secondly, Article 6(2) provides:

> On the basis of paragraph 1 [i.e. Article 6(1)], the following, in particular, shall be considered unpatentable:
>
> (a) processes for cloning human beings;
> (b) processes for modifying the germ line genetic identity of human beings;
> (c) uses of human embryos for industrial or commercial purposes;
> (d) processes for modifying the genetic identity of animals which are likely to cause them suffering without any substantial medical benefit to man or animal, and also animals resulting from such processes.

Article 6 builds on a number of recitals, most significantly, recital 38 which states:

> Whereas the operative part of this Directive should also include an illustrative list of inventions excluded from patentability so as to provide national courts and patent offices

[18] Recital 26 provides as follows:

> Whereas if an invention is based on biological material of human origin or if it uses such material, where a patent application is filed, the person from whose body the material is taken must have had an opportunity of expressing free and informed consent thereto, in accordance with national law.

[19] For analysis and discussion, see Deryck Beyleveld, Roger Brownsword, and Margaret Llewelyn 'The Morality Clauses of the Directive on the Legal Protection of Biotechnological Inventions: Conflict, Compromise, and the Patent Community' in Richard Goldberg and Julian Lonbay (eds) *Pharmaceutical Medicine, Biotechnology and European Law* (Cambridge: Cambridge University Press, 2000) 157.

with a general guide to interpreting the reference to *ordre public* and morality; whereas this list obviously cannot presume to be exhaustive; whereas processes, the use of which offend against human dignity, such as processes to produce chimeras from germ cells or totipotent cells of humans and animals, are obviously also excluded from patentability.

In other words, the examples given in Article 6(2) are to be understood as an illustrative but non-exhaustive list of inventions excluded from patentability under the morality test of Article 6(1), leaving it open to argue that patents should be denied wherever any other offence against human dignity is detected.

With the directive thus expressly tying its morality exclusion to the principle that human dignity should not be compromised, and given the particular exclusions relating to cloning humans beings and the use of human embryos,[20] the dignitarians understandably see some hope of stemming the tide of human embryonic stem cell research. However, for the dignitarians, as for the human rights theorists, the argument is not simply that there should be a morality exclusion. Rather, it is that there should be an exclusion with a particular moral content, in this case the content prescribed by the dignitarian alliance.

(ii) The claim that a morality exclusion should be applied only in the most exceptional of cases

When, in the Harvard Onco-mouse application, the European Patent Office first gave serious consideration to the application of the morality exclusion in the European Patent Convention, it approached the matter in a distinctly utilitarian way, the examiners balancing the beneficial consequences (to humans) of the development of a genetically engineered test animal for cancer research against the negative effects on animal welfare and environmental hazard.[21] However, subsequently, the jurisprudence has taken a much more restrictive approach to the application of the morality clause; the exception for morality truly is exceptional. In general, the position taken is that, in the absence of an overwhelming consensus that the exploitation of the invention would be utterly abhorrent (so much so that the granting of a patent would be inconceivable), the morality clause does not operate to bar patentability. Thus, in the more recent case of LELAND STANFORD/Modified Animal[22] (which involved a test animal for AIDS research), the Opposition Division at the European Patent Office said:

[A]s long as a claimed invention has a legitimate use, it cannot be the role of the EPO to act as moral censor and invoke the provisions of Article 53(a) EPC to refuse on ethical grounds

[20] Respectively, Article 6(2)(a) and (c). See Graeme Laurie 'Patenting Stem Cells of Human Origin' [2004] EIPR 59, and Aurora Plomer *Stem Cell Patents: European Patent Law and Ethics Report* (Nottingham, July 2006): <http://www.nottingham.ac.uk/law/StemCellProject/project.report.pdf>.

[21] OJ EPO 10/1992, 590.

[22] [2002] EPOR 2.

to grant a patent on legal research and directed to an invention indisputably associated with medical benefits. The technology underlying the present invention is undoubtedly controversial and the subject of intensive discussion in the media and among members of the public. However, there is at present no consensus in Europe[an] society about the desirability or otherwise of this technology, and public opinion is still being formed on this and related matters. It would be presumptuous for the EPO to interfere in this public debate. The provisions of Article 53(a) EPC are intended to exclude from patentability not subject-matter that is controversial, but rather that kind of extreme subject-matter (e.g. letter-bombs and anti-personnel mines) which would be regarded by the public as so abhorrent that the grant of a patent would be inconceivable.[23]

Such a restrictive reading of the jurisdiction given by the morality clause reflects the patent community's view that the regulatory tilt of the patent regime is in favour of granting patents.[24]

What would our three bioethical approaches make of this view that morality exclusions are to be applied only exceptionally and on the basis of an overwhelming consensus?

From the utilitarian perspective, if a calculable patent regime encourages research and development that generates utility-producing inventive applications, it is important that a morality exclusion does not detract from these benefits. Accordingly, for a utilitarian, the relevant caveats in relation to the application of a morality exclusion are not so much that it should be invoked only exceptionally or on the basis of an overwhelming consensus; rather, the caveats are that the application of such a clause should be predictable and not so broad as to inhibit investment in utility-producing inventive work. Given such an approach, utilitarians would tend to favour clearly identified exclusions; and, if open-ended general clauses cannot be avoided, then so far as possible the patent community should be given specific advance guidance as to the application of such provisions. Thus, the attempt to give patent offices just such guidance (however inadequate) in the EC patent directive would be broadly welcomed by utilitarians.

Turning to a human rights perspective, matters will be viewed rather differently. Granted, not every application (in fact, relatively few) will directly raise human rights issues—not every application will raise issues of informed consent as directly as, say, the Relaxin Opposition at the European Patent Office.[25] However, where human rights issues are raised, whether directly or indirectly, they must be addressed. In this sense, applications of morality exclusions might be expected, in practice, to be relatively infrequent; but this is not to treat such applications as exceptional as a matter of principle. As for the idea that applications should be limited to cases where there is an overwhelming consensus in support of rejecting the application (or revoking the grant), this is off the mark. Human rights

[23] ibid para 51.

[24] cf Deryck Beyleveld, Roger Brownsword, and Margaret Llewelyn (n 19 above).

[25] HOWARD FLOREY/Relaxin [1995] EPOR 541. For commentary, see Roger Brownsword 'The Relaxin Opposition Revisited' (2001) 9 Jahrbuch für Recht und Ethik 3.

applications are not always straightforward or uncontroversial; but those who operate the morality exclusions in a patent regime must apply human rights principles in good faith and conscientiously even if the result does not always command uniform support.

For the dignitarian alliance, the human rights view, albeit using the wrong currency, at least has the right sort of shape. In practice, it might be only occasionally that patent applications will raise issues relating to respect for human dignity. However, where such issues are presented, they must be addressed; and they must be answered by reference to the value of human dignity rather than by reliance on any positive moral consensus. Indeed, from this perspective, the possible willingness of the EPO to reject stem cell patents for dignitarian reasons, even in the face of anything but a broad European consensus, must be seen as an important step in the right direction.

The lesson of this is that, in conditions of ethical pluralism, any attempt to base a moral exclusion on consensus or convergence will marginalize the role of the exclusion; and, while this seems to favour no particular constituency within the plurality, in practice it probably plays into the hands of the utilitarians (trading on the assumption that a patent regime that is geared to granting patents will be more beneficial than one that denies patentability on contestable moral grounds). Indeed, when the EPO finally determines whether human embryonic stem cells are patentable, it will be surprising if it does not revert to the background utilitarian approach indicated by the weight of its jurisprudence.

(iii) Morality exclusion in a regional community of rights

Let us imagine that the patent regime in Europe is to serve a group of contracting nation states, each of which represents a community of rights. As I have said, an important feature of such communities is that they each subject their understanding and application of their commitments to regular review. Such communities are never complacent about their commitment to doing the right thing. Given that such communities might arrive at somewhat different answers to the many hard questions that they face, what does this tell us about their approach to morality exclusions in patent regimes?

Nationally, there is no problem. In each national patent regime, there will be a morality exclusion, tied to the community's rights commitments, and each national patent office will do its best to apply the exclusion in a way that is in line with the community's values. The problem arises where, as in current European patent regimes, an attempt is made to streamline the patent system by setting up a regional patent office. The two-part question is: would the individual nation states collectively grant any kind of moral jurisdiction to the regional office; and, if so, how extensive would that moral jurisdiction be?

With regard to the first question, so long as regulatory economy and efficiency are the only considerations,[26] the individual nation states would agree

[26] cf ch 5.

that the regional office should have a full technical jurisdiction (so that questions of inventiveness, originality, and the like, are delegated to the regional office). For similar reasons, it would make sense to confer as well a moral jurisdiction that operates on a *principle of unanimity*. Hence, if all national patent offices judge that a patent should be excluded on moral grounds, the regional office should be authorised to reject the application for this moral reason; and, conversely, if all national patent offices judge that an application is morally clean, the regional office should be authorized to make the appropriate declaration of regional moral admissibility. Assuming that the regional office is scrupulous in avoiding making any moral declaration (whether in favour of exclusion or admission) where there is any doubt about the views of the members, the attraction of this proposal is that there is a gain in regulatory economy without taking away from each community of rights the sovereignty to make its own moral judgments where those judgments are distinctively its own. The trickier question is whether a more extensive moral jurisdiction should be granted to the regional office.

It might be proposed that the principle of unanimity should be relaxed so that the moral jurisdiction of the regional office should operate on a *majoritarian principle*. If the regional office were granted such a jurisdiction, then (a) it would reject an application where the majority of Member States judged that a patent should be excluded on moral grounds and (b) it would declare the application morally clean where a majority of Member States so judged. Clearly, there would be no purpose in conferring such a moral jurisdiction on the regional office unless its declarations were treated as binding on members. The nub of the matter, therefore, is whether minority members could live with such a delegation of moral authority. Two points that might be put in favour of such a delegation are as follows. First, within a single community of rights, there will sometimes be differences of opinion which are resolved on the majoritarian principle; if this is acceptable, then why should we oppose the proposed delegation of moral jurisdiction which simply applies the principle to a larger group? Secondly, where the majority decision is in favour of granting the patent, it remains open to minority members to regulate against the commercial exploitation of the patent within their own national boundaries. As the European Patent Office has been fond of remarking, the grant of a patent is no guarantee that the invention will be commercially exploitable. Granted, where the majority decision is in favour of rejecting the patent application, it is less obvious how minority members might compensate for the regional moral exclusion against patentability. However, as the first argument reminds us, it is not uncommon within a community of rights to find minority members having to live with a moral judgment that they do not share; and, as the second argument emphasizes, the commercial exploitability of a process or product does not hinge on its patentability (so, exceptionally, minority members might take alternative regulatory action to incentivise or to assist commercial exploitation of the invention in their territory).

If neither unanimity nor majority appeals, how about the delegation of a moral jurisdiction that operates on a *minority principle*? In its most extreme form, such a principle would give each member a veto. So, even if all members bar one judged that a patent should be excluded on moral grounds, the minority member could veto the declaration of regional exclusion (but, of course, not require the issuing of a declaration of regional admissibility); and, conversely, if all members bar one judged that a patent should be granted as morally permissible, the minority member could veto the appropriate regional declaration (but not require the issuing of a declaration of regional exclusion). In the latter case, the price of granting such weight to the view of each member is that the minority veto creates significant diseconomies as the inventor now has to make applications to each of the majority patent offices. In the former case, the diseconomies are much less serious; here, the applicant knows that there is just the one national patent office that will not exclude the application on moral grounds.

Thus far, the assumption has been that each community of rights has a similar capacity for moral judgment; and, quite possibly, that even if capacities are mixed, each community should enjoy sovereignty over its own moral project. Let us suppose, however, that the members have reasons for believing that, if they pool their resources in the regional office, not only will there be a gain in regulatory economy and efficiency but also an improvement in the quality of moral judgment. Each community of rights strives to give its best interpretation of its commitments; but perhaps the regional resource appeals as a better way of rendering best judgments. In these circumstances, the members might contemplate a delegation of both full technical and *full moral jurisdiction* to the regional office. If there are some matters that members particularly wish to keep within their own moral jurisdiction, they might enter various kinds of reservation. However, given such a change in the direction of thinking, the previously considered principles of unanimity, majority, and minority, would no longer be applicable.

Characteristically, because a community of rights will regard regulatory economy and efficiency as less compelling considerations than the legitimacy of regulatory judgments, any proposed delegation that departs from the principle of unanimity will be subject to close scrutiny. Moreover, if the community values making its own moral judgments for its own sake, there will be a reluctance to cede that opportunity to the regional office.

III Moral Exclusion and Market Access

Free trade is neither an end in itself and nor is it a strategy to be pursued at all costs. It is not the former because its appeal rests on the judgment that this is the economic default position that is most likely to promote human welfare; hence, if the default position does not function as intended—and this is a matter to be kept under constant review—then we need to find another way of promoting human welfare. Neither is free trade a strategy to be pursued at all costs, for (as the UNESCO axiom reminds us) measures designed to maximize aggregate human well-being must always be compatible with respect for human rights and human dignity.[27]

Thomas Cottier has persuasively argued that there are several 'portals' in both the GATT and GATS that allow for human rights considerations to be brought into play.[28] For example, Article XX(a) GATT, and likewise Article XIV(a) GATS, recognise that a commitment to market access does not prevent a Contracting State from imposing trade-related restrictions that are necessary for the protection of 'public morals'. Of course, even if it is conceded that human rights and human dignity fall within the compass of the 'public morals' exception, the chapeau to these Articles is designed to ensure that where the moral high ground is being taken, it must be taken transparently and in good faith—in other words, protective measures must not be 'applied in a manner which would constitute a means of arbitrary or unjustifiable discrimination between countries where the same conditions prevail, or [by way of] a disguised restriction on international trade...'

Nevertheless, the jurisprudence of such moral exceptions is far from well-developed. In an extremely helpful review, Steven Charnowitz[29] begins to give some shape to the jurisprudence by drawing a key distinction between 'outwardly-directed' and 'inwardly-directed' applications of the moral exception, the former covering 'trade measures used to protect the morals of foreigners residing outside one's own country', the latter 'trade measures used to protect morals of persons in one's own country...'.[30] Although it is arguable that inwardly-directed measures are less controversial, being an exercise in cultural self-defence, Charnovitz maintains that it is wrong to suppose that Article XX(a) GATT can never be applied in an outwardly-directed manner.[31] However, to confer an unqualified licence for such application would be problematic—as Charnovitz says:

> Although a unilateral determination of morality may be appropriate for inwardly-directed concerns, it is too open-ended for outwardly-directed concerns. Some method to determine the legitimacy of a moral claim is needed in order to ensure that the exception does not begin to swallow the rules. Allowing each government to restrict imports based on its own definition of morality could disrupt trade and allow imperialism by countries with market power.[32]

By way of a solution, Charnovitz suggests that 'the WTO should use international human rights law to ascribe meaning to the vague terms of Article XX(a). Thus,

[27] Generally, for similar sentiments, see Ernst-Ulrich Petersmann (ed) *Reforming the World Trade System* (Oxford: Oxford University Press, 2005).

[28] Thomas Cottier 'Genetic Engineering, Trade and Human Rights' in Francesco Francioni (ed) *Biotechnologies and International Human Rights* (Oxford: Hart, 2007) 275.

[29] Steve Charnovitz 'The Moral Exception in Trade Policy' (1998) 38 Virginia Journal of International Law 689.

[30] ibid 695.

[31] ibid 738.

[32] ibid 742.

the moral exception could validate trade actions based on international norms while rejecting trade actions based on nationalistic aims. This solution would recognize the symmetry in our pursuit of both global commerce and global values'.[33]

Now, in the light of this, let us suppose that 'respect for human rights and human dignity' is recognized as a legitimate reason for the local imposition of trade restrictions. If so, it makes a great deal of difference whether it is human dignity as empowerment or human dignity as constraint that is the operative conception. For, if it is the latter, while there is certainly some commitment to cosmopolitan prohibition, there also seems to be ample scope for local (and quite parochial) duty-driven standards to be set up against free trade. We should not expect to find the same exceptions everywhere. Whatever we make of such dignitarian exceptionalism as a matter of ethics, this is a prospect that might occasion some concern on the part of the sponsors of free trade.[34]

On the other hand, if it is simply human rights, or human dignity as empowerment, that is the operative conception, what then? If anything, human dignity as empowerment seems to support free trade (so long as it is not the slave trade or any other kind of commerce that obviously is incompatible with respect for human rights) and it remains to be seen how far there is scope for distinctively local restrictions that are set by so many communities of rights.

To focus some thoughts about dignitarian exceptionalism, we can consider two test-cases, one involving the supply of cross-border gambling services and the other GM crops. In both cases, we will encounter the argument that market access should be denied to the relevant goods or services for reasons that, either directly or indirectly, hinge on dignitarian concerns.

1. Cross-border gambling services

We can start with the decision of the WTO Appellate Body in *United States – Measures Affecting the Cross-Border Supply of Gambling and Betting Services*.[35] The dispute in this case arose when Antigua and Barbuda complained that a set of US federal and state laws made it unlawful for suppliers who are located outside the United States to supply gambling and betting services to consumers within the US. After some filtering of the issues, the Appellate Body narrowed down the offending measures to three federal laws, the Wire Act, the Travel Act, and the Illegal

[33] ibid 742–3.

[34] Compare Robert Howse 'From Politics to Technocracy – And Back Again: The Fate of the Multilateral Trading Regime' (2002) 96 American Journal of International Law 94, at 95, for the view that the design challenge is to ensure that, if a member reneges on its commitments, this will 'not trigger a general crisis of confidence in the system, and consequently a reversion to beggar-thy-neighbour protectionism'.

[35] WT/DS285/AB/R, 7 April 2005.

Gambling Business Act,[36] these measures being targeted against the cross-border supply of gambling and betting services. Having found that these legislative prohibitions on the remote supply of gambling and betting services constituted a relevant restriction within the meaning of Article XVI of GATS, the Appellate Body then considered whether the US could avail itself of the general exception for 'measures... necessary to protect public morals or to maintain public order' under Article XIV(a). Following the view formed by the panel, the Appellate Body held that the measures in question, being 'adopted to address concerns such as those pertaining to money laundering, organized crime, fraud, underage gambling and pathological gambling',[37] fell within the exception. In the event, the US argument failed to meet the chapeau requirement in Article XIV for it did not show that the domestic Interstate Horseracing Act[38] (which seems to permit certain types of remote betting on horseracing) does not amount to arbitrary or unjustifiable discrimination against extra-territorial suppliers. There is a great deal in this decision (the pattern of which fits quite closely with the equivalent EC internal market jurisprudence)[39] to be chewed over by international trade lawyers; but, for present purposes, it is the argument on the application of Article XIV(a) that is particularly relevant.

As we have seen, the US contended that the restrictive provisions were necessary measures in order to address a range of concerns. In response to this part of the US case, Antigua objected that the panel had failed to determine whether the concerns were so serious as to touch one of the fundamental interests of society.[40] The Appellate Body saw little in this point, being satisfied that the panel had taken account of the relevant matters and did not need to make a separate and explicit determination to the effect that the standard of a serious threat posed to the fundamental interests of the society had been met.

[36] Respectively, Section 1084 of Title 18 of the US Code (the 'Wire Act'), Section 1952 of Title 18 of the US Code (the 'Travel Act'), and Section 1955 of Title 18 of the US Code (the 'Illegal Gambling Business Act').

[37] WT/DS285/AB/R, 7 April 2005, at para 296.

[38] ibid paras 361–4.

[39] Specifically with regard to the provision of internet gambling services, the pivotal ECJ decision is *Gambelli*, Case C–243/01, 6 November 2003. In *Gambelli*, despite implicit criticism of the severity of the Italian restrictions, the ECJ held that: (i) public interest (moral or social) considerations may justify restrictions set by Member States on the freedom of establishment and the freedom to provide services as provided for by, respectively, Articles 43 and 49EC; (ii) provided that such restrictions are relevant to the particular public interest objective, necessary, and proportionate; and (iii) provided that the restrictions are applied without discrimination. In practice, this means that national courts are invited to make case-by-case rulings on whether local restrictions are properly motivated (not being guided by national financial considerations, particularly about the diversion of lottery revenues) and proportionate. As one commentator has remarked, 'Post-*Gambelli*, it remains the case that European Member States may still, where they have valid moral or social grounds, restrict directly or indirectly access to foreign based gambling services...And almost three years after the judgment, and many fancy conferences later, the barriers to cross border trade in gambling services remain firmly in place': Niall A O'Connor 'From *Schindler* to *Placanica* and Beyond' <http://www.bettingmarket.com/eurolaw222428.htm> (3 May 2007).

[40] ibid paras 296–7.

However, let us forget that Las Vegas is a global gambling metropolis. Counterfactually, let us suppose that the US treated all gambling and betting as immoral—indeed, as compromising human dignity—and that it had local laws prohibiting any such activities. Just as some societies might say, 'We do not want any reproductive cloning here; it offends our idea of civilised life', the hypothesis is that the US might say, 'We do not want any gambling or betting here; it simply is not civilised'. To permit such a dignitarian exception to be pleaded under Article XIV(a) is to invite each Contracting State to immunize its distinctive local cultural identity against global commerce. Where the particular cultural feature goes to the very identity of the society, it is plausible enough to treat it as touching and concerning a fundamental interest of *that* society (not of any society but of *that* particular society). However, if the restriction in question relates to a matter that falls short of that exacting standard (might we say this about the closing down of the Laserdrome in the *Omega* case?[41]), it would not qualify under provisions such as Article XIV(a)—or, at any rate, it would not qualify qua dignitarian exceptionalism (even if it might qualify under a rights-driven argument). To this extent, the objection raised by Antigua would become a focal point, and decision-making bodies would need to be satisfied (and to make it an explicit matter of record) that the dignitarian exception was eligible because it genuinely reflected the fundamental commitments of the community in question.

With these short remarks about dignitarian exceptionalism, we can turn to the question of how far an exception for human rights would be compatible with the cosmopolitan ideal. Contrary to what we might suppose, a morality clause reflecting respect for rights would not produce a standard set of exceptions. As emphasized already, a community of rights is not a finished product so much as an ongoing interpretive enterprise. Moreover, it is an enterprise that each community must take forward in its own way—each community, as it were, must have 'ownership' of its rights project.[42] And, without attempting to be exhaustive, some of the more pressing and recurring types of questions to be addressed, debated, and (at least, provisionally) resolved within a community of rights are the following.

First, there is a large cluster of questions concerning which rights are to be recognized and what the scope of particular rights is. The international community of rights already recognizes a long catalogue of particular rights; but the

[41] *Omega Spielhallen- und Automatenaufstellungs-GmbH v Oberbürgermeisterin der Bundesstadt Bonn* (Case C–36/02) (14 October 2004); [2004] OJ C300/3. Compare Thomas Ackermann (2005) 42 CMLR 1107, at 1117: 'If respect for human dignity is a fundamental interest of society that can only be defined with reference to cultural conceptions of respect for personal identity, there is no alternative to taking national value judgments as a basis as long as the underlying conceptions vary between Member States.' However, national value judgments might be over-ridden where the interest is not of a fundamental nature. Or, to put this in the terms used by Advocate General Stix-Hackl in the *Omega* case, the restriction must be directed at a genuine and sufficiently serious threat to a fundamental interest of society (para 100).

[42] Compare Christian Tomuschat *Human Rights: Between Idealism and Realism* (Oxford: Oxford University Press, 2003).

world moves on and, as it does so, each community must decide which rights it will endorse.[43]

Secondly, where positive rights and responsibilities are recognised, there needs to be a larger debate about how extensive these responsibilities are. While a community of rights will be sensitive to matters of historical injustice and second-best conditions (which, for instance, might require affirmative action), it will also be anxious to avoid compounding unfairness—for example, by imposing disproportionate burdens of positive responsibility or by creating opportunities for free-riding.

Thirdly, there are inevitably conflicts between rights, between, say, the right to privacy and the right to freedom of expression. And, then, there are competing rights—that is, cases where two rights-holders present with the same right.

Fourthly, where a community of rights is committed to a will theory of rights, the dignity of choice includes making choices not only as to the way in which an option-giving right (such as the right to freedom of expression) is to be exercised but also as to the waiver of the benefits covered by the right. This latter kind of choice is expressed by the rights-holder's consent or, as the case might be, refusal of consent.[44] To repeat the thrust of Chapter 3, consent is an extremely important dynamic in a community of rights and the community needs to debate the terms on which a supposed 'consent' will be recognized as valid and effective.[45]

Finally, although this has already been discussed at some length,[46] it bears repetition that there is the vexed question of who has rights. Where do we draw the line between children, fetuses, and embryos? What do we make of non-human higher animals, smart robots, and, in some future world, hybrids and cyborgs of various kinds? Given the frailty of human reasoning, how precautionary should the community be? Is there a margin in which the benefit of doubt applies? If so, how wide is the margin to be?

In this catalogue of issues to be addressed by a community of rights, we see that recognizing human rights as a legitimate restriction on free trade is not recognizing an entirely predictable and unproblematic set of limitations. What is being globalized is not just the product of human rights, but equally importantly the process of deliberation and reflection that is characteristic of a community of rights. If each community is seeking, in good faith, to arrive at its best understanding of its commitment to human rights, there can be no guarantee that

[43] Compare Francesco Francioni 'Genetic Resources, Biotechnology and Human Rights: the International Legal Framework' in Francesco Francioni (ed) *Biotechnologies and International Human Rights* (Hart, Oxford, 2007) 3.

[44] For the importance of giving a refusal its due weight, see Sabine Michalowski 'Advance Refusals of Life-Sustaining Medical Treatment: The Relativity of an Absolute Right' (2005) 68 MLR 958.

[45] See, further, Roger Brownsword 'The Cult of Consent: Fixation and Fallacy' (2004) 15 KCLJ 223; and Deryck Beyleveld and Roger Brownsword *Consent in the Law* (Oxford: Hart Publishing, 2007).

[46] See ch 4.

the answers arrived at will be the same everywhere—all of which allows for the possibility of distinctive human-rights based local restrictions on trade.[47]

Where does this take us? Let me suggest that exceptions for human dignity categorically must be recognized if the compromising of human dignity connotes the harming of the essential conditions for the existence of *any* moral community, including a community of rights. Indeed, if free trade agreements permit an exception to be made for threats that strike at the fundamental interests of society, my point—and this point is a recurrent theme in the later chapters of this book—is that for any society that aspires to be a moral community, there is no more fundamental threat than one that corrodes the conditions of human dignity. While this suggestion does not serve to resolve the tension between those (moral) communities that articulate around human dignity as empowerment and those that articulate around human dignity as constraint, it points to the deep significance of respect for human dignity. On this analysis, to compromise human dignity is not to violate the principles of some particular moral code but to compromise the possibility of any form of moral life.

It follows that a particularly prescient community of rights, anticipating the corrosion of the conditions for moral community in general and a threat to a flourishing community of rights in particular, might impose some restrictions on the trade in modern technologies. Even though, elsewhere, the technologies are regarded as tokens of progress, the steps taken by the community in question are seen as an act of self-defence—the protective measures taken being designed to prevent the breakdown, not of a particular (and peculiarly local) moral order, but of the very conditions of moral order itself. Human dignity, so conceived, does indeed cut deep.

2. GM crops

Concluding an extended commentary on *European Communities – Measures Affecting the Approval and Marketing of Biotech Products*,[48] David Winickoff and his co-authors[49] assert that:

> [f]ree trade need not mean running roughshod over deeply held political and cultural values. In an age of globalization in which anxieties about cultural homogenization and

[47] Compare Joanne Scott 'On Kith and Kine (Crustaceans): Trade and Environment in the EU and WTO', in JHH Weiler (ed) *The EU, the WTO, and the NAFTA* (Oxford: Oxford University Press, 2001) 125 (especially with regard to *EC – Measures Concerning Meat and Meat Products (Hormones)*, Report of the Appellate Body, WT/DS26/AB/R, WT/DS48/AB/R, 16 January 1998, and the question of *scientific* uncertainty).

[48] WT/DS291/23 (United States), WT/DS292/17 (Canada), and WT/DS293/17 (Argentina), 8 August 2003.

[49] David Winickoff, Sheila Jasanoff, Lawrence Busch, Robin Grove-White, and Brian Wynne 'Adjudicating the GM Food Wars: Science, Risk, and Democracy in World Trade Law' (2005) 30 Yale Journal of International Law 81.

non-accountability of global governance are endemic, the political advantages of such an approach are obvious.[50]

According to Winickoff et al, there is a balance to be struck between trade liberalisation and regulatory self-determination, in the light of which the *Biotech Products* case—where three leading GM crop-growing nations challenged the de facto EU moratorium on GM crop authorization—afforded 'an opportunity to preserve a space for legitimate cultural differences in risk assessment and technology policy within the trading system'.[51] Yet, we might wonder, how could a dispute about the safety of GM crops (and GM foods) be thought to raise questions about regulatory cosmopolitanism?

In a case such as *Biotech Products*, unless the moral exception is invoked, the relevant GATT provisions (especially in the Sanitary and Phytosanitary [SPS] Agreement) channel the disputants towards arguments based on scientific evidence.[52] Where, as in *Biotech Products*, the science relating to the safety of GM crops is contested, how is the matter to be resolved? An innocent response is that the question should be determined by reference to the view supported by 'sound science', this being taken to be a neutral and reliable arbiter. However, for many commentators on the practice and politics of science, including Winickoff et al, this is a naïve view. Science just is not like that. What exactly science is like is another story and it is a matter that we need not pursue. For present purposes, it is enough to understand that scientists reasonably disagree with one another, not just about the bottom-line questions, but about matters of methodology, relevance, and focus. Science is never going to be theory-neutral (that is the whole point of the enterprise) but Winickoff et al deny that it is 'value-neutral'. Consider the case of GM crops:

> The 'products approach' to regulating GMOs assumes that no untoward risk occurs merely from applying this technology to agricultural production. GMOs are subjected to strict rules only when the end products are not substantially equivalent to their conventional counterparts. In contrast, the 'process approach' rests on the idea that genetic engineering itself may entail novel and unique risks to human health or the environment. Whereas the United States has embraced the products approach to GM agriculture, the European Union and its member states have tended to adopt the more precautionary process approach.[53]

So, if scientists on one side of the Atlantic make safety judgments by reference to the end product while scientists on the other side of the Atlantic make (different) safety

[50] ibid 123.

[51] ibid 85.

[52] See, eg, Robert Lee 'GM Resistant: Europe and the WTO Panel Dispute on Biotech Products' in Jennifer Gunning and Søren Hom (eds) *Ethics, Law and Society* (vol 1) (Aldershot: Ashgate, 2005) 131.

[53] Winickoff et al (n 49 above) at 87. Compare Árpád Pusztai and Susan Bardocz 'Nanotechnology and Nanoparticle Toxicity: A Case for Precaution' in Geoffrey Hunt and Michael Mehta (eds) *Nanotechnology: Risk, Ethics and Law* (London: Earthscan, 2006) 167, especially at 174.

judgments by reference to the process used, and if both practices are regarded in their own territories as sound science, then 'sound science' simply cannot serve as a neutral court of appeal.

In the event, the WTO disputes panel in *Biotech Products* made no attempt to settle the question of whether GM crops are safe. The question was not whether the EU position was scientifically vindicated, nor even whether it was a reasonable position as judged by common opinion. Rather, the question was the narrower and more specific one of whether the EU position was consistent with members' obligations under the SPS Agreement. In favour of the EU, it was decided that the de facto moratorium on the approval of biotech products was a legitimate response to the uncertain state of the scientific evidence—in other words, the moratorium was a legitimate provisional and precautionary measure as contemplated by Article 5.7 of the SPS Agreement.[54] However, in favour of the complainants, it was found that the EU was in breach of its obligations by failing to progress individual approval procedures without undue delay and that it was vicariously in breach of its obligations in respect of the safeguard measures taken by the six member states that represent the strongest opposition to GM crops in Europe.[55] Bearing in mind that the Commission had itself defended its own internal market principles by refusing to permit Austria (one of the group of six) to establish a 'GMO-free area', one imagines that, at least in some quarters of Brussels, the latter part of the WTO ruling was neither unexpected nor altogether unwelcome.[56]

Given that European resistance to GM crops was not straightforwardly scientific and precautionary but also was fuelled by moral concerns,[57] if we do not remit disputes such as *Biotech Products* to the court of 'sound science', are we writing a blank cheque for dignitarian exceptionalism? This is certainly not the lesson that we should draw from *Biotech Products*. On the one hand, the panel recognizes that, where there is a level of scientific uncertainty that leaves room

[54] Article 5.7 provides:

In cases where relevant scientific evidence is insufficient, a Member may provisionally adopt sanitary or phytosanitary measures on the basis of available pertinent information, including that from relevant international organizations as well as from sanitary or phytosanitary measures applied by other Members. In such circumstances, Members shall seek to obtain the additional information necessary for a more objective assessment of risk and review the sanitary or phytosanitary measures accordingly within a reasonable period.

[55] Annex C1(a) of the SPS Agreement requires members to undertake and complete 'without undue delay' procedures for checking and ensuring the fulfilment of sanitary or phytosanitary measures.

[56] Compare Sara Poli 'Restrictions on the Cultivation of Genetically Modified Organisms: Issues of EC Law' in Han Somsen (ed) *The Regulatory Challenge of Biotechnology* (Cheltenham: Edward Elgar, 2007) 156, at 160:

The Commission's scrutiny of national measures affecting the internal market traditionally is very strict, especially when it evaluates new scientific evidence. Moreover, the environmental justifications in this particular [Austrian] instance lacked force, which made the outcome of the Commission's evaluation almost inevitable.

[57] See Robert Lee (n 52 above).

for legitimate disagreement, those states that prefer to take a risk-averse approach are allowed, at least provisionally, to do so; on the other hand, where there is little room for scientific doubt, members are not to be encouraged to dress up their moral objections as if they are concerns about safety. Objecting that one does not want to gamble on GM crop safety is one thing; objecting against GM crops—or, for that matter, objecting against gambling—on moral grounds is something else.

We can infer, too, that this is not the position taken by Winickoff et al. They recognize that exceptions against free trade are open to opportunism and abuse. It is important, therefore, that any allowance made for local scientific judgments is not open to being exploited as a pretext for trade protectionism. Accordingly, it is suggested that decision-makers at the WTO should take a hard look at arguments, such as those presented by the EU in *Biotech Products*; and if, and only if, those arguments survive such a level of strict scrutiny, should they be accepted as sufficient reason for denying market access.[58] In the same way, although Winickoff et al self-consciously problematize the relationship between science, culture, and value, I take it that they would want a moral objection out in the open. In the spirit of regulatory cosmopolitanism, there must be room for legitimate local difference, whether it is a difference of scientific or social culture. And, if the relevant difference rests on a dignitarian objection, then it needs to be presented transparently and reviewed for what it is.[59]

Taking stock

Taking stock, it seems that, in principle, regulatory cosmopolitanism should be ready to recognize the following three levels of legitimate local difference: first, where a local community argues that its position is justified in order to preserve the conditions for *any* viable moral community; secondly, where a local community articulates (agreed) universal values in its own particular way; and, thirdly, where the expression of local difference falls within the sphere of either optional cultural variation or acceptable variation in scientific method, practice, and policy. Whether any particular argument is judged to pass muster is another matter, but these three kinds of arguments seem to be the ones where there should be some margin of appreciation.

[58] Winickoff et al (n 49 above) at 108–11.

[59] The need for transparency (and the encouragement of deliberative democracy) is strongly supported by Robert Howse 'Democracy, Science, and Free Trade: Risk Regulation on Trial at the World Trade Organization' (2000) 98 Michigan Law Review 2329. Concluding, at 2357, Howse argues:

> Where there is a concern that domestic regulations may constitute protectionist cheating on negotiated trade concessions, an alternative to harmonization may well be to enhance confidence in the ability to distinguish legitimate domestic regulations from protectionist cheating. Requiring that regulations be defensible in a rational, deliberative public process of justification may well enhance such confidence, while at the very same time serving, not frustrating, democracy.

IV Cosmopolitanism, Chinese Walls, and Cyberspace

For our third test case, we must imagine that a nation state identifies itself in a particular way that marks it out as different from mainstream global culture. Where the local view is permissive (against a restrictive mainstream regulatory approach), almost certainly there will be international pressure for local regulation to be brought into line. However, national sovereignty is challenged in such a case only by the pressure of international politics; and for both the superpowers and the rogue states, this is unlikely to be a serious constraint.[60] Where, by contrast, the local regulatory stance is restrictive, where local citizens are subject to prohibition when permission is the rule elsewhere, then the local regulators will have difficulty in making their policy leakproof. The leaks might occur in more than one direction, as it were, either outgoing or incoming.

The problem of outgoing leaks is partly one of regulatory tourism and partly one of regulatory arbitrage. It is a problem of regulatory tourism to the extent that consumers, with the necessary resources and determination, will travel to places where the goods or services that are restricted at home may be lawfully procured. In earlier chapters, we mentioned Diane Blood and the Whitaker family who travelled, respectively, to Brussels and to Chicago, to procure the reproductive services that were not lawfully available in the United Kingdom.[61] In the same way, end-of-life services that are not lawfully available in the United Kingdom may be procured in Switzerland, recreational drugs may be procured in Dutch cafes, experimental stem cell treatments in the Far East, and so on. So long as such tourism is a trickle rather than a flood, the local (restrictive) regulatory position is not literally breached and its credibility is not wholly undermined. Nevertheless, over time, regulatory tourism weakens the local position. Moreover, where a state engages self-consciously in regulatory arbitrage, its intention being positively to attract business, the weakening of local restrictions is likely to be much more significant. So, for example, if a state creates a permissive regulatory environment for biotechnological research and development with a view to attracting businesses that find themselves constrained by their local regulatory environments, and if such businesses relocate (or threaten to relocate), then this creates a major problem for local regulators and their restrictive policy.

The problem of incoming leaks is not a new one. Illegal cross-border trafficking of all manner of persons and commodities is hardly a new phenomenon. However, with the development of the internet, the old problem of policing one's borders seemed to be overshadowed by the new problem of regulating cyberspace. If the seminal debate between the cyberlibertarians and the

[60] Compare Gerry Simpson *Great Powers and Outlaw States* (Cambridge: Cambridge University Press, 2004).

[61] In chs 5 and 6.

cyberpaternalists was partly about the *legitimacy* of regulating the traffic that flowed through cyberspace, it was at least as much about the *possibility* of controlling that traffic. Famously, David Johnson and David Post[62] argued that nation states would have fundamentally to rethink their regulatory approach if they were to exert any control over the goods and services supplied on line, and over internet content more generally. To state the obvious, for Westphalian nation state sovereignty to prosper in the physical world, we need to have clearly marked national boundaries and flags of jurisdictional authority. In the cyberworld, we have no such markers. To be sure, there is a boundary between online and offline environments; but, as Johnson and Post highlighted, once we enter the virtual world, whatever lines we have to cross, they bear no relationship to the lines of the physical world. In cyberspace, there is scope for private governance—arguably, too much scope[63]—but the writ of local public regulation does not run so well in the virtual world.

A decade or so on from the opening shots, we can scarcely dismiss cyberlibertarianism as a spent force. For the 'Internet separatists', as Joel Reidenberg calls them,[64] seem to think that the Rule of Law (and national rules of law) simply do not apply to their online activities. Hence:

> The defenses for hate, lies, drugs, sex, gambling, and stolen music are in essence that technology justifies the denial of personal jurisdiction, the rejection of an assertion of applicable law by a sovereign state, and the denial of the enforcement of decisions...In the face of these claims, legal systems engage in a rather conventional struggle to adapt existing regulatory standards to new technologies and the Internet. Yet, the underlying fight is a profound struggle against the very right of sovereign states to establish rules for online activity.[65]

On the other hand, as Reidenberg notes, we should not underrate the resourcefulness of local regulators, particularly their willingness to become more robust in claiming jurisdiction and choice of law over extra-territorial servers (particularly where there is a technological link with local equipment). In practice, nation states have not altogether surrendered their regulatory sovereignty. Indeed, Jack Goldsmith and Tim Wu[66] have recently argued that, even with the global linking

[62] David R Johnson and David Post 'Law and Borders – The Rise of Law in Cyberspace' (1996) 48 Stanford Law Review 1367. But, for a different assessment, see eg, Jack Goldsmith 'Against Cyberanarchy' (1998) 65 University of Chicago Law Review 1199.

[63] Notably, see Lawrence Lessig *The Future of Ideas* (New York: Vintage Books, 2001) and *Code Version 2.0* (New York: Basic Books, 2006); and Joel R Reidenberg 'Lex Informatica: The Formulation of Information Policy Rules Through Technology' (1998) 76 Texas Law Review 553.

[64] Joel R Reidenberg 'Technology and Internet Jurisdicition' (2005) 153 University of Pennsylvania Law Review 1951.

[65] ibid 1953–4.

[66] Jack Goldsmith and Tim Wu *Who Controls the Internet?* (Oxford: Oxford University Press, 2006).

that is effected through the technology of the internet, local differences persist and are successfully defended. Thus:

> [H]uman beings tend to cluster geographically, based on shared cultures, languages, tastes, wealth, and values.... [D]ifferent people in different places will often demand different types of Internet experiences and... the market will often comply. Often, however, these differences are also enforced through government coercion, as when France made Yahoo keep out nazi goods, or when Australia made Dow Jones pay for libelling one of its citizens, or when the United States blocked Internet gambling from Antigua. This is the other side of globalization: the determined preservation of difference, the deliberate resistance to homogenizing influence.[67]

But, how precisely are local regulators to enforce their local restrictions against undesired incoming internet traffic? First, it should be said that the range of options available to local regulators depends upon whether the political culture is authoritarian or liberal. If the culture is authoritarian, the state will control the internet at all key layers and, in this context, it will be possible for local regulators to establish Chinese walls and filters that enable it to determine the content that is available to users.[68] Where the culture is liberal, direct control of this kind is not feasible. Essentially, liberal states seem to have three options. First, they can rely in an ad hoc fashion on measures that target relevant regulatees, or their assets, where such persons or their assets are physically within the jurisdiction—in the way, for example, that the French were able to act against Yahoo! by targeting Yahoo!'s assets in France. Secondly, they might enter into systematic cooperative arrangements with other local regulators in a scheme of the kind sketched by Lawrence Lessig. Or, thirdly, they might engage in the use of technological sanctions. We can speak briefly to each of these approaches.

Consider, again, the case of internet gambling. In many places, the local regulatory view is that gambling is immoral and should be prohibited or (at the very least) discouraged; or that, even if gambling is not immoral, it can be a source of exploitation and addictive misery and, thus, it should be heavily regulated. How are such states to respond when internet gambling service providers find a regulatory haven from which to operate extra-territorially? Colin Scott offers an informative commentary on the responses made by New York State, Australia, and the United Kingdom.[69] In New York State, as in Australia, the policy was for prohibition, but the regulatory challenge was to find a strategy that would have the desired effect in relation to providers located outside the jurisdiction. Rather than targeting the online casino operators, the New York State strategy was to enrol the local

[67] ibid 183.

[68] For a helpful review, see Ronald J Deibert and Nart Villeneuve 'Firewalls and Power: An Overview of Global State Censorship of the Internet' in Mathias Klang and Andrew Murray (eds) *Human Rights in the Digital Age* (London: Cavendish Glasshouse, 2005) 111.

[69] Colin Scott 'Between the Old and the New: Innovation in the Regulation of Internet Gambling' in Julia Black, Martin Lodge, and Mark Thatcher (eds) *Regulatory Innovation* (Cheltenham: Edward Elgar, 2005) 114.

payment intermediaries who, for the most part, agreed to refuse credit card transactions involving Internet gambling. Australian regulators sought to follow this regulatory lead but without anything approaching the same degree of success; evidently, the Australian banks did not accept that by servicing a general purpose credit facility they were acting illegally and they were unwilling to assist the regulators on a voluntary basis. By contrast, the policy in the United Kingdom was much less restrictive. In fact, the objective here was to create a regulatory environment that would encourage responsible providers, acting under licence, to offer trusted and credible online gaming facilities. While, relatively speaking, the New York State story speaks to the continuing power of smart local regulators, it would be premature to celebrate the rediscovery of local sovereignty. The New York State strategy did not work in Australia; and, even in New York State, there might yet be unintended effects as providers and users seek to evade local controls. Thus:

[I]llustrating the problems of unintended effects, the targeting of financial intermediaries appears to be creating incentives to organizations other than banks to establish themselves as financial intermediaries. The creation of this new non-banking market in supplying payment mechanisms creates the risk of generating a substantial market in payment mechanisms which are more difficult for the state to monitor and control. Thus their emergence may amplify the problem that targeting of intermediaries was designed to address and create other problems, for example creating new mechanisms for money laundering.[70]

Plus ça change. Regulators, whether they are dealing with online or offline activities, need to get smart and to stay smart.

Where cybercrime is concerned, there is a considerable emphasis on international cooperation.[71] Might there be a cooperative arrangement that would help local communities to support one another in maintaining their local identities? To be sure, the regulatory restrictions in one local community will differ from those in another; in one, the restrictions might be on gambling, in another on pornography, in another on hate speech, and so on; but, the communities have it in common that they need one another's help in enforcing local restrictions. Prompted by this, Lawrence Lessig has suggested that it might be possible to devise an arrangement in which local regulators take steps to prevent local servers supplying inappropriate content to citizens who are in other jurisdictions.[72] How would this work? First, online users would carry passports that declared their citizenship. Secondly, an international table would be drawn up in which nation states declared their local restrictions. Thirdly, local regulators would require

[70] ibid 134.

[71] The model for international cooperation is the Council of Europe's Convention on Cybercrime (Budapest, 23 November 2001). For a recent programmatic initiative, see International Telecommunication Union, *ITU Global Cybersecurity Agenda [GCA]: A Framework for International Cooperation in Cybersecurity* (Geneva, October 2007).

[72] Lawrence Lessig *Code Version 2.0* (New York: Basic Books, 2006) ch 15.

servers within their jurisdiction to respect the restrictions as laid out in the table. And, all being well, the servers would know which restrictions to apply to which users because of the required declaration of citizenship. Hence:

> The pact would look like this. Each state would promise to enforce on servers within its jurisdiction the regulations of other states for citizens from those other states, in exchange for having its own regulations enforced in other jurisdictions. New York would require that servers within New York keep Minnesotans away from New York gambling servers, in exchange for Minnesota keeping New York citizens away from privacy-exploiting servers. Utah would keep EU citizens away from privacy-exploiting servers, in exchange for Europe keeping Utah citizens away from European gambling sites.[73]

This is an elegant exercise in reciprocity and, as Lessig remarks:

> Such a regime would return geographical zoning to the Net. It would re-impose borders on a network built without those borders. It would give the regulators in Hungary and Thailand the power to do what they can't do just now—control their citizens as they want. It would leave citizens of the United States or Sweden as free as their government has determined they should be.[74]

Rather obviously, however, the restoration of borders will work only as far as reciprocity extends. If Antigua has no local culture that is under internet threat, why should it join the pact? And, if Antigua continues to allow its local servers to supply on-line gambling facilities to the citizens of Minnesota and Utah, it is a minor consolation that, further to the pact, such services are no longer supplied from sites in New York or Europe.

More to the point, for present purposes, it is not clear how far Lessig's proposal rises to the particular regulatory challenge presented by the cosmopolitan ideal. One dimension of cosmopolitanism demands that we have universal concern for our fellows. But, if zoning means that nation states are able, in Lessig's words, to 'control their citizens as they want', leaving them to be only as free as they want them to be, there must be some control over the nature of the restrictions that the contracting states are permitted to enter into the international table. The international table cannot be treated as an open invitation to flout the universal values of cosmopolitanism—or, at any rate, those values about which there is broad agreement. Needless to say, if (as is the case) the universal values are themselves contested, no state will want to enter into a pact that commits it to aiding and abetting the enforcement of standards that it believes are contrary to universal values. Mutual toleration, like reciprocity, has its limits.

If these difficulties can be resolved, there is the further matter of the citizenship passports that online users would have to carry. In the real world, we are required to carry passports that bear a great deal more information about the holder than Lessig proposes. Arguably, then, we should not be unduly concerned

[73] ibid 308. [74] ibid 309.

about any threat to the privacy of online passport holders.[75] However, in a world that is moving towards biometric identifiers, it is unwise to isolate such an online proposal from the background of much greater offline surveillance. It would be a sad day for cosmopolitanism if, in our efforts to restore effective local regulatory restriction, we undermined the values that merit universal support.

The third option for national regulators, an option highlighted by Joel Reidenberg, is to turn the technology back on the separatists.[76] If an extra-territorial operator will not comply with local rules, why not disable the offending site, or official sites in the host jurisdiction,[77] by denial-of-service measures, or the like? As Reidenberg says:

> Technology empowers sovereign states with very potent electronic tools to enforce their policies and decisions even in the absence of a wrongdoer's physical presence or tangible assets. States can use filters and packet interceptors as well as hacker tools like viruses and worms to enforce decisions and sanction malfeasance.[78]

While such measures might be effective, there are rather obvious issues of legitimacy in this technological turn. For sovereign states that are not too much bothered about the Rule of Law, effective enforcement is the priority and legitimacy is a side issue. However, if our concern (and this is certainly one of Reidenberg's concerns) is that there is a dangerous tendency to regard on-line technological measures as immune against the Rule of Law, then sovereign states that value the Rule of Law need to be very careful not to send out the wrong signals when they resort to the use of technological enforcement.

V Taking Stock: One Challenge after Another

In this and the preceding chapters, we have identified and discussed a series of challenges—challenges concerning legitimacy, effectiveness, connection, and now cosmopolitanism—that face regulators who are trying to channel conduct in relation to the technologies of our time. What does this story suggest?

I think that we can safely conclude that, in at least three respects, the development of modern technologies has increased the challenges confronting regulators. First, the challenge of maintaining regulatory connection is generic to

[75] Compare the ITU Global Cybersecurity Agenda (n 71 above), one of the objectives of which is to develop strategies for the creation and endorsement of a generic and universal digital identity system.

[76] Reidenberg (n 64 above).

[77] The thinking here is that action against official sites might encourage the host regulators to clamp down on the offending activity. One is reminded of the denial-of-service attacks, allegedly originating from Russia, that disabled Estonian government sites in 2007. Compare, also, Richard Norton-Taylor 'Titan Rain – How Chinese Hackers Targeted Whitehall' *The Guardian* 5 September 2007, p 1.

[78] Reidenberg (n 64 above) at 1963.

rapidly developing technologies and regulators are still learning how to handle this difficulty. Secondly, the development of biotechnology has sharpened and shaped ethical differences in a way that makes it very difficult for regulators to take up positions that are accepted as legitimate; and the developments that we can anticipate in both nanomedicine and neurotechnology are liable to reinforce this particular challenge. Thirdly, to the extent that the spread of new technologies has contributed to the creation of a global village, international regulators cannot easily ignore—and nor should they ignore[79]—the demands of cosmopolitanism any more than local regulators can close their borders.

While the development of new technologies might raise the regulatory bar, we should not jump to the conclusion that we are facing a regulatory crisis. In a sense, we might view regulation as in a permanent state of crisis. In particular, if we start from the hypothesis that traditional legal interventions are not particularly effective, and sometimes do more harm than good, then our expectations will not be that high. From this perspective, attempts to develop regulatory strategies that rely on instruments other than strictly legal ones, that seek out approaches that promise to be more effective than traditional command and control, should be seen as healthy signs of regulatory innovation and imagination. Regulators understand that law does not rule the world; so, even if there is a crisis, there is certainly no complacency.

The moral of the story, thus far, might be that, in the face of fresh challenges, regulators are seeking out new opportunities and options. Better regulators will find better ways. And, indeed, one way, one option, might be seen in the very technologies that are responsible for creating the selfsame challenges. If the new technologies could be exploited as regulatory instruments, might this be the answer to the regulators' difficulties? It is with this thought that we move on into the second part of the book.

[79] See the powerful argument in Geoffrey Hunt 'The Global Ethics of Nanotechnology' in Geoffrey Hunt and Michael Mehta (eds) *Nanotechnology: Risk, Ethics and Law* (London: Earthscan, 2006) 183.

II

REGULATORY OPPORTUNITY

8

Genetic Databases and the First Signs of Regulatory Opportunity

I Introduction

Having reviewed a range of issues relating to the legitimate and effective regulation of modern technologies, the focus in this second part of the book shifts to the employment of such technologies as regulatory tools. The prognosis is that state regulators will increasingly turn to such technologies in order to channel the conduct of regulatees. Sometimes, the turn to technology will be a response to the failure of other regulatory strategies, particularly a lack of effectiveness; at other times, technology will be adopted simply because this is the way that modern societies do things. As the authors of an important report for the Information Commissioner have recently maintained, the development of the surveillance society is not so much a conspiracy as 'a part of just being modern'.[1]

In such a society,[2] as the technologies of surveillance[3] become increasingly sophisticated, less obtrusive and embedded, citizens will not always be aware that they are being monitored and regulated. Thus:

> [The] continuous software-sorting of people and their life chances in cities is organised through myriad electronic and physical 'passage points' or 'choke points', negotiated through a widening number of code words, pass words, PIN numbers, user names, access controls, electronic cards or biometric scans. Some are highly visible and negotiated willingly (a PIN credit card purchase or an airport passport control). Others are more covert (the sorting of internet or call centre traffic). On still other occasions, the passage point is clear (a CCTV camera on a street or a speed camera on a motorway), but it is impossible to know in practice if one's face or car number plate has actually been scanned.[4]

More generally, the 'combination of CCTV, biometrics, databases and tracking technologies can be seen as part of a much broader exploration . . . of the use of

[1] Kirstie Ball, David Lyon, David Murakami Wood, Clive Norris, and Charles Raab *A Report on the Surveillance Society* (September 2006) para 1.6.

[2] Ball et al (n 1 above) identify the key characteristics of such a society as one in which 'we find purposeful, routine, systematic and focused attention paid to personal details, for the sake of control, entitlement, management, influence or protection' (para 3.1).

[3] For a review of the range of such technologies, see ibid at paras 9.3 et seq.

[4] ibid para 9.10.2.

interconnected 'smart' systems to track movements and behaviours of millions of people in both time and space'.[5]

In this chapter, the particular part of the modern technological complex that we will consider is that of genetic databases. Where genetic databases are constructed for forensic purposes, as a feature of the criminal justice system, this is a clear example of a modern technology being employed as a regulatory instrument. Where, by contrast, genetic databases are constructed for public health purposes, it is not so clear that we are dealing with a regulatory tool. However, there are two reasons for reflecting on the development of the latter kind of database in the context of technology as a regulatory tool. One reason is that, if we understand more about the conditions for good health (however specified) as a result of analysing the database information—just as we came to make the connection between smoking tobacco and various serious diseases—the state will surely act on this understanding to channel conduct towards healthier lifestyles. The other reason is that, in practice, it will be very difficult to maintain Chinese walls between forensic and health collections: if the state requires access to a public health database in order to prevent or detect serious crime, it will surely go right ahead to access the data in question.[6]

Having said this, in principle, there would seem to be an important difference between taking, retaining and processing human genetic samples without the consent of the source and doing so with the source's free and informed consent. To be sure, there will be some grey cases (for example, so-called 'dragnet' sampling by the police when suspicion falls on a large group; or taking samples from suspects where the choice is either to give a sample or face a penalty for opting not to give a sample)[7] where what is formally treated as a taking with consent is, in reality, a taking under pressure. However, to stick with the polar cases—at one pole, that of taking without consent and, at the other, that of taking with consent—then, whereas the former cries out for justification, the latter seems to be ethically clean—or, at any rate, this would seem to be so in what I am referring to as a community of rights.[8]

Generally speaking, where human genetic samples are taken, retained, and processed for public health purposes, this will be on the basis of free and informed consent. By contrast, although some human genetic samples might be voluntarily

[5] ibid para 9.10.3.

[6] Generally, see Jane Kaye 'Police Collection and Access to DNA Samples' (2006) 2(1) *Genomics, Society and Policy* 16; and, for a particular example, in which a New Zealand court authorized police access to the Guthrie Cards (heel prick blood spots) of two suspected murder victims, see Katie Elkin and D Gareth Jones 'Guthrie Cards: Legal and Ethical Issues' (2000) 1(2) New Zealand Bioethics Journal 22 (I am indebted to Sue Gibbons for this latter reference).

[7] See the French National Consultative Ethics Committee for Health and Life Sciences *Opinion No 98* (Biometrics, identifying data and human rights) Annex I, where it is stated that, under French law, although consent is generally required for biosampling, 'refusing to submit to biosampling' is itself an offence.

[8] See ch 1.

given for forensic purposes, characteristically such taking, retaining, and processing is not consent-based. Rather, the state's justification is taken to lie in compelling considerations of the public interest that warrant overriding the ordinary rights of citizens—most obviously the consideration that the compelled taking and retaining of DNA samples is necessary if the security of citizens against the threat of crime is to be assured.

In the light of these short reflections, the following sequence of thoughts—a classic case of the slippery slope—might be prompted:

- that, in a community of rights, the protection of the rights of potential victims of (serious) crime grounds a sound public interest justification for the compelled (non-consensual) taking, retaining, and processing of human genetic samples for forensic purposes
- that, if the rights of potential victims of (serious) crime are to be prioritized, there is an arguable case for compelled population-wide (universal) participation in such a forensic collection
- that, if there is an arguable case for compelled participation in such a forensic collection, there is also an arguable case for compelled participation in a public health collection
- that, if the rights of potential victims of serious disease are to be prioritized, there is an arguable case for compelled population-wide (universal) participation in such a public health collection
- that the logic of these ideas is that the databases should be consolidated into a single national collection, possibly into a larger regional collection, and
- that a community of rights should only back away from such steps if, for precautionary reasons, it judges that such a collection would invite abuse, and present a hostage to fortune.

In this chapter, I will track this possibly troubling sequence of thoughts in the following way. First (in Part II), I focus on forensic collections, entertaining the thought that, in a community of rights, it might be plausible to argue for a comprehensive population-wide DNA database. Secondly (in Part III), I turn to collections for public health purposes. If the state is justified in compelling the supply of DNA samples for forensic purposes, there might seem to be a case, contrary to present practice and philosophy, for compelling participation in public health biobanking projects. Moreover, if the move to population-wide forensic collections is sound, there might seem to be a case not just for compulsion but also for universal participation. While I doubt that the argument for compulsory population-wide *forensic* collections can be transposed so straightforwardly to compulsory population-wide *public health* collections, I do not reject the proposition that collections of this latter kind might be justified in a community of rights. To be sure, in a community of rights, individual autonomy is celebrated but this is also a community where individuals might be judged to have responsibilities to assist with collective projects that are designed to strengthen the conditions of security and well-being that are essential for individuals to make the most of their autonomy. Thirdly (in Part IV), I ask whether it makes sense to combine the forensic and health collections: if we are to express our solidarity by being all for one in these population-wide sets, in the interests of efficiency should we also operate with one for all? Finally (in Part V), I resort to precautionary reasoning to pull back somewhat from my provisional conclusions, my concern being that we are setting in chain a sequence of moves that might threaten the viability of moral community itself. This cues in the succeeding chapters in this part of the book in which we try to broaden and deepen our thinking about the use of technology as a regulatory tool.

II Forensic collections

How is the state to justify the compelled taking, processing, and retaining of DNA samples for forensic purposes? The short answer is that while, so far as possible, the process of policing should operate by consent, it is sometimes necessary for the state to have compulsory powers. In any liberal democracy, there will be a constant debate about striking the right balance between the imperatives of crime control and the demands of respect for due process.[9] Accordingly, there will be debate about who must supply a DNA sample, in which circumstances, and under which conditions the state may retain such samples. Where due process values are strong, police powers will be tightly circumscribed: a DNA sample will be compelled only where a suspect is arrested in connection with a serious offence and its retention will be permitted only where that person is convicted of a serious offence. Where due process values are less resilient, police powers will be wider.[10]

Broadly speaking, in the United Kingdom, under a clutch of controversial legislative provisions, the police may take a DNA sample from anyone who is arrested and detained in connection with a recordable offence (these being offences that carry the possibility of a custodial sentence plus more than 50 non-imprisonable offences). Furthermore, following the Criminal Justice Act 2003, the sample that has been taken may be retained indefinitely even though the person is not actually prosecuted or, if prosecuted, is acquitted. Hence, the National DNA Database, which already holds several million DNA profiles, includes a significant number of profiles of persons who have come into contact with the police but who are, formally speaking, 'innocent'. The breadth of these powers offends civil libertarians, who note the far more restrictive powers generally available elsewhere in

[9] Seminally, see Herbert L Packer *The Limits of the Criminal Sanction* (Stanford: Stanford University Press, 1969).

[10] See Deryck Beyleveld 'Ethical Issues in the Forensic Applications of DNA Analysis' 88 Forensic Science International 3; and Nuffield Council on Bioethics *The Forensic Use of Bioinformation: Ethical Issues* (London, 2007).

Europe (including in Scotland); and, while the profile that is retained itself does not disclose sensitive (eg medical) information about the individual,[11] the underlying sample (which is also retained) has such potential and, thus, raises questions about respect for an individual's right to privacy. Having said this, there is no doubting the utility of the collection in general (profiles of individuals being compared with samples collected from crime scenes both to eliminate and to identify suspects) and the retained profiles in particular, these having been linked with a significant number of murders, attempted murders, rapes, sexual offences, aggravated burglaries, and offences relating to the supply of drugs.[12]

In *R v Chief Constable of South Yorkshire Police, ex parte LS and Marper*,[13] the appeal courts held that section 82 of the Criminal Justice and Police Act 2001, which authorizes retention of the samples (both fingerprints and DNA samples) even where there is no prosecution or there is an acquittal, is compatible with the rights of privacy and non-discrimination as protected by the European Convention on Human Rights. While the judges in *Marper* are not quite at one in deciding whether the right to informational privacy is engaged under Article 8(1) of the European Convention on Human Rights, they have no hesitation in accepting that the state can justify the legislation under Article 8(2) by reference to the compelling public interest in the prevention and detection of serious crime.

In the Court of Appeal, Lord Woolf CJ suggests that, whether or not retention is seen as engaging the privacy right, 'depends very much on the cultural traditions of a particular state'.[14] If fingerprints are viewed as personal information, so too is DNA. This is not to deny that there might be a certain shading of opinions. As Lord Woolf puts it:

> There are no doubt a rainbow of reactions which are possible to intrusions of this nature, but at least for a substantial proportion of the public there is a strong objection to the State storing information relating to an individual unless there is some objective justification for this happening.[15]

Sedley LJ explicitly agrees, relying on the 'strong cultural unease in the United Kingdom about the official collection and retention of information about individuals'.[16] Yet, is this correct? The DNA profiles held in the National DNA Database are identifying metrics which can be employed to gather information about a particular

[11] The profiles are generated from sequences of DNA, so-called short tandem repeat (STR) sequences, that are derived from non-coding 'junk' DNA.

[12] See, eg, S Bird 'Architect who Dressed as Tramp to Attack Girls Trapped by DNA' *The Times* 15 June 2006, p 3; A Norfolk 'Shoe Rapist is Trapped by Sister's DNA 20 Years After Serial Attacks' *The Times*, 18 July 2006, p 3; and I Sample 'DNA Advances Lengthen Long Arm of the Law' *The Guardian* 9 September 2006, p 18.

[13] [2002] EWCA Civ 1275, [2004] UKHL 39. At the time of writing, Marper's challenge has been treated as admissible by the European Court of Human Rights and fast-tracked for hearing by the Grand Chamber.

[14] [2002] EWCA Civ 1275, para 32.

[15] ibid para 34.

[16] ibid para 68.

individuated agent. Where there is no match (between a profile and a crime scene sample), we can say that the individuated agent probably was not at the scene of the crime; where there is a positive match, we can say the opposite. Contrary to the views of the Court of Appeal, one might doubt whether there is a cultural unease in the United Kingdom about the state having the capacity to draw on such locating information; but, more importantly, one might question whether contingent cultural ease or unease is the right way to distinguish between privacy engagement and non-engagement.

When *Marper* was appealed, the House of Lords took a rather different approach to the engagement of privacy, distancing itself from the culturally contingent view espoused by the Court of Appeal. Giving the leading speech, Lord Steyn said:

> While I would not wish to subscribe to all the generalisations in the Court of Appeal about cultural traditions in the United Kingdom, in comparison with other European states, I do accept that when one moves on to consider the question of objective justification under article 8(2) the cultural traditions in the United Kingdom are material. With great respect to Lord Woolf CJ the same is not true under article 8(1).... The question whether the retention of fingerprints and samples engages article 8(1) should receive a uniform interpretation throughout member states, unaffected by different cultural traditions.[17]

Having rejected a custom-based approach, and having reviewed the essentially identifying metric nature of a DNA profile (the profile, as such, tells you nothing about the physical make-up, characteristics, health, or life of the individuated agent), Lord Steyn concluded that retention either does not engage Article 8(1) at all or engages it only very modestly.[18]

The strongest support for the engagement of Article 8(1) is given by Lady Hale. For example, she says:

> It could be said that the samples are not 'information'.... But the only reason that they are taken or kept is for the information which they contain. They are not kept for their intrinsic value as mouth swabs, hairs or whatever. They are kept because they contain the individual's unique genetic code within them. They are kept as information about that person and nothing else. Fingerprints and profiles are undoubtedly information. The same privacy principles should apply to all three.[19]

While the points made about the rich information-bearing potential of the DNA *samples* are extremely well-taken, it is not so clear that the same applies to the *profiles*. Arguably, the profiles are not so much 'information about that person' but information that enables us to identify who 'that person' is. Insofar as the profiles, in conjunction with crime-scene samples, yield information about an individuated agent's location, there is a question about whether the privacy right is engaged.

[17] [2004] UKHL 39, para 27.
[18] ibid para 31.
[19] ibid para 70.

However, that question needs to be squarely addressed rather than answered on the back of the privacy-engaging character of the full DNA sample.[20]

If we pause to reflect on the point at which the privacy right is engaged, how might we view the relationship between profiling and privacy? Putting the matter in a non-profiling way, do I violate your privacy rights if I observe and identify you at a particular place at a particular time? If not, what is wrong with constructing and using a profile in order to determine whether a particular person was or was not at a crime scene?

Consider the simple case of observing, identifying, and locating. For example, suppose that, one evening, as I leave college, I spot a colleague on the other side of the Strand. On the basis of this observation, I have information as to the whereabouts of this particular person at a particular time. If a crime were being committed on the other side of the Strand, I know that this particular person was present at a crime scene. Yet, would anyone argue that my colleague's privacy rights were prima facie engaged by my actions? Even if I were to record my observation in my diary, it is still doubtful, is it not, that my colleague's privacy interest is engaged? But, why not?

If we think that our privacy interest is engaged in circumstances where we have a reasonable expectation either that our space will not be invaded by others (against our will) or that we are in control of access to information about ourselves,[21] then our views about the prima facie engagement of the privacy right will hinge on our reasonable expectations. The answer to this question, I suggest, depends on whether our reasonable expectations are based on convention and practice or on some independent criterion of reasonableness.[22] If we adopt the former approach, the position will be clear where the conventions and practice are clear (and I suggest that it is pretty clear that my coincidental observation of my colleague's location either fails to engage the privacy right or involves no violation because the right is partly disengaged to the extent that one is located in a public place), but we will be in difficulty once the circumstances fall outside such clear cases. Equally, if we adopt the latter approach, there are difficulties about grounding it

[20] It should be noted that there is also an interesting privacy issue arising from so-called familial DNA profiling. In some cases, although DNA samples taken from a crime scene might not fully match any profile held in the database, they might be a near-match to a particular profile. In such a case, there is a possibility that a close genetic relative of the person who has the near-match profile will be a full match. This was so, for example, in the 'Shoe Rapist' case where the rapist was identified when a near-match showed up between crime-scene samples and the DNA profile of the rapist's sister (the sister's profile being taken in connection with a drink driving offence): see A Norfolk, 'Shoe Rapist is Trapped by Sister's DNA 20 Years After Serial Attacks' *The Times*, 18 July 2006, p 3. Quite apart from the investigative potency of familial DNA profiling, there is obviously the possibility that researching the DNA of family members might uncover embarrassing (and privacy-engaging) secrets about a person's genetic pedigree.

[21] Compare Graeme Laurie *Genetic Privacy* (Cambridge: Cambridge University Press, 2002) for the distinction between the spatial and informational dimensions of privacy.

[22] Roger Brownsword 'Knowing Me, Knowing You – Profiling, Privacy and the Public Interest' in Mireille Hildebrandt and Serge Gutwirth (eds) *Profiling the European Citizen* (Dordrecht: Springer, 2008) 362.

(where precisely do we find an independent anchoring point for the reasonableness of our expectations?) and then, inevitably, there will be elements of uncertainty as to its application.

In the light of these remarks, consider four degrees of profiling as follows:

- The profile either positively or negatively locates/links a person to a particular place at a particular time. It is not cumulative; it is just the one item. Negative locating (this person was not) there says very little about the person in most contexts, but there might be some contexts where, exceptionally, this throws the burden of explanation on that person. Positive locating normally is heavier with information but is there really a privacy issue here if I can be positively located in public places anyway?
- The profile aggregates information about a person, using items of information that taken individually do not raise a privacy issue. For example, a 12 hour GSP track or a chart of a person's shopping preferences (read off a loyalty card) tells us more about the person. But does this cumulative profile change the privacy position? Or, are we now moving into a distinct sphere of data protection?[23]
- The profile draws out a latent pattern of preferences or behaviours of which the person was not aware.
- The profile uses the pattern, whether patent or latent, to categorise the person in a particular way/to place the person in a particular group or set.

Each time that profiling is ratcheted up one more degree, the thought that the privacy right is engaged probably becomes more compelling. However, so long as the National DNA Database is using only first-degree profiling, we might hesitate, as most of the judges in *Marper* hesitated, before declaring that the privacy right is engaged.

No doubt, as profile-led policing gains ground, it is unlikely that DNA profiling will remain at the first level. If profiling works, it will surely be employed in a way that goes wider and deeper.[24] Quite how quickly profling will go deeper it is difficult to predict, but we can predict with some confidence that it will go wider quite quickly. Indeed, the then Prime Minister, Tony Blair, voluntarily provided a sample of his own DNA for the database in 1999 and, after a recent visit to the facility, he remarked that 'The number on the database should be the maximum you can get'[25]—in other words, the more database profiles the better.

[23] See Roger Brownsword 'Consent in Data Protection Law: A Vote of 'No Confidence'?' paper given at international conference on 'Reinventing Data Protection?' Brussels, 12–13 October 2007.

[24] Bert-Jaap Koops and Ronald Leenes '"Code" and the Slow Erosion of Privacy' (2005) 12 Michigan Telecommunications and Technology Law Review 115.

[25] See <http://www.timesonline.co.uk/article/0,,29389-2418045,00.html>; and *Bioethics News: Issue 91* (London: Nuffield Council on Bioethics, 27 October 2006).

In *Marper*, Lord Woolf CJ, appreciating the benefits of DNA sampling does not rule out the possibility of a population-wide collection. According to the Lord Chief Justice:

So far as the prevention and detection of crime is concerned, it is obvious the larger the databank of fingerprints and DNA samples available to the police, the greater the value of the databank will be in preventing crime and detecting those responsible for crime. There can be no doubt that if every member of the public was required to provide fingerprints and a DNA sample this would make a dramatic contribution to the prevention and detection of crime. To take but one example, the great majority of rapists who are not known already to their victim would be able to be identified.[26]

And, more recently, Stephen Sedley has alarmed civil libertarians by arguing that a population-wide collection is required as a matter of fairness.[27] Similarly, as we remarked in Chapter 1, Lord Steyn is enthusiastic about the state making use of new forensic technologies, urging the law enforcement agencies to 'take full advantage of the available techniques of modern technology and forensic science'. [28]

With some 4 million profiles now held on the National DNA Database and with the average person being caught 300 times a day on CCTV, the United Kingdom is setting the pace for profiling-led criminal justice. Arguably, the pace is too fast. Certainly, if the European Court of Human Rights—which has not only treated *Marper* as admissible but as raising such significant issues as to justify immediate referral to the Grand Chamber—decides that the UK is out of line with its convention commitments, the pace will need to slow. However, let us not anticipate too much of the future. At this point, let us leave forensic collections and turn to public health collections.

III Public Health Collections

Introducing the first Annual Report of the UK Biobank Ethics and Governance Council,[29] Alastair Campbell writes:

Biobanks—major collections of biological, environmental and health data—are set to become a major feature of health research in the future. They offer a huge potential for a rich understanding of the causes of ill-health and disease and for the development of effective therapies and preventative measures.[30]

[26] [2002] EWCA Civ 1275, para 17; similarly Sedley LJ at para 87.

[27] Steve Bird 'Judge Causes Furore by Calling for Record of Everyone's DNA' *The Times* 6 September 2007, p 25.

[28] [2004] UKHL 39, at paras 1–2.

[29] UK Biobank Ethics and Governance Council *Annual Report 2004–2005* (London). Available at <http://www.egcukbiobank.org.uk/assets/wtx032076.pdf>.

[30] ibid 2.

So it is that, in company with a number of European countries, the UK has seen the potential healthcare benefits that might flow from an improved understanding of the way in which a person's genetic make-up, their lifestyle and their environment interact.[31]

The declared aim of the UK Biobank[32] is to develop a major healthcare resource that will throw light on the interaction between genetic make-up, environment, and lifestyle, so that more effective measures for the prevention and treatment of disease might be developed. To this end, lifestyle and environmental information from some 500,000 volunteers (aged 40–69) is in the process of being collected (enrolment having started in spring 2007), such information being linked to medical records and biological samples. The reason for selecting this particular age group is that these are the persons most likely to succumb to common serious illnesses such as heart disease and stroke. Typically, participants will stay active with the project until their death (in some cases, many years after they have been first enrolled). Indeed, even after the death (or mental incapacitation) of participants they will maintain a passive involvement because UK Biobank will retain and continue to make use of their samples and data.[33]

Broadly speaking, so far as UK Biobank's relationship with participants is concerned, the Ethics and Governance Framework (EGF)[34] designs in provisions that are relatively strong on consent, weak on property (participants being informed of 'the fact that UK Biobank will be the legal owner of the database and the sample collection, and that participants will have no property rights in the samples'[35]), and reasonably protective of participants' interests in privacy and confidentiality.[36] In the present context, we need not inquire any further as to the property issue. However, we need to say a little more, first, about privacy and then about consent.

[31] For a helpful overview and critical comparative survey of the various governance structures adopted by biobanks in Europe, see Susan Gibbons 'Are UK Genetic Databases Governed Adequately? A Comparative Legal Analysis' (2007) 27 Legal Studies 312.

[32] See <http://www.ukbiobank.ac.uk>; Jean V McHale 'Regulating Genetic Databases: Some Legal and Ethical Issues' (2004) 12 Medical Law Review 70; Alastair V Campbell 'The Ethical Challenges of Biobanks: Safeguarding Altruism and Trust' in Sheila AM McLean (ed) *First Do No Harm* (Aldershot: Ashgate, 2006) 203; and Roger Brownsword 'Biobank Governance: Property, Privacy and Consent' in Christian Lenk, Nils Hoppe, and Roberto Andorno (eds) *Ethics and Law of Intellectual Property* (Aldershot: Ashgate, 2007) 11.

[33] *UK Biobank Ethics and Governance Framework* (version 2.0, July 2006) p 22, para I.B.7. Available at <http://www.ukbiobank.ac.uk/docs/EGF_Version2_July%2006%20most%20uptodate.pdf> (last visited 3 September 2007). If potential participants express the view that they would want to be withdrawn on death or mental incapacity, they will not be recruited.

[34] *UK Biobank Ethics and Governance Framework* (version 2.0, July 2006).

[35] ibid p 6, para I.B.1.

[36] Thus, ibid at p 12, para I.C.1 of the framework principles, we read: 'UK Biobank will maintain strict measures to protect confidentiality, and will ensure that data and samples are (reversibly) anonymised, linked and stored to very high standards of security. The same protection will be extended under contract for any handling or analysis of data or samples by third parties engaged to provide services necessary for developing the resource'.

In the previous part of the chapter, I drew attention to the difference between a profile based on *non-coding* regions of human DNA and an analysis based on a sequenced *coding* region of human DNA. My point was that, even if it is clear that the latter analysis engages a person's privacy interest (because it can disclose sensitive health information), it is less clear that (or, at any rate, when) privacy is engaged in the former case. Now, when a participant supplies samples to UK Biobank, when he or she authorizes access to their medical records, and so on, I take it that it is clear that the participant's privacy interest is engaged. For, the information so made available to UK Biobank is of an intensely personal nature. The reason why UK Biobank does not violate a participant's privacy rights by gathering in and analysing such intimate information is not because this is a longitudinal study that promises to yield major public health benefits but because UK Biobank acts with the volunteer's authorizing consent.

If we assume that UK Biobank collects its data without infringing privacy rights, there is still a question about third-party access to the collection. Formally, if A authorizes B to have access to A's medical records, then B does not violate A's privacy right by accessing A's medical records. However, if B then hands A's records on to C, this will be a prima facie violation of A's confidentiality interest. Unless A has consented to B passing on the records to C, by transferring the information to C, B (even if not violating A's privacy right) will be violating A's right that the information be treated as confidential. Putting this in the context of UK Biobank, participants will be informed that third-parties (including commercial entities) are expected to seek access to the database. Provided that the authorizing consents are sufficiently clear about such matters, participants will have no complaint about UK Biobank's respect for their privacy and confidentiality. However, what if, some years from now, these consents are judged to be inadequate in relation to third-party access? Will it be sufficient for UK Biobank to plead that the data is made available only in a reversibly anonymized form (as is the intention)? This is a tricky question the answer to which depends upon whether we think that A's interests in informational privacy and confidentiality have a proprietary basis. If we think that they do, then B violates A's rights by passing on (without A's consent) the information to C, even though the information is anonymized and even though C cannot link it back to A. If, however, we reject the proprietary basis for A's interests, B does not violate A's rights by passing on the information to C in a securely anonymised form.[37]

Turning from privacy to consent, it is, of course, axiomatic within bioethics that, wherever possible, participation in a research project should be on the basis of free and informed consent.[38] In line with this principle, the EGF regime seeks

[37] See, further, Roger Brownsword 'Biobank Governance: Property, Privacy and Consent' (n 32 above).

[38] See ch 3.

to ensure that participants fully understand the purpose of UK Biobank (that is, that no-one will subsequently complain about having signed up on a false prospectus), that consent is free, and that the process of maintaining consent is ongoing. Crucially, participants should understand that UK Biobank is not a healthcare programme but a research resource,[39] and that there will be a link to the medical record. As I have said, participants should also understand that commercial entities might apply to make use of the UK Biobank resource, and that the full assemblage of data will be maintained in a reversibly anonymized form.

With regard to the ongoing nature of the relationship, participants should be told that they have an unconditional right to withdraw at any time (without having to give a reason and without penalty) and that, for various reasons, they might be recontacted by UK Biobank. The right to withdraw is seen as 'essential to preserve and demonstrate the voluntary nature of participation'.[40] While the recruitment and induction of participants should emphasize the desirability of long-term participation (until death do us part, and even beyond), there is neither an obligation to participate (the initial decision to participate is voluntary) nor an obligation to stay in the project for a minimum term. Participants, so to speak, opt in and then opt to stay in.[41]

According to the governance framework, '[f]urther consent will be sought for any proposed activities that do not fall within the existing consent'[42]—or, more precisely, it will be explained to participants that they might be recontacted in order '[t]o seek consent to proposed new uses that have passed scientific and ethics review but do not fall within the existing consent'.[43] Where the scope of each participant's consent is drafted in a bespoke narrow fashion, it is easy to understand how the need for fresh authorization might arise.[44] However, where broad or blanket consents are taken, then the idea is to cover all anticipated purposes and minimize the occasions when fresh consent for secondary purposes is required. Although the employment of broad consents has attracted criticism[45] (and, to this extent, the EGF is not as strong on consent as it might be), there is

[39] But note Carolyn Johnston and Jane Kaye 'Does the UK Biobank Have a Legal Obligation to Feedback Individual Findings to Participants?' (2004) 12 Medical Law Review 239.

[40] *UK Biobank Ethics and Governance Framework* (above n 33) p. 10, para I.B.6.

[41] The most complete form of withdrawal is 'no further use' (meaning that, over and above no further contact or access, UK Biobank will destroy all samples and health information previously collected from the participant): ibid pp 10–11, para I.B.6.

[42] ibid p 7, para I.B.1.

[43] ibid p 10, para I.B.5.

[44] Compare the US National Bioethics Advisory Commission's report and recommendations, in *Research Involving Human Biological Materials: Ethical Issues and Policy Guidance* (Rockville, MD: August 1999) vol 1, Recommendation 9, 64–5. Available at <http://www.georgetown.edu/research/nrcbl/nbac/pubs.html>.

[45] See Alastair V Campbell 'The Ethical Challenges of Biobanks: Safeguarding Altruism and Trust' in Sheila AM McLean (ed) *First Do No Harm* (Aldershot: Ashgate, 2006) 203, 204–7; and Timothy Caulfield 'Biobanks and Blanket Consent: The Proper Place of the Public Good and Public Perception Rationales' (2007) 18 King's Law Journal 209.

at least explicit recognition of the need to return for further authorization if the terms of the original consent no longer apply.[46]

On the face of it, so long as participation is on an informed consent basis, there is little that requires major ethical attention. However, if recruitment is slow or if larger numbers of participants are required for the public health benefits to be realized, would it be arguable that participation is ethically *required* (akin, for instance, to jury service)? In fact, John Harris has argued for either opt out or mandatory participation in research projects (including database recruitment) where the prevention of serious harm is involved.[47] But, would such an argument be plausible in a community of rights?

In what follows, I will suggest that the argument about the prevention of serious harm—which supports compelled participation in a *forensic* collection—does not map so readily onto compelled participation in a *public health* collection. If the state has a justification for the latter, I will suggest that it is to be found not so much in preventing and detecting (criminal) acts that are a threat to the well-being of others, but in securing the complex of conditions (to a large extent environmental and informational) that make for public health and the well-being of individual agents.

(a) Preventing harm and the protection of negative rights

An attractive argument for conscription is along the lines that, if we accept that the state is justified in taking samples without consent for the purpose of understanding more about (detecting and preventing) serious crime, then we must also accept that the state is justified in requiring participation in database projects for the purpose of understanding more about (detecting and preventing) serious disease. However, on closer inspection, the move from crime prevention to disease prevention is not as straightforward as it might seem.

The state's justification for violating citizen x's privacy right (assuming that the privacy right is engaged) for *forensic* purposes is that such compulsion is required in order to prevent violations of various more important rights held by citizens y and z. Conversely, the justification for violating the privacy rights of citizens y and z is in order to prevent violations of various more important rights held by citizen x. If the state attempts to mount a similar justification in relation to the violation of x's privacy rights for *public health* purposes, it is not at all clear that compulsion is required in order to prevent violations of various more important rights held by citizens y and z. No doubt, there is a right that x should not attempt intentionally to infect y or z with a serious disease;[48] but, in general, the case for required

[46] For discussion, see Campbell (n 45 above), especially at 204–7.

[47] See Editorial 'Striking the right balance between privacy and public good' (2006) 367(9507) *The Lancet* 275.

[48] *R v Mohammed Dica* [2004] EWCA Crim 1103.

participation in a public health project does not seem to be so convincingly tied to the prevention of proximate and direct rights violations. Nevertheless, the thought occurs that we might arrive at the conclusion that there is a justification for such required participation by a rather different route—namely, by reflecting on the extent of a citizen's positive obligations in a community of rights.

(b) Positive rights and responsibilities

I take it that, in a community of rights, it will be accepted that one agent may freely put himself under a positive obligation to another. Hence, I may freely agree to participate in the UK Biobank. However, what does a community of rights make of background positive rights and responsibilities—that is to say, positive rights and responsibilities that are imposed rather than freely assumed by promise or agreement?

To take a standard example, let us suppose that A, who is an experienced swimmer, observes B, who is a novice, getting into difficulty. Does A now have a positive responsibility for B's safety? Certainly, it would seem to be insouciant in the extreme if A were to shrug off any responsibility for B's well-being. But, would a community of rights fix A with a positive obligation to assist B as a matter of its background (imposed) moral standards?

If we assume that no community of rights would reject the very idea of background positive requirements, then the real question concerns the conditions that the community would set for the recognition of background positive obligations. I suggest that the conditions set would reflect the community's understanding and application of three guiding considerations. First, there are considerations of rational prescription. In any community that accepts the basic canons of rational prescription, an agent will only be required to assist another where 'ought implies can' is satisfied. It follows that no agent will be burdened with a positive obligation unless they are capable of rendering assistance. If we are to prescribe that A ought to assist B (by swimming over to assist B, or by throwing a line to B, or by calling a lifeguard, or whatever), then the demands that we make of A should at least be within A's capabilities. Secondly, there are considerations of reasonableness (and proportionality). How much can we reasonably demand of A? In the hypothetical, it seems that it would be little more than a minor inconvenience for A to rescue B. However, the circumstances might be very different. Is there a point beyond which it would be unreasonable to impose on A? For example, if A would put his own life at risk by entering the waters, would we *require* such a heroic act (or would this be a case of supererogation)? Thirdly, there are considerations of fairness. Even in a community that recognizes positive rights, the default position is represented by 'can implies ought'—that is to say, the default expectation is that those who are capable of helping themselves should do so. So, if the roles were reversed, we would expect B, an experienced swimmer, to rely on his own resources before seeking assistance from others.

Arguably, drawing on these considerations, a four-stage test along the following lines might be formulated for the recognition of particular background prima facie positive rights and responsibilities.[49]

(i) Is A in a position to assist B?

(ii) Does A have the capability to assist B in any material respect?

(iii) Even though A is in a position to assist B and has the relevant capability, would the burden of responsibility on A be unreasonable (or disproportionate) relative to A's own essential interests?

(iv) Even though A is in a position to assist B, has the relevant capability, and the imposition of responsibility on A would not be unreasonable (relative to A's essential interests), would B be taking unfair advantage of A if A were required to assist B?

Quite clearly, there is still a great deal of interpretive work to be done on these general principles, particularly in relation to the pivotal notions of 'unreasonable imposition', 'essential interests', and 'unfair advantage taking'. Let us suppose that the community, recognizing that these are slippery notions, tries to stabilize the four-stage test by focusing on the common needs of all agents, irrespective of their particular purposes, plans, or projects—for example, the need of all agents for life and a level of basic physical and psychological well-being. With this focus, the community can say that A is not required to attempt to rescue B where this would jeopardize A's own life (this would be an unreasonable imposition) and, similarly, that A is not required to assist B where B is in no danger but simply wants A to teach him how to do the backstroke (this would be an unreasonable demand that amounts to another example of unfair advantage taking).

Even with the test stabilized in this way, the community will also be mindful of a troubling pair of puzzles that threaten to undermine the practicability of any regime of positive rights. Stated shortly, one puzzle arises where A is not the only experienced swimmer on the beach. The question then is why we should single out A as the person responsible for assisting B.[50] The converse puzzle arises where

[49] It should be emphasized that this test only takes the community as far as recognising prima facie responsibilities. Even if A is judged to have a prima facie positive obligation in relation to B, there might yet be competing or conflicting rights-based claims to be arbitrated.

[50] Compare Lord Hoffmann's remarks about omissions in *Stovin v Wise* [1996] AC 923 (HL) at 943–4:

There are sound reasons why omissions require different treatment from positive conduct. It is one thing for the law to say that a person who undertakes some activity shall take reasonable care not to cause damage to others. It is another thing for the law to require that a person who is doing nothing in particular shall take steps to prevent another from suffering harm. . . . One can put the matter in political, moral or economic terms. In political terms it is less of an invasion of an individual's freedom for the law to require him to consider the safety of others in his actions than to impose upon him a duty to rescue or protect. A moral version of this point may be called the 'Why pick on me?' argument. A duty to prevent harm to others or to render assistance to a person in danger or distress may apply to a large and indeterminate class of people who happen to be able to do something. Why should one be held liable rather than another? In economic terms, the efficient allocation of

it is not just B, but B, C, and D who are in difficulty and A simply cannot assist all three. Here, the question is why we should single out, say, B as the agent to be assisted. For sure, the lesson to be taken from these puzzles is not that A is released from his positive obligation to assist (because, in the first case, others are also able to assist or because, in the second case, he cannot assist all three distressed agents). Rather, the lesson is that the community needs to articulate some principles of relative priority in relation to the bearers of positive duties (for the first kind of case) as well as those who are positive rights-holders (for the second kind of case).

How far does this analysis take us in responding to the mooted proposal for required participation in a public health facility? If the state required the giving of blood or the donation of (cadaveric) organs in order to save the lives of injured or ill agents, or if there was a programme of compulsory vaccination against a lethal pandemic, the positive obligations analysis would work very nicely. Moreover, it would work in a way that would not require any apologia for infringing rights; the state's justification would be that it was holding citizens to their (positive) obligations. However, one senses that the justification misses the mark slightly in relation to projects such as the UK Biobank. For the UK Biobank, as it takes great pains to emphasize, is not a clinical facility; it is purely and simply a research facility that, in the longer run, aims to improve our collective understanding of the conditions for public health and individual well-being. Accordingly, if we are to find an argument that supports compelled participation, we need a justification that fits more closely.

(c) Collective responsibility and state stewardship

In a community of rights, agents take their autonomy extremely seriously. Each agent has a life to lead; but the life that they lead is the life that they individually choose to lead. Whatever life an individual agent chooses, however, it will not be a life worth leading unless the agent enjoys a level of basic well-being. And, the conditions of public health are critical for any agent's basic well-being. What precisely do we understand, however, by 'the conditions of public health'?

In his seminal study, Larry Gostin remarks that '[d]efinitions of public health vary widely, ranging from the utopian conception of the World Health Organization of an ideal state of physical and mental health to a more concrete listing of public health practices [such as preventing disease, prolonging life, and promoting physical health through focused community efforts]'.[51] Public

resources usually requires an activity should bear its own costs.... So liability to pay compensation for loss caused by negligent conduct acts as a deterrent.... But there is no similar justification for requiring a person who is not doing anything to spend money on behalf of someone else.... So there must be some special reason why he should have to put his hand in his pocket.

[51] Lawrence O Gostin *Public Health Law* (Berkeley: University of California Press, 2000) 13.

health, so understood, has more than one referent. We might speak about both the state of the public's health and the conditions that contribute, both positively and negatively, to the health of the public. Once we separate out these applications, it becomes possible, in principle, to speak about a population being healthy despite poor public health provision and, conversely, a population being unhealthy despite good public health provision. Just as the infrastructure for the London Olympics in 2012 might be the best ever, it does not follow that performances at those Olympics will be the best ever. Other things being equal, though, we might expect there to be a positive correlation between an improvement in the conditions of public health (support for Olympians) and the state of public health (Olympic performances)—in the most general terms, the vision for any public health agency must be one of healthy people in healthy communities.[52] A little more needs to be said about both the state of public health and the conditions for public health.[53]

Let us assume that there are a number of agreed criteria by reference to which we can assess the health of an individual. If we generalize this approach, we can assess the health of a larger population. This is not quite the same as assessing the state of public health in that population because this assessment needs to take account not only of the level of health of the living but also various mortality rates. What are the prospects for young children? What is the average life expectancy? What proportion of that average life expectancy is affected by morbidity? And, so on. With answers to these questions, we have a general sense of the level of public health enjoyed by the population in question—and, for that matter, as between different socio-economic sets of the larger population.[54] This is not a precisely calibrated measure (especially where quality of life judgments are involved).[55] However, provided that the criteria (or performance indicators) are constant, we can judge whether the state of public health in, say, 21st century England is an improvement on that in Victorian England as we can compare the state of public health in contemporary England with that in, say, contemporary Germany or the USA.

Turning to the all important question of the conditions for public health, where the state of public health seems to be improving (or deteriorating) or where it is superior in one population to another, how are such trends or variations to be explained? An obvious line of inquiry leads us to the background living conditions, the conditions that set the scene for the well-being of the population as a whole—think of this as being analogous to the background lighting and acoustics that

[52] Compare, Gostin (n 51 above) at 320–1.

[53] Compare Roger Brownsword 'Public Health, Private Right and the Common Law' (2006) 120 Public Health 42.

[54] See, eg, Department of Health *Tackling Health Inequalities: A Programme for Action* (July 2, 2003).

[55] See, eg, Helen N Macbeth (ed) *Health Outcomes* (Oxford: Oxford University Press, 1996); and George Teeling Smith (ed) *Measuring Health: A Practical Approach* (Chichester: John Wiley and Sons, 1988).

set the stage for a successful theatrical performance. To be sure, if the water is contaminated, the air polluted, and if medication is in short supply, there will be particular individuals who suffer a deterioration in their health. However, in principle, it could be any member of the population that is adversely affected. Conversely, where clean water is available, where pollution is reduced, and where medication is now available, this changes the background environment in a way that is conducive to the health of all members of the population.

Even with the benefit of favourable background conditions, however, there might be further ways in which the state of health of the population could be improved—for example, by redirecting adverse life-style habits (lack of exercise, over-consumption of alcohol, and the like). However, where the problem arises from an individual's choice of (unhealthy) life-style, then rectification calls for either a change in the background conditions (eg by making the option either impossible or less convenient or less attractive in some way) or direct intervention in relation to the particular individual; and the price that we pay is that there is some diminution of personal choice. In a community of rights, there will be alarm bells if the state proposes to intrude upon autonomy in this way.[56]

In the light of these remarks, if the state were to compel participation in a project such as UK Biobank, might this be judged to be legitimate in a community of rights? Put shortly, the rationale for the state's imposition is that it has a stewardship responsibility for the infrastructural conditions that make agency possible and that individual agents owe it to one another to assist in securing those conditions. Put very simply, then, a working principle in a community of rights might be that citizens have a responsibility to assist in collective database projects where:

- such projects promise to maintain or improve the infrastructural conditions for agency (albeit, we should note, largely for the benefit of future generations of agents)
- collective action is essential, and
- there is no disproportionate cost to a citizen's interests as a rights-holding agent with an interest in personal autonomy.

We arrive at a position, therefore, in which we treat the right to personal security as overriding privacy rights in relation to forensic DNA collections and collective responsibility coupled with stewardship as the basis for required participation in biobanking projects for public health purposes.

Before we leave these arguments for compelled participation, we might entertain the thought that the principle of collective solidarity might also be applicable to forensic databanks. What is more, we might also think that the solidarity justification is more attractive than one that rests on an appeal to overriding rights. However, if we extend the principle in this way, it is unclear where the boundary

[56] Compare the liberal constraints that are the starting point for the ethical framework of stewardship developed in Nuffield Council on Bioethics *Public Health: Ethical Issues* (London, 2007).

of the infrastructural conditions for agency lies. In a community of rights, we would expect agents to adopt a pretty restrictive reading of this principle; and, while it merits further consideration, for the time being we can nip the idea in the bud.

IV Just One Collection?

Let us suppose that, in a community of rights, it is accepted that, as a matter of principle, it is right that citizens should cooperate in order to make the social environment more conducive to agency. It is not so much that better placed agents have responsibilities to assist vulnerable agents but that non-vulnerable agents can, and should, mutually assist one another in order to improve the collective context for agency.

Now, once the community has arrived at this point, it will see a number of ways in which the collections might be made more effective, each step appealing as a progressive and rational development.

First, there will seem to be little sense in having two collections, one for forensic and the other for public health research purposes. A population-wide national collection—just one collection, one for all—will make perfect sense. Just as there are mergers of banks in the financial sector, so it will make economic sense to merge biobanks.

Secondly, as each nation state consolidates its biobank resources, the opportunities for, together with the advantages of, linking one national collection to another will be explored. Indeed, this kind of forward-thinking is already underway. For example, the UK police are exploring means of joining the National DNA Database with those of other countries; and, further to the Hague Programme on strengthening freedom, security and justice in the European Union,[57] the international use of databases of personal information is under consideration—thus, one of the Commission's declared priorities is that 'A high level of exchange of information between law enforcement authorities must be maintained and improved, taking into account the overall principle of availability'.[58] Once concerns about privacy have been assuaged, the way will be clear for Member States to disclose personal data to the competent authorities of other Member States for the purposes of police and judicial cooperation.[59]

Alongside developments of this kind, we should take note of the view that the next generation of epidemiological studies requires large collections of biosamples

[57] [2005] OJ C53; and the Commission's subsequent Communication *The Hague Programme: Ten Priorities for the Next Five Years* COM(2005) 184 final, Brussels, 10 May 2005.

[58] See *The Hague Programme: Ten Priorities for the Next Five Years*, priority area 7 (privacy and security in sharing information).

[59] See the publication by the European Commission of the *Proposal for a Council Framework Decision on the protection of personal data processed in the framework of police and judicial cooperation in criminal matters* (Memo/05/349, 4 October 2005); and for UK interest, see Select Committee on European Scrutiny *Thirty-Sixth Report* (2006). See, also, David Charter 'Central Fingerprint Database Plan Draws Fire from All over EU' *The Times* 16 March 2007, p 2.

and data. How is this to be achieved? According to Bartha Knoppers, Ma'n H Abdul-Rahman, and Karine Bédard:

> One solution to the problem of achieving the requisite scale of research materials needed for such initiatives is to establish frameworks, standards and norms by which existing or new database resources can be networked together. Ideally, such frameworks, standards and norms would enable datasets to be networked—and data and, where necessary, biosamples, to be transferred or shared—at both the national and international levels. Interoperability and international collaborative access to, and use of, the genomic data so created will be essential to the goal of achieving the rapid translation of research results into clinical knowledge and new therapies.[60]

In line with this vision, the Public Population Project in Genomics (the so-called P3G Project)[61] presents itself as 'an international consortium for the development and management of a multidisciplinary infrastructure for comparing and merging results from population genomic studies'. Clearly, planning for the interoperability of national public health biobanks makes a lot of sense. Moreover, in due course, it might seem perfectly sensible to plan for the interoperability of national public health and forensic collections if they have not already been merged into single collections.

Thirdly, given that a heel prick blood sample is already taken from all newly born children, we might wonder why we should not use this sample for the DNA database. Would this not be more convenient and more efficient than calling in agents to supply samples?

Not long ago, the Human Genetics Commission concluded that, in the present state of the art, the budget for public health could not possibly finance the genetic profiling of newly born children; and, even if genetic profiling were affordable, it would be highly problematic on ethical grounds—particularly because of issues relating to consent.[62] Within a community of rights, however, the first question would be whether genetic profiling would violate any prima facie rights at all. If not, the act would be permitted and consent simply would not be an issue. It would only be if the rights of the neonate or its parents were engaged that consent would be relevant.[63] If such rights were engaged, then the burden of justification would shift to those who proposed that genetic profiling would be legitimate lack of relevant consent notwithstanding.

Things are moving very quickly now and we might again start anticipating a future that takes us to a place that we do not want to be.[64] However, let us suppose

[60] Bartha Maria Knoppers, Ma'n H Abdul-Rahman, and Karine Bédard 'Genomic Databases and International Collaboration' (2007) 18 King's Law Journal 291, at 293.

[61] <http://www.p3gconsortium.org>.

[62] Human Genetics Commission *Profiling the Newborn: A Prospective Gene Technology?* (London: March, 2005).

[63] See ch 3.

[64] Compare the 'Knowing It All' scenario drawn for the Foresight Report on the *Cyber Trust and Crime Prevention Project* (London: Office of Science and Technology, 2004) 18.

that things go no further. Even with this, in a community of rights, there might be concerns about the collections being abused. Is it time for the state to call a halt by invoking some kind of precautionary proviso? This is the question to which we finally turn.

V The Precautionary Proviso

In Chapter 4, we took a hard look at the so-called precautionary principle. If we try to cast the principle in a form that is context neutral, it has something like the following shape: where some practice [P] is perceived to present a special kind of risk [R], then regulators should require that P cease (or be restricted) notwithstanding that the evidence base concerning the threat presented by P to R falls below the level that would generally be accepted as sufficient for requiring that P should cease (or be restricted). So expressed, the principle is open to many different interpretations; and, no matter how the principle is articulated, it invites the Sunstein critique to the effect that we should not overlook the fact that the taking of precautionary measures itself involves risk (sacrifice).[65]

If a precautionary approach to the development of genetic databases were to be advocated, what would be specified as the relevant risk? Perhaps the obvious (albeit not exclusive) risk is that of infringements of privacy and confidentiality, and the like;[66] or, of course, we might be deeply concerned that the national data sets might fall into the wrong hands and be abused (for example, being applied for illegitimate discriminatory or exclusionary purposes). Moreover, as Mark Rothstein and Meghan Talbott[67] have emphasized, we need to be aware of the context in which we are contemplating this expansion of state power:

> The prospect of expanded use of DNA forensics needs to be placed in context. In a world in which personal privacy is difficult to maintain against an onslaught of computer file sharing, surveillance cameras, biometric imaging, thermal imaging, and other technological 'advances', for many people, the last 'off limit' area for access to personal information is law enforcement....
>
> Assume that a hypothetical country routinely required all of its residents to submit the following items to the police: a DNA sample, a yearly photograph, handwriting exemplar, voiceprint, fingerprints, hair samples, retinal scans, bank statements, credit card information, health records, and other details of their personal life. Obviously, ready access to this information by police would help solve crimes. Nevertheless, such comprehensive information submission to law enforcement would be widely viewed as hallmarks of a repressive, totalitarian state....

[65] See Cass Sunstein *Laws of Fear* (Cambridge: Cambridge University Press, 2005).

[66] Compare Kirstie Ball, David Lyon, David Murakami Wood, Clive Norris, and Charles Raab *A Report on the Surveillance Society* (September 2006) paras 4.2–4.5 and 11.1–11.5.

[67] Mark A Rothstein and Meghan K Talbott 'The Expanding Use of DNA in Law Enforcement: What Role for Privacy?' (2006) 34 Journal of Law, Medicine and Ethics 153, at 160–1.

The point is well made and there are distinct Orwellian echoes here.[68] However, it is not the particular risk that I want to highlight. My point is not about striking the right balance between competing moral considerations—for example, between the interest in security of person and property and the interests in freedom, the integrity of families, and equal respect and non-discrimination.[69] Rather, my point is about the threat that genetic databases might present to moral sustainability itself.

In the chapters that follow, this particular risk is one that I will revisit several times. Here, it suffices to flag up one way in which the risk might be formulated. Imagine that the state has access to population-wide biobanking collections on the basis of which it develops a profiling technology that is so sophisticated and reliable that there is little chance that, where a criminal offence is committed, the offending agent will not be detected. Even if such a community has a fairly limited criminal code, the fact that almost all offenders will be detected might be a cause for concern in a community of rights.[70] But why? If the code penalizes the violation of those rights that are fundamental to a community of rights, what is the problem with such an effective detection strategy? For years, we have bemoaned the fact that where crime and punishment is concerned nothing works, so why look for problems when we find a criminal justice strategy that actually works?

One problematic feature of such a strategy is captured by Michel Foucault in the following terms:

> He who is subjected to a field of visibility, and who knows it, assumes responsibility for the constraints of power; he makes them play spontaneously upon himself; he inscribes in himself the power relation in which he simultaneously plays both roles; he becomes the principle of his own subjection.[71]

Of course, under the right conditions, such efficient self-regulation is fine. However, in a community of rights, agents expect to have more than a paper choice between

[68] Compare George Orwell *Nineteen Eighty-Four* (London: Penguin Books, 1989) 219–20 (quoted in ch 1).

[69] See, eg, Amitai Etzioni 'A Communitarian Approach: A Viewpoint on the Study of the Legal, Ethical and Policy Considerations Raised by DNA Tests and Databases' (2006) 34 Journal of Law, Medicine and Ethics 214; Robin Williams and Paul Johnson 'Inclusiveness, Effectiveness and Intrusiveness: Issues in the Developing Uses of DNA Profiling in Support of Criminal Investigations' ibid 234; and Henry T Greely, Daniel P. Riordan, Nanibaa' A Garrison, and Joanna L Mountain 'Family Ties: The Use of DNA Offender Databases to Catch Offenders' Kin' ibid 248. In their concluding remarks, Greely et al nicely capture the dilemma about the discriminatory impact of DNA databases where the criminal justice system already operates with a bias against ethnic minorities. Thus, at 260, they suggest that 'it may be wise to consider an expressly population-wide database rather than ending up with something that, through the extension to family members, becomes a large but racially biased database'.

[70] Compare Victor Tadros 'Power and the Value of Privacy' in Erik Claes, Antony Duff, and Serge Gutwirth (eds) *Privacy and the Criminal Law* (Antwerp and Oxford: Intersentia, 2006) 105 (especially Tadros's discussion of what he calls Camerania).

[71] Michel Foucault *Discipline and Punish* (London: Penguin reprint, 1991) 202–3.

compliance and non-compliance with their legal-moral criminal code; and, given the conditions set by the hypothesized profiling, while agents have the paper option of non-compliance, the reality is that they know that, if they do not obey, they almost certainly will pay. For a community of rights, the concern is whether such a state of affairs interferes with the development of agent virtue, particularly the virtue of choosing to do the right thing for the right reason. For, if agents comply only because they fear near-certain detection and punishment, there is little room for the promotion of the desired virtue.

Against this, it might be argued that such a view is 'idealistic'. Even without such profiling technology, agents rarely do the right thing for just the right reason. In practice, for many agents it is the background (albeit uncertain) threat of penal sanctions that deters the commission of crime. On this view, where agents rarely do the right thing for the right reason, profiling (by converting a low-risk threat of punishment into a high-risk threat of punishment) simply extends the logic of the existing arrangements—this is no real change in kind, simply a change in degree. Even in a morally disposed community, there has to be some sanction to compensate for weakness of the will.[72]

If we were trying to respond to this reality check without assuming that the context is that of an aspirant community of rights, we would need a robust answer to those who see little virtue in doing the right thing *for the right reason*, or who for that matter see no reason for *doing the right thing*. These are difficulties to be revisited in later chapters. At this stage, however, we need only remind ourselves that we are dealing with an aspirant moral community. If a community of rights is prepared to grant the state a stewardship jurisdiction to maintain and improve the infrastructural conditions for agency simpliciter (this perhaps being the best argument for required participation in a biobanking project), then it will certainly see the sense of charging the state with a similar responsibility with regard to the infrastructural conditions for moral agency. In this light, it will seem entirely appropriate that the state, exercising its stewardship responsibility, should monitor developments that might challenge either the physical or the moral sustainability of such a community. If, in good faith, the state judges that even the well-intentioned development of national and regional population-wide DNA collections threatens the sustainability of moral community, then this is an appropriate occasion for the precautionary proviso to be exercised.

VI Conclusion

According to John Gibb:

Databases are a product of joined-up government. Once identity card information is pooled and cross-referenced with other personal data, including Inland Revenue and

[72] Compare Ian Ayres and John Braithwaite *Responsive Regulation* (Oxford: Oxford University Press, 1992) ch 2 (arguing for a persuasive rather than a penal approach but with credible sanctions in the background). And see my discussion in ch 10.

Customs and Excise records, Criminal Records, the new and fast-growing [national DNA database], the NHS database, the huge amount of knowledge gained and stored from smart cards and credit cards, immigration records, the Department for Education database, the Passport Office, driving licences, bank records, library records and the National Register of Births, Marriages and Deaths, everything about us will be known—and that's probably more than we know about ourselves.[73]

Moreover, in this emerging surveillance society, it needs to be understood that:

[t]he more that states, organisations, communities and people become dependent on surveillance technologies, the more there is an apparent 'lock-in' which prevents other options from being considered, and a comprehension gap which increases a dependence on expertise outside the democratic system.[74]

To ask whether it is feasible to regulate the state's employment of such technologies might be to miss the point: in future, *the technology is the regulation*.

In this context of both technological acceleration and convergence,[75] we should be concerned lest we corrode the basis of moral community, in particular the dignity of moral choice. Even more apocalyptically, we might fear that these developments presage not just the end of moral community but the end of human community. As Bill Joy[76] explained the seductive power of the new technologies:

Each of these technologies also offers untold promise: The vision of near immortality . . . drives us forward; genetic engineering may soon provide treatments, if not outright cures, for most diseases; and nanotechnology and nanomedicine can address yet more ills. Together they could significantly extend our average life span and improve the quality of our lives. Yet, with each of these technologies, a sequence of small, individually sensible advances leads to an accumulation of great power and, concomitantly, great danger.[77]

Indeed, is this not precisely the point of the story told in this chapter—namely, that 'a sequence of small, individually sensible advances leads to an accumulation of great power and, concomitantly, great danger'? We start with a small genetic database for forensic purposes. Without realising quite how quickly it is growing, we find that the collection is of a size and complexion that invites a debate about expanding it into a population-wide database. At the same time, we see the launch of a major database for public health purposes. So long as participation in the latter database is voluntary, there seems little harm in scaling it up; but, already, there is the suggestion that participation might be required (as with the forensic collection) as a matter of public responsibility. Each step is incremental; each step takes us closer to a population-wide multi-purpose collection.

[73] John Gibb *Who's Watching You?* (London: Collins and Brown, 2005) 236.

[74] Kirstie Ball, David Lyon, David Murakami Wood, Clive Norris, and Charles Raab *A Report on the Surveillance Society* (September 2006) para 9.12.2.

[75] Compare Pierre Baldi *The Shattered Self* (Cambridge, Mass: MIT Press, 2002).

[76] Bill Joy 'Why the Future Doesn't Need Us' (2000) 8(4) *Wired* (<http://www.wired.com/wired/archived/8.04/joy_pr.html>) (last accessed 19 June 2006).

[77] <http://www.wired.com/wired/archived/8.04/joy_pr.html> at p 4.

For the members of a community of rights, each step needs to be carefully scrutinized; and the state has a special responsibility to ensure that the cumulative effect of the steps being taken is not inconsistent with the sustainability of moral community. In the slide down this slippery slope, I have gone over each of the individual moves far more quickly than would be decent in such a community. It might well be, therefore, that there are problems about privacy or consent or positive responsibility, and the like, that I have under-stated—and that, once identified, convince the members of a community of rights that the next step should not be taken.[78] However, while the community of rights certainly needs to debate the scope and application of the rights (and responsibilities) that it recognizes, it also needs to be mindful of the conditions that are presupposed by its very existence as a moral community.

In this chapter, I have introduced the idea that agents who aspire to moral community need to be particularly mindful of the corrosive impact of a (bio) technological approach to social control whether concerned with the prevention of crime or the promotion of public health. Such agents need to be aware that the cumulative effect of seemingly benign individual choices might represent a threat to the very conditions that make their actions morally meaningful. As I will elaborate in later chapters, if a community is to function as a moral community, it is of the essence that agents try to do the right thing for the right reason. It matters, in other words, not just that agents act *as if* they respect one another's freedom and well-being but that it is precisely because they respect one another's freedom and well-being that they act in this other-regarding way. In sum, if a (bio)technological approach to social control, whether concerned with the prevention of crime or the promotion of public health, simply reduces the risks to which agents are exposed, all well and good; but if the effect is to corrode the conditions that underlie the very project of moral community itself, then this is a risk which no community of rights can afford to ignore and which it surely will not wish to run.

[78] In this light, it is encouraging to read that the Human Genetics Commission is to hold a public inquiry into the National DNA Database: see Richard Ford 'Police Want DNA from Speeding Drivers and Litter Louts on Database' *The Times*, 2 August 2007, p 2. See, too, Magnus Linklater 'We're Not Fools—DNA Evidence is Far From Foolproof *The Times*, 19 September 2007, p 19.

9

Seizing the Regulatory Opportunity: Code and Control

Introduction

One of the assumptions in this part of the book is that the regulators of the 21st Century will be smarter than their predecessors. They will have long since learned that, while traditional command and control interventions might be attractive to politicians, they are not always an effective or efficient form of response;[1] they will know that the criminal law tends to do better at creating new offences rather than reducing the incidence of violations; they will know that private law remedies are of limited impact; and they will know that public law control exercised by agency licensing or negotiation is open to the twin charges of being too soft or being too tough.[2] Intelligent regulators of the coming century will know that they can sometimes achieve the desired regulatory effect by relying vicariously on non-governmental pressure (whether in the form of self-regulation or co-regulation by or with business or the professions, pressure exerted by consumers, the activities of pressure groups, and so on) or by relying on market mechanisms; in addition, it will be 'old hat' that careful consideration needs to be given to selecting the optimal mix of various regulatory instruments.[3] The regulators that we are particularly interested in, however, are those who are not simply streetwise, but who operate on the assumption that conduct is sometimes most effectively channelled by relying, not on norms, pressure, or financial signals, but on 'code',

[1] Generally, see Neil Gunningham and Peter Grabosky *Smart Regulation* (Oxford: Clarendon Press, 1998).

[2] See, eg, Christine Parker 'Restorative Justice in Business Regulation? The Australian Competition and Consumer Commission's Use of Enforceable Undertakings' (2004) 67 Modern Law Review 209.

[3] In addition to emphasizing the limits of single instrument approaches, stressing the need to be aware of the range of regulatory instruments, and highlighting the importance of putting in place an optimal mix, Gunningham and Grabosky (n 1 above) argue that 'a mix of instruments will work more effectively if a broader range of participants are capable of implementing them. This means the direct involvement not only of governments (first parties) but also of business and other "targets" of regulation (second parties) and a range of other interested actors (third parties), both commercial and non-commercial' (15). For a review of the state of the (post-regulatory) art, see Colin Scott 'Regulation in the Age of Governance: The Rise of the Post-Regulatory State' in J Jordana and D Levi Faur (eds) *The Politics of Regulation* (Cheltenham: Edward Elgar, 2004) 145.

on integrated technology or design—that is, as Lawrence Lessig puts it, on a West Coast rather than a (traditional) East Coast approach to regulation.[4]

Whether regulators are simply smart or techno-wise, it is common ground that they should operate in an 'evidence-based' manner backed by the philosophy that 'what works works'.[5] Provided that the ends pursued by regulators are legitimate, we might assume that this is unproblematic. Indeed, provided that regulatory purposes are legitimate, is it not all to the good that regulators strive for a more instrumentally rational approach, that they seek out more economic, efficient, and effective interventions (or non-interventions)—surely, the smarter the regulation, the better? Moreover, if the smartest style of regulation means setting the regulatory compass towards a West Coast bearing, then why not?

In this chapter, I want to sketch a particular type of West Coast approach, an ideal-type that I will term 'techno-regulation'. This ideal-type does not merely recognize code as part of the regulatory repertoire; it does not simply make use of CCTV, forensic data bases, tracking devices, and the like; instead, it relies entirely on design. So characterized, techno-regulation has importance both as a matter of theory and as a matter of practice. Indeed, as an ideal-type, techno-regulation assumes a dual *theoretical* importance, conceptual and moral, by highlighting the distinction between those regulatory strategies that rely on an engagement with the practical reason of regulatees and those that simply seek to achieve a desired pattern of behaviour. To treat East Coast and West Coast regulatory strategies *simply* as functional equivalents is to miss a matter of the first importance.[6] Lessig himself (responding to Johnson and Post's seminal paper on the distinctive regulatory space constituted by cyberspace[7]) foreshadows this fundamental theoretical point:

> Between [a] norm and the behaviour sought is a human being, mediating whether to conform or not. Lots of times, for lots of laws, the choice is not to conform. Regardless of what the law says, it is an individual who decides whether to conform.

[4] Lawrence Lessig *Code and Other Laws of Cyberspace* (New York: Basic Books, 1999) 53–4; and 'The Law of the Horse: What Cyberlaw Might Teach' (1999) 113 Harvard Law Review 501, 533–4. In 'The New Chicago School' (1998) 27 Journal of Legal Studies 661, where, at 672, Lessig says that the aim of this new version of smart regulation (in contrast to the 'old' Chicago school) is:

> [n]ot only to understand the ways in which alternatives to law regulate, but to understand how law might be used to make selections among these alternatives. How law, that is, functions as a regulator and meta-regulator; how it might direct itself, or might also co-opt, use, or regulate, these alternative modalities of regulation so that they each regulate to law's own end.

[5] Compare David Garland *The Culture of Control* (Oxford: Oxford University Press, 2001) 115–16 (on smart crime control).

[6] Compare Martin W Bauer and George Gaskell 'The Biotechnology Movement' in Martin W Bauer and George Gaskell (eds) *Biotechnology – the Making of a Global Controversy* (Cambridge: Cambridge University Press, 2002) 379, at 383:

> In a Durkheimian sense, social norms and technology are functionally equivalent 'social facts' constraining behaviour into recurrent patterns..., making some actions more likely while discouraging others. Whereas norms are enforced by social sanctions, the use of things is channelled by affordances, the action adequate for the thing or the opportunity costs from not using the thing.

[7] David R Johnson and David Post 'Law and Borders – The Rise of Law in Cyberspace' (1996) 48 Stanford Law Review 1367.

> Regulation in cyberspace is, or can be, different. If the regulator wants to induce a certain behaviour, she need not threaten or cajole, to inspire the change. She need only change the code—the software that defines the terms upon which the individual gains access to the system, or uses assets on the system. If she wants to limit trespass on a system, she need not rely simply on a law against trespass; she can implement a system of passwords....
>
> Code is an efficient means of regulation. But its perfection makes it something different. *One obeys these laws as code not because one should; one obeys these laws as code because one can do nothing else. There is no choice about whether to yield to the demand for a password; one complies if one wants to enter the system.* In the well implemented system, there is no civil disobedience. Law as code is a start to the perfect technology of justice.[8]

At a *practical* level, an awareness of the possibility of techno-regulation cautions against creeping reliance on code; it warns us that when regulators set their compass for the West, this might be less smart than it seems. In sum, whereas, on the East Coast, regulators speak to their regulatees, reasoning with them more or less successfully, on the West Coast, regulators by-pass practical reason to design-in a solution to a problem of which regulatees might not even be aware.

The chapter is in three parts. In the first part, I specify the nature of techno-regulation; in the second, I consider the objection that techno-regulation, even if it makes for safer societies, fails to respect the values of good governance, especially the values of transparency and accountability; and, in the third, I turn to the deep objection (flagged up in the previous chapter) that techno-regulation, by undermining notions of respect and responsibility, is corrosive of the conditions of moral community. From the point of view of a community of rights, these are serious objections, the former because it indicates a deficit in participatory rights and the latter because it points to a threat to the possibility of moral community.

I Regulation and techno-regulation

In this book, I have combined a narrow concept of a regulator (as an agent or agency of government authorized to control and channel conduct in a specified field)[9] with a broad concept of regulation (as encompassing whatever measures regulators take to control and channel conduct in the desired way). Although concerns about code as law are often directed at the exercise of private power, we can persist with our focus on the public dimension of power—in other

[8] Lawrence Lessig 'The Zones of Cyberspace' (1996) 48 Stanford Law Review 1403 at 1408 (emphasis added).

[9] This stipulation is not so narrow as to exclude regional and supranational *governmental* bodies or agents. However, it does exclude, at all levels, local, regional, and international, the channelling strategies of non-governmental organizations, corporations, trade associations, consumer groups, the professions, netizens, and the (non-governmental) rest.

words, we can stick with the idea that the (techno-) regulators are government agents and that (techno-) regulation is concerned with channelling the conduct of citizens.

Recalling Lawrence Lessig's identification of four key regulatory modalities (or modes of regulation)—namely: the law, social norms, the market, and architecture (or, code in the West Coast sense)[10]—and assuming that there will be an acceleration in the production of technologies that have power and potential as instruments of control, it seems plausible to predict that those regulatory options that are available by way of code or design will appeal—not least because, in larger regulatory arenas, they will promise to outperform traditional East Coast strategies.[11] Where such options are taken up, there will be a modulation in the pitch of regulation as regulators become more concerned with the pattern of regulatees' behaviour and less concerned with giving regulatees reasons for action. To grasp the significance of such a regulatory turn to the West Coast, we must first remind ourselves briefly about the idea of regulatory pitch and then we can clarify the distinctive nature of techno-regulation.

(i) Regulatory pitch

To recall our discussion in Chapter 1, the idea of 'regulatory pitch' refers quite simply to the way in which regulators seek to engage with their targets. Essentially, three pitches are available, namely: moral, practical, and behavioural.

Where the pitch is moral, regulators seek to engage with the targets' moral reason. In other words, regulators argue for compliance on the ground that the regulatory position, or the process that led to that position, is legitimate. Accordingly, regulators maintain that, by complying, regulatees will be doing the right thing. Where the moral pitch successfully engages regulatees, it is accepted either that the regulatory position is morally legitimate, or that (on

[10] *Code* (n 4 above) ch 7; and Lessig 'The Law of the Horse: What Cyberlaw Might Teach' (1999) 113 Harvard Law Review 501, 507–14.

[11] Compare John Law *Organizing Modernity* (Oxford: Blackwell, 1994). According to Law, the problem of 'social order' should be reposed as a problem about the processes of ordering (not of an achieved and stable pattern of order) implicating a variety of materials, such as 'talk, bodies, texts, machines, architectures' and so on (p 2). Drawing on actor-network theory, it is suggested that some materials travel better than others, some are more durable than others, and the like. Law, however, emphasizes that such features are themselves relational effects. Thus:

> Concrete walls are solid while they are maintained and patrolled. Texts order only if they are not destroyed *en route*, and there is someone at the other end who will read them and order her conduct accordingly. Buildings may be adapted for other uses—for instance as objects of the tourist gaze. (102)

The significance of these remarks (and of Law's analysis in general) for smart regulators who aspire to put in place regimes of global governance bears some reflection. I should add that I am not sure whether relating Law's 'materials and modes' approach to ordering (diagramatically represented at 140) to Lessig's theory of regulatory modalities would be either possible or productive. I am sure, however, that this is not the place to attempt any such thing.

moral grounds) it merits respect, or that compliance (where channelling takes this form) is morally obligatory.

Where the pitch is practical, regulators make the less demanding claim that there is 'good reason' (not necessarily or specifically moral reason) for compliance; and channelling will have the desired effect where targets share the sense of good reason (even if there is no one reason that targets uniformly recognise as good). Accordingly, no particular reason within practical reason is privileged although, in practice, the practical pitch will often appeal to the self-interest, especially the economic interests, of targets.

Where the pitch is behavioural, no attempt is made to engage with either moral reason in particular or practical reason in general. All that matters is that the channelling device that is employed engages with the targets in such a way as to achieve the desired pattern of behaviour. Hence, if the desired outcome is that x is done, the doing of x is all that matters. Those who do x need have no reasons for doing x or, if they do have reasons, they need not be responding to reasons that regulators have offered them; and regulators who employ a behavioural pitch need give no reasons to their regulatees.

With regulatory pitch in focus in this way, we can see that, while East Coast regulation (in line with traditional jurisprudential thinking) is premised on an engagement with practical reason, West Coast code is not.[12] Thus, when David Garland says of new situational criminological approaches that they aim 'to embed controls in the fabric of normal interaction, rather than suspend them above it in the form of a sovereign command',[13] what we are seemingly aspiring to, whether or not we are aware of it, is the West Coast.

(ii) Techno-regulation

What is it that is distinctive about techno-regulation, about the ideal-typical West Coast approach? It is perhaps easier to start by identifying three features that are not the key to its distinctive (ideal-typical) nature.

First, there is no suggestion that code or design cannot be applied for virtuous regulatory purposes; there is, thus, no suggestion that the East Coast is necessarily more virtuous than the West. Lessig suggests various examples of virtuous design—for instance, the architecture of Paris after the mid 19th century introduction of boulevards, the placement of the White House in relation to the Capitol, the removal of constitutional courts away from the seat of the legislative and executive branches, speed bumps, and so on.[14] However, design is not always applied with such virtuous intent—Lessig gives the example of the bridges built on

[12] If we wished to firm up these conceptual distinctions, we would have 'law' (as the moral ideal-type of regulation), 'regulation' (as any channelling strategy that engages with practical reason), and 'code' (as any channelling strategy that by-passes engagement with practical reason).

[13] Garland (n 5 above) at 129.

[14] *Code* (n 4 above) at 91–2.

Long Island by Robert Moses so that buses carrying African Americans would not be able to get through to public beaches.[15] Having said this, it is arguable that the overt regulatory approach of the East Coast make it more difficult for illegitimate purposes to be pursued, but I do not want to rest on this argument. For present purposes, we can assume that each style of regulation is capable of abuse and that there can be well-intentioned regulators on both sides of the divide.

Secondly, it is not the use of technology, or technical support, as such that characterises West Coast regulation. Where technology is deployed to monitor compliance and/or to enforce the regulatory standard, design is functioning in some regulatory dimensions but this falls short of ideal-typical techno-regulation. With techno-regulation, design operates alone in all regulatory dimensions. Moreover, it functions in such a way that regulatees have no choice (not even a paper choice of the kind left open by Orwellian surveillance) but to act in accordance with the desired regulatory pattern—it is the difference, for example, between systems that make it physically impossible to exit the Underground (or Metro) without a valid ticket and low-level barriers that make it more difficult (but not impossible) to do so. In this light, consider Garland's elaboration of the idea of controls being embedded in normal interaction:

> Rather than rely upon the uncertain threat of deterrent sentences, or the dubious ability of the police to catch villains, it [the new criminological approach] sets in place a more mundane set of reforms, designed not to change people but to redesign things and reshape situations. A thousand small adjustments are required. Replace cash with credit cards. Build locks into the steering columns of automobiles. Employ attendants in parking lots and use close circuit TV cameras to monitor city centre streets. Co-ordinate the closing times of rival clubs and discos. Lay on late night buses and special routes to and from football games. Advise retailers about security. Encourage local authorities to co-ordinate the various agencies that deal with crime. Remind citizens of the need to safeguard their property and supervise their neighbourhoods.[16]

With the exception of replacing cash with credit cards (after which cash crimes are no longer possible to commit), these examples speak to making the criminal option more difficult to take with success (as with steering locks, and where security measures are adopted by retailers and citizens), more likely to be detected (as with parking attendants and CCTV), or less likely to present itself (as where football supporters are segregated and given their own dedicated routes to and from matches). This is not to say that these are not intelligent responses (albeit responses that are far from free of a variety of ethical concerns, some much more obvious than others).[17] To be sure, this is smart regulation in action; but by

[15] ibid 92.

[16] Garland (n 5 above) at 129.

[17] See Andrew von Hirsch, David Garland, and Alison Wakefield (eds) *Ethical and Social Perspectives on Situational Crime Prevention* (Oxford: Hart Publishing, 2000).

leaving regulatees with the option of non-compliance, both on paper and (for the most part) in practice, this is not yet techno-regulation.

Thirdly, while techno-regulation might focus on designing the environment in which regulatees act, it is not so restricted; it is not co-extensive with situational crime prevention.[18] In principle, techno-regulation might focus on designing people, products, or places. If Lessig sees emerging design responses in the field of information and communications technology, and if Garland sees it in situational crime prevention, then a revolution in biotechnology or in neurotechnology might one day offer a further suite of design options, one that tackles people rather than products or environments. Again, consider Garland's remarks to the effect that the emphasis of the new criminological approach is on 'social order as a problem of *system* integration'.[19] Thus:

> It isn't people who most need to be integrated, but the social processes and arrangements that they inhabit. Instead of addressing human beings and their moral attitudes or psychological dispositions, the new criminologies address the component parts of social systems and situations. They consider how different situations might be redesigned so as to give rise to fewer opportunities for crime, how interacting systems... might be made to converge in ways that create fewer security weaknesses or criminological hot spots. For these frameworks, social order is a matter of aligning and integrating the diverse social routines and institutions that compose modern society. It is a problem of ensuring co-ordination—getting the trains to run on time—not of building normative consensus.[20]

In the paragraph immediately following this, Garland continues:

> The criminologies of everyday life thus offer an approach to social order that is, for the most part, amoral and technological. They bypass the realm of values and concentrate on the routine ways in which people are brought together in time and space. Their conception of social order is a matter not of shared values but of smart arrangements that minimize the opportunities for disruption and deviance. This is a very self-conscious, very sophisticated approach to social order in a complex, differentiated society. It flies in the face of traditionalist ideas that see order as emerging out of moral discipline and obedience to authority.

This is now very close to the mark. Techno-regulation approaches the problem of social order in a way that does not rely on building a normative consensus; it is amoral (or, at any rate, even if the regulatory classes engage in moral debate before imposing a pattern of conduct, they do not engage in any kind of moral discourse with regulatees); it does by-pass the

[18] There is a sense in which techno-regulation embraces both the mainstream 20th century criminological approach that views the 'proper target of crime prevention [as]...the...processes bearing upon the formation of criminal character' and that of situational crime prevention which targets 'the situational dynamics that produce particular criminal events', see David Garland, 'Ideas, Institutions and Situation Crime Prevention' in Andrew von Hirsch et al (n 17 above) 1 at 5.

[19] Garland (n 5 above) at 183.

[20] ibid.

realm of values (again, with the caveat just entered); and it does not rely on moral discipline or obedience to authority. However, this is not because techno-regulation favours non-moral reason over moral reason, but more dramatically *because it by-passes practical reason altogether*. Unlike the new criminological approach, though, this is no adaptation to crime as a normal feature of social existence; to the contrary, far from normalizing crime, techno-regulation seeks to eliminate it as an option.

If we turn these negative features round, we can express the distinctive nature of techno-regulation in the following way. Where the ideal-type of techno-regulation is instantiated regulators, having identified a desired pattern of behaviour (whether morally compliant or not), secure that pattern of behaviour by designing out any option of non-conforming behaviour. Such measures might involve designing regulatees themselves, their environments, or the products that they use in their environments, or a combination of these elements. Where techno-regulation is perfectly instantiated, there is no need for either correction or enforcement.

To this, it might be objected that techno-regulation so specified will never be instantiated because there will always be counter-technologies devised in response to techno-regulatory attempts. Charles Fried, for example, purports to deflate Lessig's claims about the controlling impact of code by reference to the development of DeCSS (by a Norwegian teenager) as a response to the CSS encryption and copy-protection scheme for DVDs:

> The story of CSS and DeCSS illustrates why, contrary to Lessig's assertion, code need not be a technology of perfect control after all: as in physics, so in cyberspace—for every particle there seems to be an antiparticle.[21]

No doubt, games will be played; in response to new (regulatory) technologies, hackers and crackers will emerge from Norwegian woods; and, sometimes, regulatees might themselves start the game by adopting a technological strategy of avoidance (such as P2P file-sharing as an exploitation of the limits of traditional copyright law).[22] However, it would be complacent to assume that the West Coast will never be perfectly realized. Even if it is only a remote possibility, we need to consider why we should be concerned about techno-regulation.

[21] Charles Fried 'Perfect Freedom, Perfect Control?' (2000) 114 Harvard Law Review 606, 628. Compare, also, Hans Fischer 'Technology Perspectives on Code' in Egbert Dommering and Lodewijk Asscher (eds) *Coding Regulation* (The Hague: TCM Asser Press, 2006) 17.

[22] For extended discussion, see Tim Wu 'When Code Isn't Law' (2003) 89 Virginia Law Review 679. See, also, Amitai Etzioni 'Implications of Select New Technologies for Individual Rights and Public Safety' (2002) 15 Harvard Journal of Law and Technology 257, for the dialectic that starts with 'liberalizing' technologies (such as cell phones, the internet, and strong encryption) and then leads to the responsive development of 'public protective' technologies (such as Carnivore (to monitor e-mail traffic) and the Key Logger System and Magic Lantern (to retrieve passwords)).

III Transparency, accountability, and democratic deficit

Imagine that societies are ordered by techno-regulators who are philosopher kings, who have a perfect grasp of what is right and wrong in human interactions, and who control the conduct of their regulatees in such a way that doing wrong is never an option. Is this a regulatory arrangement that should inspire us or concern us? Lee Tien[23] sounds the following warning note:

> Architectural regulations are at the extreme perceived more as conditions than as rules to be followed or disobeyed consciously. Unlike ordinary sanction-backed rules, architecture achieves compliance by default rather than through active enforcement. To the extent that legitimacy and public deliberation are integral to our notion of law, the surreptitious enactment and enforcement of norms via architecture should give us pause.[24]

In this part of the chapter, we can follow up on Tien's warning by considering a set of 'public law' concerns that object to the lack of transparency and accountability on the West Coast before moving on in the next part to more deep-seated concerns about the preservation of the infrastructural conditions for moral community.

It is axiomatic that good (democratic) governance entails transparent governance. Minimally, transparency demands that the formal regulatory position should be declared. If regulators have formally prohibited act x, then regulatees who do x should know that they are doing a prohibited act. If, however, act x is permitted, then regulatees who are contemplating doing x should be able to proceed, in reliance on the declared regulatory position, and confident in the knowledge that (at least so far as regulators are concerned) they do no wrong. Why is it important that regulatees should be so informed? From the point of view of regulators (*sic*), it is arguable that the declaration of the regulatory position is a prerequisite for effective governance (but this assumes that regulation will be some kind of East Coast attempt). More importantly, from the point of view of regulatees, autonomy is frustrated where the regulatory position is unclear and, in the absence of regulatory guidance, those who see the virtues of good citizenship can only guess at what it requires.

Over and above the bare declaration of the regulatory position, transparency enjoins regulators to declare their objectives. Where regulators declare that act x is prohibited, it will often be perfectly clear what the regulators' objectives are. However, this is not necessarily so; the regulators might have a hidden agenda. For example, the regulatory position might be that the consumption of alcohol is prohibited while, in practice, regulators make little attempt to enforce the prohibition. Here, there is a lack of congruence between the formal regulatory

[23] Lee Tien 'Architectural Regulation and the Evolution of Social Norms' (2004) 9 International Journal of Communications Law and Policy 1.

[24] ibid 7.

position (which is seen by regulators as a symbolic gesture to appease a particular constituency) and the regulators' real objectives (which are to permit alcohol to be consumed).[25] Where the formal regulatory position is that act x is permitted, the background regulatory objectives might again be more nuanced, regulators supplementing the permission with measures reflecting various degrees of encouragement (or discouragement). For example, where gaming is formally permitted but, as a matter of the private law of contract, gaming agreements are treated as unenforceable, the permission is laced with discouragement; conversely, if gaming machines, displaying inventive steps, are treated as patentable, the permission is laced with encouragement.[26] Why should it matter that, in addition to knowing the regulatory position, regulatees should also know what the regulatory objectives are? The short answer is that this matters for the purposes of accountability. Good (active) citizenship and political freedom imply an engagement between regulators and regulatees as to the purposes of the regulation. Unless the regulators' purposes are transparent, there can be no meaningful debate about the acceptability of the measures taken.[27]

Now, as regulators turn towards the West Coast, these values of good governance are put at risk. Recognizing this risk, Lessig remarks:

> Indirection misdirects responsibility. When a government uses other structures of constraint to effect a constraint it could impose directly, it muddies the responsibility for that constraint and so undermines political accountability. If transparency is a value in constitutional government, indirection is its enemy.[28]

The example of access to the public beaches on Long Island is a good one. If regulators declare openly and directly that African Americans are not permitted to use the beaches, the regulatory position and, concomitantly, the regulatory objectives —however abhorrent—are perfectly transparent. If, instead, regulators pursue the same objective indirectly—and it should be said that design is not the only indirect strategy; but, for present purposes, it is the one that matters—by constructing narrow bridges or the like, then (depending on the context)[29] it might be much less clear what is going on. Similarly, Lessig recounts that, after the decision of the US Supreme Court in *Shelley v Kraemer*[30] (striking down direct segregation

[25] See eg, Robert S Summers *Instrumentalism and American Legal Theory* (Ithaca: Cornell University Press, 1983).

[26] See, further, Roger Brownsword 'Regulating Human Genetics: New Dilemmas for a New Millennium' (2004) 12 Medical Law Review 14.

[27] See, also, Etzioni (n 22 above).

[28] *Code* (n 4 above) at 96; and Lessig 'The Law of the Horse: What Cyberlaw Might Teach' (1999) 113 Harvard Law Review 501, 541–3.

[29] In some contexts, it will be clear enough that a regulatory intervention, albeit by design, is taking place—no one supposes, as Lessig points out, that speed bumps ('sleeping policemen') are accidental (ibid at 98). Nor is anyone in any doubt about the regulatory objective (although there might be more debate about the background objectives—road safety or revenue raising— associated with speed cameras).

[30] 334 US 1 (1948).

effected by private restrictive covenants), the transparent racism of local communities was replaced by 'a thousand tiny inconveniences of architecture and zoning'[31] designed indirectly to maintain segregation. If smart regulation leads to a reduction in transparency and a diminution in accountability, perhaps this is less smart than it seems.[32]

Let us suppose that the regulators of tomorrow, mindful of the values of transparency and accountability, propose a West Coast solution which is then presented to citizens for debate and decision. In other words, the regulators present a designed response to a problem but they will not introduce it unless specifically mandated to do so by the informed choice of their citizens. Let us suppose that what the regulators propose is a fully automatic car as a guarantee of safe transportation. When their biometrically identified owners enter these vehicles of the future, they simply instruct the vehicle to proceed to a given destination. The onboard computer or motorobot does the rest; and the vehicle duly transports its passengers safely to their destination. Road traffic accidents, road traffic offences, drink-driving,[33] and, let us suppose, car crime too are things of the past. What owners give up is the opportunity to drive their cars; but, if they so wish, they can experience the thrill, and practise the skill, of driving in the comfort and safety of simulated virtual environments.[34] Citizens debate their options. There is some resistance to the fully automatic car because many who thought that they had jobs for life (driving instructors, driving examiners, traffic police, and so on) will need to retrain. However, the majority of citizens, weary of the toll taken by road traffic accidents and the risks associated with motoring, vote for the designed solution; they freely choose the West Coast; and driven vehicles, like dinosaurs, become museum pieces.

So far, surely, so good. The regulatory objective is transparent and the means of achieving it have been fully debated and specifically authorized. To be sure, once the designed solution is in place, practical reason is by-passed; but regulators have made every effort to engage their regulatees' practical reason before settling on the West Coast. Is there, nevertheless, cause for concern?

[31] *Code* (n 4 above) at 97.

[32] While *Thornton v Shoe Lane Parking Ltd* [1971] 2 QB 163 is not generally perceived in these terms, with hindsight, it actually offers an interesting analogue in private law. There, the architecture of the car-park was unusual for that time in that it, quite literally, channelled motorists up to the entry point where entry was automated (no parking attendant was present). It would have been perfectly clear to motorists of the 1960s that the design of the car-park was no accident. Although the architecture of the car-park might have troubled contract lawyers (because it channelled motorists towards acceptance), the Court of Appeal was more concerned about the lack of transparency with regard to the car-park operators' exclusions of liability for negligence. Less convincingly, such terms were also regarded as unusual.

[33] To this extent, the fully automatic car would overtake such attempted technological fixes as the so-called alco-lock (which is designed to prevent a car being started up if the device detects any trace of alcohol on the breath of the driver): see *The Guardian* 5 August 2004, p 7.

[34] For a vision of a virtual future, see Susan Greenfield *Tomorrow's People* (London: Allen Lane, 2001).

Recall David Garland's remark that the everyday criminological school on the West Coast aims to embed regulatory controls in the fabric of normal interaction rather than rely on normative prescription. When the fully automatic car is introduced, it is not only non-automatic cars that disappear; a whole raft of road traffic law is rendered obsolete. For first generation automatic car users, for those who actually participated in the great debate, there is still the recollection of failed road traffic laws; and, for some time thereafter, the repealed road traffic laws might still be part of the collective memory and the cultural heritage. However, the cultural code is changing.[35] The very embeddedness of the fully automatic car means that downstream generations simply see this hi-tech object as a car (the distinction between an automatic and a non-automatic car has been lost; this is just a car; what else could there be?); and the sense of transportation actually being regulated is also lost—whereas the first generation made a self-conscious choice between East Coast and West Coast regulation, for later generations this is just how you are transported from East to West.[36]

Pulling these threads together, we can detect two rather different West Coast challenges to transparency and accountability. One threat arises from regulators who, favouring indirect over direct approaches, and insouciant to the values of transparency and accountability, deviate from the canons of good governance. The other arises from the embedded nature of West Coast solutions; even where regulators act with meticulous concern for transparency and accountability, designed solutions might become so embedded in everyday life that it is only outsiders and historians who can trace the invisible hand of regulation.

Such concerns, however, are not the end of the story; it is not just transparency and accountability that are at risk. Techno-regulation operates by reducing the options available to regulatees. On one view, this is undesirable; autonomous agents flourish in a context where their options are extended, not contracted. Arguably, however, the more serious concern is that options are being reduced in a way that impacts on the authenticity of moral decision-making. What we must now consider, therefore, is an objection to techno-regulation that focuses

[35] Compare Lawrence Lessig 'The New Chicago School' (1998) 27 Journal of Legal Studies 661, at 685. In the context of information technology, Bauer and Gaskell (n 6 above, at 383) observe:

> [T]he rise of the personal computer has increased keyboard writing and has probably decreased the intensity and quality of handwriting. Thus technology structures behaviour [and, I want to say, perceptions], both individually and collectively, bringing both opportunities and threats to human pursuits.

[36] As James Boyle puts it in 'Foucault in Cyberspace: Surveillance, Sovereignty, and Hardwired Censors' (1997) 66 University of Cincinnati Law Review 177 at 205:

> [T]he attraction of technical solutions is that they apparently elide the question of power—both private *and* public—in the first place. The technology appears to be 'just the ways things are'; its origins are concealed, whether those origins lie in state-sponsored scheme or market-structured order, and its effects are obscured because it is hard to imagine the alternative. Above all, technical solutions are less contentious; we think of a legal regime as coercing, and a technological regime as merely shaping—or even actively facilitating—our choices.

on the significance of having the option to do wrong as well as the preconditions for such essentially moral notions as those of respect and responsibility.[37] We can begin this process of reflection in the next part of the chapter and then continue it in the following chapter.

IV Responsibility, respect, and human dignity

In a moral community, judgments speak to matters of both act morality and agent morality. Act morality concerns the status of the act itself, whether it is morally permitted or required (and, thus, 'moral') or prohibited (and, thus, 'immoral'). Agent morality expresses judgments relative to the agent who acts. An agent who attempts to do the right thing and who acts on the right considerations will be judged to be acting like a moral agent; by contrast, an agent who does not attempt to do the right thing or who acts on improper considerations will be judged to deviate from the standard of agent morality. Ideal-typically, the fully moral action will involve an agent doing the right thing (as a matter of act morality) for the right reasons (as a matter of agent morality). However, there are deviations from this ideal-typical case, where judgments of act and agent morality are not in alignment. Notoriously, agents who (as a matter of agent morality) try to do the right thing might (as a matter of act morality) do the wrong thing, and vice versa. In principle, some might argue that it is act morality that ultimately matters and that, if a choice has to be made, we should prioritize act morality over agent morality. However, in a community of rights, where the self-conscious absence of assumed moral omniscience is a key feature in our specification, judgments of agent morality matter a great deal in practice.[38] This is not to say that agents will be readily excused, on agent morality grounds, where they flout settled standards; but, where there is reasonable disagreement about the right standard or the right action, practical judgments necessarily will focus on considerations of agent morality. It follows that any developments that threaten to undercut the sense of an agent trying to do the right thing are a serious matter for a community of rights.

In the light of this thumbnail sketch of moral judgment, we can return to the West Coast where we can pick up the tale of automatic transportation. Let us suppose that the desired regulatory pattern is achieved. The roads are now safe places.

[37] For a hint as to how situational crime prevention might threaten moral responsibility, see RA Duff and SE Marshall 'Benefits, Burdens and Responsibilities: Some Ethical Dimensions of Situational Crime Prevention' in Andrew von Hirsch et al (n 17 above) 17 especially at 20–1. And for concerns that (private) exclusion and profiling by-passes agency, see Andrew von Hirsch and Clifford Shearing 'Exclusion from Public Space', ibid at 77.

[38] Compare Peter Cane *Responsibility in Law and Morality* (Oxford: Hart, 2002), one of the recurring themes of which is that, whereas the criminal law paradigm, because it is concerned with stigmatizing and punishing wrongdoers, tends to be agent (offender)-orientated, the civil law paradigm, because it is concerned with remedy and repair, tends to be directed more to the protection of victims.

If owners were in control of their cars, we would say that as a matter of act morality their driving evinces respect for the legitimate interests of fellow road users, motorists and pedestrians alike—cars are driven as act morality requires (or permits). *If owners were making a conscious (albeit fallible) effort to drive carefully and with regard to the safety of fellow road users*, we would judge that they at least conform to the standards of responsible agent morality. But, on the West Coast, car owners do not actually drive their vehicles; they are the passive beneficiaries of safe passage not its active producers. What, then, can we say? How far does moral judgment remain available and meaningful? Can we say much more than that the observed regulatory effect is in line with act morality?

In the context of (what we now see as) East Coast regulation, HLA Hart famously distinguishes between the perception of the (epistemologically) external observer of a rule-governed road traffic situation and that of an insider.[39] Whereas the former observes only a pattern of behaviour (for example, motorists stopping when the traffic lights turn to red), the insider interprets this as compliance with a rule requiring traffic to observe the signals. If not (for Hart) quite the sovereign's command suspended at the traffic lights, it is at least the primary rules of the criminal law that are in play. For those insiders who internalize the rules, for those who have a critical and reflective attitude towards compliance, deviants are rightly held responsible for non-compliance. Moreover, in the Hartian analysis, where legal rules are viewed by insiders as having the right moral credentials, such insider judgments of legal responsibility track their judgments of moral responsibility.

This contrasts sharply with life on the West Coast. There, as we have seen, it is characteristic of techno-regulation that rules and reasons are dispensed with; patterned behaviour is what matters; and it is not only the external observer who might be unaware of the situation being a regulated one—motorists, too, might lack such awareness. Crucially, on the West Coast, regulators leave no room for judgments of moral responsibility. When regulators design people, products, or places in such a way that regulatees have no choice but to act in whatever way is judged to be appropriate, we cannot meaningfully speak about them being morally responsible agents, to be credited with acts that respect others and to be blamed where they fall short of moral requirements.[40]

In Chapter 4, I identified two preconditions for moral community, namely: first, the vulnerability of agents (the fact that agents have legitimate interests capable of being harmed; or that others have the capability and opportunity to inflict harm of this kind); and, secondly, the perception that agents are responsible for their actions (in the sense that agents are legitimately held to account for their

[39] HLA Hart *The Concept of Law* (Oxford: Clarendon Press, 1961).

[40] Compare Ronald Dworkin *Sovereign Virtue* (Cambridge, Mass: Harvard University Press, 2000) at 446 for the view that it would be a confusion to suppose that 'even the most dramatic shifts in the chance/choice boundary [via genetic engineering] somehow challenge morality itself'. While genetic engineering surely weakens the judgments of responsibility that are central to agent morality, it does not eliminate the meaningfulness of act morality.

wrongdoing). In its most well-intentioned form, techno-regulation aspires to make communities safer places by designing out the option of inflicting harm on rights-holders or designing out their vulnerability. The desired pattern of behaviour will simulate that of a realized act morality but the context is transformed so that agents are no longer active participants in a moral community.[41] Agents who are techno-regulated simply do what they do; what they do is not harmful; it cannot be harmful; but the idea of rights now makes little sense (to regulatees) and, once rights lose their sense, so too does the idea of responsibility.

Of course, if West Coast regulation ends with the automatic motor car, many opportunities will remain for choosing agents to respect the vulnerability of others. The culture will still code for respect and responsibility. However, the corrosion of moral community is already underway. On the one side, there is no reason to think that regulators, encouraged by their success, will stop at safe roads and every reason to suppose that techno-regulation will move on from safe roads to safe cities and (no longer moral) safe communities. On the other side, one might wonder how regulatees will react. As David Smith has pointed out in an insightful paper, technology 'may have a moralising or alternatively a demoralising effect'.[42] Thus:

> A system which delivers a strong and consistent symbolic message... may have the effect of creating or reinforcing norms, strengthening belief in them, and making it harder for people to disengage their self-controls from these norms. By contrast, a system which removes all personal choice may tend to weaken self-controls, for a variety of reasons. If people are denied any autonomy, then they perceive that the moral responsibility lies entirely with the system, and they no longer retain any obligations themselves.[43]

Consider, too, the parallel concerns sometimes expressed about the administration of methylphenidate (Ritalin) and amphetamine (Adderall) to children whose conduct is outside the range of acceptability. In its report, *Beyond Therapy*,[44] the President's Council on Bioethics expresses just this concern in the following terms:

> Behavior-modifying agents circumvent that process [i.e. the process of self-control and progressive moral education], and act directly on the brain to affect the child's behavior

[41] Notice, too, how commentators on situational crime prevention detect a reconfiguration of trust once there is an expectation that targets will take defensive measures. In 'Situational Crime Prevention, Urban Governance and Trust Relations', (n 17 above) 193, at 193–4, Adam Crawford puts the point in the following way:

> SCP constructs symbolic representations of 'orderly environments': through notions of territoriality, exclusivity, surveillance, protection and defensiveness. At the same time, SCP inscribes distrust into the physical environment through the modification, design and manipulation of situational attributes. These interventions result in a reconfiguration of what can be trusted, by producing new abstract systems and symbolic tokens.

See, also, John Kleinig 'The Burdens of Situational Crime Prevention: An Ethical Commentary' (n 17 above) 37.

[42] David J Smith 'Changing Situations and Changing People', (n 17 above) 147 at 170.

[43] ibid. Smith is making this important point in the context of automatic ticketing systems that are designed to reduce fare evasion by users of public transport.

[44] President's Council on Bioethics *Beyond Therapy* (Washington: Dana Press, 2003).

without the intervening learning process. If what matters is only the child's outward behavior, then this is simply a more effective and efficient means of achieving the desired result. But because moral education is typically more about the shaping of the agent's character than about the outward act, the process of learning to behave appropriately matters most of all. If the development of character depends on effort to choose and act appropriately, often in the face of resisting desires and impulses, then the more direct pharmacological approach bypasses a crucial element.... By treating the restlessness of youth as a medical, rather than a moral, challenge, those resorting to behavior-modifying drugs might not only deprive [the] child of an essential part of this education. They might also encourage him to change his self-understanding as governed largely by chemical impulses and not by moral decisions grounded in some sense of what is right and appropriate.[45]

In other words, once we rely on design or architecture, or take an interventionist biotechnological or neurotechnological approach, to respond to (or manage) our social problems, there is a danger that, as the President's Council puts it, 'we may weaken our sense of responsibility and agency'.[46] If so, as the East gives way to the West, such a demoralising effect might give the smartest of regulators pause. Is any space being left for regulatees to exercise moral choice and moral responsibility?

Let us suppose that techno-regulation has moved on from safe roads to safe communities more generally. Even so, the sphere of techno-regulated life is not co-extensive with the life of the community. As on the East Coast, so too on the West Coast there is a line between state regulated conduct and conduct that is unregulated. Of course, on both coasts, private regulators might see the attractions of a technological approach. However, for the sake of argument, let us suppose that, even on the West Coast, there is a sphere of action that is not techno-regulated. Moreover, let us suppose that this is a sphere in which agents adopt and act on (or sometimes break) an informal moral code. The state, let us imagine, does not care whether agents break promises in their own homes or engage in acts of duplicity with friends and relatives. If this is the context, then West Coast regulators who wonder whether they have gone too far will need to ask two questions. First, is the space that is left for moral community sufficient? If not, might it be enhanced without engaging in a regulatory U-turn—for example, by enabling games players to confront moral dilemmas in simulated virtual environments; or by debating moral hypotheticals in high school? Secondly, if the space is sufficient, do regulatees still have the capacity to engage in moral reason? The point is that the particular control strategies that have been employed to secure the required pattern of behaviour in the techno-regulated sphere might be incompatible with the exercise of moral reason in the unregulated sphere. For example, if agents have been genetically coded to be other-regarding, can this coding be switched off as regulatees move from the regulated sphere to the unregulated sphere? Perhaps

[45] ibid pp 105–6. [46] ibid 106.

this is clutching at straws. At this stage, it is best not to blur the bottom line—which is, quite simply, that a fully techno-regulated community is no longer an operative moral community.

Ultimately, then, the question boils down to this: if we are regulated so that we can only do the right thing, does it matter that we lose the opportunity to do the wrong thing? To which, some might be inclined to respond: if techno-regulators know how to stop us from being bad but only by, at the same time, stopping us from being good, maybe the East Coast, for all its imperfections, has something going for it.[47]

V Conclusion

There is a view that it is technical fixes rather than legislation that largely account for improvements to the quality of life.[48] If we adopt this view, the idea of regulating by technical fix rather than by legislation will appeal. However, before we migrate to the West Coast, we should reflect upon the caution that the 'progress' claimed for scientific and technological innovation is often a mixed blessing.[49] In the case of techno-regulation, the progressive reduction of crime is accompanied by the reduction of choice—not the elimination of all choice but a reduction of the opportunities to choose between doing right or doing wrong. In its most favourable instantiation, a techno-regulated society presents itself as a community that acts morally (always), as a community that acts responsibly and with respect; and yet it is a community in which moral currency has been all but eliminated, a community that no longer codes for respect and responsibility. If the passing of such a community (that is, a community that codes for respect and responsibility) is a cause for concern, the East Coast is where we should stay.

Of course, in less favourable instantiations, a techno-regulated society will look distinctly dystopian. If we fear abuse of power, corruption, and evil on the West Coast we might think that the prospects are better on the East—whether because we judge that such risks are less likely to arise where governance tends towards transparency or because we believe that, if such risks were to arise, it would be easier to respond to them on the East. These are not unimportant considerations and an argument advocating the East over the West for just such reasons might well be made out. However, this is not an argument on which I am

[47] Compare the reservations of Castle, the sceptical philosopher, in BF Skinner *Walden Two* (Upper Saddle River, NJ: Prentice Hall, 1948, 1976) especially at 161 and 227.

[48] Matt Ridley 'We've Never Had it so Good – and it's All Thanks to Science' Guardian Life 3 April 2003, 8.

[49] Alain Touraine 'The Crisis of "Progress"' in Martin Bauer (ed) *Resistance to New Technology* (Cambridge: Cambridge University Press, 1995) 45. See, also, Michael Levi and David S Wall 'Technologies, Security, and Privacy in the Post-9/11 European Information Society' (2004) 31 Journal of Law and Society 194.

relying.[50] What I want to draw out is the West Coast vision in its most favourable instantiation. If we reject the most favourable option on offer from the West, then we will certainly not accept any less favourable offer.

So, which regulatory approach is it to be, the East Coast or the West Coast? Should the members of a community of rights favour the safe and secure environment of the West or the social, if not always sociable, environment of the East? It is a remarkably difficult call because the choice reflects a tension between two larger visions of progressive human development. On the one hand, there is the celebration of instrumental rationality where 'rational individuals... build a reasonable society thanks to the resources created by science and technology' coupled with a confidence in the 'parallelism between scientific and technological achievements on the one hand, and abundance, freedom and happiness on the other'.[51] On the other hand, there is the Kantian view of the cultivation of moral agency, of moral will yielding authentic freedom and responsibility. While the West Coast approach is in line with the (former) technocratic view that we can make things better by working on (and minimizing) the natural and social adversities that present us with problems of justice (scarcity of resources) and social order, the East Coast approach is in line with the (latter) view that what ultimately matters is how we, as humans, address these adversities.[52]

To eschew the technological solution seems perverse; how could members of a community of rights turn their backs on a regulatory regime that guarantees full compliance with whatever pattern of conduct the regulatory classes judge to be properly other-regarding? And yet, there is a sense that the West Coast is a place to avoid. After all, if one aspires to be an actively participating member of a moral community, regulatees on the West Coast are seriously disenfranchized.[53] If only there could be a synthesis that brought together the attractions of the respective regimes. If only there could be a third way. With the thought that there might be such a way out of the stark choice between East and West, we can move on to the next chapter.

[50] I do touch on such prudential considerations in 'What the World Needs Now: Techno-Regulation, Human Rights and Human Dignity' in Roger Brownsword (ed) *Global Governance and Human Rights* (Oxford: Hart, 2004) 203.

[51] Touraine, (n 49 above) at 51.

[52] Compare RA Duff and SE Marshall (n 37 above).

[53] For a glimpse of Lessig's own reservations about the 'dark character' of the New Chicago School, see 'The New Chicago School' (1998) 27 Journal of Legal Studies 661, at 691.

10

Code and the Corrosion of Moral Community

I Introduction

In Anthony Burgess's remarkable novel, *A Clockwork Orange*,[1] it is not altogether clear who is to be regarded as the principal villain of the piece. Is it Alex, the teenage thug? Or, is it Dr Brodsky, who pioneers the use of Ludovico's Technique (a programme of aversion therapy) at the State Institute for the Reclamation of Criminal Types? The chaplain has little doubt that it is the latter who represents the real danger to society. Observing the successful results of Alex's treatment, the chaplain laments:

> He has no real choice, has he? Self-interest, fear of physical pain, drove him to that grotesque act of self-abasement. Its insincerity was clearly to be seen. He ceases to be a wrongdoer. He ceases also to be a creature capable of moral choice.[2]

To which Dr Brodsky responds:

> These are subtleties... We are not concerned with motive, with the higher ethics. We are concerned only with cutting down crime....[3]

However, for the chaplain, the higher ethics really do matter. In his assessment, the principal objection to Ludovico's Technique is not that it might misfire, but that it works; and that, when it works, it succeeds in depriving the reclaimed person of the capacity for moral choice. Indeed, the chaplain would go as far as to say that it is better that a person should choose to do wrong than that they should be conditioned to do right.

Even if we are with the chaplain rather than Dr Brodsky, it surely is ultra-provocative to suggest that it is better that people should choose to do wrong than that they should be conditioned to do right. For this ranks the interest in having the opportunity to lead an authentic moral life above the interest in having any kind of life. Alex's interest in having the capacity to be an authentic moral person, freely to choose to do the right thing, is extremely important; but it is not obviously more

[1] (London: William Heinemann Ltd, 1962). My page references are to the Penguin Classics edition, 2000.

[2] ibid 94.

[3] ibid.

important than Alex's interest (like the interests of his victims) in having a level of basic well-being. Before there can be a moral life, there has to be life. Accordingly, to be less provocative, what the chaplain should say is *not* that it is better that people should choose to do *wrong* than that they should be conditioned to do *right*, but that it is better that people should choose to do *right* (for the right reason) than that they should be conditioned to do *right*. From the chaplain's perspective, so modified, we certainly want people to do the right thing rather than the wrong thing; however, it matters not only that they choose to do the right thing but also that they so choose for the right reason—for the chaplain, it is not sufficient that a person chooses to act in line with moral requirements where this is motivated by considerations of self-interest or fear, or the like; characteristically, a person with the capacity for moral choice chooses to act in line with moral requirements because, quite simply, it is accepted that one's actions should conform to one's moral judgments.

Even this modified version of the chaplain's view, however, might seem too high-minded. After all, if a person is to have the opportunity to choose to do right, this implies that the choice to do wrong must also be available. If we cannot be good without also having the opportunity to be bad, there must be a risk that harm will be done to others. Why, then, should we value the opportunity to choose between good and bad (the opportunity, that is, to lead an authentic moral life) over a series of conditioned responses that eliminate the risk of harming one another? And, even if we say, as I am inclined to say, that this very matter of having the opportunity to lead an authentic moral life takes us right to the essence of human dignity, it is not clear why we should prioritize this value over values such as physical well-being or respect for property and the like.

The significance of these remarks, of course, is this: as technologies—whether biotechnology, ICT, the technologies associated with the new brain sciences, nanotechnology, AI, and the like—bring on stream enhanced mechanisms for social control, regulators will have increasingly sophisticated tools for managing the risk of crime. If, like Dr Brodsky, regulators are interested, not in higher ethics but only in what succeeds in controlling or reducing crime, then the imperative to turn to technological interventions will be strong. My question is not whether the chaplain's view will prevail against the Brodskys of a high-tech future but whether, in a community of rights, there is a point at which regulators should, for the sake of a higher ethics, draw back. How far should regulators go with panopticon surveillance? How far should they go with techno-regulatory total control?

The chapter is in four parts. In the first part, I rehearse the contrast that I have drawn in the previous chapter between a regime of total control (the West Coast) and a standard criminal justice regime (the East Coast). If neither option looks wholly attractive, we might be tempted either to allow some technological intervention on the East Coast or to reduce the degree of technological control exercised on the West Coast; we might be tempted, in other words, to develop a mid-West kind of regime. In the second part, taking the East Coast as my starting point, I consider the temptation to move some way to the West, to make use of regulating technologies. The question is how far we could take such a regime before we prompted the chaplain's objection. In the third part, I consider a revised contrast in which the West Coast model is compared not with the typically ineffective East Coast model[4] but an East Coast community that fulfils the chaplain's aspirations, citizens doing the right thing for the right reason. If the East Coast environment is every bit as safe and secure as the West Coast, is there any reason to prefer one regulatory model over the other? Finally, I ask whether the chaplain's view is compatible, first, with an East Coast commitment to human rights and individual freedom—a commitment that rejects the kind of cultural conservatism that is often articulated in the name of respect for human dignity[5]—and, secondly, with scientific developments that cast doubt on the very idea of Alex or anyone else having a 'real choice'.

II Two Regulatory Models: the East and the West

Consider our two regulatory models. One, the East Coast model, is an approximation of the way in which regulators operate in modern societies; the other, the West Coast model, is a thought-experiment, purely ideal-typical. In the former, regulators rely on a mix of regulatory strategies—traditional legal command and control techniques, informal social and peer pressure, market adjustment, and so on,[6] in the latter, regulation is of an entirely technological kind—risk-management is handled exclusively by technological design of one kind or another. Whereas, in the East Coast community, Alex and his friends would not be out of place, in the West Coast community, there would be no place for people like Alex. Not only would the West Coast regulators either design-out people like Alex or design-in a control mechanism that eliminates the risk that Alex otherwise would present, they also would design-out the characteristic East Coast choice between doing right and doing wrong. By coding for only certain kinds of (approved) conduct, the regulators on the West Coast make theirs a safe community; but the price is that regulators do not speak to, or reason with, their regulatees.

In the previous chapter, I stipulated that the regulators on the West Coast would always act in a morally well-intentioned way. Indeed, I might even propose that, for the purposes of making a choice between the two regulatory models,

[4] For a classic critique of traditional criminal justice systems, see Richard Danzig 'Towards the Creation of a Complementary Decentralised System of Criminal Justice' (1973) 26 Stanford Law Review 1.

[5] Compare Deryck Beyleveld and Roger Brownsword *Human Dignity in Bioethics and Biolaw* (Oxford: Oxford University Press, 2001); and Roger Brownsword 'Bioethics Today, Bioethics Tomorrow: Stem Cell Research and the "Dignitarian Alliance"' (2003) 17 Notre Dame Journal of Law, Ethics and Public Policy 15.

[6] Lawrence Lessig *Code and Other Laws of Cyberspace* (New York: Basic Books, 1999) 53–4; and 'The Law of the Horse: What Cyberlaw Might Teach' (1999) 113 Harvard Law Review 501, 533–4.

we should assume that the West Coast regulators will design-in compliance with whatever moral code the choosing party wishes to specify. Even with the benefit of that assumption, it is far from clear that a prospective regulatee should opt for the West Coast. Granted, the assumption of perpetually benign West Coast regulators strains the imagination. Even so, why the resistance to the West? Why the lingering affection for the imperfect East?[7]

Surely, it is perverse to cling to the East? Anyone who encounters Alex and his friends is unlikely to see much attraction in a style of regulation that prohibits without being able to prevent their brand of thuggery. What is the use of civilizing influences such as libraries, one might think, if gangs of young Alexes simply take it into their heads to rough up elderly library-users and destroy their books? So, what is it that the East Coast has going for it?

Essentially, there are two positive features to the East Coast model of regulation (that is to say, over and above the commitment to respect for human rights and fundamental freedoms that I am assuming as a feature of East Coast regulation).[8] First, if we assume that the East Coast is committed to such modern public law virtues as those of transparency, accountability and participation, then citizens have an opportunity to contribute to the discourse and debate of public regulation. Depending upon how effectively such public law ideals are translated into practice, citizens have a real role to play in the formation of the regulatory positions that govern their community. Secondly, where the regulatory positions that are adopted on the East Coast prohibit certain actions or require citizens to behave in certain ways, citizens again exercise a choice as to compliance or non-compliance. In other words, citizens have two relevant chances to contribute to the moral character of their community, first by having a say as to what the rules are to be and, secondly, by electing to act in line with those rules. On the West Coast, by contrast, these chances and choices are denied.

The spectre of Alex persists, however. Is there no way of combining the best of both worlds? In a world of third-ways, is there not a mid-West option—a regulatory model that is either Alex-free or at least one in which potential victims are Alex-proof but where the essential features of moral community are retained? Even if regulators on the East Coast should not adopt a full-scale West Coast approach, should they not at least move some way in that direction? This question, this invitation to head West, takes us to the second part of the chapter.

[7] Compare the reservations of Castle, the sceptical philosopher, in BF Skinner, *Walden Two* (Upper Saddle River, NJ: Prentice Hall, 1948, 1976) especially at 161 and 227.

[8] This assumption is made to bring the East Coast model even closer to those regulatory regimes with which we are familiar; and, in the final part of the chapter, the East Coast commitment to human rights is deployed to provoke a question concerning the consistency of the East Coast credo—a question that arises purely by way of immanent critique. I am conscious, however, that the East Coast commitment to human rights might be turned, too, on the West Coast model. Arguably, as we argued in the previous chapter, there is a serial violation of human rights on the West Coast insofar as regulatee citizens are systematically excluded from participation in public governance.

III Neither East Nor West

In this part of the chapter, I want to consider how East Coast regulators might take advantage of technological channelling devices without sacrificing the essential features of moral community that they prize. The question is whether a middle-way approach is feasible, either in principle or in practice. Or, to put this another way, the question is whether, once East Coast regulators start to head West, there is any stopping point short of the West Coast itself.

Let me sketch two proposals that might be put forward on the East Coast with a view to enabling the community to introduce a degree of techno-enhancement into its traditional regulatory repertoire. To assist with getting a fix on these proposals, perhaps we can imagine that regulators consider three points for technological intervention: (i) ex ante, to eliminate the possibility of wrongdoing; (ii) at the point of wrongdoing, to detect the offence and to identify and apprehend the wrongdoer; and (iii) ex post, at the stage of correction. If the technical fix is adopted ex ante, agents can do no wrong; if the fix is adopted at the second stage, agents can do wrong but they cannot get away with it; and if the technical fix is adopted ex post, agents will be disabled from doing wrong again. It goes without saying that each proposal adopts a minimalist approach because of East Coast nervousness about diminishing the role of moral choice.

(i) Two proposals

The first proposal is that technology should be focused on detecting non-compliance, identifying offenders and bringing such persons before the courts.[9] Moreover, this proposal explicitly limits techno-assistance to this one segment of the regulatory process. It follows that regulators should never rely ex ante on technology in order to design-out conduct that is not acceptable or to design-in the required conduct—and this restriction applies equally to persons who have not yet committed a crime as to those who have a record of criminality. Accordingly, if it were possible, say, genetically to engineer individuals so that any predisposition towards violence would be removed,[10] this is not a step that regulators should take (neither ex ante nor ex post the commission of an offence). However, provided that the regulatory standard is set in the usual way, it is legitimate for regulators to make use of technology in monitoring compliance and in enforcing

[9] Possibly, sponsors of this proposal would be encouraged by Lord Steyn's remarks in *R v Chief Constable of South Yorkshire Police, ex parte LS and Marper* [2004] UKHL 39 at paras 1–2 (where his Lordship stresses that 'law enforcement agencies should take full advantage of the available techniques of modern technology and forensic science' and declares that 'it is a high priority that police forces should expand the use of such [technologically assisted] evidence where possible and practicable').

[10] For a valuable discussion, see the Nuffield Council on Bioethics *Genetics and Human Behaviour: the Ethical Context* (October, 2002).

against non-compliance.[11] Under this proposal, the good news for Alex and his gang is that they are born free to choose a life of crime and, even after committing offences, they will not be subjected to any kind of technological regime that seeks to eliminate future criminality—there will be no use of Ludovico's Technique or the like. However, the bad news is that, provided that the technology is up to the job, each of Alex's infractions will be detected, he will be identified as the offender, he will be brought before a court, and he will be punished.

The second proposal does not balk at the use of technology in any segment of the regulatory process. However, it sets a threefold limit to technological assistance. First, although there is no veto on ex ante designing-out conduct as such, the limit is that technology should be used only to design-out conduct that presents the most serious kind of threat to the basic interests of citizens. This allows East Coast regulators to code against the most dangerous class of acts; and, provided that the community is convinced that there is really no room for debate about the wrongfulness of such acts, the design-out might even be of a permanent and irreversible (eg biotechnological) nature. Secondly, where technology is used to monitor compliance and identify offenders, it should not be unduly intrusive. Thirdly, if offenders are to be subjected to regimes of treatment, of the kind suggested by Ludovico's Technique, then this should be only on the basis of the offender's informed consent. Under this proposal, the good news for Alex and his gang is that they will have the opportunity to lead a life of minor mischief-making; but the bad news is that they will not have the option of inflicting serious harm on fellow citizens.

What might we expect the citizens of an East Coast community of rights to make of these proposals? Would they be persuaded that either of these invitations to go West makes sense? Or, if not, is there some way of stitching these proposals together that has more appeal without adopting the full-blown West Coast model?

(ii) Evaluating the first proposal

In relation to the first proposal, East Coasters will appreciate the determined effort that is made, first, to maintain the processes of participatory democracy (of open and inclusive regulatory dialogue) and, secondly, to present individuals with the option of doing the right thing. Even repeat offenders are given repeated opportunities to mend their ways. However, there seem to be three deficits with this proposal.

First, echoing the concerns that we expressed in Chapter 8, if the technology of surveillance and detection approaches anything like the level of reliability and effectiveness to which regulators aspire, then this seriously distorts the choice between compliance and non-compliance. The idea on the East Coast is that

[11] For reflections on just how smart and successful intelligent environments might be, see 'Dark Scenarios in Ambient Intelligence' <www.securitytaskforce.org/dmdocuments/SWAMI.pdf>.

citizens make a virtuous decision to do the right thing, that they elect compliance because they understand the moral case for compliance. However, if citizens are complying only because they fear certain detection and punishment, there is little promotion of the desired virtue.

By way of rebuttal, a number of arguments spring to mind. One such counter-argument is to the effect that much East Coast compliance is already to be accounted for in just these terms. For many East Coasters, it is precisely the background threat of penal sanctions that deters the commission of crime. On this view, East Coasters rarely do the right thing for the right reason and the proposal to convert a low-risk threat of punishment into a high-risk threat of punishment simply extends the logic of the existing arrangements—this is no real change in kind, simply a change in degree.

If, however, it is conceded that the new surveillance approach on the East Coast would be more than a change of degree, we might still attempt to rebut the objection by highlighting the opportunities that remain for agents to do the right thing for the right reason. Here, we might identify two such spheres of opportunity. One, as indicated in the previous chapter, is that sphere of conduct that lies beyond the reach of state regulation. In the unregulated zone, it might be contended, the environment is still compatible with moral community. How far this rebuttal is convincing depends on the particular circumstances of East Coast life. The other opportunity turns again to the state regulated sphere. Here, the argument is that, if the penal threat is merely background and does not intrude too much into the foreground, it will still be perfectly feasible for a morally disposed community to cultivate moral virtue. Support for such a view is offered by the leading regulatory theorists Ian Ayres and John Braithwaite who conceive of socially responsible deliberation—by 'directors of nursing who deliberate in terms of the well-being of patients instead of self interest, mine managers pondering how to secure maximum safety for their employees, [and] factory managers weighing how to minimize the pollution caused by their operation'[12]—in the shadow of the background penal law. So, for example:

> As [Smith] sits surrounded by receipts, a method of cheating to reduce his tax enters his head. Almost simultaneously, the idea of getting into trouble with the tax authorities crosses his mind. This is enough to stop the cheating idea in its tracks. He does not go on to calculate rationally the chances of the spectre of 'trouble with the Tax Office' eventuating or what the actual penalties might be. Rather, within an instant of this spectre crossing his mind, another thought has occupied the foreground of his deliberation. This is that it is morally wrong to violate the tax laws; he remembers his self-concept as an honest taxpayer; turning his mind to careful calculation of the risks and benefits of cheating would be a distasteful mode of deliberation for him.[13]

[12] Ian Ayres and John Braithwaite *Responsive Regulation* (Oxford: Oxford University Press, 1992) 47.

[13] ibid.

So Smith does the right thing and he duly does it for the right reason. What is more, as Ayres and Braithwaite present it, such a sequence of thinking (cheating, trouble, honesty) is most likely to take place in a milieu where the background threat is perceived to be awesome and invincible.

Against this view, though, many maintain that the first proposal is incompatible with a morally progressive evolution on the East Coast. The foreground in the surveillance society is just too dense with the threat of retaliation and punishment. Instead of Smith the taxpayer, recall Smith the employee at the Ministry of Truth; instead of the Tax Office, recall Big Brother. When the threat of detection and punishment is relatively low, there is still space for moral reason to play a part in influencing the decision to comply or not. Indeed, in the Platonic fable of the Ring of Gyges,[14] it was precisely where there was no risk of detection and punishment that moral reason came into its own. If, by extreme contrast, the threat of detection and punishment is overwhelming, this prudential consideration will dominate practical reason—inevitably, in most cases, the right thing will be done but not for the right reason.

Secondly, by restricting any technological assistance to detection and enforcement, the first proposal invites Alex and his friends to obey or (certainly) pay in respect of every provision of the criminal code. Whether Alex is out for an evening of minor mischief-making or gang rape or murder, the first proposal presents Alex with the same option: obey or pay. This, critics of the first proposal maintain, leaves East Coasters exposed to too many serious risks. To take the most serious risk, the loss of life, no payment by Alex can ever fully redeem the loss of the innocent victim's life; and, more generally, a community that lives in fear of Alex and his ilk is seriously disabled.[15] To present Alex with the obey or pay option, in the hope that this will cultivate the virtue of his doing the right thing for the right reasons, is not a cost-free exercise; and, where serious crime is involved, particularly involving the loss of life or personal injury, the price is simply too high. Just imagine, say critics, how the Alex reformers would feel if, having finally set Alex on the right road, some other unreformed young Turk promptly chose Alex as his first victim. No, the East Coast should use technology to control the worst kind of vice before questing after virtue.

Thirdly, the first proposal does not seem to have any learning capacity. If Alex and company are to be invited to obey or pay, why repeat the invitation when it is quite clear that they do not take the option of compliance seriously? East Coast regulators do not view the penal sanction as a tax on permissible conduct, or as something akin to pay per view; they clearly prefer citizens to obey. However, the East Coast culture prizes compliance for the right reason and so the option is presented. Even so, when it becomes apparent that an individual is a hopeless repeat offender, the preference for obedience should be hardened up. If, at that stage, it

[14] Plato *The Republic* Book II.

[15] Compare Robert Nozick *Anarchy, State, and Utopia* (Oxford: Basil Blackwell, 1974).

is possible to use a technological fix that disables future offending (a technology that removes the previous obey or pay option) by that particular individual, it surely makes sense to use it. At that stage, the disabled party has had his chance, several times over, and he has persistently abused it.

In sum, then, this evaluation of the first proposal judges that while too much use of technology is proposed in relation to monitoring, detection, and enforcement, too little use is made in relation to eliminating more serious crime and disabling recidivists.

(iii) Evaluating the second proposal

The second proposal has a rather different scale of priorities. It starts from the need for a relatively secure environment. East Coasters value their freedom, the opportunity to pursue their own life plans and projects in their own way, compatible with like freedom for others. While there is plenty of room for debate about the details of East Coast regulation, it is absolutely plain that a core of essential conditions must be secured before any kind of freedom can be productively utilized. So long as Alex and his mates lurk round the corner, East Coasters will find their plans and projects prematurely terminated or frustrated, and they will be diverted into a defensive counter-culture. If something can be done to fix this problem, if the essential conditions can be technologically secured, then the second proposal advocates taking such measures. No doubt, there will be debate about where precisely the line is to be drawn between serious and less serious crime, between what is dangerous (or too dangerous not to attract a technological response) and what is not; but, by and large, this second proposal responds to what seems to be the most troublesome deficit in the first proposal. Under the second proposal, there is no denying that the state is tough on serious crime, nor that it is tough on the causes and conditions of crime (which are, in effect, to be eliminated).

The remaining features of the second proposal represent significant attempts to address the other deficits identified in the first proposal. It is now proposed that the use of technology in relation to monitoring, detecting and enforcing against non-compliance should draw back from the panopticon strategy of the first proposal. But, of course, with dangerous crimes to be designed-out under the second proposal, the limit on surveillance will operate only in relation to less serious offences. In these less serious regions of the criminal code, Alex and his friends will be invited to obey or pay in a setting in which there is some chance of non-compliers avoiding payment. It is also proposed that repeat offenders should be given the chance to consent to a technological intervention that will terminate their career in crime. Critics might complain that, for a proposal that purports to be security-sensitive, this is far too indulgent towards the criminal classes. Again, however, provided that the technology employed in the background design-out strategy is effective, the only career in crime to be terminated or continued will be one of, relatively speaking, petty criminality.

No doubt, critics of the second proposal will snipe at it by complaining that there is a grey area dividing the class of dangerous acts from those acts that are not to be subjected to a design-out technology; and that the practice of obtaining informed consent from repeat offenders will fall short of its promise. It might also be objected that the second proposal no longer seems committed to the chaplain's credo. There are restrictions on the use of technology but it is not wholly clear what drives the limitations. However, so long as the particular control strategy that is applied to exclude the option of dangerous action does not also remove the capacity for moral choice, the defenders of the second proposal seem to have a fair case for saying that they are leaving ample opportunity for Alex and others to cultivate moral virtue and experience moral community. Beyond the techno-regulated zone, there is a large class of state-regulated and unregulated activity where moral life can continue. Accordingly, if the critics of the second proposal are to do real damage to it, they need a better objection. Is there an objection that goes right to the heart of this second proposal?

What is distinctive of the second proposal is that it bites the bullet, judging that the security of East Coasters comes first. The risks presented by young Alex and his friends have to be controlled. Alex and company are not denied all opportunity to do the right thing for the right reason—to repeat, the regulative technology permitting, when it comes to doing less significant right things, they may still choose to do so for the right reason; but what is not to be tolerated is that they have the chance to do significantly wrong things in the hope that they might one day see the light and do right for the right reason. Is this not plausible? Is this not the basis for a coherent mid-West regulatory position?

Those who are not persuaded by this second proposal might articulate their fundamental objection in something like the following terms. For members of the East Coast community, it is plain that there needs to be mutual recognition and respect for the most basic conditions of agency, of purposeful action. Generally speaking, as a member of the community, Alex is not required to assist fellow members in pursuing their plans or contribute in any way to their projects. Other things being equal, Alex is not required to share the passion of those who use the local library to cultivate their interest in literature any more than they are required to share Alex's passion for Beethoven's music. Each to his own. However, it is a precondition of agents being able to do their own thing in their own way that they respect one another's basic interests. Agency needs a protective and supportive regulatory setting within which individuals may confidently build their own projects; but this will only be possible where each agent recognizes the importance of acting in ways that are compatible with respect for the agency-realizing framework conditions. The attraction of the second proposal is that it targets these very conditions for technological support. Yet, this, the objectors complain, is also its fatal weakness. The point is that doing the right thing for the right reason is not an empty virtue. To do the right thing alone leaves the agency infrastructure intact; but to do the right thing for the right reason is to understand that it is the protection of the agency infrastructure that drives the argument for mutual respect. If the second proposal carries the day, the exhortation to do the right thing for the right reason is weakened because it is taken away from its paradigmatic context, from the context in which it is most rationally compelling.

By articulating the objection in these terms, however, the defenders of the East Coast put their case in a seemingly instrumental way. The reason why we should each do the right thing is that this enhances the opportunities for the flowering of individual and co-operative projects; it is a win-win formula. But, if this is the bottom line defence of the East Coast regulatory model, it challenges the West Coast technological model purely on instrumental grounds. The question becomes whether the East Coast or the West Coast style of regulation has better prospects of delivering an environment that is supportive of agency. This seems like a very dangerous gambit for the East Coast, where the sense is that the virtue of doing the right thing for the right reason has more to it than instrumental value. Is there, then, a better way of articulating this objection?

The spirit of the chaplain's view that informs the East Coast approach is that the doing of the right thing for the right reason speaks to what it is to be human. As Terry Eagleton puts this way of thinking:

> Being human is something you have to get good at, like playing snooker or avoiding the rent collector. The virtuous are those who are successful at being human, as a butcher or jazz pianist are successful at their jobs. Some human beings are even virtuosi of virtue. Virtue in this sense is a worldly affair; but it is unworldly in the sense that success is its own reward.[16]

But, if East Coasters defend their regulatory style by reference to what it is to be essentially human, or by asserting that the moral life is its own reward, this is liable to be rejected as mystical, or metaphysical, or just plain puzzling. The danger with arguing that the virtue of doing the right thing has an expressive value is that we reduce what East Coasters prize to little more than a modus vivendi, leaving advocates of this way of life simply to preach to the converted.

Where the advocates of the East Coast are addressing others who aspire to moral community, even if not to precisely the kind of moral community that I am treating as a community of rights, it is accepted that the moral way of life is the good life; moralism itself is not challenged. However, if the advocacy is to persuade those who are not morally committed, it needs to be put in more compelling terms. Is this possible?

To try one more time for the benefit of those who are sceptical about moralism, East Coasters are committed to the idea that their regulatory framework should present agents with the option of doing the right thing for the right reason. In turn, agents should learn to act in other-regarding (fellow agent-respecting) ways because they understand that this is morally required. In a sense, agents

[16] Terry Eagleton *After Theory* (London: Allen Lane, 2003) 125.

who do the right thing for the right reason self-regulate. But how are East Coasters to respond to amoralists who simply insist that self-interest is the only interest that rationally matters? East Coasters might point out, as Amartya Sen observes, that such 'wise-guy scepticism makes huge idiots out of Mohandas Gandhi, Martin Luther King Jr., Mother Teresa, and Nelson Mandela, and rather smaller idiots out of the rest of us';[17] and they might point to various cultures of cooperative practice, not least in business life where self-interested economic man supposedly rules. However, this will not do; it is not enough to point to counter-examples, heroic or routine; it is not enough to demonstrate that amoralism is not representative of the practical disposition of many agents. Nor is it enough to show that amoralism is eccentric or exceptional in practice. To silence the amoralist, it must be shown that amoralism itself is irrational.

It is for this reason that the argument—high tariff and controversial though it is—first outlined by the Chicago moral philosopher, Alan Gewirth, is so important; for this is an argument that aspires to demonstrate that it is irrational for an agent to deny being bound by other-regarding principles; that it is irrational for an agent to deny a responsibility to respect fellow agents.[18] Stated very shortly, the argument is that an agent, A, reflecting on the conditions of effective agency, must accept the logic of having a positive attitude towards the freedom and basic well-being on which its agency rests (the agent's generic conditions, irrespective of its particular purposes); and, correlatively, A must accept that the only rational position is for an agent to have a negative attitude towards actions that amount to an unwilled interference with those generic conditions. Even an amoralist must agree with this. However, the argument does not end here. To continue, an agent, A, knowing (true to amoralism) that it is implausible to assume that other agents will be guided by prioritizing the former agent's interests (ie, A's interests), must frame the demand for non-interference in a way that cannot be rejected as simply self-serving. I suggest that the most plausible way for A to put this claim is to demand that, irrespective of the identity of the claiming agent, the generic conditions of agency should be respected. Even if A's claim is, in practice, rejected by agents to whom it is put (again, as an amoralist might anticipate), A is now rationally bound to respect the rights of other agents—because, in defending himself against unwilled interference with his freedom and basic well-being, A has had to commit himself to the general principle that the generic conditions of agents should be respected *irrespective of whose agency benefits thereby*.

This argument can be presented in more than one way,[19] but the critical question is whether it is substantively valid. If the substance of this argument (regardless of

[17] Amartya Sen *Identity and Violence: The Illusion of Destiny* (London: Penguin, Allen Lane, 2006) 21.

[18] Seminally, see Alan Gewirth *Reason and Morality* (Chicago: University of Chicago Press, 1978).

[19] In addition to Gewirth's own presentations, the most careful presentations have been given by Deryck Beyleveld: see, in particular, Deryck Beyleveld *The Dialectical Necessity of Morality: An Analysis and Defense of Alan Gewirth's Argument to the Principle of Generic Consistency* (Chicago: University

the particular way it is presented) is correct, it follows that the East Coast commitment to doing the right thing is far more than a modus vivendi; doing the right thing is rationally required. However, although this argument develops the idea of an infrastructure for agency, East Coasters may legitimately reject the claim that the reason for doing the right thing is instrumental. To the contrary, the reason for doing the right thing is not that this is in the longer-term interest of all agents (even though it might well be)[20] but that it is, so to speak, in the agent's own interests as a rational being—an agent who does the right thing for the right reason maintains its own integrity as a rational being.

Where does this leave us? First, there is an argument for the proposition that agents are rationally bound to accept, and act on, principles that reflect mutual respect for the essential conditions of agency. To be sure, it is a complex and contested argument. Secondly, if this argument holds, then East Coasters can reject the idea that their way of life is merely a modus vivendi. Thirdly, again if this argument holds, they can also reject the idea that the case for doing the right thing is simply instrumental. Although, if the argument works, this seems to be an adequate defence of the East Coast regulatory culture, there is a complication. Recalling the distinction drawn in the previous chapter between act and agent morality, the question is whether it matters that agents simply conform to moral requirements (satisfying 'act morality') or whether agents must also strive to do the right thing (satisfying 'agent morality').[21] Given that, on the East Coast, the requirements of act morality are contested, that agents do not see themselves as morally omniscient, it looks plausible to suggest that agent morality is extremely important to the practical life of the community. If so, extreme caution needs to be exercised before a technical fix is used to deprive an agent of the option of doing x, where x is what that agent in good faith judges to be morally required. Put this way, the principal objection to the second proposal becomes that its ex ante interventions might encroach too severely on the functioning of agent morality.

Viewing the main objection to the second proposal in this way, if there is any room for technological design-out, perhaps it should be focused on less serious rather than more serious crime (on less serious rather than more serious matters of agent morality). For example, the kind of annoying conduct targeted by Anti Social Behaviour Orders (ASBOs),[22] or their equivalents, might be countered by technological innovation of one kind or another, leaving more serious crime to

of Chicago Press, 1991). And, for a recent, more discursive presentation, see Henrik Palmer Olsen and Stuart W Toddington, *The Architecture of Justice* (Aldershot: Ashgate, 2007).

[20] Compare the strategy in David Gauthier *Morals by Agreement* (Oxford: Oxford University Press, 1986).

[21] This distinction is elaborated in Deryck Beyleveld and Roger Brownsword *Law as a Moral Judgment* (London: Sweet and Maxwell, 1986; reprinted Sheffield: Sheffield Academic Press, 1994).

[22] For a very helpful review and critique of the use made of ASBOs, see Stuart Macdonald 'A Suicidal Woman, Roaming Pigs and a Noisy Trampolinist: Refining the ASBO's Definition of "Anti Social Behaviour"' (2006) 69 MLR 183.

set the stage for cultivating the doing of the right thing for the right reason. Such an inversion of the second proposal is worthy of further consideration; but, on the face of it, it is unlikely to appeal to East Coasters as the sensible step to take in the direction of the West Coast.

(iv) Design-out and design-in

We seem to have a stalemate. On the one hand, East Coasters are attracted by the prospect of a technologically secured safe environment (as per the second proposal); but, on the other hand, the case for educating each agent to appreciate the vulnerability of each and every fellow agent and to understand the need to respect the basic conditions of agency is fundamental to East Coast philosophy (as per the first proposal). Is it possible to break the stalemate by discriminating between technologies that design-out the option of offending and those that design-in protection for a potential victim? If it were possible, so to speak, either to take out Alex's sword or to equip his targets with a shield, would this be a choice that mattered?

Let us suppose that the second proposal contemplates the use of a technology that gives East Coasters an immunity against actions that are life-threatening or physically harmful. Perhaps nanotechnology facilitates the development of a lightweight non-removable flak-jacket, or the like; and let us suppose that, if Alex or his mates attempt to assault a person who is nano-protected, they will feel like they have struck into a brick wall. On this assumption, Alex and his friends are left free to elect between doing right or doing wrong, at all points on the criminal scale; but where they elect to do wrong, as a result of the designed-in protection, the act will be rendered harmless (or, the only harm done will be to potential wrongdoers). The thought is that this strategy is more attractive than a technological design-out that gives Alex no choice, that simply disables him from making what would be the wrong choice. To be sure, this assumption presupposes a very high level of technological sophistication; but then, whichever way we look at it, the assumption is of an extraordinarily high-tech future.

This question of design-in or design-out certainly merits further consideration; and, in the concluding chapter, I will return to the question of design variations and their significance for the moral aspirations of a community of rights. However, for present purposes, suffice it to suggest that the proposed fine-tuning of the second proposal is probably susceptible to the objection that by rendering Alex's 'wrongful' acts as harmless, the context of wrongdoing is fundamentally altered. If Alex cannot occasion any real harm to his victims, the sense in which his act is one of wrongdoing is attenuated. To have any chance of cultivating the required virtue in Alex, there has to be a real opportunity to inflict real harm on fellow agents. In short, it will be argued, agents will not learn to do right for the right reasons unless they can also do real wrong.

IV 'East or West?' Revised and Revisited

If there is no obvious mid-West regulatory model, perhaps we should return to the original choice between the East Coast and the West Coast regulatory models. However, if we are to do this, we should take steps to even up the odds. In specifying the West Coast model, we have assumed that the regulators would faithfully apply whatever moral script was stipulated. Clearly, if different choosers were to stipulate different moral codes (as they might well do), the West Coast specification would fail. To overcome this objection, therefore, let us make the weaker assumption that the regulators on the West Coast will always try to regulate in accordance with their best understanding of moral requirements. Even with this weakening, the West Coast model is painted in a very favourable light.

By contrast, the original East Coast specification is much less generous. On the East Coast, regulators struggle to combat crime, little seems to work, and any audit of the criminal justice system makes for depressing reading. Let us, however, paint the model in a more favourable light. Let us suppose that, on the East Coast, by and large, the community is self-regulating: East Coasters do the right thing and they do it for the right reason. Occasionally, offences are committed by one or two rogue Alexes; but, this is exceptional and the resources of the criminal justice system are so under-stretched that an effective response is usually made. In other words, let us suppose that the East Coast is a safe harbour and that its environment can pretty well match that on the West Coast for its security.

On these assumptions, what is the essential difference between the East Coast and the West Coast? Both communities are highly developed technological societies. However, there are two obvious differences. First, whereas the West Coast is a divided community, the regulatory elite debating and setting the required pattern of conduct, regulatees simply acting in whichever ways are designed-in, on the East Coast there continues to be an inclusive and open dialogue between regulators and regulatees. Secondly, East Coasters understand and know what it is to do wrong; and they see in themselves the developed capacity to do right for the right reason. If we want participatory democracy and moral community on top of technological sophistication, the East Coast must be the choice. Moreover, if we want a response to those who complain that, in the present day, our moral faculties are not developing at the same pace as our technological capacities, then the East Coast, not the West, seems to be the way to go.

Is there any way in which we might modify the West Coast specification to respond to these apparent deficits when it is compared with the now crime-free East? Is there any reason, for example, why the regulatory class must keep its technological secrets to itself? If West Coasters are genetically engineered in certain ways that assure a secure environment, why not make this an open secret? Why not tell regulatees that the environment is technologically managed? Rather obviously, if regulators on the West Coast let regulatees into their secret, there is a risk that regulatees will 'rebel', or want to be included in the regulatory processes. Having said this, the level of technological sophistication that we are crediting to the West Coast might allow regulators to design round such risks. In other words, in principle, we can imagine that West Coast regulators will be able to let regulatees know the regulatory score without this disrupting their peaceful pattern of conduct. Even so, there is no way that West Coast regulators can genuinely include regulatees in their moral deliberations without taking the community a step back towards the East Coast. The most that West Coast regulators can do is disclose to their regulatees that they do not have any say; if regulatees, as on the East Coast, are to be given a genuine voice, this is no longer the West Coast.

There is also the question of moral virtue that distinguishes the East from the West. If regulatees on the West Coast, upon learning about the regulatory reality, demand the opportunity to cultivate the virtue of freely doing the right thing, regulators cannot accede to that demand without, again, moving away from the West Coast. Regulators might offer regulatees the opportunity of experiencing, in a virtual environment, the conditions that put moral virtue to the test. However, ex hypothesi, such an environment is virtual, and it can never match the East Coast for the genuine article.[23] And, even allowing for some future blurring of the virtual and the real,[24] we might assume that, in order to develop moral virtue, regulatees really must have the opportunity to do the wrong thing.

On this analysis, it looks as though the East Coast model has more going for it than the West Coast model. Having said this, in both these perfectly realized safe and secure communities, where agents no longer need to worry about the risks presented by fellow agents (there is no need to fear that an agent will act in a way that is wholly self-regarding and gives no consideration to the legitimate interests of fellow agents) agents will be primarily concerned with 'getting a life' rather than heroically struggling to lead a moral life. To this extent, morality rather slips into the background. This does not mean that the choice between the East Coast and the West should be treated with indifference. The East Coast preserves a visible and inclusive public moral discourse—the importance of which should not be understated, for (as I have already stated many times) a flourishing community of rights is a community that engages in a reflective and ongoing way on the best interpretation of its commitments. However, on both Coasts, the communities have, in their different ways, rather grown out of celebrating displays of moral virtue.

Such remarks, however, might seem altogether too futuristic. It is all very well to say that there is little to choose between the perfectly realized versions of the West and East Coast. However, what are the chances of such realization? The fact of the matter is that, at the moment, our only option is the East Coast; and the only choice that matters is whether we try to make the East Coast a safer place by

[23] Compare Ruth Gledhill 'Lead Us Not into Cyber-Temptation as Missionaries Enter Second Life' *The Times* 30 July 2007, p 8.

[24] Susan Greenfield *Tomorrow's People* (London: Allen Lane, 2003).

adopting techno-assistance or by working on moral virtue. Is it sensible to prefer morality to (im)mortality? In the final part of the chapter, therefore, we must return to the present tense: is the East Coast taking a coherent approach by sticking with the chaplain's view?

V Human Dignity and the Virtue of Doing the Right Thing for the Right Reason

If the East Coast is judged to have better credentials than the West purely because it takes the chaplain's view seriously, there are two final objections to consider. One is the objection that the East Coast obsession with the dignity of humans doing the right thing for the right reason is not compatible with the respect for human rights and fundamental freedoms that I am taking to be characteristic of East Coast morality generally. The other is the objection that the East Coast obsession with 'real choice', with agents making authentic moral choices, is based on bad science. If the very idea of an agent having a real choice is rejected by the findings of, say, human genetics or neuroscience, then the regulatory model on the East Coast is based on flawed premises.

(i) The commitment to human rights

On the East Coast, let us suppose that there is a commitment to human rights and fundamental freedoms. Nevertheless, as modelled, the East Coast is first and foremost a moral community and it is deeply conscious that a moral community will survive only if certain characteristic conditions are protected. Although East Coasters value the right to make their own individual choices (particularly in matters of life-style and life-plans)—echoing Mill, they believe that the majority should not be allowed to dictate how the minority live their lives, nor vice versa—the range of legitimate choice has to be regulated and, in the final analysis, it is not the capacity for choice that matters so much as the capacity for moral choice. The choices involved in living the moral life, however, are layered. First, one chooses to aspire to the moral life. Secondly, one participates in setting standards, in choosing the appropriate regulative principles. Thirdly, one chooses to follow those standards rather than to act on other practical considerations. If one is not able to choose at any one of these levels—and, it is worth emphasizing that, on the West Coast, regulatees are not given the relevant choice at all three levels—one is denied some opportunity to participate in and experience the moral life. If we are looking for a striking way of registering this kind of deficit, this is where we might say that there is a denial of human dignity. Accordingly, on this analysis, East Coasters are deeply committed to the idea that, above all, human dignity should not be compromised. For East Coasters, human dignity is expressed precisely in doing the right thing for the right reason.

Is there not a contradiction, then, in an East Coast community of rights holding that, while they are fundamentally committed to the principle that human dignity should not be compromised, they reject the dignitarian claim that a whole raft of particular practices and pursuits (for example, prostitution, sado-masochism, surrogacy, abortion, euthanasia, embryo selection, reproductive and therapeutic cloning, dwarf-throwing, 'killing games', reality television shows, and so on) should be prohibited as compromising human dignity?[25] Not at all. The East Coast commitment to human dignity is as a precondition for any kind of moral community; but its particular vision of a moral community is one that is governed by respect for individual autonomy, human rights and fundamental freedoms. By contrast, a different moral community—let us call it the South Coast model—might have a vision that employs the notion of human dignity as a constraint on freedom of action, emphasizing the duties of its members rather than their rights. Whether the moral vision of the South Coast is more defensible than that of the East Coast is another matter.[26] The point here is that there is no contradiction in either community developing its moral vision in its own way. What would be contradictory would be if either community, claiming to be a moral community, acted in ways that corroded the dignity preconditions for the existence of any kind of moral community.

To put this slightly differently, there is a difference between simple cultural conservatism (of the South Coast dignitarian variety) and conservation of the generic conditions of moral community.[27] The East Coast, as an aspirant moral community, is necessarily dignitarian in the latter sense; but not in the former sense; and there is no contradiction in this position.[28]

Nevertheless, even if there is no contradiction between insisting that human dignity should not be compromised at the level of the possibility of any kind of moral community and, at the same time, rejecting certain dignitarian articulations of moral community, is there not still a certain cultural conservatism on the East Coast? Is the East Coast attachment to the concept of the moral life (albeit a contested concept) not indicative of a deep cultural conservatism? This, it seems, is another way of suggesting that the East Coast way of life is simply a modus vivendi which,

[25] For a general commentary, see Deryck Beyleveld and Roger Brownsword *Human Dignity in Bioethics and Biolaw* (Oxford: Oxford University Press, 2001) chs 1–2. For a discussion of the particular question of embryo selection, see Roger Brownsword 'Happy Families, Consenting Couples, and Children with Dignity: Sex Selection and Saviour Siblings' (2005) 17 CFLQ 435. And, for the particular instances of (i) 'dwarf throwing' and (ii) 'killing games', see: (i) *Ville d'Aix-en-Provence* 1996 Dalloz 177 (Conseil d'Etat) req nos 143–578; *Cne de Morsang-sur-Orge* 1995 Dalloz 257 (Conseil d'Etat) req nos 136–727; and (ii) *Omega Spielhallen- und Automatenaufstellungs- GmbH v Oberbürgermeisterin der Bundesstadt Bonn* (Case C–36/02) (14 October 2004); [2004] OJ C300/3.

[26] Compare, eg, Roger Brownsword 'Bioethics Today, Bioethics Tomorrow: Stem Cell Research and the "Dignitarian Alliance"' (2003) 17 Notre Dame Journal of Law, Ethics and Public Policy 15; and 'Stem Cells and Cloning: Where the Regulatory Consensus Fails' (2005) 39 New England Law Review 535.

[27] Compare ch 7.

[28] See, also, Roger Brownsword 'Human Rights – What Hope? Human Dignity—What Scope?' in Jennifer Gunning and Søren Holm (eds) *Ethics, Law and Society: Volume I* (Aldershot: Ashgate, 2005) 189.

for no good reason other than their preference for it, East Coasters want to cling on to. However, to hark back to our earlier discussion, if the moral life is *rationally* compelling in a community of agents, if it would be irrational to espouse amoralism—and, it is perhaps worth interjecting that, relative to agent morality, regulatees on the West Coast are amoralists—then East Coasters are only culturally conservative to the extent that reason dictates that they should be so. And, even if culturally conservative, the East Coast need not apologize for this.

(ii) The belief in the possibility of real choice

Amoralism is not the only form of scepticism that throws down the gauntlet to the East Coast; there is also a long-standing question-mark about agents being 'in control', or having a 'real choice', or 'being able to act otherwise than they do', or having 'free will',[29] and so on. Doubts of this kind niggle at the presuppositions of our responsibility practices—holding an agent 'responsible' to compensate on a strict liability basis is one thing, but holding an agent responsible in the full-blooded stigmatizing criminal justice sense is another matter.[30] If agents cannot really help doing what they do, should we be holding them to account for their wrongdoing? To be sure, we can take the robust Aristotelian approach to the effect that, so long as no other person is physically moving my limbs (no third-party is holding and guiding my hand as I plunge the dagger into my victim), then my act is free; but, in a universe gripped by science, this no longer suffices to assuage our concerns—and the more that science uncovers law-like patterned behaviour in both the physical and the social worlds, the less confident we are about our belief in control and choice.[31] The challenge is well put by Deborah Denno:

> Ultimately, the criminal justice system must confront the significance of the mounting evidence concerning the biological bases of behavior, weigh its importance, evaluate its strengths and weaknesses, and recommend a policy for its use. The direction of that policy will depend upon our notions of human nature, our assumptions of causality, and, undoubtedly, the politics and potentially broad applicability of the biological deficiency argument.[32]

What, then, should East Coasters make of all this?

Stated very simply, there seems to be a stark choice: either our actions are random or they are caused. Whichever way we look at it, we are in trouble. If we try to escape

[29] For an accessible introduction, see DJ O'Connor *Free Will* (London: Macmillan, 1972).

[30] For the distinction between criminal law responsibility and the compensatory responsibilities of private law, see Peter Cane *Responsibility in Law and Morality* (Oxford: Hart, 2002); and, for general discussion of the former, see, eg, Alf Ross *On Guilt, Responsibility and Punishment* (London: Stevens, 1975).

[31] See Sidney Hook (ed) *Determinism and Freedom in the Age of Modern Science* (New York: Collier, 1961).

[32] Deborah W Denno 'Human Biology and Criminal Responsibility: Free Will or Free Ride?' (1988) 137 University of Pennsylvania Law Review 615, at 618 (Denno goes on to question, inter alia, the adequacy of the causal accounts presented by biological explanations).

the clutches of determinism by treating our actions as random, then we are conceding that we are not in control. If our actions 'just happen'—in effect, if they just happen to us—then this will not do; the East Coast view needs agents to be active not passive. So randomness definitely is not an option. On the other hand, if we accept that our actions are caused, it is unclear how our acts are relevantly different from the movements of other objects in the world. Hence, if presented with this classical fork, randomness or causation, East Coasters must opt for the latter.

Clearly, we are moving into extremely difficult philosophical territory. How are we to construct a coherent account of agency that treats actions as caused and yet, at the same time, can give meaning to the ideas of choice, control, and responsibility that we want to salvage?[33] What we seem to be after is an account that treats an agent's reasons as the causes of action, with the agent originating such action by engaging in practical reason; and, if we feel the need to find a place for free will, then we might follow Kant in conceiving of the will being free when an agent acts on *moral* reason.[34]

But, if practical reason is some kind of black box from which particular willed acts originate, is this taking the account back towards randomness? Arguably it is not because we are still able to distinguish between agents acting for reasons, and objects that seem to act neither for reason nor for any rhyme or reason. As Richard Taylor puts it:

> [Such a characterization] does deny that there are conditions sufficient for the occurrence of all events that occur. But it does not deny that there is an explanation or reason for every event... for there are ways of explaining a man's conduct otherwise than by a recitation of causal conditions. The concept of agency, then, is quite unlike that of a thing whose behavior (sic) is arranged to coincide with the random selections of a roulette; for, assuming the wheel to be causally undetermined, there is *no* ultimate explanation for the roulette's behavior, whereas there is for the agent's. Moreover, saying of an agent that *he* acts makes sense; but we cannot conceive of a wheel—no agent at all—as 'deciding' what is to be 'done'.[35]

If this is the kind of account that East Coasters must adopt, then the pressing question is whether it can survive whatever light the new brain sciences might throw on the way that the black box, the brain processor, functions.

According to modern brain science, equipped with powerful scanning and imaging machines and with a focus on the development of smart psychoactive drugs, there is some plausibility in the claim (as Nikolas Rose puts it) that '[m]ind is simply what

[33] Compare Richard Taylor 'Determinism and the Theory of Agency' in Hook (n 31 above) at 224.

[34] Immanuel Kant *Groundwork of the Metaphysic of Morals* (trans HJ Paton as *The Moral Law*) (London: Hutchinson University Library, 1948). In the modern canon, note Martin Hollis *Models of Man* (Cambridge: Cambridge University Press, 1977); and Deryck Beyleveld and Paul Wiles 'How to Retain Your Soul and be a Political Deviant' in David Downes and Paul Rock (eds) *Deviant Interpretations* (Oxford: Martin Robertson, 1979) 122.

[35] Taylor (n 33 above) at 229–30.

the brain does'.[36] If, as Rose has suggested, this invites a shift in our perception of human ontology, then the proposition that we are agents who are generally in control of our conduct (and accountable for our actions) is liable to come under fire. Again, we might meet fire with fire, holding to a robust agency-based view. As Thomas Buller remarks:

> If Jones throws a brick through a shop window it is no excuse to say that his brain did it. Since all our psychobehavioral states correlate in some fashion with neurophysical states, we should either jettison completely the belief that we are intentional rational agents or deny neuroscience any broad explanatory role in the normal case.[37]

Adopting the latter of Buller's options, Stephen Morse[38] has argued that 'until currently unimaginable [neuro]scientific advances convince us otherwise, we are fully entitled to believe that we are ordinarily conscious, intentional, and potentially rational creatures' and that determinism gives us no reason 'to abandon current responsibility criteria and practices'.[39] What then should we make of this difference in reading? Does more work in the brain sciences look set to cut across the view, characteristically found in a moral community, that we are each responsible for our actions?

Let us go back, with Morse,[40] to some East Coast basics:

> Law guides human conduct by giving citizens prudential and moral reasons for conduct. Law would be powerless to achieve its primary goal of regulating human interaction if it did not operate through the practical reason of the agents it addresses and if agents were not capable of rationally understanding the rules and their application under the circumstances in which the agent acts.
>
> Responsibility is a normative condition that law and morality attribute only to human beings. We do not ascribe responsibility to inanimate natural forces or to other species. Holding an agent responsible means simply that it is fair to require the agent to satisfy moral and legal expectations and to bear the consequences if he or she does not do so; holding an agent non-responsible means simply that we do not believe the agent was capable in the context in question of satisfying moral and legal expectations. The central reason why an agent might not be able to be guided by moral and legal expectations is that the agent was not capable of being guided by reason.[41]

[36] Nikolas Rose *The Politics of Life Itself* (Princeton, NJ: Princeton University Press, 2007) 192. Generally, see David Nutt, Trevor W Robbins, Gerald W Stimson, Martin Ince, and Andrew Jackson (eds) *Drugs and the Future* (London: Academic Press, 2007).

[37] Thomas Buller 'Brains, Lies, and Psychological Explanations' in Judy Illes (ed) *Neuroethics* (Oxford: Oxford University Press, 2006) 51, at 56.

[38] Stephen J Morse 'Moral and Legal Responsibility and the New Neuroscience' in Judy Illes (ed) *Neuroethics* (Oxford: Oxford University Press, 2006) 33.

[39] ibid 47. Even if it is conceded that Morse is correct, however, our phenomenology might tell us a different story; see Joshua Greene and Jonathan Cohen 'For the Law, Neuroscience Changes Nothing and Everything' (2004) 359 *Phil. Trans. R. Soc. Lond.* B 1775.

[40] Stephen J Morse 'Uncontrollable Urges and Irrational People' (2002) 88 Virginia Law Review 1025.

[41] ibid 1065–6.

Now, building on this view, in the ideal-typical moral community, members set standards that concretize their judgments of what it is that should be done if we are to do the right thing and they expect to judge themselves and others by reference to these standards. Where there are deviations from the standards, where there is wrongdoing, those who so deviate are expected to account for their actions. Characteristically, members hold one another responsible for their wrongdoing.

As we understand more about particular brain formations and functions, it is possible that we will see that some brains simply lack the parts that are required for engagement in moral reason, or that they lack the apparatus to engage in practical reason more generally. Given such abnormality, any person so equipped is disabled from participating in the moral community as well as lacking the means to act like a practically rational agent.[42] Cases of this kind will need to be debated. The community will need to decide how far it is appropriate to hold such persons responsible for their 'wrongdoing' in the way that one would otherwise hold a member of the community to account. Even if the new brain sciences reveal that quite a large number of humans are disabled in this way, this does not yet undermine the possibility of moral community.

Where a person who is neither in a recognized disabled class nor suffering from some cognitive defect deviates from a moral standard, might the new brain sciences give us any reason to have second thoughts about holding such a person responsible for their wrongdoing? Let us suppose that we are persuaded that this is a case where there has been some malfunction of the brain. On this occasion, the neurotransmitters have failed to prioritize the signal that the act in question violates moral standards and should not be done. If we view the deviation in this way, this might lead us to rethink the way in which we hold the wrongdoer responsible. We might think that it is inappropriate to shame and blame this person—even if the brain scientists believe that stigmatizing wrongdoers has some useful feedback effect, a moral community might nonetheless judge that such a response is unfair or unreasonable.[43] Instead, the appropriate response might be thought to be to reinforce the moral standards, much in the way that the community deems it appropriate to respond to children who break the moral rules. Although such a modification in the community's responsibility practices is significant, and although the community's view of agency is becoming more nuanced,[44] we can agree with Morse that practical and moral reason is not yet dead.

[42] See Patricia Smith Churchland 'Moral Decision-Making and the Brain' in Judy Illes (ed) *Neuroethics* (Oxford: Oxford University Press, 2006) 3. Compare Buller (n 37 above).

[43] This would not be altogether unprecedented. For example, where agents act under extreme duress or necessity, even though they remain responsible for their acts, criminal law regimes may recognize the conditions as excusing.

[44] Compare Neil Levy *Neuroethics* (Cambridge: Cambridge University Press, 2007) especially ch 7.

What would it take for brain science to close the curtains on moral community? According to Morse, so long as we see ourselves as 'social creatures whose interactions are not governed primarily by innate repertoires', that is, as creatures who 'are able to guide our behavior in light of reasons we may have for acting and [who] do not solely and blindly follow instinct',[45] then brain science might erode some of our social practices but it would not fundamentally change them. If the brain sciences were to come up with an account that eliminated practical (or moral) reason from the script, that would be pretty extraordinary. However, what if research in the brain sciences were to indicate that practical or moral reason is epiphenomenal? That, is to say, what if research showed that, while we get to know what we are going to do a little before others, our sense of choosing is not actually part of the material causal sequence that connects brain and body to act?[46] Again, to say the least, that would be a startling finding and, if it were not for the fact that choice no longer seems significant, we would say that, in the light of this finding, the aspirant moral community would face a tough choice.[47]

Do concerns of this kind suggest that we should immediately curtail any further work in the new brain sciences? I think that we can be confident that such demands would fall on deaf ears. The impulse to understand more about ourselves is compelling. To be sure, brain scientists might one day reflect on the way in which the wiring of the human brain led the species into a quest for improved self-understanding that resulted in the undermining of moral community. With the benefit of hindsight, future generations might think that it is not only cats that need to be careful about their instinct for curiosity.

What does this imply for the choice between the East Coast and the West? Even if, as neuroscience eventually shows, the East Coasters are living a noble lie, the West gains little by exposing that reasons are not causes and that humans are never in control. For, if regulatees on the East Coast cling on to the idea of a real choice being made (and, concomitantly, of right choices being made for the right reasons), then regulators on the West Coast seem equally wedded to the notion that, in setting the pattern of West Coast regulation, they exercise real choice, freely choosing to do the right thing. Accordingly, for the critics of the East Coast to attack it in this way is a nuclear option.

[45] Stephen J Morse, 'New Neuroscience, Old Problems: Legal Implications of Brain Science' (2004) 6 *Cerebrum* 81, at 82.

[46] Although the famous study conducted by Benjamin Libet does not go as far as showing that intention and choice are not implicated in the relevant causal sequence (see Morse (n 38 above) at 42–3), one might imagine post-Libet research generating such a view. But, compare Buller (n 37 above) especially at 54, where he points out that, even if Libet's studies 'do show that my conscious decision to raise my arm was preceded by brain activity', it does not follow that we should abandon an agency-based normative view. According to Buller, this is not to deny Libet's findings, 'it is only to say that their importance depends upon a prior commitment to the ontological and explanatory success of neuroscientific reductionism'.

[47] See Smith Churchland (n 42 above).

VI Conclusion

In the foreword to the 1946 edition of *Brave New World*,[48] Aldous Huxley reflected that he perhaps should have offered the Savage (and readers) a third option, neither the centralized order of the Fordist World State nor the primitive condition of the Reservation. With the benefit of such an option, the Savage might have chosen a middle way in which, inter alia:

> Science and technology would be used as though, like the Sabbath, they had been made for man, not (as at present and still more so in the Brave New World) as though man were to be adapted and enslaved to them.[49]

Alas, lacking such an option, the Savage fails to create an acceptable space, physically within the World State but without its controlling features, and he comes to a sad end. For readers, too, the straight choice between the World State and the Reservation, not unlike the straight choice between the West Coast and the East Coast (although I must not press the analogy too strongly), is an unattractive one.

In this chapter, I have considered whether there is a mid-West option that promises a more effective (technology-assisted) regulatory approach without compromising the rights of agents and without damaging the very possibility of moral community. However, far from finding a simple solution that clearly makes sense as a matter of both principle and practice, we have identified some fundamental questions about the coherence of the East Coast project. In particular, do we think that moral virtue has both intrinsic (expressive) and instrumental value? Do we think that the reason why a moral community is a good thing is because it sets the stage for agents to increase their utility? Or, is there more to moral virtue and moral community than this? The chaplain, like the East Coast denizens, believes that morality is not just instrumental—morality truly expresses the good life; it is not simply a vehicle for enjoying the good life. However, this leaves the East Coast on the horns of a dilemma.

If East Coasters think that the moral life is not an end in itself, if they think that it is merely an instrument for establishing a safe context for agent interactions, there is no reason to stick with the East Coast regulatory style if a more effective strategy is available. On this analysis, smart regulators might well argue in favour of a more intrusive technological strategy that performs better than any alternative strategies.

However, if, like the chaplain, East Coasters think that moral community is something to be valued for its own sake, as the ultimate expression of human dignity, the East Coast project is one that we must persist with and the struggle

[48] London: Flamingo, Harper Collins, 1994, first printed London: Chatto and Windus, 1932.
[49] ibid foreword.

to integrate technology in a way that does not compromise human dignity will continue. On such an analysis, however, the East Coast preference for the moral life might look uncomfortably like a *deeper* version of the dignitarian cultural conservatism that it otherwise condemns.

So long as the debate is limited to those who aspire to some kind of moral community, East Coast advocates can get off these various hooks. However, to broaden the range of the argument, the East Coast model needs to be grounded in a line of thinking that teases out, purely by logically underwritten steps, the normative implications of agency. If, as a matter of rational necessity, agents must accept other-regarding responsibilities, then they have good reasons for espousing the moral life. Yet, even this is not the end of the matter. For, there is still the question of whether we assume (as I have done in relation to the community of rights) that agents are not morally omniscient. So long as we make this assumption, the practical life of the community is shaped to a very considerable extent by agent morality—that is, by each agent making its own sincere and good faith judgments as to moral requirements and then acting on those judgments—and, in such a context, technological channelling is problematic. On the other hand, if we were to assume moral omniscience, or if we assumed that regulators at least were morally omniscient, would it matter that agents were simply coded for conformity with the requirements of act morality?

The immature Alex, we can be sure, would advise us to lighten up and spend more time at the Korova Milkbar or the Duke of New York, where we could ease our burdens with a cocktail of some kind or another. But what, we might wonder, would the mature Alex have to say? Would he agree with the chaplain? And, in the unlikely event of a Habermassian encounter, how would Alex respond to an interlocutor who asks: '[W]hy shouldn't complex societies simply drop their normative foundations entirely, and switch over to systemic(!) (or, in the future, biogenetic) steering mechanisms?'[50] What would the mature Alex make of our regulatory dilemma? Would he head East or would he head West?

[50] Jürgen Habermas *The Future of Human Nature* (Cambridge: Polity Press, 2003) 92–3. Habermas continues:

> Today, the relevant controversy is played out between a naturalistic futurism, committed to a technical self-optimization of human beings, and anthropological conceptions whose 'weak naturalism' has them accept the views of neo-Darwinism (and scientific views in general) without scientistically undermining or constructivistically outstripping the normative self-understanding of speakers and actors, for whom reasons still count.

11

Regulating Technologies: Challenge and Opportunity

Introduction

How shall we conclude this book? If the book were a present, we could wrap it up, tie some decorative ribbon around it, make the gift, and delete the item from our 'to do' list. However, the writing of this book is an exercise that defies any such tidy completion. The roll-out of new technologies, we can safely assume, will continue apace; for example, even during the four years that I have been working on this book, there has been a marked surge of interest in both neurotechnology and nanotechnology, as well as in the development of biometrics, databases, and data profiling.[1] For regulators and regulatees, as for commentators on the regulatory process, the scene is a rapidly changing one. I might be able to, indeed I must, draw a line under the book but the underlying project remains one of work in progress.

The underlying project, and its expression in this particular book, began with the sense that, as we crossed from one millennium to another, this was a special time. There were seemingly great leaps forward in both human and animal genetics, and the internet was transforming the cultural, commercial and, quite possibly, political worlds. Yet, it was not clear that these were unqualified goods. Concerns (unfounded as it proved) about a Y2K computer crash raised questions about the wisdom of an increasing reliance on digital data; and the prospect of reproductive cloning, even if acceptable in Edinburgh sheep, was not one that humans would necessarily welcome in their own species. Stephen Cutliffe captured the ambivalence of this millennial mood in the following way:

> At the turn of the millennium, society is faced with both the promises and the dangers of scientific and technological endeavors such as the human genome project and electronic communication systems, developments that must surely change our lives, either for better or for worse, but most likely for both.[2]

[1] For speculation about the trajectory of modern technologies, including their 'compound interest' characteristics, see Joel Garreau 'The Next Generation' *Washington Post* 26 April 2002, p C01.

[2] Stephen H Cutliffe *Ideas, Machines, and Values* (Lanham, Maryland: Rowman and Littlefield, 2000) viii.

Clearly, on this analysis, the role of regulators is to intervene in ways that are designed to ensure that the changes brought about by such technologies are for the better rather than for the worse. Or, as UNESCO constantly declares, we need regulatory environments that enable humans to enjoy the benefits of science and technology while, at the same time, ensuring that human rights, human dignity, and fundamental freedoms are fully respected and protected. But, we know that this is all much easier said than done.

As a first step, I roughed out a list of questions that seemed to me to form the agenda for the underlying project. As work on the book proceeded, the list was revised and expanded somewhat, so that the agenda now looks something like this:

- There is a sense that modern technologies are significantly different to their predecessors. But is this right? If so, in what sense are such technologies radically different or revolutionary? And why is this a matter of relevance to regulators?
- Is the fact that these new technologies (information and communication technologies and biotechnology, as well as neurotechnology and nanotechnology) are in some way implicated in the processes or phenomenon of globalization significant? If so, how? And, at the same time, is the development of global governance a relevant consideration?
- Spheres of regulation beyond the nation state have developed rapidly in recent years but the nature of regulation within nation states (and regulatory theory that accompanies it) is also undergoing major change. How does this bear on questions concerning regulation and technology?
- In pluralistic societies, how are regulators to defend the positions that they take up (and, in morally sceptical communities, how are they to justify their regulatory positions as legitimate)? The challenges of legitimation and legitimacy get more acute, do they not, as regulatory zones move beyond nation states to cover regions and even larger (worldwide) jurisdictions. How are these challenges to be met?
- How are moral caveats (such as moral exclusions against patentability, or the general exceptions for 'public morals' in international trade agreements) to be operationalized?
- There is scepticism about the effectiveness of traditional legal strategies of command and control. Smart regulation explores all the options. Even so, compliance cannot be taken as read. If laws are ineffective within nation states, how are they likely to fare in regional and international regulatory spaces let alone cyberspace?
- How can we design regulatory institutions in such a way that they respond to all desiderata—flexibility with calculability, independence with accountability, expertise with detachment, speed with due deliberation, and so on?

- How are regulators to respond to a lack of trust (to a crisis of confidence) in experts? How is the public to be engaged?
- How is regulation able to stay 'connected' to rapidly developing technologies? Is law able to evolve with the technology or is it destined to be chasing it?
- Is there something special about the regulatory space occupied by new technologies (especially cyberspace?); and is there anything distinctive about the kind of crimes (eg cybercrime) or torts (eg genomic torts) associated with these technologies?
- Are there generic lessons to be learnt (so that we do not keep reinventing the regulatory wheel) or does each technology import its own regulatory ground rules?
- What happens if we join up concerns about the way that technologies might be deployed in the private sector with concerns about reliance on technology by the state as a regulatory instrument?
- When the state embraces new technologies as regulatory tools, is this a step towards the dystopian orders depicted by Orwell and Huxley?
- Should we be troubled by the thought that, with technological sophistication and a culture of prevention and risk management, the Rule of Law might be replaced by the Rule of Technology? Would this be such a bad thing?

In conjunction with these questions, I also started with a sketch and a general story-line for what has become this book.[3]

The frame for my sketch was Francis Fukuyama's *Our Posthuman Future,*[4] the fundamental thesis of which is that modern biotechnology represents an insidious threat to human dignity and it needs to be regulated accordingly. As for the gist of the story that I told in counterpoint to Fukuyama's manifesto, it was along the lines that regulators, in their efforts to regulate new technologies, would learn a great deal about the strengths and weaknesses of traditional regulatory instruments, but also would spot the potential of these technologies as regulatory tools, supplementing and even supplanting traditional modes of regulation.[5] In other words, this was a short and embryonic version of the story now told in this book.

[3] See Roger Brownsword 'What the World Needs Now: Techno-Regulation, Human Rights, and Human Dignity' in Roger Brownsword (ed) *Human Rights* (Oxford: Hart, 2004) 203.

[4] London: Profile Books, 2002.

[5] At that time, in 2003, some of the suggestions that caught my eye were: the use of scannable microscopic computer chips embedded in high value bank notes (to combat forgery); vehicle number-plate recognition technology to enable cars to be matched against an insurance database (to combat driving without insurance); joined up information systems (following the murder of Victoria Climbié, to identify children at risk); and tagging paedophiles using global satellite positioning technology. On the first, see Andrew Osborn, 'Computer Chip Plan to Fight Banknote Fraud' *The Guardian* 9 June 2003, p 4; on the second, Sean Coughlan 'Driving Home the Hot-Spot Danger Zone' *The Guardian* (Jobs and Money) 13 September 2003, p 6; on the third, Michael Cross 'Eyes on the Child' *The Guardian* (Life) 18 September 2003, p 16; and, on the fourth, Jamie Doward '500 Paedophiles to be Tracked by Satellite Tags' *The Observer* 21 September 2003, p 1.

The book, I should emphasize, does not attempt to respond to all the questions posed by the underlying agenda. Rather, the book, as is always the case—at any rate, in my experience—has taken on something of a life of its own in the writing. Nevertheless, in that process, a very clear answer has emerged to the first and last questions in the list (this being a two-sided answer that, as it were, closes the circle). In response to the first question, the position taken in the book is that, as lawyers, we need not agonize about whether the technological changes that are underway are revolutionary in relation to the underlying science, or the like. What is significant is that the employment of these technologies could represent a fundamentally different way of going about the business of regulating—indeed, just as some might contend that the employment of information technology represents a fundamentally different way of going about the business of lawyering.[6] A regulatory environment that is dense with these new technologies is a very different place to an environment that relies on compliance with norms that are either legally or morally expressed or simply implicit in custom and practice. If this is the regulatory environment of the future then, in response to the last question, we should certainly be worried about the breakdown in the procedural values of the Rule of Law, in the lack of transparency and accountability, and the like. However, the fundamental concern for any aspirant moral community is that a reckless adoption of a technology-led regulatory style will erode the conditions that are essential for the community to make sense of its moral mission. The technological revolution, in other words, overthrows not just law but the *moral* law.

With these introductory remarks, we can conclude, first (in Parts II, III, and IV), by dipping into the underlying agenda to sketch how we might now respond to the questions and then (in Part V) by reflecting on what we would now make of Fukuyama's plea for active regulatory engagement with biotechnology.

II The Regulation of Technology (Regulating *Technologies*)

From the questions that relate to the regulation of technology, let me isolate the following for short consideration: (i) Are there generic lessons to be learned about the regulation of new technologies? (ii) Is there anything distinctive about the

The introduction of 'smart' ID cards is another important indicator of this tendency: see Alan Travis and Patrick Wintour 'ID Cards are on the Way' *The Guardian* 12 November 2003, p 1. As the book nears completion, more recent examples are: Richard Ford 'Traffic Spies to Join Fight Against Crime' *The Times* 18 July 2007, p. 1 (plans to use smart cameras associated with road pricing technology to assist in the prevention and detection of crime); Ben Webster 'New Cycle Lane Cameras to Hit Wayward Drivers with £120 Fine' *The Times* 24 July 2007, p 8; and Richard Ford 'Police Want DNA from Speeding Drivers and Litter Louts on Database' *The Times* 2 August 2007, p 2.

[6] See, eg Richard Susskind *Transforming the Law* (Oxford: Oxford University Press, 2003).

regulatory space occupied by particular technologies? (iii) In pluralistic societies, how are regulators to achieve positions that are perceived to be legitimate? (iv) How does globalization and global governance bear on the regulation of technologies?

(i) Are there generic lessons to be learned about the regulation of new technologies?

Without doubt, the outstanding generic challenge presented by new technologies is that of regulatory connection. Indeed, if we define 'new technologies' by reference to the speed of their development, this might be no more than the statement of an analytic truth; but, even if we do not secure the truth of the proposition in this definitional way, the fact is that experience indicates that the technologies in which we have an interest do develop and move on in ways that create difficulties for regulators. So much for the generic regulatory challenge: what, if any, generic lessons do there seem to be?

First, is there a clear-cut answer to the regulator's question, 'How are we to keep the regulation connected to the technology?' As we saw in Chapters 5 and 6, the ideal regulatory response seems to be one that enables the regulation to bind to the technology and to evolve with it. In pursuit of this ideal, regulators face a choice between taking a traditional hard law approach or leaving it to self-regulation and, concomitantly, a softer form of law.[7] Where the former approach is taken, the hard edges of the law can be softened in various ways—especially by adopting a 'technology neutral' drafting style,[8] by delegating regulatory powers to the relevant minister and by encouraging a culture of purposive interpretation in the courts. Conversely, where self-regulation and softer law is preferred, the regime can be hardened up by moving towards a form of co-regulation. However, no matter which approach is adopted, there is no guarantee that it will be effective and the details of the regulatory regime will always reflect a tension between the need for flexibility (if regulation is to move with the technology) and the demand for predictability and consistency (if regulatees are to know where they stand). To this extent, therefore, there is no straightforward generic lesson to be

[7] On the soft law approach to the regulation of genetic testing, see Philippa Gannon and Charlotte Villiers 'Regulation of Genetic Testing' in Laura Macgregor, Tony Prosser, and Charlotte Villiers (eds) *Regulation and Markets Beyond 2000* (Aldershot: Ashgate, 2000) 125, at 130. See, also, John Huntley, Paul Carlyle, and John Caldwell 'Competition in the Telecommunications Sector' in Macgregor et al, op cit, 99 at 119 (for the insight that the technology itself introduces an element of competition, driving out the need for ex ante regulation and encouraging a 'light touch at the tiller').

[8] As advocated, for instance, in relation to electronic signatures (see eg, Pamela Samuelson 'Five Challenges for Regulating the Global Information Society' in Christopher T Marsden (ed) *Regulating the Global Information Society* (London: Routledge, 2000) 316, at 320–1) and electronic money.

drawn; it is not as though, having identified the problem, we now have a template for responding.

Secondly, where a regulatory framework becomes disconnected, there is no denying that this might be undesirable relative to considerations of regulatory effectiveness and/or regulatory economy. With regard to the former (regulatory effectiveness) the problem is that, once regulation becomes disconnected, regulatees cannot be quite sure where they stand—and this will create difficulties irrespective of whether the regulatory environment is intended to support and promote certain activities (for example, human embryonic stem cell research) or to prohibit them (for example, human reproductive cloning). Here, we might pause to note an irony: the more that regulators (in an attempt to let regulatees know where they stand) try to establish an initial set of standards that are clear, detailed, and precise, the more likely it is that the regulation will lose connection with its technological target (leaving regulatees unclear as to their position). With regard to regulatory economy, the point is that, where regulation becomes formally disconnected, it is wasteful to expend either legislative or judicial resource in declaring expressly and for the avoidance of doubt that the regulatory position is as it was clearly intended to be.

Having said this, we should not forget the point that I laboured in Chapter 6. This is that it is a mistake to assume that (ex post) regulatory disconnection is necessarily and inevitably a bad thing and that, when it happens, every effort should be made to close the gap. Sometimes, in the interests of regulatory legitimacy and democracy, it is important to take time out to debate the developments that have taken place and to determine how the regulatory framework should be adjusted.

Thirdly, even if there are no simple prescriptions for effective and legitimate regulatory connection, there is a growing awareness that there is a serious problem that requires attention. So, for example, one of the recommendations made in the Royal Society and the Royal Academy of Engineering's report on nanotechnology is that 'the Chief Scientific Advisor should establish a group that brings together the representatives of a wide range of stakeholders to look at new and emerging technologies and identify at the earliest possible stage areas where potential health, safety, environmental, social, ethical and regulatory issues may arise and advise on how these might be addressed'.[9] This proposal, it should be emphasized, is directed at emerging technologies in general, not just nanotechnologies. Such a group should ensure, not only that regulators are forewarned but also, as experience is gathered, that regulators are forearmed. Regulators, too, are waking up to the fact that sustainability is a problem and there are encouraging signs of imaginative solutions being sought. So, for example, in the House of Commons Science and Technology Select Committee's report on hybrid and

[9] The Royal Society and the Royal Academy of Engineering *Nanoscience and Nanotechnologies: Opportunities and Uncertainties* (London: The Royal Society, 2004) (RS Policy document 19/04) para 9.7.

chimera embryos,[10] it is suggested that the regulatory agency should be given a broad licensing power to authorize the use of inter-species embryos as research tools but that, if a particularly controversial use or wholly uncontemplated type of embryo is proposed, the regulatory framework should 'contain a provision to enable the Secretary of State to put a stop to the procedure for a limited period while deciding whether or not to make regulations'.[11] While this is no more than a sketch of an idea, the details of which would need to be properly worked through, it is an interesting exercise in joint regulation, with the breadth of the agency's licensing powers being geared for flexibility and connection, and the Secretary of State's stop and review powers designed for both clarity and legitimacy.

Although the Committee's suggestion was not taken forward by the government in the Draft Human Tissue and Embryos Bill 2007, the Bill, in its own way, endeavours to incorporate a number of novel anti-disconnection measures. For example, clause 65(2) of the Bill gives the Secretary of State prior authorization to regulate against the selling, supplying, or advertising of sperm sorting kits (if and when DIY sperm sorting kits come on stream);[12] and, in a similar fashion, clause 34 pre-authorizes the making of regulations to cover procedures that make it possible to create human embryos from genetic material provided by two women. Inevitably, there will be technological developments that legislatures simply cannot foresee; but the thinking behind the Bill is that, where certain technological developments are foreseen, then an anticipatory regulatory regime should be agreed ready for roll-out. Subject to two provisos, this seems an intelligent piece of forward planning. The first proviso is that the scenarios and powers in question need to be fully debated and authorized at the time of enactment. In other words, the advance authorization needs to pass muster, as best it can, relative to the criteria of legitimacy. Secondly, the scenarios and the scope of the powers need to be sufficiently clear to enable the debate to be adequately informed. Otherwise, a well-intended effort to try to be ahead of the game will prove to be a false regulatory economy. In the light of these provisos, we might be less sanguine about clause 14(5) of the Bill which empowers the Secretary of State, where it appears to be 'necessary or desirable to do so in the light of developments in science or medicine' to extend the statutory definitions of embryos, eggs, sperm, or gametes

[10] House of Commons Science and Technology Select Committee *Government Proposals for the Regulation of Hybrid and Chimera Embryos* (Fifth Report of Session 2006–07) (HC 272–I, 5 April 2007).

[11] ibid para 100. This idea has some support, too, in The Academy of Medical Sciences *Inter-Species Embryos* (London, July 2007) at 39; and in House of Lords House of Commons Joint Committee on the Human Tissue and Embryos (Draft) Bill *Human Tissue and Embryos (Draft) Bill*, HL Paper 169–I, HC Paper 630-I (London: Stationery Office, 1 August 2007), where a regime of 'devolved regulation' is favoured.

[12] Although the Joint Committee on the Human Tissue and Embryos (Draft) Bill expresses 'sympathy with the intention behind clause 65', it judges that the provision would be 'unenforceable in practice' and recommends that the clause be removed from the draft Bill (n 11 above) para 284.

in order to include 'things...which would not otherwise fall within the [relevant] definition'.

There is no guarantee, of course, that advance measures of this kind will be effective when they are activated. To some extent, it makes a difference whether the regulatory intervention is designed to prohibit some conduct or to permit it. In the case of DIY sperm sorting kits, we are dealing with an intended prohibition. Compliance cannot be taken for granted. Couples who do not accept the legitimacy of this restriction might try to source the kits on the black market; and we can be fairly confident that they will be assisted by internet suppliers who operate outside the UK. This does not mean that activating the regulatory powers would be a complete waste of time; but the effectiveness of the intervention is likely to be limited.[13] By contrast, where regulation declares some activity (such as egg donation for mitochondrial replacement only) to be permitted, then there is perhaps less of an issue about effectiveness—or, at any rate, this is so unless the intention is not merely to permit but to permit *and to promote*. Nevertheless, a permissive provision of this kind might agitate the dignitarians; and, although the signals from the appeal courts have hardly given the dignitarians any encouragement, we should not discount the possibility that the exercise of such new-style powers might be tested through judicial review.

(ii) Is there anything distinctive about the regulatory space occupied by particular technologies?

One of the principal ideas associated with the underlying agenda is that, each time a new technology appears, or an established technology assumes a fresh significance or moves forward in some way, we should not, so to speak, have to reinvent the regulatory wheel. Moreover, this sentiment chimes in with the oft-heard view that we should not repeat the mistakes (especially the mistake of genetic reductionism) that we might have made with biotechnology. On the other hand, this idea needs to be counter-balanced by the thought that the technologies, while having some similarities as regulatory targets, are nevertheless different—the thought that each new technology has its own distinctive identity. Hence, even if we do not need to reinvent the regulatory wheel, we do need to refine our regulatory intelligence to bring it into alignment with the characteristics of each particular technology.

One way of trying to implement this sense of similarity and difference is to think about the regulatory space occupied by a particular technology.[14] If we had a set of variables that enabled us to plot a regulatory space, we should be able to

[13] See, further, ch 7; and Roger Brownsword 'Red Lights and Rogues: Regulating Human Genetics' in Han Somsen (ed) *The Regulatory Challenge of Biotechnology* (Cheltenham: Edward Elgar, 2007) 39.

[14] This is an exercise carefully undertaken in relation to information technology in Andrew Murray *The Regulation of Cyberspace* (Abingdon: Routledge-Cavendish, 2007).

figure out quite quickly, and in an organized way, in which respects the technology in question was a routine regulatory target and in which respects it was distinctive and special. But, what would those variables be? Given that this is an exercise in the application of regulatory intelligence, the key variables must be those factors that we take to be of regulatory significance. Accordingly, I suggest that the starting point should be to treat the main variables as those relating to legitimacy, effectiveness (including economy and efficiency), connection, and cosmopolitanism.

What, then, is it that makes a particular technology, or the regulatory space that it occupies, different and distinctive? If, as I have suggested, connection is a generic challenge, we can assume that each technology will be developing at a rate that threatens disconnection. To be sure, some technologies will develop even more quickly than others; but, generally, this will not be where the relevant difference is to be found.

At an early stage of their development, some technologies might be purely domestic in their significance such that there is not yet a cosmopolitan challenge to be addressed. If so, there will, at this juncture, be a distinction between the technologies that raise a cosmopolitan challenge and those that do not. However, where technologies are designed to deliver benefits, but where they also present risks, we can be sure that it will not be long before cosmopolitan questions arise. On the face of it, then, the particular differences are likely to relate to legitimacy and effectiveness.

In Chapter 1, I remarked that while, for some technologies, legitimacy seems to be the regulatory 'hot-spot', for others it is effectiveness. Following up this thought, we might say that the regulatory space in which information technology is located differs from that occupied by, say, red biotechnology or neurotechnology because, in the former, it is effectiveness that is problematic while, in the latter, it is legitimacy that is the principal source of regulatory difficulty. However, while this characterization of difference might be on the mark at the moment, values and views might change as might the features of the technological targets once convergence occurs. For example, we might say that, while effectiveness is likely to be the principal regulatory challenge in relation to nanotechnology (how can you regulate for safety when the risks involved in the technology are not clear?), the regulatory difficulty might switch to legitimacy once nanomedical applications are developed; and, over a period of time, quite possibly, things might change again as the technology is accepted. Or, to take another example, because each technology emerges against an existing regulatory background, there will be a question about whether fresh or dedicated regulatory provisions need to be introduced for the emerging technology. Just as it was asked whether existing contract law provisions might suffice to regulate e-commerce, it is now being asked whether existing health and safety regulations will suffice to cover nanotechnology.[15] Sooner or later, however, the answer to the question becomes

[15] See, eg, the Royal Society and the Royal Academy of Engineering (n 9 above), ch 8; and Jean McHale 'Nanotechnology, Small Particles, Big Issues: A New Regulatory Dawn for Health Care

clearer and what was once an issue is no longer so. In other words, the features that distinguish a particular regulatory space at a particular time are neither intrinsic to the technology nor enduring. Regulatory spaces are shifting scenes.

The lesson to be drawn from this, therefore, is that we should try to recognize common regulatory challenges for what they are. However, while, in the interests of regulatory economy, we should avoid reinventing the wheel, we should not suppose that we can mechanically transport a regulatory regime from one regulatory space to another any more than we should assume that the pressure points on regulators will remain constant.

(iii) In pluralistic societies, how are regulators to achieve positions that are perceived to be legitimate?

The opening chapters of the book highlight two key points that bear on the challenge of regulatory legitimacy. One point concerns the difficulties that regulators have in accommodating the various constituencies that make up an ethical plurality; and the other concerns the mistaken assumption that certain ethical concepts are neutral and unproblematic (even in a plurality). In both cases, plurality is the problem. However, there are different degrees of plurality and we need to understand the significance of this matter.

In what I have been calling a community of rights, there is a baseline of agreement with regard to the shape and character of the community's ethic. Nevertheless, at various points in the discussion, I have been at pains to emphasize that, even in a community of rights, there is plenty of scope for disagreement. For instance, there might be disagreement about the scope and application of agreed rights or about who qualifies as a rights-bearer, or about the appropriate way of treating those who are not rights-holders. To this extent, there is a plurality within the singularity that is a community of rights. Potentially, however, even this degree of plurality could be destabilizing. It is critical, therefore, that members of a community of rights not only agree on the general shape of their ethical commitments but also agree upon the processes that will be employed to resolve their disagreements. In other words, the community of rights needs to develop a politico-legal framework, orientated towards the community's basic ethic, that facilitates the provisional settlement of the community's differences.[16] If this trick can be pulled off, the expectation is that disputants will accept that there are reasonable differences of moral opinion (within the accepted parameters) and that provisional settlement must be respected. Or, to put this another

Law and Bioethics?', paper delivered at Twelfth Annual Interdisciplinary Colloquium on *Law and Bioethics*, University College London, 2 July 2007.

[16] Compare Deryck Beyleveld and Roger Brownsword *Law as a Moral Judgment* (London: Sweet and Maxwell, 1986; reprinted Sheffield: Sheffield Academic Press, 1994) where precisely such a framework is elaborated.

way, it means that regulators who act within the terms of the agreed politico-legal framework can respond shortly to those who challenge the legitimacy of their decisions. Essentially, the community is at one in trying to elaborate and act on the best interpretation of its commitments; where a 'best interpretation' is contested and needs provisional settlement, regulators who set the standard need not claim that the position adopted is in line with everyone's interpretation; it suffices to stand on the authority to make the decision and a good faith attempt to discharge the responsibility of taking a public position on the matter.

Once we depart from a relatively safe haven of this kind, we are in serious difficulty.[17] Plurality now spells disagreement of a more fundamental nature. The basic ethical principles and parameters are themselves disputed. To some extent, we might be able to cover over the disagreements by drafting consensus declarations in suitably vague or abstract terms; but, as soon as a concrete issue needs to be addressed, the divisions break out. We might also find happenstance agreement in some cases; but such consensus is fragile, unpredictable, and exceptional. Moreover, as I explained in Chapter 4, because the differences go so deep, the prospects for a procedural solution are poor. In short, when regulators are dealing with this degree of plurality, there is no easy way of rising to the challenge of regulatory legitimacy.

The crucial sticking point is that the plurality (the bioethical triangle) includes duty-led dignitarians who believe that certain acts and practices are categorically wrong. Liberals sometimes think that they can talk the dignitarians out of their restrictiveness by arguing along the following lines: 'We take a permissive view of this practice (say, therapeutic cloning); but you want to prohibit it. Clearly, we cannot have both permission and prohibition (unless we have independent zones of regulation). We are not telling you what you can and cannot do; so neither should you try to dictate what we can and cannot do. It follows that, while you are perfectly entitled to be restrictive in your private lives, you should not try to impose your restrictive principles on others as a matter of public regulation'. Unfortunately, even if this liberal plea did not beg the question in favour of its permissive approach (by presupposing optionality), the dignitarians are not buying it anyway.

Before we settle on a rather painful prognosis for regulatory legitimacy, we might seek comfort in the larger picture. We might think, for example, that if the renaissance of dignitarianism owes something to what Gregory Stock calls 'European sensitivities',[18] then it will probably fall away as quickly as it has asserted itself.[19] Yet, there is reason for thinking otherwise. In particular, neither the

[17] See the discussion of the problem of 'external authority' in Deryck Beyleveld and Roger Brownsword 'Principle, Proceduralism and Precaution in a Community of Rights' (2006) 19 Ratio Juris 141.

[18] Gregory Stock *Redesigning Humans* (London: Profile Books, 2002) 13.

[19] After all, it is little more than 30 years since philosophers could write that human dignity 'seems to have suffered the fate of notions such as virtue and honor, by simply fading into the past': see Michael Pritchard 'Human Dignity and Justice' (1972) 82 Ethics 299, at 299.

utilitarian nor the human rights perspective gives much support to the interests of conservatism, constancy, and stability. And, as the pace of new technology accelerates, we should not underrate the felt need to find a way of registering a concern that the world, if not standing still, should at least slow down. Alongside this concern, there is the fear of the unknown. According to Manuel Castells:

> The greatest fear for people ... is the oldest fear of humankind: fear of the technological monsters that we can create. This is particularly the case with genetic engineering, but given the convergence between micro-electronics and biology, and the potential development of ubiquitous sensors and nanotechnology, this primary biological fear extends to the entire realm of technological discovery.[20]

Admittedly, we might not think that constraint for the sake of constraint, nor for that matter irrational fear, has much to recommend it; but, as I have argued throughout the later chapters of the book, any aspirant moral community needs to be careful that the adoption of new technologies does not have the effect of undercutting the very conditions upon which its aspirations are predicated.

The lesson here, then, is not encouraging. Depending upon the particular configuration of power and plurality, a failure to rise to the challenge of regulatory legitimacy might or might not be politically problematic. Be that as it may, one of the facts of regulatory life is that there is no easy way out of deep moral disagreement. It is a problem that has taxed moral and political philosophers; and it is a problem that will continue to plague the regulation of new technologies.

(iv) How does globalisation and global governance bear on the regulation of technologies?

In Chapter 7, I explored a number of issues that I took to be elements of the challenge of regulatory cosmopolitanism, the challenge of doing justice to the twin ideals of universal concern and respect for legitimate difference. Let us suppose, however, that the question is not so much about accommodating both universal and local values as about the possibility of putting in place a global regulatory regime for a particular technology. If this were feasible, the regulatory environment for the research, development, and application of, say, green biotechnology would be the same whether the location was Austria or Switzerland, or Argentina or China. The question is, what might stand in the way of putting such a plan into practice? Or, to put this another way, in what sense does regulating technology, in a global regulatory context, represent a more complex challenge than regulating it in a domestic nation state context?

First, we cannot assume that there will be agreement in all regulatory zones (local, regional, and international) as to the benefits to be derived from the technologies (in some places, techno-optimism will prevail, in others the mood will

[20] Manuel Castells *The Internet Galaxy* (Oxford: Oxford University Press, 2001) 280.

be one of techno-pessimism).[21] In consequence, we are likely to find different regulatory thresholds in different societies. Michael Kirby has put this point in the following way:

> [T]he achievement of effective global regulation of a pervasive scientific development is extremely difficult to attain. Quite apart from the different interests of different societies, there are often different starting points for the very idea of regulation. In some societies, the view is adopted that science carries risks and should not be permitted unless scientists can demonstrate affirmatively that there is no risk, or that the risks are negligible. In other societies, there is a presumption that science should be free to advance and will ultimately benefit humanity, as it has generally done in the past.[22]

But, even if we agree that our regulatory mind-set towards science should be neutral (neither low benefit/high risk nor high benefit/low risk in its predisposition), we still need to agree on the limits within which science and technology should be permitted to operate. This takes us to the second point of difficulty.

Secondly, following through on our discussion of regulatory legitimacy, we cannot assume that there will be consensus as to the nature of human rights and human dignity, or the balance to be struck between facilitation and protection (the different attitudes towards data protection and privacy rights in the US and Europe is a case in point).[23] The fact that there are contested conceptions of human dignity is not just a philosophical puzzle; it bears on the politics and practice of regulation, on effectiveness as well as on legitimacy.

Thirdly, to recall a point made in Chapter 7, if there is significant regulatory variation from one zone to another, compliance becomes problematic for the more restrictive regimes—not just in the sense that research and development of the technology can be transferred from the more restrictive to the more permissive zones, but in the sense that the knowledge that this is so weakens the position of those regimes wishing to take a restrictive approach.[24]

[21] For a helpful general overview and, at the same time, a valuable corrective against an invention-centric view of technological development and spread, see David Edgerton *The Shock of the Old* (London: Profile Books, 2006). More particularly, see Matt Ridley 'We've Never had it so Good – and it's all Thanks to Science' *Guardian Life* 3 April 2003, 8. And compare the contrasting assessments in, respectively, Europe (negative) and the United States (positive) as to the benefits of GM crops—largely replicated in relation to the perceived promise of nanotechnology: see Kirsty Mills 'Nanotechnologies and Society in the USA' in Geoffrey Hunt and Michael Mehta (eds) *Nanotechnology: Risk, Ethics and Law* (London: Earthscan, 2006) 74.

[22] The Hon Justice Michael Kirby 'Human Freedom and the Human Genome: The Ten Rules of Valencia' (paper given at international workshop on Freedom and Risk Situations, Valencia, Spain, 25 January 1999) p 13.

[23] See, eg, Andrew Charlesworth 'Data Privacy in Cyberspace: Not National vs. International but Commercial vs. Individual' in Lilian Edwards and Charlotte Waelde (eds) *Law and the Internet* (2nd edn, Oxford: Hart, 2000) 79.

[24] cf Marcus Radetzki, Marian Radetzki, and Niklas Juth *Genes and Insurance* (Cambridge: Cambridge University Press, 2003) (re offshore insurance).

Fourthly, where national economies need research and development in new technology, politicians will be nervous about regulation that discourages investment. Hence, there was pressure to pave the way, legally speaking, for e-commerce; and the economic agenda behind the UK's liberal regulatory framework for embryonic stem cell research is an open secret.[25] Local regulation, in other words, can operate only in the shadow of whatever local political will prevails; and the prospect of regulatory arbitrage between jurisdictions competing to host technology-based business militates against the adoption and enforcement of regional or international minimum standards.

Fifthly, as Francis Fukuyama rightly remarks in his most recent book, '[a]ll international institutions face the same design tradeoffs...: institutions that are regarded as legitimate...are not terribly effective, while those that are effective are not regarded as legitimate'.[26] One of Fukuyama's illustrations of this tension (which, of course, is also a tension found in national governance) is the Internet Corporation for Assigned Names and Numbers (ICANN). The short history of assigning and registering internet addresses, from Jon Postel's legendary notebook to the establishment of ICANN in 1998, has been one of relative informality. Unfortunately, while ICANN might claim to have been reasonably effective in handling internet addresses, in resolving domain name disputes, and so on, 'it came to be regarded as totally illegitimate by many of the Internet's important stakeholders, especially non-Americans, who had no idea of how this body was making decisions that ultimately affected them'.[27] But, there is no easy answer: for if, instead, ICANN's functions were to be handed over to a global body (such as the International Telecommunications Union) that scores better for accountability and legitimacy, there would surely be a correlative loss of effectiveness.

Such considerations suggest that regulatory tourists will find a patchwork of regulation, ranging from outright prohibition to unqualified permission, with various compromises forged along the way. To be sure, there will be international agreements (to which individual national sovereign states subscribe) that relate in one way and another to new technologies; and, to this extent, we can talk up global governance.[28] However, the idea that all nation states, first, might agree that the regulatory environment for new technologies should be the same in all places, secondly, might actually sign off a package of regulatory standards to constitute that environment and, thirdly, might actually comply with the standards, to say the least, seems fanciful. The international community might be on the way

[25] See, eg, *Scientific Research: Innovation with Controls* (Better Regulation Task Force, London, 2003) 26.

[26] Francis Fukuyama *After the Neocons* (London: Profile Books, 2007) 163.

[27] ibid 170.

[28] Or, on occasion, talk it down: compare Margaret Llewelyn 'The Legal Protection of Biotechnological Material: Concord in Discord' in Douglas Lewis (ed) *International and Regional Organisations* (Oxford: Hart, 2006) 151 at 153, where the TRIPs Agreement is characterized 'more as a *Dis*agreement on Trade Related Aspects of Intellectual Property Rights'.

to becoming a global village but it is not yet ready for an international version of *gemeinschaft* regulation.

III Regulatory Design

Where regulatory decisions are being made about new technologies, the form and style of the regulation and its institutional array needs very careful consideration. There is a huge amount to be said about institutional design, much of it not at all specific to new technologies. Once again, I can only begin to scratch the surface.[29]

To earth these short remarks, consider the case of the Human Fertilisation and Embryology Act 1990 together with the Human Fertilisation and Embryology Authority that was set up by that Act. It is frequently said that this is a model regulatory scheme. Yet, what is model about it? The legislation has been outrun by developments in embryology; it is a textbook example of regulatory disconnection. More to the point for present purposes, the regulatory authority is thought by its various critics to be too slow and bureaucratic in its decision-making, unrepresentative in its membership (dignitarians are not welcome), prone to capture by its licensees from whom the authority draws its funds, and largely unaccountable.[30] In the light of our discussion of productive and unproductive disconnection, we might mount a reasonable defence to the criticism of the legislation but what should we think about the kind of criticisms that are made of the regulatory agency itself?

Currently, the government is set on saving public funds by reducing the number of arm's length agencies. Accordingly, one proposal is to merge the Human Fertilisation and Embryology Authority and the recently-formed Human Tissue Authority, these two agencies being reconstituted as the Regulatory Authority for Tissue and Embryos (RATE). This plan to create one super agency has plenty of critics, not least because it entrusts the new authority with a responsibility for a very wide sweep of activities running from assisted reproduction to state of the art research—indeed, the Joint Committee on the Human Tissue and Embryos (Draft) Bill found the evidence against RATE so 'overwhelming and convincing' that it recommended that the government should abandon its plan.[31] However, the merits of the proposed merger and the eventual fate of RATE is not the present issue. Rather, what is of interest is the regulatory requirement placed on RATE by clause 10 of the draft Human Tissue and Embryos Bill 2007. Here, RATE

[29] For helpful regulatory 'maps', see Julia Black 'De-centring Regulation: Understanding the Role of Regulation and Self-Regulation in a "Post-Regulatory" World' (2001) 54 Current Legal Problems 103, especially at 134-5; and Colin Scott 'Accountability in the Regulatory State' (2000) 27 Journal of Law and Society 38.

[30] See, eg, Sarah Boseley 'MPs Hit at Fertility Watchdog over Designer Baby' *The Guardian*, 18 July 2002.

[31] Inter-Species Embryos (n 11 above) at para 297.

is required, first, to 'carry out its functions effectively, efficiently and economically'; and, secondly, to carry out its functions in such a way that has 'regard to the principles of best regulatory practice (including the principles under which regulatory activities should be transparent, accountable, proportionate, consistent and targeted only at cases in which action is needed)'—in other words, to act in accordance with the principles of good regulation as set out by the Better Regulation Task Force.

The idea that RATE might be judicially reviewed for a failure to comply with the requirements of effectiveness, economy, or efficiency is surely only a paper possibility. Just to take one scenario: suppose that the efficiency curve for RATE shows that the optimal gearing is at a point of rather low agency activity. At this level, RATE does not carry out inspections or audits of licensed facilities. In due course, following a scandal or two, and a media campaign complaining about the agency's inadequate supervision, RATE is judicially reviewed for failure to carry out its duties effectively. RATE's response is that, if it is to be more effective, its performance will be less efficient (not to mention being less economical). I imagine that, if the initial application for judicial review were granted, the ruling would be that it is for RATE, not the High Court, to accommodate these values; and that, provided this is done in a way that satisfies undemanding *Wednesbury* reasonableness,[32] RATE must proceed as it thinks best. Be such matters as they may, our particular interest is in the second requirement.

As is well known, the Better Regulation Task Force advocates the five principles of good regulation as specified in the above mentioned clause 10.[33] As a 'back of an envelope' list, each of the principles, and the set as a whole, is plausible. However, each principle invites elaboration. For example, when transparency is unpacked, we find that it includes requirements for clarity of regulatory purpose and clear communication of that purpose, consultation, clear penalties for non-compliance, clear drafting of regulations, and information, support, and guidance for those subject to the regulation as well as time to comply. Similarly, when we read beyond the headings for proportionality and targeting (necessity), we find that these principles are geared to counteracting the tendency towards over-regulation in a risk averse society.[34] Already we have a sense that holding RATE to account in relation to these principles will not be entirely straightforward. However, the bearing of the better regulation principles on the matter of institutional design is much more complex than this. Let me simply note four aspects of this unstated complexity.

[32] *Associated Provincial Picture Houses Ltd v Wednesbury Corporation* [1948] 1 KB 223; and, for discussion of the reasonableness standard in judicial review, see John N Adams and Roger Brownsword *Understanding Law* (4th edn, London: Sweet and Maxwell, 2006) ch 8.

[33] See *Scientific Research: Innovation with Controls* (Better Regulation Task Force, London, 2003) Appendix C, p 36.

[34] ibid p 3: 'The UK has a proud history of scientific research and innovation, but in an increasingly risk averse society this is in danger of being undermined by excessive regulation'.

First, to ask a naïve question, which bit of regulatory design is it that the better regulation principles have as their target? By and large, the principles are not directed at the substantive standards set by regulators. Granted, there is an agenda here about over-regulation (for which we should read regulatory prohibition or requirement); but, in general, the principles are not about writing the regulatory script itself. Rather, for the most part, the principles seem to be about the operational practice of regulators. The principles, in other words, are less concerned with telling regulators what standards they should or should not set as with telling regulators how to go about setting standards. In their practice, regulators should act in a way that is transparent (with all that this principle implies), consistent, and so on. Having said this, the principle of accountability seems to speak to a different concern. Here, the concern is not about the standards that are actually to be set, nor about how standards are set, but about making regulators answerable for their actions. What we detect, then, is that the better regulation principles straddle matters that speak not only to the way in which an agency is constituted (particularly relating to the way that an agency is held to account) but also to the way in which an agency operates. But, once we begin to separate out these aspects of regulatory design, we might wonder whether the principles expressed by the Task Force give us the full story.

This takes us to the second point. In a brilliant paper, Michael Trebilcock and Edward Iacobucci identify 10 design desiderata which they then marshal as five oppositional pairs.[35] Although the focus of the paper is on regulatory design in the context of competition law, it seems to me that what Trebilcock and Iacobucci say is of general application. The five key pairs of opposition are between independence and accountability, expertise and detachment, transparency and confidentiality, efficiency and due process, and predictability, and flexibility. Once again, these desiderata seem to straddle agency constitution (especially, independence, accountability, expertise, and detachment) and agency operation (particularly, transparency, confidentiality, efficiency, due process, predictability and flexibility); but, wherever we look, the oppositional pairs suggest tensions that are implicated in regulatory design. In this light, three of the principles proposed by the Better Regulation Task Force look one-sided: transparency needs to be balanced with confidentiality, accountability with independence, and consistency (or predictability) with flexibility. This, however, is not yet the end of the complexity because, as Trebilcock and Iacobucci point out, many of the values 'interact with each other in polycentric, mutually reinforcing or antithetical ways. For example, accountability may be antithetical to administrative efficiency by proliferating appeal or review processes, while expertise may enhance administrative efficiency. Confidentiality and flexibility

[35] Michael Trebilcock and Edward Iacobucci 'Designing Competition Law Institutions' Cambridge Lectures (for the Canadian Bar), Queen's College, Cambridge, July 2001.

may be antithetical to due process, but due process in turn may be in tension with expertise'.[36]

Thirdly, although neither the better regulation principles nor the Trebilcock and Iacobucci desiderata are directed at the substance of regulatory standards (which is where we find the ethical plurality most vociferously at odds with itself), we should not infer that questions of regulatory design are value-free or ethically neutral. Questions of regulatory legitimacy arise here too; and, inevitably, we soon run into the problems of plurality. For example, the opposition between efficiency and due process tends to be underwritten by the opposition between utilitarian ethics (for efficiency) and rights ethics (for due process); and the Task Force's agenda against 'over-regulation' of science is implicitly underwritten by a utilitarian ethic that is prioritized against the rights constituency that demands (as utilitarians see it) burdensome consent and data protection practice as well as against the dignitarian red-light ethic. Mapping the ethics that support the principles and desiderata would be a major exercise; but it would serve to underline the complexity of the matter.

Fourthly, we have, thus far, posed the question of regulatory design in relation to just a single agency. However, RATE, or any another agency, typically will form part of an institutional set, comprising the agency, the legislature, the executive, and the courts. The significance of this is that we want the set as a whole, not simply the agency in isolation, to make regulatory sense. For example, if we were to criticize the design of the courts as conferring too much independence on judges and leaving the judicial branch insufficiently accountable to electors, the obvious response would be that we see good regulatory sense in the current design when put alongside the accountability of the political branch. Or, again, as we saw in recent debates about the licensing powers of the HFE Authority, we need to think about the interaction between the various parties that make the regulatory environment what it is.

Finally, when we turn from regulatory design in general to regulatory design in the particular context of new technologies, we see that there is a pressing challenge. For, in some parts of the world, it would be no exaggeration to say that there is now a crisis of confidence in both the practitioners and the custodians of new technology; scientists and regulators alike are no longer trusted. How is this breakdown in trust to be repaired? How are trusted institutions to be rebuilt? As Onora O'Neill has astutely observed, we can introduce processes that are designed to manifest trustworthiness (processes that are geared for transparency and accountability and the like) but this does not necessarily engender trust.[37] Paradoxically, procedures that are designed for trustworthiness—including

[36] ibid 9.

[37] Onora O'Neill *Autonomy and Trust in Bioethics* (Cambridge: Cambridge University Press, 2002) ch 6.

procedures for public participation—might contribute even more to the breakdown of trust.

The lesson of all this is clear: if regulatory institutions are to enjoy the trust and confidence of the public (where there are concerns about the technology) as well as meeting the demands of their political and technological stakeholders, there are major design challenges ahead.[38]

IV Technology as a Regulatory Tool (*Regulating* Technologies)

The final three questions in the underlying agenda express a common concern: what are the implications of new technologies being adopted as regulatory tools? In the second half of the book, I have tended to jump ahead in an attempt to anticipate what the concerns are likely to be once regulation assumes what is predominantly a technological trajectory. This is not to say that I regard present concerns, especially about privacy, as trivial. Far from it, these are vital concerns in a community of rights[39]—concerns that are even voiced by the police.[40] Nor should it be thought that I foresee the technological revolution happening overnight; rather it will be an incremental and uneven process.

To take up this latter point, we already see a technological approach being employed within the framework of traditional 'obey or pay' forms of regulation. The technology might be designed to discourage non-compliance or to improve the chances of detection, or both; it might be pretty crude (for example, speed bumps or other traffic calming measures within restricted areas)[41] or it might be more sophisticated (for example, CCTV, smart cards, tracking devices, DNA data bases, and so on). In order to tighten the technological grip, the technology of

[38] cf Kirby (n 22 above) at 18–19:

> Without global institutions, talk about prohibitions, regulations and moratoriums will be just that: talk. The absence of effective inhibitions amounts to a permit for science to go where any individual researcher chooses... Ultimately, we require effective institutions of regulation and lawmaking which render the genomic scientist and the technologist, like everyone else, answerable to the law.
>
> ...One of the biggest challenges to the freedom of humanity in the coming century will be to build more effective national and international institutions which can respond with appropriate speed and expertise to the challenges of science and technology.

Compare, too, the remarks made by the Joint Committee on the Human Tissue and Embryos (Draft) Bill (n 11 above) especially at paras 130–3.

[39] Compare, eg, *Peck v United Kingdom* (2003) 36 EHRR 719. The court held that the actions of a local authority in releasing CCTV footage that captured a suicide attempt by Peck engaged his Article 8 right under the convention. And, whilst the local authority may have been well-intentioned in its desire to publicize the success of its CCTV scheme, its failure either to mask Peck's identity or to obtain his consent meant that its interference with his convention right was disproportionate and unjustified.

[40] See, eg, Rachel Williams '"Orwellian" CCTV in Shires Alarms Senior Police Officer' *The Guardian* 21 May 2007, 6.

[41] For relatively straightforward design initiatives, see Neal Kumar Katyal 'Architecture as Crime Control' (2002) 111 Yale Law Journal 1039.

surveillance and detection has to be—and, it clearly is becoming—more sophisticated and pervasive[42] and/or non-compliance must simply be designed out (whether by focusing on products, people, or places). Whether the technological initiative is for detection or design-out, my point is that we need to be alert to the threats that this might present to aspirant moral communities—not because regulatory practices of this kind are immoral (although they might well be judged to be so) but because they threaten the sustainability of moral community itself.

To pick up three questions for further consideration: (i) is the particular way in which a design-based regulatory approach impacts on an agent's choice significant; (ii) what precisely should we understand by the stewardship jurisdiction that I am proposing should be accorded to the regulatory state; and (iii) is the prospect of techno-regulation really feasible (can ambient law ever be as smart and flexible as traditional law)?

(i) The details of regulating by design

I have drawn a broad distinction between two classes of regulatory technologies, those (panopticon) technologies that are designed to monitor and detect non-compliance and those (exclusionary) technologies that are designed to eliminate the option of non-compliance. I have also floated the possibility that, in relation to the latter class of technologies, there might be some distinction between those technologies that design-out the possibility of deviance (by coding potential offenders) and those that design-in an immunity (for the protection of 'victims') against the harms associated with deviations from the required pattern of conduct. However, as Karen Yeung has highlighted in a very helpful analysis of design-based approaches to regulation, there is a range of design-based strategies and the way in which particular designs impact on moral choice is nuanced and bears further consideration.[43]

In a community of rights, agents will face more than one kind of moral dilemma. One kind of dilemma will be that in which the agent is striving to do the right thing but it is not clear what action is required; for example, this is the dilemma of an agent who is not sure whether the right thing is to tell the truth or to tell a white lie, whether to respect a confidence or to inform another of a risk, and so on. However, it is another kind of dilemma that is relevant to our thinking about the impact and import of design-based regulation. This is the dilemma of an agent who believes that the morally required action is x (say, keeping a promise) but who is inclined, for reasons of non-moral self-interest, to do not-x (say, breaking the promise in order to make a financial gain). As

[42] See, eg, Clive Norris and Gary Armstrong *The Maximum Surveillance Society: The Rise of CCTV* (Oxford: Berg, 1999) ch 10; and John Gibb *Who's Watching You?* (London: Collins and Brown, 2005).

[43] Karen Yeung 'Towards an Understanding of Regulation by Design' in Roger Brownsword and Karen Yeung (eds) *Regulating Technologies* (Oxford: Hart, 2008) (forthcoming).

Kantians would put it, this is the case of an agent whose will is in conflict, the autonomous moral will being contested by the heteronomous will of inclination and desire. More prosaically, we can identify the following four key elements in this conflicted situation:

(i) the agent is aware that doing x is the morally required action
(ii) however, the agent is inclined, or desires, to do not-x
(iii) this conflict arises in circumstances where a choice between doing x and doing not-x presents itself to the agent as a real practical issue, and
(iv) the circumstances also allow, in practice, for the doing of not-x.

In principle, regulators might target any one of these elements in order to design around or design out the difficulty. The question is whether, in a community of rights, anything rides on which element of the situation regulators target.

Assuming that the agent is aware that doing x is morally required, then where an agent might be tempted to defect, regulators might seek to reinforce the agent's moral resolve against defection. In most communities, social pressure together with the possibility of censure and criticism works quite well to keep agents on the moral straight and narrow. However, we are contemplating regulators who employ new technologies to reinforce the moral line. Let us suppose, then, that regulators introduce into the food or water supply a cocktail of smart drugs that has the desired effect. With this supplement, agents find it much easier to empathize and sympathize with others and to overcome their immoral inclinations; and, as a result, they do the right thing.[44] Would such a regulatory strategy (assuming that it is known that this is what regulators are doing) be problematic in a community of rights? One thought, a thought articulated by Yeung, is that this kind of approach might be judged to interfere with authentic, unaided, moral action. Other things being equal, we certainly might intuitively prefer that moral action is unaided rather than artificially assisted; but, unless the injunction that agents should do the right thing for the right reason also implies that there should be a certain degree of hardship or adversity involved in doing the right thing, it is not clear that this intuition is reliable. To be sure, if the regulatory intervention makes it so easy for agents to do the right thing that they experience no resistance to doing that thing, then there is no element of overcoming and there is a risk that agents lose the sense that they face a choice (between right and wrong).

If, instead of boosting the moral will, regulators target their strategy at suppressing the inclination to defect, would this make any difference? Let us suppose, once again, that a regime of smart drugs will have the desired effect. On the face of it, this does not seem to be materially different from the first approach. If the

[44] We might recall Mustapha Mond's conversation with the Savage in Aldous Huxley *Brave New World* (London: Flamingo, Harper Collins, 1994), where Mond points out that, in place of all the effort associated with hard moral training, anyone can be moral by swallowing a small amount of soma. As Mond puts it (at 217), 'Anybody can be virtuous now. You can carry at least half your morality about in a bottle. Christianity without tears—that's what soma is'.

suppressants are so powerful that they eliminate all desire to defect, then there might be a question mark against such an intervention; and, we might also question this approach if we harbour a sense of moral virtue that involves a certain degree of overcoming (where the intervention, if not eliminating the desire to defect, suppresses it to a level that makes it simply too easy for the agent to claim any merit in doing the right thing). So, provided that agents are not given a 'walk-over' or such a favourable weighting with regard to the ratio between willing x and willing not-x that they can hardly fail to do the right thing, a design strategy of this kind might be judged acceptable.

Having said this, in both cases, I am assuming that the intervention is general rather than agent specific, and that it applies across a broad spectrum of acts rather than in relation to one particular kind of act. Where the intervention is agent specific and restricted to one particular type of act (say, paedophilia), a community of rights might judge that elimination of desire (or major ramping up of moral resolve) is acceptable provided that the agent otherwise enjoys a 'normal' moral life.

Turning to the targeting of the circumstances rather than the agent, what should we make of a design that simply eliminates the difficulty? For example, as Jonathan Zittrain suggests:[45]

> One might put flagstones on a grassy quadrangle precisely where people tend to walk, rather than trying to convince people to use paths that do not track where they would like to go, to mitigate the damage to the turf.

This might not be in the longer-run interest of *regulators* because, where keeping off the grass really matters, regulators will need to find ways of being 'more insistent and creative in influencing behavior'.[46] However, the present question is whether such putative smart regulation is in the interest of *regulatees*. Where resources are in short supply, but where additional resources can be provided, is it always smart to supply to demand? For instance, do we think that it is smart parenting where, in order to avoid conflict, children are given their own televisions, their own computers, their own rooms, and so on? The effect of this strategy is to reduce the opportunities that children have to learn how to share, how to cooperate, how to compromise. If they have adequate opportunities elsewhere, then why not make the home a haven for their self-regarding individualism? And, in a community of rights, we might entertain similar thoughts. If we keep on eliminating situations where we need to be other-regarding, will the community be capable of responding in the right (moral) way if and when the need arises? Unless we are other-regarding by nature (which evokes a further, the fourth, possibility), we need some practice at being moral; children need to be nurtured in a moral direction, and we all need the opportunity.

[45] Jonathan Zittrain 'A History of Online Gatekeeping' (2006) 19 Harvard Journal of Law and Technology 253, at 255.

[46] ibid.

Fourthly, there is the possibility that regulators might target the practical opportunity for defecting from the moral code. As I have said, where techno-regulation simply eliminates the possibility of deviating from the required pattern of conduct, where the only practical option is to do the right thing, then the conditions for moral community are compromised. If this is the default strategy for regulators, then a red line has been crossed. Even if some of the other instances of a design-based approach might be acceptable in a community of rights, systematic targeting of the practical opportunity for defection is off limits: in general, regulators should not try to exclude the possibility of doing wrong.

This prompts further reflection on the distinction between design-out and design-in strategies to which I alluded in Chapter 10. If it is wrong for regulators to eliminate the possibility of doing wrong, does it matter whether they target potential violators (by design-out measures) or their victims (by design-in measures). To clarify, regulators might be able to design agents so that they simply do not have the capacity or the will to deviate from the required pattern of conduct; or, lacking this technological expertise, regulators might be able, through various technological means, to immunize victims against violations. In the former case, the design-out means that agents are coded to act like saints; in the latter case, agents are still free to sin but any harm associated with sinning is neutralised.

I suggested in Chapter 10 that a community of rights might think that this is a distinction without a difference because deviants who know that they can never inflict any real harm on others might as well not have the inclination or the will to deviate in the first place. However, this is not the only plausible response. Alternatively, a community of rights might reason that there is a significant difference between design-out and design-in because, in the former case, agents are only dimly aware (if at all) that they are doing right rather than wrong, while in the latter case agents will be aware that they are deviating. In the former case, agents make no attempt to deviate; but, in the latter case, agents not only can attempt to deviate but be aware that they are acting against the preferred regulatory pattern of conduct. Even with this second bite at the cherry, it is not clear whether the distinction between design-out and design-in really matters for a community of rights.

(ii) State stewardship

I have argued that, in a community of rights, the state is entrusted with a stewardship responsibility for the moral welfare of the community. Like any form of stewardship, this responsibility implies an obligation not only to present members of the community but also to future generations. The most precious thing that an aspirant moral community can hand on to the next generation is an environment that is conducive to a moral way of life, to a way of life that hinges on agents trying to do the right thing, trying to respect the legitimate interests of fellow agents, and being held responsible for their actions. At its most profound, the state's stewardship responsibility is to ensure that the enthusiasm that regulators begin to display for technological instruments of control does not insidiously undermine the conditions that give moral life its meaning.

However, I have touched on stewardship more than once in the book, introducing the idea, first, in Chapter 4, and I am conscious that this is an idea that could invite a regulatory approach that is quite at odds with what would be acceptable in a community of rights. Accordingly, let me try to pull together the threads in order to clarify the basis and the boundaries of stewardship.

To start with the basis of stewardship: in a community of rights, we can assume that the state will need special reasons for interfering with acts that seem to be permitted—whether because they do not obviously impinge on the rights of others or because the relevant others have consented and there is no impingement on non-consenting third parties. Moreover, we can assume that where individual agents act, alone or in concert, in ways that seem to be permissible, the state has the burden of justification if it is to intervene against such acts. To license the state to intervene on the grounds that the acts in question *might* be damaging to rights-holders or *might* be damaging to the community is to put a considerable trust in both the sound judgment and the good faith of the state. Nevertheless, this is what a stewardship responsibility implies.

To take a step back, if it is agreed that the state needs special reasons for interfering with prima facie permitted acts, we might argue for a lower or a higher threshold for legitimate state intervention. If we argue for the higher threshold, we are, in effect, treating the state as no different to an agent. In the absence of consent, the state should not prohibit or otherwise impede an agent's act unless this is necessary for the sake of more compelling rights. By contrast, if we argue for a lower threshold, our view is that, in addition to the reasons that are adequate relative to the higher threshold, the state may (indeed, should) exercise a stewardship responsibility. Quite possibly, those who view the state as an unwelcome extension of private relationships will tend towards the former view, while those who start with a public law perspective will tend towards the latter view. Clearly, however, whether our mind-set is private or public, we will want to see the boundaries of stewardship closely defined.

What, then, are the boundaries of stewardship? I have suggested three circumstances in which stewardship might legitimately be invoked. First, given that the members of a community of rights do not regard themselves as morally omniscient, the state has some margin to cater for the fallibility of the community. Accordingly, if it is argued that an action should be prohibited because it might put at risk the interests of *possible* rights-holders or because it might *indirectly* be damaging to rights-holders, the state might intervene (if only temporarily) on stewardship grounds. Secondly, the state has a responsibility to protect and promote the conditions that are conducive to flourishing agency. In Chapter 8, I specified public health as such a case. Stewardship certainly requires the state to keep citizens informed about risks to their health and a community of rights might well judge that it is legitimate for the state to exercise stewardship by requiring participation in programmes that are intended to improve the conditions of public health. Thirdly, to return to my basic point, the state has a stewardship responsibility to protect and promote the conditions that are constitutive of a meaningful moral community.

(iii) The feasibility of techno-regulation

The discussion in the second part of the book would be truly academic if there was no possibility that the technologies might develop in a way that enables regulators to code and design for compliance. In this light, we should recognize that many researchers in the biosciences are sceptical that the science and technology needed to support the kind of control implicit in such a regulatory vision is, at best, on a distant horizon. To master the coding and circuitry of the brain and the body, let alone our interactions with others and the environment, is a challenge of massive proportions. Perhaps if we were engaging in this kind of speculative discussion at the turn of the next millennium, or the millennium after that, it would have a little more practical purchase. I take the point, but I think that I can live with it—if, for once, our moral deliberations are getting ahead of the technology (even a very long way ahead), this does not strike me as such a bad thing. It might, however, be argued that, even if technology advances far more rapidly than we expect, it simply is not feasible to techno-regulate in the subtle way that traditional rules regulate.[47]

Consider the case of a railway carriage that is set aside as a quiet zone. Although it is the recent development of the mobile phone that has prompted the practice of designating quiet coaches, the current regulatory practice is highly traditional. Typically, notices are displayed in the carriage, reminding passengers that this is the quiet coach and prescribing that 'passengers should not use mobile phones or make any other unnecessary noise', or some such form of words. Generally, social pressure suffices to enforce compliance with the rule. However, if it were felt that a stiffer sanction was called for, say a fixed fine, we might look to technically-minded regulators to implement this scheme. In the not too distant future, when each railway passenger is biometrically identified, when smart cards operate multi-functionally as tickets, as entry and exit tokens, and as payment instruments, and when CCTV is routinely embedded in transport systems, this might look like a reasonably straightforward brief for the designers. Basically, if passengers act improperly in the quiet carriage, they will only be able to exit the carriage once

[47] Compare Richard Susskind *Transforming the Law* (Oxford: Oxford University Press, 2000) especially chs 7 and 8. At 170, Susskind identifies five dimensions of feasibility: technical possibility, jurisprudential soundness, commercial viability, organizational suitability, and strategic appropriateness. In the text, I have assumed technical possibility and then focused exclusively on the issue of jurisprudential soundness.

the fixed penalty payment has been deducted from their payment cards. However, even if this sounds perfectly feasible as a technical challenge, is it so clear that the technology can be mapped onto the background rule?

The rule, as currently drafted, is open-textured.[48] Even if there is not much doubt about what qualifies as a mobile phone (although would a child playing with a toy mobile phone break the rule, would a BlackBerry count as a mobile phone?), there is some vagueness about what qualifies as 'use' of a mobile phone (would an adult using his or her mobile to text a friend or to take photographs break the rule?). More seriously, the catch-all supplementary phrase 'or make any other unnecessary noise' is wide open to interpretation. The intention of the rider clearly is to catch other activities that violate the spirit (if not the letter) of the rule, but we can imagine a host of activities that might or might not be caught depending upon how we interpret the phrase and especially how we interpret the word 'unnecessary'. For example, would a passenger listening to a personal music player be in breach of the rule if the background 'chink-a-chink' is audible? Would it be a breach of the rule to talk with a colleague in an animated fashion, or to bring a crying child or a barking dog into the quiet coach, and so on?

This is not the end of the matter, for whatever traditional legal rules might mean on paper, there is often a practice around the rules that is quite different.[49] The paper rules are one thing; the real rules are something else. Expectations relative to the paper rules do not always coincide with expectations encouraged by custom and practice. So it is with quiet coaches. If we are guided by custom and practice, the paper rule seems to be disapplied in certain circumstances—for example, when a train is over-crowded and there is standing room only in the quiet coach, when a train is severely delayed and passengers want to use their mobiles to let friends and relatives know that they are running late, and (or so I assume) if there were an emergency needing a rapid 999 response. One might argue that some of these exceptions are implicitly written into the rule, that the prohibition is not on the use of mobiles but on the unnecessary use of mobiles. However, this hardly improves the position because, whichever way we look at it, what the rule means depends on a raft of conventions, linguistic and social, and the conventions are sometimes fuzzy as well as being susceptible to change.

In the light of this, the question is whether the ambient regulatory environment of the high-tech quiet carriage could be modulated to reflect these various scenarios. Insofar as we are able to specify the various scenarios and the application of the rule (applied or disapplied) in those scenarios, I assume that expert systems will be able to track old-fashioned law. However, there seem to be two sources of serious difficulty: one is that we are not able to foresee or anticipate the full set of scenarios; and the other is that, over time, we change our minds about

[48] Classically, see HLA Hart *The Concept of Law* (Oxford: Clarendon Press, 1961).

[49] Compare Stewart Macaulay 'The Real and the Paper Deal: Empirical Pictures of Relationships, Complexity and the Urge for Transparent Simple Rules' (2003) 66 MLR 44.

how the rule should be applied. Yet, these difficulties do not look insuperable. In response to the former, the obvious response surely is to equip the system with a default rule. Whether the default should be for application or for disapplication is a matter to be settled; but, once the default is installed, the system knows what to do even if the scenario is not specifically anticipated. In response to the latter, we could minimize the difficulty by agreeing that we will not change our minds on the hoof. If we then have an outcome that we judge to be unacceptable—arising from a classic hard case such as an elderly person, carrying a mobile phone, but failing to appreciate that there are restrictions in the quiet coach—we should make the necessary adjustments to the system and possibly compensate the passenger; but, in general, so long as the penalty for violation is a relatively minor and reversible one, this might seem to be a reasonable price to pay for submitting to the rule of the technology. Of course, it might be protested that the technology can never match the law because the beauty of the latter is that we can make it up as we go along. However, this seems like a quixotic inversion of what we usually take to be the virtue of the Rule of Law, namely that making it up as we go along is precisely what we do not do. Insofar as the Rule of Technology checks against just that temptation, some might think that, not only is regulation by technology feasible, but indeed desirable.[50]

V Fukuyama Revisited: Two Technologies, Two Dystopias

As is well known, Francis Fukuyama has argued that, with the collapse of the communist bloc, one version of the end of history has fallen by the wayside. In future, with the drive towards modernization, the only political trajectory is towards liberal democracy.[51] At the same time, with the breakdown of communism, we have embarked on a fresh phase of globalization, spreading liberal democracy, spreading respect for human rights and human dignity, spreading trade and spreading technology.

Yet, as Fukuyama reminds us in *Our Posthuman Future*,[52] the current phase of globalization carries forward two dystopian visions that caution us as to the relationship between technology and fundamental human values. First, there is the Orwellian vision of the panoptican state and then there is Huxley's vision of a brave new world. Does information technology create a pathway to the former and biotechnology, coupled with the daily dose of soma that neurotechnology can offer, a pathway to the latter? According to Fukuyama, the answer to the first

[50] Compare Mireille Hildebrandt 'A Vision of Ambient Law' in Roger Brownsword and Karen Yeung (eds) *Regulating Technologies* (Oxford: Hart, 2008).

[51] Francis Fukuyama *The End of History and the Last Man* (New York: Free Press, 2006).

[52] Note 4 above.

question is negative; but, to the latter, it is positive unless regulation succeeds in closing off the dystopian avenues.

It is easy to be wise after the event, but it is clear that, even if communism is no longer a serious candidate, Fukuyama's prognosis that liberal democracy has the field to itself is apt to be misinterpreted. For, the global situation remains complex and contested; and, whether our reading is relatively positive[53] or negative, it still looks like a long haul for liberal democracy. However, this is something of a side issue: our principal interest is in the claims that Fukuyama makes about information technology and biotechnology. Do we agree with his position?

(i) Information technology

According to Fukuyama, information technology is largely benign calling only for light regulation. Of personal computers and the internet, he says:

> [T]hese new forms of information technology (IT) promised to create wealth, spread access to information and therefore power around more democratically, and foster community among their users. People had to look hard for downsides to the Information Revolution; what they have found to date are issues like the so-called digital divide (that is, inequality of access to IT) and threats to privacy, neither of which qualify as earth-shaking matters of justice or morality.[54]

To be sure, Fukuyama is not alone in highlighting the opportunities for redistribution and community that are created by freeing the production and circulation of information from the market—indeed, this is precisely the view more recently presented by Yochai Benkler.[55] Nevertheless, on several scores, we might want to take issue with Fukuyama's upbeat yet relatively low-key reading of the Information Revolution.

First, it might be argued that Fukuyama's view underrates the significance of the internet-enabled transformation of the global centres of economic power as well as the potential for state appropriation of this medium. With regard to the former, we should note Manuel Castells's perceptive remarks:

> The fundamental digital divide is not measured by the number of connections to the Internet, but by the consequences of both connection and lack of connection....[T]he Internet...is not just a technology. It is the technological tool and organizational form that distributes information power, knowledge generation, and networking capacity in all realms of activity....[W]ithout an Internet-based economy and management system,

[53] See, eg, the markedly non-apocalyptic reading in Amitai Etzioni *From Empire to Community* (New York: Palgrave Macmillan, 2004); and Amartya Sen's critique of the 'clash of civilisations' thesis as betraying 'a remarkably impoverished understanding of different civilizations and their similarities, connections, and interdependence in science, technology, mathematics, literature, trade, commerce, and political, economic, and social ideas' in *Identity and Violence: The Illusion of Destiny* (London: Penguin, Allen Lane, 2006) 58.

[54] Note 4 above, at 182.

[55] Yochai Benkler *The Wealth of Networks* (New Haven: Yale University Press, 2006).

there is little chance for any country to generate the resources necessary to cover its developmental needs, on a sustainable ground—meaning economically sustainable, socially sustainable, and environmentally sustainable.[56]

In other words, the internet is not necessarily a case of power to the people;[57] it is a case of power being concentrated in a handful of global nodes. As for the potential for state appropriation, we should hardly be sanguine about governments that are prepared not only to filter the medium but to ensure that the medium is effectively the government's messenger.[58] Contrary to Fukuyama, such a development surely is distinctly Orwellian.

Secondly, even if we take the view that the cyber-libertarians underestimated the ability of nation states to respond to the regulatory challenges presented by the internet and that, despite predictions to the contrary, the internet has not proved to be lawless,[59] we can hardly be sanguine about the extent to which malware of one kind and another is threatening the integrity of the system. The concerns about privacy that Fukuyama rightly notes are now part of a much larger concern about what Jonathan Zittrain calls the 'generative' (flexible and open) design of the end-to-end net, coupled with a parallel flexibility and openness in the design of PCs.[60] As Zittrain reads the situation:

The modern Internet is at a point of inflection....[Its] generativity, and that of the PC, has produced extraordinary progress in information technology, which in turn has led to extraordinary progress in the development of forms of artistic and political expression....

The challenge facing those interested in a vibrant global Internet is to maintain the core of that experimentalist spirit in the face of growing pressures.[61]

In other words, if we are not to return to 'tethered appliances' and to closed intranets, the regulatory challenge is to 'try to maintain the fundamental generativity of

[56] Manuel Castells *The Internet Galaxy* (Oxford: Oxford University Press, 2001) at 269.

[57] Which is not to deny that there are conspicuous examples of community power: see, for one candidate, Andrew Murray *The Regulation of Cyberspace* (Abingdon: Routledge-Cavendish, 2007) at 154–7 (concerning the pressure applied by netizens in reaction to what they saw as the Live 8 ticket scandal). And see Benkler (n 55 above). See, further, Kathy Bowrey *Law and Internet Cultures* (Cambridge: Cambridge University Press, 2005) especially ch 7.

[58] We should note the analysis in Jack Goldsmith and Tim Wu *Who Controls the Internet?* (Oxford: OUP, 2006).

[59] Perri 6 'Global Digital Communications and the Prospects for Transnational Regulation' in David Held and Anthony McGrew (eds) *Governing Globalization* (Cambridge: Polity Press, 2002) 145.

[60] Jonathan Zittrain 'The Generative Internet' (2006) 119 Harvard Law Review 1974. We should note, too, the concerns about the threats to security and, concomitantly, the undermining of trust in cybersystems in the Foresight Report on the *Cyber Trust and Crime Prevention Project* (London: Office of Science and Technology, 2004).

[61] Zittrain (n 60 above) at 2039–40. For evidence of international concern and planned response, see International Telecommunication Union *ITU Global Cybersecurity Agenda [GCA]: A Framework for International Cooperation in Cybersecurity* (Geneva, October 2007).

the existing grid while taking seriously the problems that fuel enemies of the Internet free-for-all'.[62]

Thirdly, there is also the view that certain offline evils (child pornography and grooming, for example) are transformed and amplified by the internet.[63] Whether or not such evils qualify as 'earth-shaking' moral concerns, they are certainly a serious cause for concern and we should not be complacent about them.

Finally, in line with the argument in the second part of this book, it is in liberal democracies no less that we need to keep a very careful eye on the insidious advance of information technology in the evolution of the surveillance society. Famously, as Michel Foucault reminds us, the panopticon:

> [m]ust be understood as a generalizable model of functioning; a way of defining power relations in terms of the everyday life of men....[T]he panopticon must not be understood [merely] as a dream building: it is the diagram of a mechanism of power reduced to its ideal form; its functioning, abstracted from any obstacle, resistance or friction, must be represented as a pure architectural and optical system: it is in fact a figure of political technology that may and must be detached from any specific use.[64]

In this light, we should understand that the panopticon society represents as much of a threat to moral community as the biotechnologically engineered society that Fukuyama fears.

(ii) Biotechnology

Turning to the regulation of biotechnology, Fukuyama poses three important questions: first, whether we should regulate biotechnology; secondly, if so, why we should do so; and, thirdly, if we do try to do so, whether we have any prospect of regulating the technology effectively.

(i) Does biotechnology present a risk that needs to be regulated?

In response to the first question, Fukuyama observes that, whereas some technologies are relatively benign (as we have just seen, he suggests that the development of the Internet falls into this category), others are dangerous. Further, in this latter category, whereas some technologies are obviously and transparently dangerous (for instance, nuclear technology), others are less obviously dangerous (but, ex hypothesi, dangerous nevertheless). Anticipating the

[62] ibid 2040.

[63] See, eg, Bela Bonita Chatterjee 'Pixels, Pimps and Prostitutes: Human Rights and the Cyber-Sex Trade' in Mathias Klang and Andrew Murray (eds) *Human Rights in the Digital Age* (London: Cavendish Glasshouse, 2005) 11; and Marie Eneman 'The New Face of Child Pornography' op cit, 27.

[64] Michel Foucault *Discipline and Punish* (London: Penguin reprint, 1991) 205.

answer that he will give to the second question, Fukuyama places biotechnology in this latter division, from which it follows that he advocates a vigilant approach by the regulators.

(ii) What sort of risk is it?

Addressing the second question, Fukuyama suggests that the distinctive reason why we should regulate biotechnology is not that it is unsafe (otherwise it would be a transparently dangerous technology) but that it is an insidious threat to our way of life.

Let us suppose, suggests Fukuyama, that we ask the following question: What exactly is wrong with the biotechnologically engineered and pharmacologically controlled world depicted by Huxley?[65] If respondents were guided by the bioethical triangle, they would probably say that, while utilitarians would be comfortable with the Fordist World State (which, after all, is geared for the production and maintenance of happiness), rights theorists would regard Bokanovsky's Process as a clear violation of an agent's right to an open future, and dignitarians would be appalled at the commodification of human life (including the exploitation of corpses as a source of phosphorus). However, according to Fukuyama, the A grade answer runs along the following lines:

> [T]he people in *Brave New World* may be healthy and happy, but they have ceased to be human beings. They no longer struggle, aspire, love, feel pain, make difficult moral choices, have families, or do any of the things that we traditionally associate with being human. They no longer have the characteristics that give us *human dignity*.[66]

And, indeed, this would be a smart answer because it is a long way into the book before this feature of life in the World State is explicitly underlined—namely, when Mustapha Mond reminds the Savage that '[i]n a properly organized society... nobody has any opportunities for being noble or heroic'.[67] Be that as it may, none of this implies that biotechnology offers no benefits for human health and well-being. Rather, Fukuyama's point is that our deepest concerns about biotechnology cannot be captured by a utilitarian calculation. Thus:

> While it is legitimate to worry about unintended consequences and unforeseen costs, the deepest fear that people express about [bio]technology is not a utilitarian one at all. It is rather a fear that, in the end, biotechnology will cause us in some way to lose our

[65] We might note, with Matt Ridley, that Huxley's dystopia actually 'owes nothing to nature and everything to nurture. It is an environmental, not a genetic, hell. Everybody's fate is determined, but by their controlled environment, not their genes. It is indeed biological determinism, but not genetic determinism. Aldous Huxley's genius was to recognize how hellish a world in which nurture prevailed would actually be'. See Matt Ridley *Genome* (London, Fourth Estate, 1999) 304.

[66] Note 4 above, at 6, emphasis supplied. To similar effect, see Bill McKibben *Enough: Genetic Engineering and the End of Human Nature* (London: Bloomsbury, 2003).

[67] Note 44 above, at 216.

humanity—that is, some essential quality that has always underpinned our sense of who we are and where we are going [ie human dignity]...[68]

In short, we need the concept of human dignity to articulate our deepest concerns about the biotechnological revolution—and, as we very well know, many would join with Fukuyama in contending that the reason why human reproductive cloning, germ-line gene therapy, genetic enhancement, embryonic stem cell research, and the like must be regulated (meaning, by and large prohibited) is precisely that such practices compromise human dignity.[69]

What precisely does Fukuyama's version of human dignity amount to? Fukuyama rejects the idea that the essence of humanity (which grounds dignity) can be reduced to any one capacity, such as the ability to reason, or to communicate, or to make moral choices, or the like. Instead, he suggests that human dignity refers to a complex of such capacities including a range of characteristically human emotions.[70] Most importantly, it is the survival of this range of emotions, the human emotional gamut, that is put at risk by a utilitarian-inspired biotechnology. Thus:

That aspect of our complex natures most under threat has to do with our emotional gamut. We will be constantly tempted to think that we understand what 'good' and 'bad' emotions are, and that we can do nature one better by suppressing the latter, by trying to make people less aggressive, more sociable, more compliant, less depressed. The utilitarian good of minimizing suffering is itself very problematic. No one can make a brief in favor of pain and suffering, but the fact of the matter is that what we consider to be the highest and most admirable human qualities... are often related to the way that we react to, confront, overcome, and frequently succumb to pain, suffering, and death. In the absence of these human evils there would be no sympathy, compassion, courage, heroism, solidarity, or strength of character. A person who has not confronted suffering or death has no depth. Our ability to experience these emotions is what connects us potentially to all other human beings, both living and dead.[71]

How should we interpret these remarks? Seemingly, Fukuyama's script is not utilitarian—or, at any rate, if it is utilitarian, it is only indirectly so. The more obvious candidates are a rights-based approach (which fits quite well with much of Fukuyama's thinking) or some version of duty-driven dignitarianism (possibly of a communitarian kind). However, on this occasion, we need not linger over this question, for the most significant feature of Fukuyama's take on human dignity is the way in which he sees, first, that the variety of human emotions can be

[68] Note 4 above, at 101.

[69] Roger Brownsword 'Bioethics Today, Bioethics Tomorrow: Stem Cell Research and the "Dignitarian Alliance"' (2003) 17 Notre Dame Journal of Law, Ethics and Public Policy 15; and ch 2.

[70] Note 4 above, at 171–4.

[71] ibid 172–3. See, also, the concerns of the Nuffield Council on Bioethics *Genetics and Human Behaviour* (London: October 2002) with regard to the medicalization of conditions within the 'normal' range of behaviour.

experienced only in a certain kind of context and, secondly, that this is a context that might be biotechnologically threatened. What Fukuyama rightly appreciates is that humans cannot experience the dignity of dealing with adversity, and the emotional gamut that goes with it, unless the context of human social existence is one that presents the relevant forms of adversity.[72] While this is not the same contextual dependence (between moral community and the conditions of vulnerability and dignity) that I focus on in the second part of the book, the shape of the argument is similar: namely, that where humans aspire to and value a particular form of life, then regulators need to be alert to the possibility that modern biotechnology might (unless checked) erode the conditions that make that form of life a possibility.

(iii) Should we regulate biotechnology?

Finally, with regard to the third question, Fukuyama is well aware that doubts have been expressed about the capacity of regulators to hold biotechnology in check, especially when globalization permits the technology to be developed in safe regulatory havens.[73] Nevertheless, he argues that the values at stake here are too important to be abandoned to the technology. This does not mean that Fukuyama believes that the regulators can turn back the tide of technological advance; but he believes that they can at least intervene to control the speed and spread of the technology.[74]

Whether we are pessimistic about traditional forms of regulation or realistic about their limitations in a global context, or in the face of new technologies, or both, the critical question is how we respond. One response is, in effect, to abandon regulation (resigning ourselves to a regulatory race to the bottom and the prospect of technological might dictating what is right). A second response is to try at least to hold the regulatory line, concentrating resources on the most serious violations.[75] And then there is a third response, one that represents the great paradox. Here, regulators turn to the new technologies to assist their projects. While these new regulatory instruments might not assist greatly in controlling the new

[72] Compare the pre-Enlightenment idea of the dignity of the nobles: see Michael J Meyer 'Introduction' in Michael J Meyer and William A Parent (eds) *The Constitution of Rights: Human Dignity and American Values* (Ithaca, NY: Cornell University Press, 1992) 1; and Deryck Beyleveld and Roger Brownsword *Human Dignity in Bioethics and Biolaw* (Oxford: Oxford University Press, 2001).

[73] Lee Silver *Remaking Eden* (London: Weidenfeld, 1998).

[74] But compare Glenn Harlan Reynolds 'Nanotechnology and Regulatory Policy: Three Futures' (2003) 17 Harvard Journal of Law and Technology 179, at 192:

> [A] prohibitionist approach that prevents only 99.999% of nanotechnology [or biotechnology] research, while allowing a few underground projects sponsored by rogue states to slip through its net, would likely do just as much harm with no corresponding benefits. Indeed, it would only make things worse, because these rogue states would then have a monopoly on a powerful technology, while the civilized world would lack the wherewithal to deploy countermeasures.

[75] cf Perri 6 (n 59 above) at 160, for a dispassionate analysis of what we can reasonably expect from our regulators.

technologies themselves, they appeal greatly as a more effective instrument of general social control. Further, if the regulators fail to control these technologies so that they become even more powerful tools for general regulatory purposes, the regulators will hardly complain. Every regulatory cloud, it seems, has a silver lining.

(iii) Overview: Fukuyama and the final word

Revisiting the end of history, Fukuyama identifies a number of challenges that stand in the path of smooth progression to liberal democracy, of which the power and potential of bio-(and neuro)technologies is one.[76] Again, he repeats his warning that the threat presented by such technologies is a subtle one. After all, as Matt Ridley has argued, technical fixes have been employed to make people healthier, wealthier, and wiser; and, by and large, what improves the quality of life is invention rather than legislation.[77] Nevertheless, the spectre of social engineering is not far away; and regulators might well conclude, therefore, that what the world needs now is hi-tech social control (after hi-tech war comes hi-tech law). If so, where technology is deployed in support of traditional measures of prevention and enforcement, respect for human rights and human dignity continues to be relevant to the lines that we draw around the acceptable use of the technology (by the regulators). However, if regulators go beyond this, systematically relying on a technological strategy in place of traditional forms of social control, then, as I have argued in this book, whatever our moral take, whatever we make of human rights or human dignity, the preconditions for moral debate and discourse are diminished.

In a community of rights, it is not enough that a regulatory technology works (that it achieves the desired regulatory effect). Nor is it enough that the technology respects privacy and confidentiality, or has been authorized by processes that satisfy the requirements of free and informed consent. In a community of rights, the fundamental question is whether the technology threatens to change the cultural environment in a way that no aspirant moral community can live with. If there is a real concern that the technology presents such a threat, regulators, as stewards for the moral community, should go no further with that kind of strategy. When regulators trade technologically guaranteed compliance for legitimacy, we cannot even say that they have entered into a pact with the Devil; because when regulators strike this deal, in effect, they dispense with the distinction between right and wrong. The regulatory challenge presented by new technologies can become, and is already being seen as, a significant opportunity; but, unless we are ready for what Jürgen Habermas describes as 'the coldness of a form

[76] Note 51 above at 353-4.

[77] Matt Ridley 'We've Never Had it so Good – and it's All Thanks to Science' *Guardian Life* 3 April 2003, 8.

of life not informed by moral considerations',[78] it is hard to imagine a challenge that is more fundamental than that presented by this self-same opportunity.

And so we reach the final curtain. I am not sure whether to make the last word one of optimism or one of pessimism; and, for some time, I have been uncertain whether to accentuate the positive (that regulators are likely to get better at their art) or the negative (that regulators might become over-reliant on technological instruments). Perhaps I should simply say, as others have said, that our technological future is 'dangerous but open'.[79] However, whatever the last word in this book—and I leave that to the reader's own disposition and good judgment—it is clear that this is no more than an opening shot. Even if the book is finished, the underlying project is only just underway.

[78] Jürgen Habermas *The Future of Human Nature* (Cambridge: Polity Press, 2003) at 73.

[79] To adopt Paul Rabinow's phrase in his Introduction to *The Foucault Reader* (London: Penguin reprint, 1991) at 27, where Rabinow finds a commonality between Weber and Foucault in that both proffer 'a heroic refusal to sentimentalize the past in any way or to shirk the necessity of facing the future as dangerous but open'.

Index

Lightning Source UK Ltd.
Milton Keynes UK
UKOW05n1928230414

230469UK00001B/33/P